ENGLISH POETRY
OF THE
FIRST WORLD WAR
A Bibliography

Catherine W. Reilly

ST. MARTIN'S PRESS

NEW YORK

FOR THE ORIGINAL THESIS ON WHICH THIS WORK IS BASED,
THE AUTHOR WAS GRANTED THE FELLOWSHIP OF THE
LIBRARY ASSOCIATION

Laurence Cotterell, who writes the foreword, is on the one hand a
member of the Military Commentators' Circle, and a regular
reviewer of militaria for *The Times*; and on the other a published
'war poet' of the 1939–45 conflict, and a Vice-President of the
Poetry Society. He serves on the Literature Panel of the Arts
Council, and is an acknowledged authority on the world of book
publishing.

All rights reserved. For information write:
St. Martin's Press, Inc., 175 Fifth Avenue, New York, N.Y. 10010
Printed in Great Britain
Library of Congress Catalog Card Number 77–95261
ISBN 0–312–25517–9
First published in the United States of America in 1978

CONTENTS

iii

FOREWORD

Some years ago I noticed Edmund Blunden, L.P. Hartley and Henry Williamson, all septuagenarians, standing together at a party, laughing and joking as if they had not a care in the world. In another corner of the room stood three successful young authors looking about as gloomy as three rich young authors could. I put the difference down to the fact that the older trio had all been through the most night-marish experience in history to be suffered by men for crawling weeks and months that lengthened into years — the trench warfare of the 1914-18 conflict. These three were glad to be alive. They were living on borrowed time, and they knew it and relished it.

It was inevitably a politician and not a soldier who wrote cynically that he agreed with the proposition that war brought out the best in men, adding "and it stays out!" Both the original statement and the rider are oversimplifications. The Great War was an immense agony for whole nations and innumerable individuals — an intolerable waste and a sanity-shattering joke of an evil god if it left nothing except a disordered world, drained of its best young blood, for greedy and insensitive non-combatant statesmen to snarl over.

One legacy that helped to make the situation just bearable — to make man feel there was something (though not enough) on the credit side — was the immense tide of poetry that surged up out of the minds of the fighting men, especially, but also of civilians in widely differing circumstances.

Those whose living relies to any extent on a wide reading of military history and the poetry of war might have come across the work of, say, some 300 poets of the First World War. How staggering it is, then, and what a salutary lesson in humility, to find no fewer than 2,225 English poets identified in this bibliography — 2,225 poets of

v

England, Ireland, Scotland and Wales, servicemen and civilians, men and women, who experienced the 1914-18 war personally.

I have never before come across a bibliography — a mere listing one might think — which could be picked up and read from page to page as if it were a narrative. One leafs through the work, amazed at the industry and detective powers of the compiler not only in finding a host of obscure or virtually unknown poets to add to the famous names, but also in many cases finding a few words about the author and brief publication details.

We find the unlikely entry of Horatio Bottomley, editor, notorious swindler and sometime friend of the great, followed (with much in between) by reference to the work of a demobilised and unemployed soldier. We find Lieutenant Gray, who was killed in 1917, with his *Souvenir of the war,* and a little later on a listing of a couple of broadsides by Private Hadley, who was wounded at the Dardanelles. Fascinating and tantalising entries by the hundred.

Of course the Grenfells and Owens are here along with their equally famous compatriots, whether they wrote lyrically of peaceful subjects, or in horror of what they saw and experienced, or with the zest of the ruthless romantic. And, among others, the non-combatant romancers are here, Housman and the rest, with their heroic verses. But most notably (and perhaps for the scholar most valuably) there are so very many beguiling entries that tempt one into further investigation: poems and verses (and the difference must lie in the eye and the reaction of each individual reader) by long-forgotten men and women whose works were either published in books also long forgotten, or issued privately in pamphlets, broadsides and modest little volumes. The majority of those listed here were indeed
>"Not the great nor well-bespoke,
>But the mere uncounted folk
>Of whose life and death is none
>Report or lamentation . . . ."

It is not often that we (of certain age especially) find a whole new vista of reading opening up before us, but that is precisely the prospect that Catherine Reilly's diligence, scholarship and imagination have provided for us.

Laurence Cotterell   *1977*

ACKNOWLEDGMENTS

I am indebted to many people for their help in the preparation of this bibliography.

I thank Professor J.A.V. Chapple, University of Hull, for his constant advice and encouragement; my colleagues from several departments in the Manchester Public Libraries, particularly the staff of the Language and Literature Library; Mr. V. Rigby, Deputy Head, Department of Printed Books, Imperial War Museum; Mrs. Shirley Edrich, of I.D. Edrich (Bookseller), Wanstead; Professor J.M. Carroll, College of the Holy Cross, Worcester, Massachusetts, a fellow-bibliographer; Mr. W. Taylor, City Librarian of Birmingham, and Mr. E.B. Irving, Chief Librarian of Wallasey, who allowed me special access to the collections in their custody; Mr. D.I. Colley, City Librarian of Manchester, who afforded me study, typing and binding facilities; and the Director of Reader Services, British Museum, who made it possible for me to examine a large number of books in a short period of time.

Finally, I thank Miss Jean Gwynn and Mrs. Edith Wilshaw for their typing skills (Miss Gwynn with the first draft, Mrs. Wilshaw with the final copy), and Mr. Alan Taylor for binding the completed work.

February 1973   C.W.R.

ABSTRACT

This bibliography collects together poetry and verse on the theme of the First World War, written by English poets (i.e. poets of England, Ireland, Scotland and Wales), servicemen and civilians, who experienced the war. It is restricted to printed material in the form of book, pamphlet, card, or broadside.

It comprises three sections, each arranged in alphabetical order: Anthologies; Individual Authors; Title Index. Appended is a supplementary list of war poets of other English speaking nations — Australia, Canada, New Zealand, South Africa, United States of America.

The object of the bibliography is to identify the many English poets of the First World War and their work, and so provide a research tool for students of the poetry, history and sociology of the period.

INTRODUCTION

Scope

It has always been known that the First World War produced a phenomenal number of poets who wrote a vast quantity of verse — good, bad and indifferent. " 'War poet' and 'war poetry' are terms first used in World War 1 and perhaps peculiar to it" (Robert Graves in "The common asphodel : collected essays on poetry, 1922 – 1949" p. 307). Several interpretations of the phrase 'war poetry' can be and have been made. It could mean all the poetry published during the war, whether on a war theme or not. It could mean poetry, not necessarily on the theme of war, by servicemen who were killed in action — the lost generation of subalterns. The usual connotation is poetry by servicemen (particularly the soldier poets or trench poets) written out of their experiences in the war of 1914-1918.

My interpretation for the purpose of this bibliography is poetry on the theme of the First World War by English poets (i.e. the poets of England, Ireland, Scotland and Wales) both servicemen and civilians, who experienced the war. This has meant examining several thousand volumes of poetry and verse published from the outbreak of war in August 1914 to the present day — a total of almost sixty years. The resultant bibliography is confined to printed material in the form of book, pamphlet, card, or broadside. It is a guide to comment on the war in poetry or verse, whether meritorious or not. The British Museum General Catalogue attempts to categorize each volume of poetry as either 'poems' or 'verses', a difficult distinction to make in many cases. I have used the generic term 'poem' throughout.

Many war poems were first published in newspapers and other periodicals; indeed some were only ever published in this form. Periodicals are excluded here, apart from certain annually published anthologies, as in practice the vast majority of periodical publications (either the original copies or micro-filmed copies) can be examined at the British Museum Newspaper Library at Colindale and in the largest public and university libraries. Regimental magazines and school magazines are also a good source and can usually be seen at the organizations concerned.

Omitted is poetry which deals exclusively with the Irish question and the Rising of 1916. Some Irish patriotic poets saw their war as being with England, not Germany. Excluded are American and British Empire poets. A list of these is appended, compiled from the many anthologies examined and from examples of the poets' work to be found in libraries in this country. At the turn of the twentieth century there was a great deal of emigrant movement. Many of the Commonwealth poets were born in the United Kingdom but taken abroad in infancy or early childhood and so do not qualify here as English. It is largely a matter of the social and cultural influences affecting the stance of a particular poet. An example of this is Robert W. Service, who was born in England in 1876, emigrated to Canada at the age of twenty-one and eventually became known as "the Canadian Kipling". Conversely, many American and Empire poets joined the British armed forces and so have a place in this bibliography. Also excluded is the work of contemporary poets who have written convincingly of World War 1 although they were born after the war ended. Special mention might be made of Edward Lucie-Smith's "Gallipoli : fifty years after", Peter Porter's "Somme and Flanders" and Vernon Scannell's "The Great War".

Arrangement

The bibliography is in three parts: Section A Anthologies; Section B Individual Authors; Section C Title Index.

The abbreviation at the end of each entry in Section A and B denotes the particular library where the item has been seen, but by no means implies that this is the only library holding a copy. See ABBREVIATIONS OF LIBRARY LOCATIONS (p. xxxi) for complete list. When it is known from a reliable source (see SOURCES (p. xxi) that a particular work exists, but a copy has not been traced, this is indicated by the phrase 'Not seen'. However, American editions which are re-impressions or else sheets from English editions bound with American publishers' title-pages, are omitted even though they feature in such reliable series as the Soho bibliographies.

A simplified version of a standard library catalogue entry is used but the data given is sufficient to identify any item. Square brackets are used around details not found on title-page (recto or verso) or in colophon.

Authors' names are given in their most complete form as ascertained from the bibliographical sources consulted, followed by any pseudonyms used. When the name given on a title-page is other than an author's real name, then the pseudonym is repeated in the entry, e.g. EVANS, William, (Wil Ifan, pseud.) Songs of the heather heights: [poems]; by Wil Ifan. Every pseudonym is placed alphabetically in sequence and is followed by a cross reference to the author's real name, e.g. IFAN, Wil, pseud. see EVANS, William, (Wil Ifan, pseud.). Cross references are also made from joint authorships and from other forms of name. Married women are listed under married name, with reference from maiden name when this has also been used. Noblemen are listed under family name, with reference from their title. Double-barrelled, hyphenated names are listed under the first part of the name, with reference from the second part.

All titles are those of first editions unless otherwise indicated. The statement of other editions than the first follows the title in each entry. The pagination of later 'editions' is often identical to that of the first edition, implying no substantial change in the text. Any difference is usually in the wording of the preface, foreword or introduction. However, as it was not often possible to examine editions of the same work together and there was no time for full collation, I have therefore simply taken the publisher's statement of edition. It seemed useful to describe all 'editions' if only to show the probability that their texts are identical.

The place of publication is London unless otherwise stated. Publishers' names are given in abbreviated form but one which is sufficient for identification, e.g. 'William Heinemann, Ltd' becomes 'Heinemann' and 'George Allen & Unwin, Ltd' becomes 'Allen & Unwin'. Privately published works are described 'Privately publ.'.

When the date of publication is not printed inside the book, the supposed publication date is given, in square brackets, from allusions in the text or from bibliographies. If there is some doubt about the supposed date this is indicated by a question mark, e.g. [1917?].

The number of pages in one-volume works is given in Arabic numerals, counting the colophon page and any blank pages preceding the colophon page, and preliminary matter is usually separately paged by means of Roman numerals, e.g. xvi, 92p. Unnumbered pages are given in square brackets.

Works in more than one volume are given separate entries when individual volumes have distinct titles. When individual volumes are not distinctively titled then only one entry is made for the multi-volume work. In this case, only the number of volumes is indicated and the pagination of individual volumes is not given.

When an illustrator's name is found on the title-page, the name is given as part of the entry in the following form:— il. (by Sybil C. Williams).

When a book belongs to a series, the name of the series is given in curved brackets at the end of the entry, followed by the serial number, if any, e.g. (Initiates series of poetry by proved hands, 2).

The annotations to the entries give supplemental information of many kinds. The following examples represent the type of annotation most commonly found:—

(a) Bibliog. (author's works) 4p.
   [These bibliographies have all been checked and in many cases the information given has led to the discovery of further items that come within the purview of this bibliography].
(b) Title from cover.
(c) Cover title is "The mad dog of Potsdam".
(d) A broadside [or card or postcard].
   [These terms describe items consisting of a single page, printed on one side only].
(e) Limericks referring to the Kaiser.
(f) 'Written in barracks between parades' — preface.
(g) In Cockney dialect.
(h) A limited edition of 100 hand-printed copies.
(i) Printed for private circulation.
(j) Printed on one side of leaf only.
(k) Reprinted from the *Devon and Exeter Gazette,* 16th December 1918.
(l) In aid of the Lord Mayor's War Fund and the Belgian Relief Fund.
(m) 'Dedicated to the memory of my kindest critic and dearly-

loved brother, Captain Maurice Tweedale of the 7th King's Liverpool Regiment, killed in action at Festubert, May 15th, 1915'.

Section A : Anthologies

This is necessarily a selective list. Every anthology covering English twentieth century poetry includes at least one or two examples of First World War poetry, usually that of Rupert Brooke, Wilfred Owen and Siegfried Sassoon. Each of the 131 anthologies included here has been selected for one or more of the following reasons:— it covers First World War poetry exclusively; it contains a section of First World War poetry, often distinctively titled; it covers war poetry of all ages including that of the First World War; it was published during or soon after the First World War and so contains a preponderance of its poetry; it contains relevant contributions by poets not represented elsewhere; it contains soldier songs and verses, usually anonymous, of the First World War; it represents the First World War poetry of a national element (e.g. (3) BELL, Sir Harold Idris, & BELL, Charles Christopher, eds & trs. Welsh poems of the twentieth century in English verse) or a regional element (e.g. (129) WRIGHT, S. Fowler, ed. Contemporary Devonshire and Cornwall poetry).

Anthologies containing both poetry and prose are included only when the poetry contribution is substantial and/or significant. Annual compilations such as "Georgian poetry", "Oxford poetry", and "Wheels", often cited in bibliographies as examples of war poetry anthologies, are included if only to demonstrate how little war poetry they actually contain.

Omitted are the volumes of consolatory verse specifically designed to comfort those bereaved by the war. This verse was usually of a religious or spiritual nature and made no mention of the war. Also omitted are the many volumes of patriotic verse published mainly during the first two years of war, consisting of poetry taken from other periods and other wars.

Entries in this section are numbered and arranged in alphabetical order of editor or compiler and under the title where no editor or compiler is given. Annually published anthologies are also placed under the title. Cross references are made from pseudonyms and from joint editorships. Contributors to each anthology are listed in alphabetical name order after the main entry. The names of American and Empire poets who are represented in some of these anthologies are omitted, only English poets being listed. Only initials of forenames are given here but full names, where ascertained, are given in the Individual Authors section. Titles of all anthologies are listed in the Title Index.

Section B : Individual Authors

This is a single alphabetical sequence in author order, then title order of individual works, followed by 'see also' references to the serial numbers of the specific anthologies from Section A in which a poet's work is represented. The latter give a fair indication of the popularity of a particular poet. (Some poets are only represented in the anthologies). Anonymous works are listed under title. Works containing both poetry and prose are included only when the poetry contribution is substantial and/or not found elsewhere. Brief biographical details of each poet, particularly his war time activities, are given where these details were readily available, for instance mentioned in a preface or introduction, e.g. COOK, Leonard Niell (M.C. 2nd Lieutenant, Royal Lancashire Regiment. Killed in action 7th July 1917).

Each work listed is either a single war poem or is a volume of poems containing at least one example of war poetry. The sub-title [poems] is used where the title of a collection *is not* the title of a specific poem, and [and other poems] where the title of a collection *is* that of a specific poem. When this device is not used the implication is that the work consists of only one poem (long or short) bearing that title.

Many of the items included were privately printed. Where the printer's name was evident I have used this in the entry, e.g. Printed Hove : Cliftonville P. London printers often gave the district where their workshop was located and this information is given here, thus making the entry more interesting as it often denotes the area where a poet lived, e.g. Printed Kilburn: Hunt & Clark. The punctuation of some of these locally produced broadsides and cards is rather strange. They were obviously printed by jobbing printers assisted by in-experienced apprentices, and title-pages are liberally sprinked with unnecessary question marks, inverted commas, exclamation marks, etc. However, they are typical of their kind, so title-pages have been copied exactly, including the bad punctuation and occasional wrong spelling.

Section C : Title Index

Title entries are given for all works having distinctive titles by individual poets, for anonymous works and for *all* anthologies.

Anthology titles are distinguished by the serial number in curves at the end of each entry. Cover titles are given, but not alternative titles. Where several titles appear on a title-page, entries are given for all war poems. An entry is given for the first title if it is a distinctive one, even though it is not war poetry, e.g. FORD, Ford Madox "The good soldier; Selected memories; Poems". In this instance, a title entry is made for "The good soldier" although it is a novel.

Supplement : War Poets of Other English Speaking Nations

These are arranged alphabetically, with entries under pseudonyms as well as real names, and prefixed by abbreviation for nationality. A few poets are so minor it was impossible to trace their nationality with any certainty. This is indicated by a question mark after the supposed nationality. Some poets served in ANZAC (Australia and New Zealand Army Corps). Where the country of origin is unspecified, this is indicated by AU?.

Conclusion

Subject in poetry is always difficult to trace. Granger's and other poetry indexes are helpful, but generally refer only to the best known poems by the best known poets. The main volume of Granger lists fifty-eight poems on the theme of World War I. Of these, only twenty-four are English. Of these twenty-four, five are by Wilfred Owen, three by Siegfried Sassoon, one each by Rupert Brooke, Robert Graves and Isaac Rosenberg, and the remaining thirteen by lesser poets.

This bibliography identifies 2,225 English poets (although some only by pseudonym or initials). Of these 2,225, at least 532 were women and at least 417 served in the armed forces or other uniformed organizations such as the Red Cross, the Special Constabulary, and the Voluntary Aid Detachment. 619 poets are only represented in the anthologies. In addition to the anthologies, 3,104 works by individual poets are listed, 28 of these works being anonymous. It is obvious from the annotations that a large proportion of verse was published to aid war charities or to commemorate relatives and friends who were killed in action.

The War Poetry Collection at Birmingham Central Library contains a fair number of broadsides and cards. It seemed reasonable to include these as they are now quite rare. Most libraries did not trouble to collect them, regarding them as ephemeral. I believe they emerge as one of the most interesting aspects of the bibliography. The cards are small enough to be carried in the pocket or in a soldier's pay book and this is how they were meant to be used. The postcards were probably published in issues of at least one thousand copies and so must have reached a very wide circle of readers. The British Museum has several collections of broadsides and cards housed in guard books. They are entered in the General Catalogue under EUROPEAN WAR, 1914-1918. The most important of these is in two volumes under the 'blanket' title [A collection of poems on the European War; by various writers]. There are so many items that they are not listed inside the guard book cover according to usual British Museum practice, nor do they appear under individual authors in the General Catalogue. To my knowledge this bibliography provides the only key to their contents. Further research in this field would be profitable, as many broadsides and cards are likely to be found in the local author collections of public libraries all over the United Kingdom.

It is axiomatic that every subject bibliography can only be a 'contribution' and I am conscious that it may be so in this case. There must surely be some volumes of poetry and verse published privately in limited editions, which did not go through the usual trade channels, were not deposited at the Copyright Office and so remain unrecorded. This theory is supported by the fact that the antiquarian booksellers, I. D. Edrich Ltd. of London, during several years of systematic searching for English First World War poetry, traced nineteen items by individual authors which are not be to be found in the British Museum or any other library to which I have had access.

The only similar list printed is Birmingham Public Library's "Catalogue of the War Poetry Collection" published in 1921, but this is restricted to that Library's holdings and covers war poetry of all nations, including European in foreign languages.

So this bibliography is unique in several ways:— it separates English First World War poetry from that of other nations and in so doing quantifies the corpus of English First World War poetry for the first time; it lists works containing the First World War poetry of prolific major writers like Thomas Hardy and Rudyard Kipling; it identifies many English minor poets hitherto unknown; it gives a library location for the vast majority of works listed. As a reference tool it has an obvious usefulness not only to the student of First World War poetry, but to the student of twentieth century English poetry in general, the librarian, the antiquarian bookseller, the social historian and the war historian.

SOURCES

The research for this bibliography has been carried out at the British Museum; at the Imperial War Museum; at Birmingham Central Library, the repository of a unique and important War Poetry Collection; at Manchester Central Library, which is especially rich in twentieth century poetry; at Wallasey Central Library, which collects English poetry within the subject specialization scheme of the North Western Regional Library Bureau; at the John Rylands Library, Manchester; at the University of Manchester; and at the antiquarian booksellers, I.D. Edrich of Wanstead, London, who hold a large collection of poetry of both World Wars. Many items have been borrowed from other libraries via the North Western Regional Library Bureau, the National Central Library, and the Scottish Central Library.

Apart from the anthologies listed in Section A the following works are the main reference sources consulted:—

ADCOCK, Arthur St. John
For remembrance : soldier poets who have fallen in the war. Revised ed. Hodder & Stoughton. [1920].

ALEXANDER, W.F., & CURRIE, A.E., eds
A treasury of New Zealand verse. 2nd ed. Whitcombe & Tombs. [1926].

BERRY, Francis
Herbert Read. Revised ed. Longmans, Green. 1961. (Bibliographical series of supplements to *British Book News* on writers and their work).

BIRMINGHAM PUBLIC LIBRARIES. REFERENCE DEPART-MENT
Catalogue of the War Poetry Collection presented by an anonymous donor in memory of Private William John Billington. Birmingham Printers. 1921.
Also Microfilm of additions, 1967.

BLUNDEN, Edmund
A booklist on the War, 1914-1918. National Home Reading Union. [1930?].
Reprinted from *The Reader*.

The BOOKMAN, 1914-1920.

The BOOKMAN [American], 1914-1920.

BRITISH MUSEUM
General catalogue of printed books. BM. 1961-66. 263v.
Also Ten-year supplement, 1956-1965, publ. 1968. 50v.

The BRITISH NATIONAL BIBLIOGRAPHY, 1950-70. B.N.B.

BURKE, W.J., & HOWE, Will D.
American authors and books : 1640 to the present day. Vane. 1963.

CARTER, John, & SPARROW, John
A.E. Housman : an annotated hand-list. Hart-Davis. 1952. (Soho bibliographies).

CRONE, John S.
A concise dictionary of Irish biography. Longmans, Green. 1928.

CROUCH, Edward Heath
A treasury of South African poetry and verse. Scott. 1907.

DICTIONARY of American biography. Oxford U.P. [1929-37]. 20v.
Also Supplement (to December 31, 1935).

DICTIONARY of national biography. Oxford U.P.

FIFOOT, Richard
A bibliography of Edith, Osbert and Sacheverell Sitwell. Hart-Davis. 1963. (Soho bibliographies).

GRANGER, Edith
Index to poetry. 5th ed., completely revised and enlarged, indexing anthologies published through June 30, 1960. Ed. by William F. Bernhardt. New York : Columbia U.P. 1962.

HARDIE, Alec M.
Edmund Blunden. Longmans, Green. 1958. (Bibliographical series of supplements to *British Book News* on writers and their work).

HELPS, Edmund Arthur, ed.
Songs and ballads of Greater Britain. Dent. 1913.

HIGGINSON, Fred H.
A bibliography of the works of Robert Graves. Vane. 1966.

HOUSMAN, Laurence, ed.
War letters of fallen Englishmen. Gollancz. 1930.

KEYNES, Geoffrey
A bibliography of Rupert Brooke. 2nd ed. Hart-Davis. 1959. (Soho bibliographies).

KEYNES, Geoffrey
A bibliography of Siegfried Sassoon. Hart-Davis. 1926. (Soho bibliographies).

KREYMBORG, Alfred, ed.
An anthology of American poetry : lyric America, 1639-1930. New ed. New York : Tudor Publ. Co. 1935.

KUNITZ, Stanley J., & HAYCRAFT, Howard, eds
Twentieth century authors : a biographical dictionary of modern literature. New York : Wilson. 1942.
Also First supplement, 1955.

LANG, John, & LANG, Jean, eds
Poetry of Empire : nineteen centuries of British history. Jack. [1910].

LANG, Frederick William Theodore, & BERRY, William Turner, eds
Books on the Great War : an annotated bibliography of literature issued during the European conflict. Grafton. 1915-16. 4v.

MARKHAM, Edwin, ed.
　　The book of American poetry. Harrap. [1940?].

MOORE, T. Sturge
　　Some soldier poets. Grant Richards. 1919.

MURDOCH, Sir Walter, ed.
　　A book of Australasian verse. 2nd ed. Oxford U.P. 1928.

MYERS, Robin, ed.
　　A dictionary of literature in the English language. Compiled for the National Book League. Pergamon P. 1970.

OSBORN, E.B.
　　The new Elizabethans : a first selection of the lives of young men who have fallen in the Great War. Bodley Head. 1919.

POETRY REVIEW, 1914-1920.

POETRY SOCIETY
　　Anthologies of the 1914-1918 war poets; and, The poets of the 1914-1918 war. [1936?].
　　(Typescript. Copy in MPL).

POETRY SOCIETY OF AMERICA
　　Anthology. New York : Fine Editions P. 1946.

PROTHERO, Sir George Walter
　　A select analytical list of books concerning the Great War. H.M.S.O. 1923.

SERLE, Percival
　　A bibliography of Australasian poetry and verse : Australia and New Zealand. Melbourne U.P. 1925.

SLATER, Francis Carey, ed.
　　The centenary book of South African verse, 1820-1925. Longmans. 1925.

SMITH, Arthur James Marshall, ed.
　　The book of Canadian poetry : a critical and historical anthology. 2nd ed. Chicago U.P. 1948.

SPENDER, Stephen, & HALL, Donald, eds
　　The concise encyclopedia of English and American poets and poetry. 2nd ed. Hutchinson. 1970.

STEVENS, Bertram, ed.
An anthology of Australian verse. Macmillan. 1906.

STEWART, James McG.
Rudyard Kipling : a bibliographical catalogue. Dalhousie U.P.;
Toronto U.P. 1959.

WADE, Allan
A bibliography of the writings of W.B. Yeats. 3rd ed. revised
and ed. by Russell K. Alspach. Hart-Davis. 1968. (Soho bibliographies).

WALLACE, W. Stewart, comp.
A dictionary of North American authors deceased before 1950.
Toronto : Ryerson P. 1951.

WARNER, Charles Dudley, ed.
Biographical dictionary and synopsis of books, ancient and
modern. Akron : Werner. 1965 reprint.

WHO was who, 1897-1950. Black. 4v.

BIBLIOGRAPHICAL NOTES ON CRITICISM

There are many critical works on the individual major poets of the First World War. The war poets are discussed as a 'genre' in most histories of twentieth century English literature and in many periodical articles. The few monographs, all published in recent years, are of a particularly high order. These are:—

BERGONZI, Bernard
Heroes' twilight : a study of the literature of the Great War. Constable. 1965. 235p.

Chapters on the fiction and autobiography of the period, but largely concerned with the poets, including Richard Aldington, Laurence Binyon, Edmund Blunden, Rupert Brooke, Ford Madox Ford, Robert Graves, Julian Grenfell, Ivor Gurney, Thomas Hardy, F.W. Harvey, Rudyard Kipling, Frederic Manning, Robert Nichols, Wilfred Owen, Herbert Read, Edgell Rickword, Isaac Rosenberg, Siegfried Sassoon, Osbert Sitwell, Charles Hamilton Sorley, Edward Thomas, Arthur Graeme West, W.B. Yeats. A chapter is devoted to David Jones's "In parenthesis".

BLUNDEN, Edmund
War poets, 1914-1918. New ed. Longmans, Green. 1964. 43p. por. (Bibliographical series of supplements to *British Book News* on writers and their work, 100).
Bibliog. 5p.
Publ. for the British Council and the National Book League.
Rupert Brooke, Julian Grenfell, Wilfred Owen, Siegfried Sassoon, Charles Hamilton Sorley, Arthur Graeme West. Brief mentions of Robert Graves, F.W. Harvey, Ivor Gurney, Robert Nichols, Isaac Rosenberg. Modestly, the author does not include himself.

JOHNSTON, John H.
English poetry of the First World War : a study in the evolution of lyric and narrative form. Oxford U.P. 1964. xvi, 354p.
Bibliog. 6p.
Chapters on "The early poets" (Rupert Brooke, Julian Grenfell, Robert Nichols, Charles Hamilton Sorley) and on Edmund Blunden, David Jones, Wilfred Owen, Herbert Read, Isaac Rosenberg, Siegfried Sassoon. Brief mentions of Laurence Binyon, Leslie Coulson, Gilbert Frankau, Thomas Hardy, W.N. Hodgson, Francis Ledwidge, Edward Thomas.

SILKIN, Jon
Out of battle : the poetry of the Great War. Oxford U.P. 1972. x, 366p.
Bibliog. 6p.
Richard Aldington, Edmund Blunden, Rupert Brooke, Ford Madox Ford, Julian Grenfell, Ivor Gurney, Thomas Hardy, David Jones, Rudyard Kipling, Wilfred Owen, Herbert Read, Isaac Rosenberg, Siegfried Sassoon, Charles Hamilton Sorley, Edward Thomas.

Some of the modern anthologies included in this bibliography provide useful background material, notably:—

(33) **GARDNER, Brian,** comp. Up the line to death.
Includes an introductory note and an appendix of short biographical notes on the poets represented. The poems are arranged under headings denoting aspects or phases of the war, e.g. 'Field Manoeuvres', 'Home Front', 'Behind the Lines'.

(50) **HUSSEY, Maurice,** ed. Poetry of the First World War.
In three sections 'Before Marching', 'Marching', 'After Marching', each section prefaced by editor's critical notes. Concludes with biographical notes on the poets.

(80) **PARSONS, I.M.,** ed. Men who march away.
Prefaced with a short critical introduction. Arranged in seven sections, which reflect the chronological progress of the war and the changing emotional attitudes of the poets towards it. Concludes with biographical notes on the poets.

ABBREVIATIONS

anon.	anonymous
b.	born
bibliog.	bibliography/bibliographical
C.B.	Companion of the Bath
Co.	Company
col.il.	coloured illustration(s)
comp.	compiled/compiler
D.C.M.	Distinguished Conduct Medal
D.S.C.	Distinguished Service Cross
D.S.O.	Distinguished Service Order
ed.	edited/edition/editor
facsim.	facsimile(s)
G.H.Q.	General Headquarters
gen. tab.	genealogical table(s)
Hon.	Honourable
il.	illustrated/illustration(s)
intro.	introduction
M.C.	Military Cross
M.V.O.	Member of the Victorian Order
mp	map
mps	maps
P.	Press
p.	pages
por.	portrait(s)
pseud.	pseudonym
publ.	published/publishing/publishers
repr.	reprint/reprinted
sic.	so
St.	Saint
U.P.	University Press
v.	volume(s)

ABBREVIATIONS OF LIBRARY LOCATIONS

BM	British Museum
BPL	Birmingham Public Libraries
BUPL	Burnley Public Libraries
CPL	Cheltenham Public Libraries
CWR	Bibliographer's copy
ECPL	Eccles Public Libraries
EDR	I.D. Edrich (Bookseller), Wanstead, London E11 2QF
EPL	Edinburgh Public Libraries
IWM	Imperial War Museum
JRL	John Rylands Library, Manchester
LPL	Liverpool Public Libraries
MPL	Manchester Public Libraries
NCL	National Central Library
PPL	Paisley Public Libraries
QUB	Queen's University, Belfast
SCL	Scottish Central Library
SCO	Staffordshire County Libraries
SOPL	Southampton Public Libraries
SPL	Salford Public Libraries
UD	University of Durham
UE	University of Exeter
UM	University of Manchester
UN	University of Newcastle
WCL	Wigtownshire County Libraries
WEPL	Westminster Public Libraries
WPL	Wallasey Public Libraries

SECTION A: ANTHOLOGIES

1   **AIR** Force songs and verses. *Aeronautics.* 1927. 40p.
    'All profits to go to the R.A.F. Memorial Fund'.   IWM

2   **ANDREWS, Clarence Edward,** comp.
    From the front: trench poetry. With an intro. New York:
    Appleton. 1918, xxx, 220p.

    H.A., G. Alchin, H. Asquith, C.W. Blackall, R. Brooke,
    E.T. Cooper, N.M.F. Corbett, L. Coulson, C.G.L. Du Cann,
    G. Frankau, A.F. Graves, R. Gurner, A.P. Herbert, W.N.
    Hodgson, W.K. Holmes, S. King-Hall, J.H. Knight-Adkin,
    J. Lee, D.O. Lumley, W.S.S. Lyon, C.A. Macartney,
    P. MacGill, H.A. Nesbitt, R. Nichols, W.G. Shakespeare,
    H. Steele, J.E. Stewart, J.W. Streets, T. Tiplady, G. Waterhouse,
    A.E. Whiting-Baker, E.F. Wilkinson, E.A. Wodehouse.   BM

    B., L.L., comp. see **H., G.E., & B., L.L.,** comps (44)

    BELL, Charles Christopher, ed. & tr. see **BELL, Sir Harold
    Idris, & BELL, Charles Christopher,** eds & trs (3)

3   **BELL, Sir Harold Idris, & BELL, Charles Christopher,**
    eds & trs
    Welsh poems of the twentieth century in English verse.
    With an historical and critical essay on Welsh poetry by
    H.I. Bell. Wrexham: Hughes 1925. x, 139p.

    Section *Poems of the War:* W.J. Gruffydd, G. Jones,
    D. Owen, W. Parry, J.R. Williams   MPL

4   **BLACK, Edward Loring,** ed.
    1914-8 in poetry: an anthology. London U.P. 1970. 157p.

1

R. Aldington, H. Asquith, L. Binyon, E.C. Blunden,
R. Brooke, G.K. Chesterton, W.N. Ewer, W.W. Gibson,
R. Graves, J. Grenfell, I. Gurney, T. Hardy, A.P. Herbert,
W.N. Hodgson, A.E. Housman. P. Johnstone, R. Kipling,
E.A. Mackintosh, R. Nichols, W. Owen, M. Plowman,
H. Read, E. Rhys, E. Rickword, I. Rosenberg, S. Sassoon,
O. Sitwell, C.H. Sorley, E. Thomas, R.E. Vernède.   MPL

5   **BLUE CROSS FUND**
A book of poems for the Blue Cross Fund (to help horses
in war time). Jarrolds. 1917. vi, 90p.

J.A. Anderson, N.M. Armstrong, H.B., H.T.M. Bell, G.A.
Congreve, M. Crosbie, P. Crozier, O.P. Downes, A.W.
Drewett, Equites, pseud., L. Fieldhouse, G. Fuller, S.R.
Gibson, H.J. Greenaway, R.S. Henrey, E.F. Holland,
L. Jousiffe, A. Joyce, E. Knott, M.F. Larkin, L. Lawrence,
D. Legge, B. Locock, A.M., Minor, pseud., L.G. Moberly,
A. Morley, A.G. Nichols, Old Hunter, pseud., M. Ponsonby,
J. Pope, J. Preston, C.S. Purves, I. Quilter, H.D. Rawnsley,
J. Rhoades, H. Robinson, Scots Grey, pseud., B. Sheen,
E. Strickland, K. Summers, H.T., R. Voss, H.F.W., Z.F.A.
West, B. Wilson, Yorkshire Girl, pseud., A. Young, N.E.Z.   BPL

BOOTH, Mary, comp. see **EDWARDS**, Mabel C., & **BOOTH**,
Mary, comps (25)

BRERETON, Frederick, pseud., comp. see **SMITH**,
Frederick Thomson, (Frederick Brereton, pseud.),
comp. (96)

6   **BROPHY**, John, & **PARTRIDGE**, Eric, eds
The long trail: what the British soldier sang and said in
the Great War of 1914-18. Deutsch. 1965. 239p. il.
   Bibliog. note 2p.
   A new presentation of "Songs and slang of the British
soldier: 1914-18".   MPL

7   **BROPHY**, John, & **PARTRIDGE**, Eric, eds
The long trail: soldiers' songs and slang, 1914-18. [New]
ed. Sphere. 1969. 189p.
   Bibliog. note 2p.
   A new presentation of "Songs and slang of the British
soldier: 1914-18".   Not seen

8 **BROPHY, John, & PARTRIDGE, Eric**, eds
Songs and slang of the British soldier: 1914-18. Scholartis P.
1930. viii, 200p.
> A limited ed. of 1,000 copies.
> With "Glossary of soldiers' slang".   BPL

9 **BROPHY, John, & PARTRIDGE, Eric**, eds
Songs and slang of the British soldier: 1914-1918. 2nd ed.
Scholartis P. 1930. viii, 222p.
> With "Glossary of soldiers' slang".   BM

10 **BROPHY, John, & PARTRIDGE, Eric**, eds
Songs and slang of the British soldier: 1914-1918. 3rd ed.
Scholartis P. 1931. viii, 383p.
> With "Glossary of soldiers' slang".   BM

11 **BRYDEN, H.G.**, ed.
Wings: an anthology of flight. Faber. 1942. 320p.

Section *War:* P. Bewsher, E. Daryush, G. Frankau, E.V.
Hall, J.L. Hitchings, S. Sassoon, W.J. Turner, W.B. Yeats.
Includes "Songs they sang in the R.F.C., 1914-1918".   MPL

12 **CASE, Carleton Britton**, comp.
Wartime and patriotic selections for recitation and
reading. Chicago: Shrewesbury Publ. Co. [1918]. 159p.

L. Binyon, R. Bridges, C.W. Brodribb, R. Brooke, P.R.
Chalmers, F. Coutts, A. Dobson, A.C. Doyle, W.N. Ewer,
W.W. Gibson, Growler, pseud., M.C.D.H., G.R. Hamilton,
M. Hewlett, H. Ingamells, J.H. Knight-Adkin, J. Lee, W.M.
Letts, P. MacGill, F. Niven, E. Phillpotts, C.F. Smith,
K. Tynan, R.E. Vernède, L.M. Watt.   BPL

13 **CHAPMAN, Guy**, ed.
Vain glory: a miscellany of the Great War, 1914-1918,
written by those who fought in it on each side and on all
fronts. With an intro. Cassell. 1937. xviii, 762p.

Mainly prose contributions, but includes poems by V.M.
Brittain, W.W. Gibson, L.W. Griffith, P. Johnstone,
W. Owen, I. Rosenberg, P. Shaw-Stewart, I. Zangwill.   BM

14 **CHAPMAN, Guy**, ed.
Vain glory: a miscellany of the Great War, 1914-1918,
written by those who fought in it on each side and on all

fronts. With an intro. 2nd ed. Cassell. 1968. xviii, 762p.
Contents as 1st ed. BPL

15 CINQUANTE Quatre: Flying Corps songs. Cambridge:
Bowes. 1918. [iii], 16p. il.
Anonymous words to be sung to well known tunes. MPL

[First printed privately in 1917. No copy of this ed.
traced].

16 **CLARKE, George Herbert, ed.**
A treasury of war poetry: British and American poems of
the World War, 1914-1917. With intro. and notes. First
series. Boston (Mass.): Houghton Mifflin. 1917. xxx, 282p.

H. Asquith, P. Bewsher, F. Bickley, L. Binyon, F.W.
Bourdillon, R. Bridges, R. Brooke, P.R. Chalmers, C.E.
Chesterton, G.K. Chesterton, L. Coulson, M. Dalton,
W. De La Mare, W.M. Dixon, A. Dobson, A.C. Doyle,
J. Drinkwater, A.N. Field, G. Frankau, J. Freeman,
J. Galsworthy, W.W. Gibson, J. Grenfell, G.R. Hamilton,
T. Hardy, J. Helston, M. Hemphrey, M. Hewlett, W.N.
Hodgson, G. Howard, D. Hussey, H.W. Hutchinson,
H. Jones, R. Kipling, J.H. Knight-Adkin, J. Lee, W.M.
Letts, E.V. Lucas, F. Manning, J. Masefield, C.L. Morgan,
H. Newbolt, R. Nichols, A. Noyes, W.H. Ogilvie, S. Oswald,
E. Owen, B. Pain, M. Peterson, S. Phillips, E. Phillpotts,
A.V. Ratcliffe, H.D. Rawnsley, A. Robertson, R. Ross,
O. Seaman, C.F. Smith, C.H. Sorley, J.E. Stewart, E.W.
Tennant, K. Tynan, R.E. Vernède, J. Walker, G. Waterhouse. BPL

17 **CLARKE, George Herbert, ed.**
A treasury of war poetry: British and American poems of
the World War, 1914-1919. With intro. and notes. Second
series. Boston (Mass.): Houghton Mifflin. [1919]. xxxviii,
362p.

H. Asquith, R.G. Barnes, H.H. Bashford, M.A. Bell,
P. Bewsher, L. Binyon, F.W. Bourdillon, R. Bridges, C.W.
Brodribb, R. Brooke, M. Byrde, R.L. Carton, P.R. Chalmers,
G.K. Chesterton, N.M.F. Corbett, W.L. Courtney, R.O.A.
Crewe-Milnes, M. Dalton, M.J.G. Day, E. De Stein,
A. Dobson, A.C. Doyle, W.H. Draper, J. Drinkwater,
G. Frankau, J. Freeman, W.C. Galbraith, J. Galsworthy,
W.W. Gibson, R. Graves, T. Hardy, F.W. Harvey, H. Head,
J. Helston, E.M. Hewitt, M. Hewlett, W.N. Hodgson,

4

J. Hogben, W.K. Holmes, M. Huxley, G. Kendall, J.H.
Knight-Adkin, K. Knox, F. Ledwidge, J. Lee, R. Le Gallienne,
W.M. Letts, W.S.S. Lyon, P. MacGill, F. Manning,
J. Masefield, N. Munro, A.E. Murray, A.T. Nankivell,
H. Newbolt, R. Nichols, A. Noyes, N.J. O'Conor, W.H.
Ogilvie, C.H. Oldfield, E. Owen, N. Oxland, B. Pain,
A.L. Phelps, E. Phillpotts, E.J.M.D. Plunkett, H.D.
Rawnsley, G.E. Rees, C. Roberts, M. Roberts, R. Ross,
G.W. Russell, S. Sassoon, O. Seaman, W.G. Shakespeare,
E. Shillito, C.F. Smith, C.H. Sorley, E.W. Tennant, B.F.
Trotter, K. Tynan, E. Underhill, J. Walker, G.O. Warren,
W. Watson, L. Whitmell, M. Wilson, M.A. Wilson, T.P.C.
Wilson, E.A. Wodehouse, M.L. Woods, E.H. Young.   BPL

18 **CLARKE, George Herbert**, ed.
A treasury of war poetry: British and American poems of
the World War, 1914-1919. With intro. and notes. Hodder
& Stoughton. [1919]. 448p.

H. Asquith, M. Baring, R.G. Barnes, H.H. Bashford,
M.A. Bell, P. Bewsher, F. Bickley, L. Binyon, F.W.
Bourdillon, R. Bridges, C.W. Brodribb, R. Brooke, R.L.
Carton, P.R. Chalmers, C.E. Chesterton, G.K. Chesterton,
N.M.F. Corbett, L. Coulson, W.L. Courtney, R.O.A. Crewe-
Milnes, M. Dalton, M.J.G. Day, W. De La Mare, E. De Stein,
W.M. Dixon, A. Dobson, A.C. Doyle, W.H. Draper,
J. Drinkwater, A.N. Field, G. Frankau, J. Freeman, W.C.
Galbraith, J. Galsworthy, W.W. Gibson, R. Graves,
J. Grenfell, T. Hardy, I.W. Harper, F.W. Harvey, H. Head,
J. Helston, E.M. Hewitt, M. Hewlett, W.N. Hodgson,
J. Hogben, W.K. Holmes, H.W. Hutchinson, M. Huxley,
D.F.G. Johnson, H. Jones, G. Kendall, G.A.S. Kennedy,
T.M. Kettle, R. Kipling, J.H. Knight-Adkin, K. Knox,
F. Ledwidge, J. Lee, R. Le Gallienne, W.M. Letts, E.V.
Lucas, W.S.S. Lyon, P. MacGill, E.A. Mackintosh,
F. Manning, J. Masefield, C.L. Morgan, N. Munro, A.E.
Murray, A.T. Nankivell, H. Newbolt, R. Nichols, A. Noyes,
N.J. O'Conor, W.H. Ogilvie, C.H. Oldfield, E. Owen,
N. Oxland, B. Pain, S. Phillips, E. Phillpotts, E.J.M.D.
Plunkett, H.D. Rawnsley, G.E. Rees, C. Roberts,
M. Roberts, R. Ross, G.W. Russell, S. Sassoon, O. Seaman,
W.G. Shakespeare, E. Shillito, C.F. Smith, C.H. Sorley,
E.W. Tennant, B.F. Trotter, K. Tynan, E. Underhill, R.E.
Vernède, A. Vickridge, J. Walker, G.O. Warren, W. Watson,
L. Whitmell, W.L. Wilkinson, M. Wilson, M.A. Wilson, T.P.C.
Wilson, E.A. Wodehouse, M.L. Woods, E.H. Young.   MPL

COUCH, Sir Arthur Quiller-, ed. see QUILLER-COUCH,
Sir Arthur, ed. (88)

19 CUNLIFFE, John William, comp.
Poems of the Great War. Selected on behalf of the
Belgian Scholarship Committee. New York: Macmillan.
1916. xxii, 297p.

G. Alchin, R. Aldington, E. Alexander, H. Allsopp,
H. Asquith, H. Begbie, L. Binyon, W. Blair, H.W. Bliss,
F.W. Bourdillon, R. Bridges, R. Brooke, G.A.J.C., P.R.
Chalmers, A.V. Chartres, G.K. Chesterton, P.B. Clayton,
W.L. Courtney, R.O.A. Crewe-Milnes, T.W.H. Crosland,
G.H. Crow, W. De La Mare, J. Drinkwater, A.M.F.R.
Duclaux, G. Faber, J.B. Fagan, A.S. Falconer, G. Frankau,
J. Freeman, H.R. Freston, V.H. Friedlaender, L. Gard,
H.C. Gardner, W.W. Gibson, B. Gilbert, V. Gillespie,
G. Goddard, A.P. Graves, J. Grenfell, N. Griffiths, N.M.H.,
C. Hamilton, T. Hardy, H.C. Harwood, M. Hewlett,
D. Hussey, V. Jacob, E. Jenkins, E. John, W.M. Letts,
E.V. Lucas, H. Lulham, O.M., J.A. Mackereth, J. Masefield,
M.G. Meugens, A. Meynell, E. Nesbit, J.A. Nicklin,
A. Noyes, W.H. Olgivie, S. Oswald, B. Pain, S. Phillips,
J. Pope, R. Ross, J.H.S., E.T. Sandford, O. Seaman,
E. Shillito, F. Sidgwick, M. Sinclair, I.G. Smith, C.H. Sorley,
J. Stephens, A. Stodart-Walker, A.J. Stuart, F. Taylor,
G. Thomas, G.E. Tollemache, D.H. Tripp, K. Tynan,
A. Vickridge, T.H. Warren, W. Watson, L.M. Watt, I.A.
Williams, M.L. Woods, F.B. Young.   BPL

20 DAVISON, Edward, comp.
Cambridge poets, 1914-1920. Cambridge: Heffer. 1920.
xii, 217p.
    Bibliog. 3p.

S. Bellhouse, R. Brooke, G. Bullett, G.F. Fyson, A.M.
Harrison, D.B. Haseler, D.F.G. Johnson, J.H.F. McEwen,
J.D. Macleod, S. Sassoon, J.C. Squire, C.B. Tracey, K.M.
Wallace, E.H. Young.   MPL

21 D'ERLANGER, Emile Beaumont, Baron, comp.
Les soldats-poètes de l'Angleterre: poëmes de Rupert
Brooke, Julian Grenfell et Siegfried Sassoon. Récités à
L'Army and Navy British Leave Club de Paris.[Paris?].
1919. [29]p.
    In English, with French translations.   BM

6

22 **DICKINSON, Patric,** comp.
Soldiers' verse. Muller. 1945. viii, 119p. col. il. (by
William Scott). (New excursions into English poetry).

E.C. Blunden, G.K. Chesterton, R. Church, E.L. Davison,
W. De La Mare, T. Hardy, A.E. Housman, R. Kipling,
A. Meynell, H. Newbolt, W. Owen, E. Rhys, S. Sassoon,
C.H. Sorley, E. Thomas, W.J. Turner.   MPL

23 **DONALD, Mary,** comp.
A garland of patriotism: an anthology. Edinburgh:
Nimmo, Hay & Mitchell. [1917]. viii, 88p.

Section *Poems suggested by the present war:* A. Barry,
H. Begbie, H. Chappell, T. Hardy, W.J. Mathams, L.G.
Moberly, A.L.O.P., J.L. Robertson, C.A. Salmond,
O. Seaman, W. Watson.   BPL

24 **EATON, William Dunsheath,** ed.
The war in verse and prose. With intro., notes and original
matter. Chicago: Denison. [1918]. 199p.

H.A., J.G. Bower, W.A. Briscoe, R. Brooke, L. Coulson,
M.B.H., B.H.M. Hetherington, J.H. Knight-Adkin,
F. Ledwidge, W.M. Letts, P.H.B. Lyon, H.J.M., E. Owen,
V. Perowne, O.C. Platoon, pseud., A.W. Pollard, G.E.R.,
S. Sassoon, W.G. Shakespeare, G. Waterhouse,
L. Whitmell, T.P.C. Wilson.   BPL

25 **EDWARDS, Mabel C., & BOOTH, Mary,** comps
The fiery cross: an anthology. Grant Richards. 1915. 96p.
   Sold for the benefit of the Red Cross.

H. Allsopp, L. Binyon, M. Booth, F.W. Bourdillon, W.S.
Boyle, R. Brooke, H. Chappell, G.K. Chesterton, D. Clark,
C. Congreve, F.R. Coulson, W.L. Courtney, R.O.A. Crewe-
Milnes, T.W.H. Crosland, A. Dobson, H.P. Eden, J.B. Fagan,
A.S. Falconer, M. Gower, C.L. Graves, D.F. Gurney,
T. Hardy, P. Haselden, E.G.V. Knox, L.B. Lyon, M.G.
Meugens, A. Meynell, H. Newbolt, A. Noyes, J. Oxenham,
B. Pain, J. Pope, H.D. Rawnsley, O. Seaman, K. Tynan,
T.H. Warren, W. Watson, M.L. Woods.   MPL

26 **ELLIOTT, H.B.,** ed.
Lest we forget: a war anthology. Foreword by Baroness
Orczy. Jarrolds. 1915. 139p. il.
   Compiled to aid the Queen Mary Needlework Guild.

J.W. Allen, W. Archer, L. Binyon, M. Booth, F.W.
Bourdillon, A.W. Bustridge, A.V. Chartres, C.E.
Chesterton, F. Chesterton, G.K. Chesterton, P.B. Clayton,
W.L. Courtney, J.E. Flecker, J. Frankau, J. Freeman, R.L.
Gales, L. Gard, L. Gomme, M. Gower, A.P. Graves,
C. Hamilton, T. Hardy, M. Hewlett, W.N. Hodgson, G.H.
Leonard, J.H. McCarthy, E. Nesbit, A. Noyes, B. Pain,
M. Peterson, S. Phillips, E. Phillpotts, H.D. Rawnsley,
O. Seaman, F. Sidgwick, H. Simpson, D.S.S. Steuart,
D.M. Stuart, G.E. Tollemache, K. Tynan, W. Watson,
A.E. Whiting-Baker.   MPL

FORD, S. Gertrude, comp. see **MACDONALD, Erskine,**
& FORD, S. Gertrude, comps (63)

27   **FORSHAW, Charles Frederick,** ed.
One hundred of the best poems on the European War. v. 1.
By poets of the Empire. Elliot Stock. 1915. 192p. por.
   Cover-title is "One hundred best poems on the war".
   Dedicated to Lieutenant William Thomas Forshaw, V.C.,
9th Battalion, Manchester Regiment.

A. Aaronson, G. Abel, F. Anderson, J. Baker, R.H. Banks,
H.E. Bannard, W. Bargery, J. Batteson, H.T.M. Bell, R.G.
Bell, A. Bennett, W.C. Blaker, W.A. Boyd, F.T. Bramston,
J.C. Brittain, J.A. Brooke, J.J. Brown, W.M. Bryden,
H. Chappell, L.A. Compton-Rickett, F.S.J. Corbett, H.J.
Cox, A. Crocket, W. Cryer, S.G. Dodsley, C. Donner,
L. Dowdall, E. Dynes, A.C. Farrington, G.R. Fetherston,
N. Fleming, J.G.S. Flett, J.M. Foster, A.J. Freeland,
S. Gasking, J.G. Gibson, C. Goff, F.H.B. Graves, F.G.
Greenwood, T. Grey, T. Grice, D.A. Griffiths, F.P.
Halsall, R. Hanbury, W.D. Harding, J. Hartley, H. Henderson,
C.F. Hobday, A. Holdsworth, E. Holdsworth, F. Hood,
A. Houston, H.K. Hudson, J. Hunter, M. Hyslop, R.J.
Kerr, J.J. Lane, E. Lee, J. Lill, T.J. Linekar, T.W. Little,
W.H. Lloyd, L. Longfield, G.H. Longrigg, S.S. McCurry,
R. McDonnell, J.W. Marshall, W. Maudslay, J.R. Meagher,
A. Morris, H.C.G. Moule, J. Nicol, O. Norman, A.H.
Osborne, J.R. Palmer, C. Powell, G.P. Quick, H.D.
Rawnsley, F.T. Read, R. Ross, J. Rowlands, E.G.
Sargent, J. Silvester, H.S. Spencer, C.P. Stevenson, F.S.
Stevenson, J. Storrie, J. Taylor, T. Telford, A.A. Toms,
A.R. Tremearne, W. Trend, E. Urwick, F.W.O. Ward,
J.C.D. Whelan, T. Whitehead, L. Williams, G.H.
Williamson, G.H. Wilson, L.H. Winn, H. Yeandle.   MPL

FORSHAW, Charles Frederick, ed.
One hundred of the best poems on the European War. v.2.
By women poets of the Empire. Elliot Stock. 1916. 170p.
por.
   Cover-title is "One hundred best poems on the war".
   Dedicatory poem by Henry Chappell, to Private Thomas
Garrett Forshaw, 17th Battalion, Cheshire Regiment.

H. Abercromby, P. Bate, H. Bolland, J. Bonnyman, E.M.
Briggs, B.A. Brock, M. Brodie, B. Brownsword, E. Budgen,
B. Bunting, L.D. Burke, E.M. Buskin, V.D. Chapman,
G.T. Clarke, F. Clee, M. Clephane, K.M. Coates, H.H.
Colvill, E.M. Crawford, N.M. Crawford, A.R. Cron, E.M.
Cruttwell, A.I. Curwen, N. Davidson, C. Deas, J. Donnan,
M. Du Deney, A. Duxbury, E. Edis, K. Everest, A.V.
Gandy, E.C. Gerrard, M.E. Gibson, P. Grant, E. Gray,
E. Guy, M. Hall, M.E. Hall, F. Harden, A. Hartley, R.A. Hayden,
L. Henley-White, E. Hind, L. Hoare, E. Jenkinson, G.E.G.
Jewitt, T. Leslie, E. Ling, M.C. Lufkin, I. Macintire,
L. Mallett, A. Mann, L. Marcus, S. Masefield, G.M. Mason,
O.G. Mather, M. Milnes, E.J. Montgomerie, C. Morgan,
M. Mostyn, L.L.A. Panter, E.F. Parr, M.W. Paton, J.E.
Pemberton, K. Pickard, F.H. Poole, E. Postlethwaite,
M. Pratt, J. Precious, E. Pressimer, L. Prior, F. Radcliffe,
J. Rayner, G. Renny, L. Riddell-Webster, G. Roberts,
A. Rooker, E. Rose, A.E. Rowe, M. Royce, C.E. Sharpley,
K.O. Simmonds, A. Squires, G.P. Stanley, F.C. Steel,
E.M. Stephenson, D.E. Stevenson, E.M. Stratton, C.P.
Thomson, A. Tillyard, G. Turnley, M. Tyrrell-Green,
E. Vaughan, L.E. Ward, I.E.T. Warner, I. Warry, L.A.
Whitworth, H.F. Wilkins, M.A. Woods, A.M. Workman.   MPL

FORSHAW, Charles Frederick, ed.
Poems in memory of the late Field-Marshall Lord
Kitchener, K.G. Bradford: Institute of British Poetry.
1916. vi, 252p. il., por.
   Cover-title is "Poetical tributes to the late Lord Kitchener".

N. Abraham, R. Ambrose, N. Ansell, M. Askew, H.F.B.
Aumonier, A.S.B. Badminton, B.B. Baily, E. Ballard,
W. Bargery, P. Bate, A.J. Begbie, A. Bennett, L.E. Bent,
J. Black, H. Bolland, J. Bonnyman, A.J. Bramman, F.T.
Bramston, R. Bridges, J.C. Brittain, B.A. Brock, R. Brock,
J.A. Brooke, H.J. Bulkeley, F.R. Burrow, B.C. Busbridge,
E.M. Buskin, M. Cameron, V.D. Chapman, F.W.G. Clarke, F. Clee,
J.E. Cook, H.A. Corser, J. Coutts, F.I. Cowles, E. Crabtree,

E.M. Crawford, N.M. Crawford, A. Crocket, F. Croft, M.M.
Curchod, A.I. Curwen, E. Denby, D.M. Dillon, E.M. Dixon,
J.W. Dobson, J. Donnan, A.W. Drewett, M. Du Deney,
R.F. Eldridge, B.A. Eyre, T. Farrar, A.C. Farrington, G.P.
Findlay, N. Fleming, J.G.S. Flett, C.F. Forshaw, R.H.
Forster, A.A. Foster, J.M. Foster, A.J. Freeland, S. Gasking,
W. Gell, E.C. Gerrard, F.B. Girling, W.J. Gomersall, H.G.
Gorst, M. Gower, F.H.B. Graves, F.G. Greenwood, D.A.
Griffiths, C.H. Grinling, J.H. Grove, G. Hadgraft, M. Hall,
M.E. Hall, F. Harden, W.D. Harding, A. Hartley,
H. Henderson, D. Henkel, L. Henley-White, E. Hind, L.J.
Hobbs, E. Holdsworth, F. Hood, A.A. Hopper, J.C. Hunter,
E. Jenkinson, I. Jennings, G.E.G. Jewitt, F.B. Keate, A.H.
Kellett, W.A. Kingston, G. Kitching, J.J. Lane, L. Lawrence,
G.A. Le Bert, M.C. Lufkin, A.W. Mair, R. Mallett, A. Mann,
W.E. Manning, L. Marcus, C.S. Marriott, J.W. Marshall,
S. Masefield, A.A. Miller, J.S. Mills, A.G. Mitchell, J.T.
Monteith, M. Mostyn, J. Mountain, G.G. Napier, E. Ness,
J. Nicol, D.M. Nicoll, J.N. Noble, R. O'Neal, H. Palmer, J.R.
Palmer, L.L.A. Panter, M.W. Paton, J.E. Pemberton, F.H. Poole,
D. Preston, S.A. Preston, L.Pritt, F. Radcliffe, J. Ramsay,
S. Randall, G.M.L. Reade, P. Rennie, H. Reseigh, J. Rhoades,
F. Richards, L. Riddell-Webster, G. Roberts, A.E. Rowe,
J. Rowlands, C.M. Savage, J.S. Scotland, D. Scott,
N. Scrymgeour, O. Seaman, C.E. Sharpley, J. Silvester,
J. Simpson, W.T. Smellie, T.N. Smith, J. Sorby, A. Squires,
E. Stanley, G.P. Stanley, F. Stephens, E.M. Stephenson,
E.M. Stratton, E. Summers, J.C. Sutcliffe, A.C. Symons,
T. Telford, W. Thornyhill, E.E. Todd, M. Tucker,
E. Vaughan, K. Veasey, S. Walbank, W.S. Walker, L.E.
Ward, E.E. Warren, I. Warry, J.C.D. Whelan, D.R.
Williamson, A. Winnifrith, A.M. Workman, G.G. Wylie.   BPL

30   **FOSTER, Alfred Eyde Manning**, comp.
Lord God of battles: a war anthology. Cope & Fenwick.
1914. 80p.

R. Bridges, H. Chappell, M. Cope, W. De La Mare, A.C.
Doyle, M. Goldring, A. Gyles, T. Hardy, H.D. Smith,
H.A. Vachell.   BPL

31   **FOXCROFT, Frank**, ed.
War verse. 5th [ed.]. New York: Crowell. 1918. xii, 303p.
   Back of title-page states 5th printing but may be 5th ed.

J.W.A., I. Adair, M. Allen, B. Allhusen, A.V. Arnold,

H. Asquith, A.J.B., P.B., H. Begbie, L. Binyon, F.W.
Bourdillon, J.G. Bower, R. Bridges, R. Brooke, M. Byrde,
V.D. Chapman, C.E. Chesterton, G.K. Chesterton,
E. Chilman, A. Cochrane, H.H. Colvill, L. Coulson,
F. Coutts, S.D. Cox, B. Cregan, R.O.A. Crewe-Milnes,
R.A. Crouch, E. De Stein, A. Dobson, A.C. Doyle,
J. Drinkwater, R. Duffin, P.J. Fisher, E.C. Forman,
E. Fuller-Maitland, W.H. Gadsdon, W.C. Galbraith, W.W.
Gibson, G. Greenland, J. Grenfell, N.G.H., G.R.
Hamilton, T. Hardy, B.H.M Hetherington, B. Hill, W.N.
Hodgson, J. Hogben, W.G. Hole, R. Hope, M. Huxley,
W.E.K., A.G. Keown, j.H. Knight-Adkin, W.L., R.H.
Law, J. Lee, W.M. Letts, A. Lindsay, P.H. Loyson,
H. Lulham, P.H.B. Lyon, P.S.M., M.A. Macdonald, F.E.
Maitland, L. Masterman, T. Maynard, J.N. Milne, N. Munro,
A.E. Murray, G.D. Nash, E. Nesbit, B.P. Neuman,
H. Newbolt, W.B. Nichols, F. Niven, A. Noyes, W.H.O.,
W.H. Ogilvie, Orellius, pseud., M. O'Rourke, J. Oxenham,
E. Phillpotts, E.J.M.D. Plunkett, A.G. Prys-Jones,
R. Raleigh, pseud., H.D. Rawnsley, J. Rhoades, C. Roberts,
G. Robertson-Glasgow, R. O'D. Ross-Lewin, G.W.
Russell, M. Sackville, S. Sassoon, O. Seaman, E. Shillito,
W. Sichel, E. Simms, C.F. Smith, J.C. Squire, L. Thanet,
H. Trench, K. Tynan, E. Underhill, R.V., G.E.M.
Vaughan, F.A. Vicars, B.H.W., E.M. Walker, W. Watson,
L. Whitmell, T.P.C. Wilson and several anon.   IWM

2   FOXCROFT, Frank, ed.
War verse. 7th [ed]. New York: Crowell. 1918. xvi, 373p.
   Back of title-page states 7th printing but editor's note
states 7th ed.

J.W.A., I. Adair, B. Allhusen, A.V. Arnold, H. Asquith,
A.J.B., P.B., H. Begbie, L. Binyon, A. Blundell, F.W.
Bourdillon, J.G. Bower, R. Bridges, R. Brooke, M. Byrde,
R. Capell, V.D. Chapman, C.E. Chesterton, G.K. Chesterton,
E. Chilman, A. Cochrane, H.H. Colvill, W.A. Cook,
L. Coulson, F. Coutts, S.D. Cox, B. Cregan, R.O.A.
Crewe-Milnes, R.A. Crouch, E. De Stein, A. Dobson, A.C.
Doyle, J. Drinkwater, R. Duffin, M. Few, P.J. Fisher,
E.C. Forman, E. Fuller-Maitland, W.H. Gadsdon, W.C.
Galbraith, W.W. Gibson, G. Greenland, J. Grenfell, N.G.H.,
G.R. Hamilton, T. Hardy, A.P. Herbert, B.H.M.
Hetherington, B. Hill, W.N. Hodgson, J. Hogben, W.G.
Hole, R. Hope, M. Huxley, W.E.K., A.G. Keown, J.H.
Knight-Adkin, W.L., R.H. Law, J. Lee, W.M. Letts,

A. Lindsay, S. Low, P.H. Loyson, H. Lulham, P.H.B.
Lyon, P.S.M., C.A. Macartney, M. McClymont, M.A.
Macdonald, B. McMaster, F.E. Maitland, L. Masterman,
T. Maynard, A. Meynell, J.N. Milne, N. Munro, A.E.
Murray, G.D. Nash, E. Nesbit, B.P. Neuman, H. Newbolt,
E. Newton, W.B. Nichols, F. Niven, A. Noyes, W.H.O.,
W.H. Ogilvie, Orellius, pseud., M. O'Rourke, J. Oxenham,
E. Phillpotts, E.J.M.D. Plunkett, A.G. Prys-Jones, R. Raleigh,
pseud., H.D. Rawnsley, J. Rhoades, N. Richardson,
C. Roberts, G. Robertson-Glasgow, D.A. Robison, R.O'D.
Ross-Lewin, G.W. Russell, M. Sackville, S. Sassoon,
O. Seaman, E. Shillito, W. Sichel, E. Simms, C.F. Smith,
J.C. Squire, J. Tenison, L. Thanet, D. Tovey, H. Trench,
K. Tynan, E. Underhill, R.V., G.E.M. Vaughan, F.A.
Vicars, B.H.W., E.M. Walker, K.M. Wallace, P. Warren,
W. Watson, L. Whitmell, T.P.C. Wilson and several anon.   BPL

[No other eds traced. These are the only ones recorded
in the American "National Union Catalog: Pre-1956
Imprints"].

G.E.H., comp. see H., G.E., & B., L.L., comps (44)

33   **GARDNER** , Brian, comp.
Up the line to death: the war poets, 1914-1918: an
anthology, with an intro. and notes. Foreword by Edmund
Blunden. Methuen. 1964. xxvi, 188p.

R. Aldington. M. Armstrong, H. Asquith, M. Baring,
L. Barnes, P. Bewsher, L. Binyon, E.C. Blunden, R. Brooke,
L. Coulson, M.J.G. Day, G. Dearmer, E. De Stein,
J. Drinkwater, J.G. Fairfax, G. Frankau, J. Freeman,
C. Garstin, W.W. Gibson, R.Graves, J. Grenfell, L.W.
Griffith, T. Hardy, F.W. Harvey, A.P. Herbert, W.N.
Hodgson, A.E. Housman, P. Johnstone, D. Jones, T.M.
Kettle, R. Kipling, F. Ledwidge, P.H.B. Lyon, D.S.
MacColl, P. MacGill, E.A. Mackintosh, R.B. Marriott-
Watson, A.A. Milne, H. Monro, H. Newbolt, R. Nichols,
W. Owen, N. Oxland, R. Palmer, M. Plowman, E.J.M.D.
Plunkett, H. Read, E. Rickword, I. Rosenberg, S. Sassoon,
R.H. Sauter, E. Shanks, P. Shaw-Stewart, O. Sitwell, C.H.
Sorley, E.W. Tennant, E. Thomas, E.J. Thompson, W.J.
Turner, R.E. Vernède, A. Waugh, W. Weaving, I.A.
Williams, T.P.C. Wilson, W.B. Yeats, E.H. Young,
F.B. Young.   MPL

34   **GEORGIAN** poetry, 1913-1915. Poetry Bookshop. 1915.
[x], 244p.
   Bibliog. 4p.

   R. Brooke, J. Drinkwater, W.W. Gibson.   MPL

35   **GEORGIAN** poetry, 1916-1917. Poetry Bookshop. 1918.
[x], 186p.
   Bibliog. 4p.

   H. Asquith, M. Baring, W. De La Mare, J. Freeman, W.W.
Gibson, R. Graves, R. Nichols, S. Sassoon, J.C. Squire,
W.J. Turner.   MPL

36   **GEORGIAN** poetry, 1918-1919. Poetry Bookshop. 1919.
[x], 196p.
   Bibliog. 4p.

   J. Freeman, T. Moult, S. Sassoon, W.J. Turner.   MPL

37   **GILKES, Martin,** comp.
Tribute to England: an anthology. Hutchinson. 1939.
255p.

   Section *The Great War, 1914-1918:* L. Binyon, R. Brooke,
T. Hardy, R. Nichols, W. Owen, S. Sassoon.   BM

38   **GLASIER, John Bruce,** comp.
The minstrelsy of peace: a collection of notable verse
in the English tongue, relating to peace and war, ranging
from the fifteenth century to the present day. With notes
and an introductory essay on 'Poetry and war' and
'Peace in English poetry'. Manchester: National Labour P.
[1918]. xlvi, 177p.

   Section *The European War:* W.N. Ewer, W.W. Gibson,
G.W. Russell, M. Sackville, S. Sassoon, M. South.   MPL

39   **GLASIER, John Bruce,** comp.
The minstrelsy of peace: a collection of notable verse in
the English tongue, relating to peace and war, ranging
from the fifteenth century to the present day. With notes
and an introductory essay on 'Poetry and War' and 'Peace in
English poetry'. 2nd ed. Manchester: National Labour P.
[1920]. xlvi, 177p.
   Contents as 1st ed.   BM

40 **GOODCHILD, George,** comp.
England, my England: a war anthology. Jarrolds.1914.
224p.

Section *Poems inspired by the present war, 1914:* H.W.
Bliss, F.W. Bourdillon, A.V. Chartres, J.B. Fagan, W.E.
Grogan, T. Hardy, E.G.A. Holmes, I. Tree.   MPL

41 **GOODCHILD, George,** comp.
England, my England: a patriotic anthology. New ed.
Jarrolds. [1914]. 224p.
    Contents as 1st edition.   BPL

GOODCHILD, George, ed. see also **TREVES, Sir Frederick,**
& GOODCHILD, George, eds (110)

42 **GRAHAM, Peter Anderson,** ed.
The *Country Life* anthology of verse. *Country Life;*
Newnes. 1915. xviii, 208p.

Section *The days of war:* R.G.T. Coventry, J. Drinkwater,
A.M.F.R. Duclaux, A.S. Falconer, V.H. Friedlaender,
L. Gard, N. Griffiths, G. James, M. Leigh, M.A. Macdonald,
M.G. Meugens, W.H. Ogilvie, E. Shillito.   MPL

43 **GWYNN, Stephen, & KETTLE, Thomas Michael,** comps
Battle songs for the Irish Brigades. Dublin: Maunsel.
1915. 32p.

J.I.C. Clarke, A.C. Doyle, S. Gwynn, T.M. Kettle.   MPL

44 **H., G.E., & B., L.L.,** comps
At the front: a pocket book of verse. Warne. 1915. iv, 60p.

F.W. Bourdillon, R. Brooke, P.R. Chalmers, J. Grenfell,
O. Seaman, G.C. Siordet.   BPL

45 **HALLIDAY, Wilfred Joseph,** comp.
Pro patria: a book of patriotic verse. Dent. 1915. xvi, 221p.

H. Begbie, H.T.M. Bell, R. Bridges, G. Cannan, W.L.
Courtney, T. Hardy, M. Hewlett, W.M. Letts.   BPL

46 **HARDIE, John Lipp,** comp.
Verse of valour: an anthology of shorter war poems of sea,
land, air. Glasgow: Art & Educational Publ. 1943. xvi,
129p. il.

H. Asquith, M. Baring, P. Bewsher, L. Binyon, R. Bridges,
P.R. Chalmers, M.J.G. Day, J. Drinkwater, J. Freeman,
H.R. Freston, W.W. Gibson, G.R. Hamilton, T. Hardy,
W.N. Hodgson, A.E. Housman, A.L. Jenkins, R. Kipling,
J. Masefield, I.M. Mills, A. Noyes, J.S. Phillimore,
E. Phillpotts, E.J.M.D. Plunkett, S. Sassoon, C.F. Smith,
M. Smith, W. Watson, W.B. Yeats.   BM

47   **HOLMAN, Carrie Ellen,** comp.
     In the day of battle: poems of the Great War. Toronto:
     Briggs. 1916. 166p.

     H.A., E. Alexander, H. Asquith, H. Begbie, L. Binyon,
     M. Booth, R. Brooke, H. Chappell, D. Clark, R.O.A.
     Crewe-Milnes, E. De Stein, R. Duffin, W.N. Ewer, J.B.
     Fagan, G. Frankau, H.R. Freston, W.W. Gibson, C. Hamilton,
     M.L. Haskins, C.H. Herford, M. Hewlett, R. Le Gallienne,
     G.H. Leonard, W.M. Letts, H. Lulham, H. Mackay, F.E.
     Maitland, J.N. Milne, R.R. Morgan, H. Newbolt, A. Noyes,
     A. O'Connor, E. Owen, M. Peterson, S. Phillips, H.D.
     Rawnsley, C.A. Renshaw, G. Robertson-Glasgow, W.F.
     Robinson, G.W. Russell, M. Sackville, E.T. Sandford,
     O. Seaman, W.G. Shakespeare, C.F. Smith, S.G. Tallents,
     W. Thorley, R.V., M. Webb, L. Whitmell, H. Wyatt.   BM

48   **HOLMAN, Carrie Ellen,** comp.
     In the day of battle: poems of the Great War. 2nd ed.
     Toronto: Briggs. 1917. 180p.

     H.A., E. Alexander, H. Asquith, H. Begbie, L. Binyon,
     M. Booth, R. Brooke, H. Chappell, D. Clark, R.O.A. Crewe-
     Milnes, E. De Stein, R. Duffin, W.N. Ewer, J.B. Fagan,
     G. Frankau, H.R. Freston, W.W. Gibson, J. Grenfell,
     C. Hamilton, G.R. Hamilton, M.L. Haskins, C.H. Herford,
     M. Hewlett, R. Kipling, R. Le Gallienne, G.H. Leonard,
     W.M. Letts, H. Lulham, H. Mackay, F.E. Maitland, J.N.
     Milne, R.R. Morgan, H. Newbolt, A. Noyes, A. O'Connor,
     E. Owen, M. Peterson, S. Phillips, H.D. Rawnsley, C.A.
     Renshaw, G. Robertson-Glasgow, W.F. Robinson, G.W.
     Russell, M. Sackville, E.T. Sandford, O. Seaman, W.G.
     Shakespeare, C.F. Smith, S.G. Tallents, W. Thorley,
     R.V., M. Webb, L. Whitmell, H. Wyatt.   IWM

49   **HOLMAN, Carrie Ellen,** comp.
     In the day of battle: poems of the Great War. 3rd ed.
     Toronto: Briggs. 1918. [ii], 224p.

'All profits from the sale of this edition will be sent to Lady Drummond for the King George and Queen Mary Maple Leaf Clubs'.

H.A., E. Alexander, H. Asquith, S.M. Bainbridge, H. Begbie, L. Binyon, M. Booth, R. Brooke, H. Chappell, G.K. Chesterton, D. Clark, R.O.A. Crewe-Milnes, E. De Stein, R. Duffin, W.N. Ewer, J.B. Fagan, G. Frankau, H.R. Freston, W.W. Gibson, J. Grenfell, M.B.H., C. Hamilton, G.R. Hamilton, M.L. Haskins, C.H. Herford, M. Hewlett, R. Kipling, R. Le Gallienne, G.H. Leonard, W.M. Letts, H. Lulham, S.R. Lysaght, H. Mackay, F.E. Maitland, J.N. Milne, R.R. Morgan, H. Newbolt, A. Noyes, A. O'Connor, M. O'Rourke, E. Owen, J. Oxenham, M. Peterson, S. Phillips, H.D. Rawnsley, C.A. Renshaw, G. Robertson-Glasgow, W.F. Robinson, G.W. Russell, M. Sackville, E.T. Sandford, O. Seaman, W.G. Shakespeare, C.F. Smith, C.H. Sorley, S.G. Tallents, E.W. Tennant, W. Thorley, R.V., R.E. Vernède, M. Webb, L. Whitmell, H. Wyatt.   BPL

50   HUSSEY, Maurice, ed.
Poetry of the First World War: an anthology. Longmans. 1967. xvi, 180p. (Longmans' English series).
   Bibliog. 1p.

R. Aldington, H.T.M. Bell, P. Bewsher, L. Binyon, E.C. Blunden, R. Brooke, L. Coulson, M.J.G. Day, W.N. Ewer, F.M. Ford, G. Frankau, J. Freeman, W.W. Gibson, R. Graves, J. Grenfell, I. Gurney, T. Hardy, F.W. Harvey, W.N. Hodgson, L. Housman, D. Hussey, J. Joyce, R. Kipling, D.H. Lawrence, F. Ledwidge, E.A. Mackintosh, F. Manning, A. Meynell, H. Monro, R. Nichols, E. Owen, W. Owen, H.E. Palmer, E. Phillpotts, M. Plowman, H. Read, E. Rickword, I. Rosenberg, S. Sassoon, O. Sitwell, C.H. Sorley, E.W. Tennant, E. Thomas, H. Trench, W.J. Turner, R.E. Vernède, W. Watson, A.G. West.   MPL

INGERSLEY, R.M., pseud., ed. see MARKLAND, Russell, (R.M. Ingersley, pseud), ed. (65)

JACKSON, Cyril Henry Ward-, ed. see WARD-JACKSON, Cyril Henry, ed. (116) (117)

51   [JAQUET, E.R.], comp.
These were the men: poems of the war, 1914-1918. Marshall. [1919]. 100p.

16

C.A.A., L. Binyon, C. Blake, B. Brice-Miller, R. Brooke,
C.E.C.H. Burton, I.J. Cornwall, N.D., M. Dalton, C. Darling,
A.C. Doyle, J.M. Edmonds, H.C.F., G. Frankau, J. Grenfell,
A.P. Herbert, W.N. Hodgson, M. Huxley, H. Ingamells,
E.J., J.H. Knight-Adkin, W.M. Letts, H. Lulham, P. MacGill,
W.F. de B. Maclaren, H.A. Nesbitt, H. Newbolt, W.H.
Ogilvie, E. Owen, H.V.P., O.C. Platoon, pseud., J. Rhoades,
O. Seaman, H. Severez, W.G. Shakespeare, E.W. Tennant,
K. Tynan, R.E. Vernède, W. Watson, F.E. Weatherly,
L. Whitmell and several anon.   BPL

52   **JENKINSON, Editha,** comp.
     The Malory verse book: a collection of contemporary
     poetry for school and general use. Erskine Macdonald.
     1919. 239p.

     Part II. *The heart of the nation:* P. Bewsher, L. Coulson,
     J.M. Courtney, S.D. Cox, R.O.A. Crewe-Milnes, J.E.
     Crombie, G.H. Crump, A. Dodd, M. Few, D.K. Gardiner,
     V. Gillespie, M.E. Graham, J. Grenfell, J. Gurdon, E.M.
     Heath, M. Hemphrey, G. Howard, D. Hussey, E. Jenkinson,
     J. Lodge, J.A. Mackereth, T. Maynard, G.C. Michael,
     C. Mitchell, M. Painter, A.G. Prys-Jones, C.A. Renshaw,
     N. Richardson, C. Roberts, F.W. Smith, J.W. Streets,
     G. Thomas, R.N. Tinkler, E.F. Wilkinson.   MPL

     JONES, Arthur Glyn Prys-, ed. see **PRYS-JONES, Arthur
     Glyn,** ed. (85)

53   **JONES, Donald Lewis,** ed.
     War poetry: an anthology. With intro. and commentaries.
     Pergamon P.   1968. xii, 142p. (Commonwealth and
     international library).

     L. Binyon, R. Brooke, G.K. Chesterton, T. Hardy, W. Owen,
     S. Sassoon, E. Thomas, W.B. Yeats.   MPL

     KETTLE, Thomas Michael, comp. see **GWYNN, Stephen,
     & KETTLE, Thomas Michael,** comps (43)

     KING'S COLLEGE. GEORGIAN GROUP see **LONDON
     UNIVERSITY. KING'S COLLEGE. GEORGIAN GROUP** (62)

54   **KNIGHT, William Angus,** comp.
     Pro patria et rege: poems on war, its characteristics and
     results. Selected in aid of the Belgian Relief Fund from

British and American sources. With an explanatory
preface. Century P. 1915. 218p.
Dedicated to Lord Roberts.

M. Armstrong, R. Bridges, C.W. Brodribb, W.B. Carpenter,
W.L. Courtney, A. Dobson, R.H. Forster, T. Hardy,
R. Kipling, A. Meynell, H. Newbolt, A. Noyes, W.H. Ogilvie,
H.D. Rawnsley, J.L Robertson, O. Seaman, I.G. Smith,
I. Tree, W. Watson.   MPL

55 **KNIGHT, William Angus**, comp.
Pro patria et rege: poems on war, its characteristics and
results: Selected in aid of the Belgian Relief Fund from
British and American sources. With an explanatory
preface. Second series. Century P. [1915]. 204p.
Dedicated to Herbert H. Asquith, M.P., Prime Minister
of Great Britain.

E. Alexander, H. Begbie, L. Binyon, A.K. Clarke, R.O.A.
Crewe-Milnes, B. Dobell, J.A. Fort, J. Grenfell,
M. Huxley, F.E. Maitland, H. Newbolt, A. Noyes,
J. Oxenham, H.D. Rawnsley, E. Shillito, D.M. Stuart,
K. Tynan, T.A. Warren, W. Watson, A.J. Whyte.   MPL

56 **[KYLE, Galloway]**, comp.
Soldier poets: songs of the fighting men. Erskine
Macdonald. 1916. 106p.

H.D'A.B., J.M. Courtney, S.D. Cox, E.J.L. Garstin,
J. Grenfell, W.J. Halliday, G.R. Harvey, M. Hemphrey,
W.N. Hodgson, G. Howard, D. Hussey, E.H. Lloyd,
J. Lodge, G.C. Michael, E. Morgan, S. Oswald, A.V.
Ratcliffe, A. Robertson, C.H. Sorley, H. Spurrier, J.W.
Streets, G. Waterhouse, E.F. Wilkinson.   BM

57 **[KYLE, Galloway]**, comp.
Soldier poets: songs of the fighting men. Trench ed.
Erskine Macdonald. 1916. 106p.
Contents as 1st ed.   MPL

58 **[KYLE, Galloway]**, comp.
Soldier poets: more songs by the fighting men. Second
series. Erskine Macdonald. 1917. 144p.

P. Bewsher, C. Brooks, C. Carstairs, E.K. Challenger,
E. Chilman, A.N. Choyce, R.F. Clements, L.N. Cook,
G.M. Cooper, L. Coulson, S.D. Cox, J.E. Crombie,

18

G.H. Crump, R.C.G. Dartford, E. De Banzie, C.J. Druce,
H.S. Graham, W.J. Halliday, D.H. Harris, M. Hemphrey,
B. Hill, M. Hill, H.J. Jarvis, D.T. Jones, R.W. Kerr, F.C.
Lewis, P.H.B. Lyon, M. McClymont, I.H.T. Mackenzie,
C.J.B. Masefield, J. Mason, R.L. Megroz, A. O'Connor,
D.C.M. Osborne, J. Peterson, R. Raleigh, pseud., R.H.
Spring, J.E. Stewart, E.F. Wilkinson, W.L. Wilkinson.   MPL

L.L.B., comp. see **H., G.E., & B., L.L.**, comps (44)

59 **LEONARD, Sterling Andrus, ed.**
Poems of the war and the peace. With a foreword and
notes. New York: Harcourt Brace.1921. xviii, 162p.

R. Aldington, H. Asquith, L. Binyon, F.W. Bourdillon,
R. Brooke, E. Crawshay-Williams, A. Dobson, A.M.F.R.
Duclaux, W.N. Ewer, G. Frankau, J. Galsworthy, W.W.
Gibson, R. Graves, J. Grenfell, G.R. Hamilton, F.W.
Harvey, V. Jacob, F. Ledwidge, J. Lee, W.M. Letts, E.V.
Lucas, P.H.B. Lyon, H. Newbolt, R. Nichols, A. Noyes,
W. Owen, E.H. Physick, G.W. Russell, M. Sackville,
S. Sassoon, O. Seaman, W.G. Shakespeare, F. Sidgwick,
M. Sinclair, C.F. Smith, C.H. Sorley, E.W. Tennant,
R.E. Vernède.   WEPL

60 **LLOYD, Bertram, ed.**
The paths of glory: a collection of poems written during
the War, 1914-1918. Allen & Unwin. 1919. 120p.
   Bibliog. 2p.

R. Aldington, P. Bewsher, H.F. Constantine, E. Crawshay-
Williams, G. Dearmer, W. De La Mare, T.W. Earp,
E. Farjeon, W.W. Gibson, L. Golding, E. Gore-Booth,
L. Housman, H. Read, G.W. Russell, M. Sackville,
S. Sassoon, D.S. Shorter, F. Shove, O. Sitwell, T. Van Beek,
A. Waugh.   MPL

61 **LLOYD, Bertram, ed.**
Poems written during the Great War, 1914-1918: an
anthology. Allen & Unwin. 1918. 112p.
   Bibliog 2p.

O. Baker, P. Barrington, L. Binyon, E. Crawshay-Williams,
W.N. Ewer, W.W. Gibson, E. Gore-Booth, H.C. Harwood,
E.H. Physick, G.W. Russell, J.H. Russell, M. Sackville,
H.S. Salt, S. Sassoon, E. Shillito, O. Sitwell, J.C. Squire,
I. Tree, D.H. Tripp, I. Zangwill.   MPL

62 [LONDON UNIVERSITY. KING'S COLLEGE.
GEORGIAN GROUP]
King's verse: poems of a new poetry society. Erskine
Macdonald. 1918. 63p.

D.L.G. Joseph, K.M. King, I.C. Major.   MPL

63 [MACDONALD, Erskine, & FORD, S. Gertrude], comps
A crown of amaranth: a collection of poems to the
memory of the brave and gallant gentlemen who have
given their lives for Great and greater Britain,
MCMXIV-MCMXVII. New ed. Erskine Macdonald. 1917.
84p.

I. Adair, M.B., L. Binyon, J.A. Brooke, R.O.A. Crewe-
Milnes, R. Duffin, H.P. Eden, Eton, pseud., V. Gillespie,
J. Grenfell, J. Gurdon, J. Helston, A.G. Herbertson, B.H.M.
Hetherington, D. Hussey, M. Huxley, G. Kelly, F.E.
Kenneth, A.B.L., B.A. Lees, I. May, A. Meynell, W. Meynell,
A.M. Northwood, M. Plowman, C. Roberts, H.S., E. Shillito,
H. Simpson, G.C. Siordet, W. Stewart, J.W. Streets,
E.M.T., F.I. Taylor, K. Tynan, R.V., I.A. Williams.   MPL

[No copy of 1st ed. traced].

64 MACKLIN, Alys Eyre, ed.
The Lyceum book of war verse. Erskine Macdonald.
1918. 58p.

L.G. Ascher, M. Beazley, L.M. Belletti, S. Bristowe,
S.R. Canton, F. Chapman, F.M. Close, J.C. Cohen,
D. Curtois, B. De Bertouch, S. Duff, V.L. Esson, M.H.J.
Henderson, H. Kendall, A. Law, M. Lawrence, T.M.
Mackenzie, A.E. Macklin, J.H. Macnair, A. Mends-Gibson,
G. Mount, H.E. Phillp, L.J. Rowe, S. Ruskin, J. Solomon,
E. Spensley, M. Stanley-Wrench, M.C. Stopes, C. Strachey,
S. Stuart, V. Tillie, H.M. Waithman, E.R. Wheeler,
E. Wigram.   BPL

65 MARKLAND, Russell, (R.M. Ingersley, pseud.), ed.
The glory of Belgium: a tribute and a chronicle. With a
preface by Emile Cammaerts. Erskine Macdonald. 1915.
137p.
    Publ. in aid of the Belgian Repatriation Fund.

Part 1. *Since the Great War, August, 1914:* W. Akerman,
W. Archer, B.B. Baily, W. Benington, L. Binyon,
H. Birkhead, W. Blair, H.W. Bliss, F.W. Bourdillon, G.K.

Chesterton, F. Clee, W.J. Courthope, R.O.A. Crewe-
Milnes, H. Dayne, J. Donnan, J. Drinkwater, A.M.F.R.
Duclaux, S.G. Ford, A.K. Gill, V. Gillespie, A.P. Graves,
D.W. Greaves, A.R. Hamilton, W.G. Hole, C. Kernahan,
F. Langbridge, H. Lilley, H. Lulham, W. Madden,
R. Markland, P. Marks, J.R. Palmer, S. Phillips, H.D.
Rawnsley, R.K. Risk, C. Roberts, D.P. Saunders, N.W.
Sibley, F.W.O. Ward, W. Watson.   MPL

66   MOULT, Thomas, comp.
     Cenotaph: a book of remembrance in poetry and prose for
     November the eleventh. Cape. 1923. 223p. il.

     M. Baring, L. Binyon, F.V. Branford, R. Brooke, G.K.
     Chesterton, L. Coulson, W.N. Ewer, R. Graves, T. Hardy,
     J. Lee, E.A. Mackintosh, A. Meynell, T. Moult, N. Munro,
     J.M. Murry, R. Nichols, G.W. Russell, S. Sassoon,
     E. Thomas, K. Tynan, M.L. Woods, I. Zangwill.   MPL

67   NETTLEINGHAME, Frederick Thomas, comp.
     More Tommy's tunes: an additional collection of
     soldiers' songs, marching melodies, rude rhymes and
     popular parodies, composed, collected, and arranged on
     active service with the B.E.F. Erskine Macdonald. 1918.
     98p.   MPL

68   NETTLEINGHAM[E], Frederick Thomas, comp.
     Tommy's tunes: a comprehensive collection of soldiers'
     songs, marching melodies, rude rhymes, and popular
     parodies, composed, collected, and arranged on
     active service with the B.E.F. Erskine Macdonald. 1917.
     91p.   MPL

69   NETTLEINGHAM[E], Frederick Thomas, comp.
     Tommy's tunes: a comprehensive collection of soldiers'
     songs, marching melodies, rude rhymes, and popular
     parodies, composed, collected, and arranged on active service
     with the B.E.F. 2nd ed. Erskine Macdonald. 1917. 93p.   BPL

70   NICHOLS, Robert, comp.
     Anthology of war poetry, 1914-1918. Nicholson & Watson.
     1943. 156p.
        Bibliog. 4p.

     E.C. Blunden, R. Brooke, J.E. Flecker, R. Graves,
     J. Grenfell, W.N. Hodgson, T.M. Kettle, E.A. Mackintosh,

R. Nichols, W. Owen, E. Rickword, S. Sassoon, C.H. Sorley,
F.B. Young.   MPL

71 **NORTHERN** numbers: representative selections from
certain living Scottish poets. Foulis. 1920. 130p.
     Some poems in Scots dialect.

J. Buchan, C.M. Grieve, V. Jacob, R.W. Kerr, J. Lee,
N. Munro, W.H. Ogilvie.   MPL

72 **OSBORN, Edward Bolland,** ed.
The muse in arms: a collection of war poems, for the most
part written in the field of action, by seamen, soldiers,
and flying men who are serving, or who have served, in
the Great War. Murray. 1917. xxxviii, 296p.

G. Alchin, H. Asquith, R. Brooke, N.M.F. Corbett,
L. Coulson, R.M. Dennys; G. Frankau, H.S. Graham,
R. Graves, G.W. Grenfell, J. Grenfell, I. Gurney, F.W.
Harvey, A. Herbert, W.N. Hodgson, R.A. Hopwood,
D. Hussey, L. Hutcheon, I.C. Imtarfa, A.J., W.M. James,
A.L. Jenkins, J. Lee, W.H. Littlejohn, P. MacGill, E.A.
Mackintosh, R. Nichols, O., pseud., R. Palmer, V. Perowne,
C.E.A. Philipps, D. Plowman, M. Plowman, A.V.
Ratcliffe, A. Robertson, J.M. Rose-Troup, S. Sassoon,
C.E. Scott-Moncrieff, E. Shanks, O. Sitwell, C.H. Sorley,
R.W. Sterling, J.W. Streets, E.W. Tennant, W. Weaving,
E.F. Wilkinson, B. Winder, C.W. Winterbotham.   MPL

73 **OXFORD** poetry, 1914-1916. Oxford: Blackwell. 1917.
viii, 190p.

G. Elton, H.C. Harwood, L.P. Jones, R.S. Lambert.   IWM

74 **OXFORD** poetry, 1915. Ed. by G.D.H.C. [George Douglas
Howard Cole?] and T.W.E. [T.W. Earp]. Oxford:
Blackwell. 1915. viii, 72p.

G. Elton, H.C. Harwood, L.P. Jones, R.S. Lambert.   MPL

[OXFORD poetry, 1916 contains no war poetry].

75 **OXFORD** poetry, 1917. Ed. by W.R.C. [Wilfred Rowland
Childe], T.W.E. [T.W. Earp], and D.L.S. [Dorothy L.
Sayers]. Oxford: Blackwell. 1917. iv, 60p.

F. St. V. Morris.   MPL

76 **OXFORD** poetry, 1918. Ed. by T.W.E. [T.W. Earp],
E.F.A.G. [E.F.A. Geach], and D.L.S. [Dorothy L.
Sayers]. Oxford: Blackwell. 1918. vi, 56p.

M. Leigh.   MPL

77 **OXFORD** poetry, 1919. Ed. by T.W.E. [T.W. Earp],
D.L.S. [Dorothy L Sayers], and S.S. Oxford: Blackwell.
1920. vi, 62p.

T.H.W. Armstrong, V.M. Brittain, H.I. Burt, J.B.S.
Haldane, H.J. Hope, C.B.H. Kitchin.   BPL

78 **OXFORD** poetry, 1920. Ed. by V.M.B. [Vera Mary
Brittain], C.H.B.K. [Clifford Henry Benn Kitchin],
A.P. [Alan Porter]. Oxford: Blackwell. 1920. vi. 58p.

V.M. Brittain, E. Rickword.   BPL

79 **OXFORD** poetry, 1921. Ed. by Alan Porter, Richard
Hughes, Robert Graves. Oxford: Blackwell. 1921. [viii],
64p.

E. Rickword.   BPL

80 **PARSONS, I.M., ed.**
Men who march away: poems of the First World War.
Chatto & Windus. 1965. 192p.

R. Aldington, H. Asquith, L. Binyon, E.C. Blunden,
R. Brooke, G.K. Chesterton, W. De La Mare, J. Freeman,
W.W. Gibson, R. Graves, J. Grenfell, I. Gurney, T. Hardy,
F.W. Harvey, A.P. Herbert, A.E. Housman, R. Kipling,
D.H. Lawrence, C. Mew, H. Monro, R. Nichols, W. Owen,
H. Read, I. Rosenberg, S. Sassoon, F. Shove, F. Sidgwick,
O. Sitwell, C.H. Sorley, E. Thomas, A.G. West, T.P.C.
Wilson, W.B. Yeats.   MPL

PARTRIDGE, Eric, ed. see **BROPHY, John, &**
PARTRIDGE, Eric, eds (6) (7) (8) (9) (10)

81 **POCOCK, Guy Noel, ed.**
Modern poetry. Dent. 1920. 159p. por. (Kings
treasuries of literature).

Section *The Great War:* J. Drinkwater, W.W. Gibson,
R. Graves, J. Grenfell, T. Hardy, C.F. Kenyon, R. Nichols,
H.E. Palmer, G.N. Pocock, S. Sassoon.   BPL

82   **POEMS** of the Great War. Chatto & Windus. 1914. 40p.
      Publ. on behalf of the Prince of Wales's National Relief Fund.

      H. Begbie, L. Binyon, R. Bridges, C.E. Chesterton, G.K.
      Chesterton, J. Drinkwater, J.B. Fagan, J. Freeman,
      M. Hewlett, R. Kipling, L.G. Moberly, H. Newbolt, A. Noyes,
      O. Seaman, R.E. Vernède, W. Watson.   BPL

83   **POEMS** of the Great War. 2nd ed. Chatto & Windus. 1914.
      40p.
      Publ. on behalf of the Prince of Wales's National Relief Fund.
      Contents as 1st ed.   MPL

84   **POEMS** of the Great War. 3rd ed. Chatto & Windus. 1914.
      40p.
      Publ. on behalf of the Prince of Wales's National Relief Fund.
      Contents as 1st ed.   BPL

85   **PRYS-JONES, Arthur Glyn**, ed.
      Welsh poets: a representative English selection from
      contemporary writers. Erskine Macdonald. 1917. 94p.

      H.I. Bell, B. Rhys, C. Roberts, G. Thomas, I.A. Williams.   MPL

86   **PUNCH**
      An alphabet of the war. Jarrolds. 1915. [30]p. il.
        Cartoons, with brief anonymous verses.
        Reprinted from "*Punch* almanac, 1915".   MPL

87   **PUNCH**
      Poems from *Punch,* 1909-1920. With an introductory
      essay by W.B. Drayton Henderson. Macmillan. 1922.
      xxx, 278p.

      Section *The War:* C.H. Bretherton, C.H. Brown. C.K. Burrow,
      P.R. Chalmers, D. Clark, N. Davey, S.J. Fay, C. Garstin, D. Garstin,
      A.B. Gillespie, A.P. Herbert, W.K. Holmes, A.L. Jenkins,
      G.M. Mitchell, W.H. Ogilvie, C.T. Pezare, E.W. Pigott,
      G. Robertson-Glasgow, C.F. Smith, A.F. Trotter,
      H.E. Wilkes.   MPL

88   **QUILLER-COUCH, Sir Arthur**, ed.
      The Oxford book of English verse, 1250-1918. New ed.
      Oxford U.P. 1939. xxxii, 1167p.

      L. Binyon, R. Brooke, J. Grenfell, T. Hardy, A.E.
      Housman, W. Owen, S. Sassoon.   MPL

89 **REEVES, James,** comp.
Georgian poetry. Harmondsworth: Penguin Books. 1962.
175p. (Penguin poets).

E.C. Blunden, R. Brooke, R. Graves, I. Gurney, W. Owen,
S. Sassoon, C.H. Sorley.   MPL

90 A **RHYMERS'** ring: poems by [various writers]. Oxford:
Blackwell. 1922. viii, 138p.

E. Hockliffe, M. Hockliffe, E. Upcott.   BM

91 **ROBB, William,** comp.
A book of twentieth-century Scots verse. Gowans & Gray.
1925. xvi, 259p.
    All in Scots dialect.

J. Buchan, A. Dodds, I.W. Hutchison, R.J. Maclennan,
T. McWilliam, N. Munro, C. Murray, J.L. Robertson,
M. Symon, W. Wingate.   MPL

92 **ROYAL NAVAL DIVISION**
Rhymes of the R.N.D. [Royal Naval Division]. Methuen.
1917. [viii], 54p.
    All anon.   MPL

93 **ROYAL NAVAL DIVISION**
Rhymes of the R.N.D. [Royal Naval Division]. 2nd ed.
Methuen. 1918. [viii], 54p.
    All anon.   BPL

94 **SEYMOUR, William Kean,** ed.
A miscellany of poetry — 1919. Palmer & Hayward. 1919.
136p. il. (by Doris Palmer).

F.V. Branford, G.K. Chesterton, G. Dearmer, W.W.
Gibson, L. Golding, R. Macaulay, M. Sackville, W.R.
Titterton.   MPL

95 **SIDGWICK & JACKSON, Ltd.**
A selection of poems from recent volumes published by
Sidgwick & Jackson, Ltd. Sidgwick & Jackson. 1916. 25p.

H. Asquith, R. Brooke, J. Drinkwater, F.W. Harvey,
E. Jenkins, E. Owen, W.G. Shakespeare, E. Shanks,
K. Tynan.   BM

96 **SMITH, Frederick Thomson, (Frederick Brereton, pseud.),**
comp.
An anthology of war poems; compiled by Frederick
Brereton. Intro. by Edmund Blunden. Collins. 1930. 192p.

R. Aldington, H.D'A.B., P. Bewsher, L. Binyon, E.C.
Blunden, F.V. Branford, R. Brooke, P.R. Chalmers, M.P.
Cole, L.Coulson, M.J.G. Day, G. Dearmer, W.N. Ewer,
F.M. Ford, J. Freeman, J. Galsworthy, E.J.L. Garstin,
W.W. Gibson, A.B. Gillespie, R. Graves, J. Grenfell,
I. Gurney, T. Hardy, F.W. Harvey, A.P. Herbert, B. Hill,
W.N. Hodgson, G. Howard, R. Kipling, F. Ledwidge,
H.S. Mackintosh, C.J.B. Masefield, G.C. Michael, G.M.
Mitchell, L.G. Moberly, R.H. Mottram, S. Oswald, W. Owen,
F. Prewett, H. Read, A. Robertson, I. Rosenberg, S. Sassoon,
C.H. Sorley, J.E. Stewart, J.W. Streets, E.W. Tennant,
E. Thomas, S. Vines, G. Waterhouse, A.G. West,
L. Whitmell, W.L. Wilkinson, I.A. Williams, T.P.C. Wilson,
F.B. Young.   MPL

97 **SOME** Imagist poets, 1916: an annual anthology. Boston
(Mass.): Houghton Mifflin. 1916. xvi, 98p.
   Bibliog 2p.

R. Aldington, F.S. Flint, D.H. Lawrence.   MPL

98 **SOME** Imagist poets, 1917: an annual anthology. Boston
(Mass): Houghton Mifflin. 1917. viii, 92p.
   Bibliog. 2p.

R. Aldington, F.S. Flint.   MPL

99 **SONGS** and sonnets for England in war time: a collection
of lyrics by various authors inspired by the Great War.
Bodley Head. 1914. xiv, 96p.

A.St.J. Adcock, W. Archer, R.G. Barnes, H. Begbie,
L. Binyon, R.R. Buckley, P. Bussy, G.C., G. Cannan, C.E.
Chesterton, G.K. Chesterton, W.L. Courtney, F. Coutts,
R.H. Forster, R.M. Freeman, A.K. Gill, H.E. Goad, M.H.,
T. Hardy, M. Hewlett, E.L. Hicks, W.M.L. Hutchinson,
H. Jones, M. Jourdain, C. Kernahan, R. Kipling, W.M.
Letts, J.H. McCarthy, N. Munro, H. Newbolt, B. Pain,
S. Phillips, E. Phillpotts, H.D. Rawnsley, J. Rhoades,
O. Seaman, W. Sichel, H. De V. Stacpoole, D.M. Stuart,
E. Underhill, R.E. Vernède, W. Watson and one anon.   MPL

[No copy of 2nd ed. traced].

00 **SONGS** and sonnets for England in war time: a collection
of lyrics by various authors inspired by the Great War. 3rd ed.
Bodley Head. 1915. xvi, 96p.
    Contents as 1st ed.   BPL

01 **SONGS** and sonnets for England in war time: a collection
of lyrics by various authors inspired by the Great War.
4th ed. Bodley Head. [191-]. xvi, 96p.
    Contents as 1st ed.   BPL

02 **SQUIRE, Sir John Collings**, ed.
Selections from modern poets. Martin Secker. 1921. viii,
480p.

    M. Baring, R. Brooke, J. Freeman, R. Graves, J. Grenfell,
    I. Gurney, F. Ledwidge, R. Nichols, W. Owen, S. Sassoon,
    E. Shanks, C.H. Sorley, E.W. Tennant, W.J. Turner, I.A.
    Williams, F.B. Young.   MPL

03 **SQUIRE, Sir John Collings**, comp.
Younger poets of to-day. Martin Secker. 1932. vi, 550p.

    R. Aldington, C. Bax, E.C. Blunden, F.V. Branford,
    G. Dearmer, H.S. Mackintosh, R.H. Mottram, A.G. Prys-
    Jones, S. Sassoon.   MPL

04 **STEVENSON, Burton Egbert**, comp.
The home book of modern verse: an extension of "The
home book of verse": a selection from American and
English poetry of the twentieth century. 2nd ed. New York:
Holt, Rinehart & Winston. 1953. xlx, 1124p.

    Section *Shadows of war:* O. Baker, G. Dearmer, J.E.
    Flecker, F.M. Ford, J. Freeman, L. Golding, L. Housman,
    T.M. Kettle, W.M. Letts, P. MacGill, R. Nichols, W. Owen,
    C. Roberts, S. Sassoon, C.H. Sorley, J.C. Squire, E.W.
    Tennant, H. Trench, T.P.C. Wilson, F.B. Young.   MPL

05 **SULLIVAN, John F.**, comp.
Poetry in English, 1900-1930. Arnold. 1965. xiv, 177p.
(World of English: poetry).

    L. Binyon, R. Brooke, G.K. Chesterton, W.W. Gibson,
    I. Gurney, T. Hardy, A.E. Housman, T.E. Hulme, R. Nichols,
    W. Owen, I. Rosenberg, J.C. Squire, E. Thomas, A.G. West,
    W.B. Yeats.   MPL

106 **SYMON, Julian,** comp.
An anthology of war poetry. Penguin Books. 1942. 189p.
por. (Pelican books).

Section *The World War (1914-1918):* R. Brooke, G.K.
Chesterton, F.M. Ford, R. Graves, T. Hardy, H. Monro,
W. Owen, I. Rosenberg, S. Sassoon, E. Thomas, W.B.
Yeats and several anon.   MPL

107 **TAIT, Samuel Brown,** comp.
Chambers's patriotic poems for the young. Chambers.
1915. 192p.
A school text book.

A.C. Doyle, T. Hardy, E.G.A. Holmes, B. Pain, O. Seaman,
L.M. Watt.   BPL

108 **The TIMES**
War poems from *The Times*, August 1914-1915. *The Times*.
1915. [8]p. il.
Supplement issued with *The Times,* 9th August 1915.

L. Binyon, R. Bridges, C.W. Brodribb, D. Clark, W. De La
Mare, J. Grenfell, T. Hardy, R. Kipling, F.E. Maitland,
H. Newbolt, R. Nichols, A. Noyes, G.W. Russell, W. Watson.   MPL

109 **The TIMES**
War poems, reprinted from the supplement, Aug. 9th,
1915. Printed Chiswick: Belmont School P. 1919. [22]p.
Cover-title is "Pro patria: a little book of verse".

L. Binyon, R. Bridges, C.W. Brodribb, D. Clark, W. De La
Mare, T. Hardy, F.E. Maitland, H. Newbolt, R. Nichols,
W. Watson.   BPL

110 **TREVES, Sir Frederick, & GOODCHILD, George,** eds.
Made in the trenches: composed entirely from articles
and sketches contributed by soldiers. Allen & Unwin. 1916.
240p. il., col. il.
A limited ed. of 150 copies.
Largely prose but includes some 'soldier verse' reprinted
from *The Searchlight.*

R.F.C., W.A.C., R.W. Campbell, J.P. Ede, J.G.G., J.T.
Henderson, Jap, pseud., J. Lee, C. Milligan, C.M.R.,
N. Ramsay, J.W. Streets, Strozzi, pseud., Twopence, pseud.,
A.E. Whiting-Baker.   BPL

11   **TROTTER, Jacqueline Theodora, ed.**
Valour and vision: poems of the war, 1914-1918. Longmans,
Green. 1920. xii, 146p.

E. Alexander, C.A. Alington, H. Asquith, M. Baring,
R.G. Barnes, P. Bewsher, L. Binyon, F.W. Bourdillon,
J.G. Bower, B. Brice-Miller, E. Bridges, R. Brooke, M.W.
Cannan, D. Clark, L. Coulson, R.O.A. Crewe-Milnes, T.W.H.
Crosland, W.H. Davies, M.J.G. Day, G. Dearmer, W. De La
Mare, E. De Stein, J. Drinkwater, H.P. Eden, J.G.
Fairfax, J.E. Flecker, G. Frankau, J. Freeman, C. Garstin,
W.W. Gibson, R. Graves, J. Grenfell, T. Hardy, F.W.
Harvey, A.P. Herbert, W.N. Hodgson, R.A. Hopwood,
A.E. Housman, S. Hussey, R. Kipling, F. Ledwidge,
P.H.B. Lyon, R. Macaulay, P. MacGill, J.H. Macnair, R.B.
Marriott-Watson, N. Munro, A.T. Nankivell, H. Newbolt,
R. Nichols, A. Noyes, E. Owen, N. Oxland, B. Pain,
R. Palmer, F.J. Patmore, E.J.M.D. Plunkett, J. Rhoades,
S. Sassoon, O. Seaman, E. Shanks, E. Shillito, F. Sidgwick,
C.F. Smith, C.H. Sorley, J.C. Squire, D.M. Stuart, E.W.
Tennant, E. Thomas, J. Thomas, A.F. Trotter, K. Tynan,
E. Underhill, R.E. Vernède, A. Waugh, L. Whitmell,
M. Wilson, T.P.C. Wilson, E.H. Young, F.B. Young.   MPL

12   **TROTTER, Jacqueline Theodora, ed.**
Valour and vision: poems of the war, 1914-18. New ed.
Hopkinson. 1923. xvi, 184p.
    'Profits from the sale will be given to the Incorporated
Soldiers & Sailors Help Society'.

R. Aldington, E. Alexander, C.A. Alington, M. Armstrong,
H. Asquith, M. Baring, R.G. Barnes, P. Bewsher, L. Binyon,
E.C. Blunden, F.W. Bourdillon, J.G. Bower, B. Brice-Miller,
E. Bridges, R. Bridges, R. Brooke, M.W. Cannan, G.K.
Chesterton, L. Coulson, R.G.T. Coventry, R.O.A. Crewe-
Milnes, T.W.H. Crosland, W.H. Davies, M.J.G. Day,
G. Dearmer, W. De La Mare, E. De Stein, J. Drinkwater,
H.P. Eden, J.G. Fairfax, J.E. Flecker, F.M. Ford, J. Freeman,
C. Garstin, W.W. Gibson, E. Gore-Booth, R. Graves,
J. Grenfell, T. Hardy, F.W. Harvey, A.P. Herbert, W.N.
Hodgson, R.A. Hopwood, A.E. Housman, E. Jenkins,
R. Kipling, F. Ledwidge, P.H.B. Lyon, R. Macaulay, P. MacGill,
J.H. Macnair, R.B. Marriott-Watson, A. Meynell, N. Munro,
H. Newbolt, R. Nichols, A. Noyes, E. Owen, W. Owen,
N. Oxland, B. Pain, R. Palmer, F.J. Patmore, E.J.M.D.

Plunkett, G.W. Russell, S. Sassoon, O. Seaman, E. Shanks,
E. Shillito, F. Sidgwick, M. Sinclair, O. Sitwell, C.F. Smith,
C.H. Sorley, J.C. Squire, D.M. Stuart, M. Stuart, E.W.
Tennant, E. Thomas, A.F. Trotter, W.J. Turner, K. Tynan,
E. Underhill, R.E. Vernède, A. Waugh, L. Whitmell, I.A.
Williams, M. Wilson, T.P.C. Wilson, H. Wolfe, W.B. Yeats,
E.H. Young, F.B. Young and one anon.   MPL

113 **TUTING, William Chomel,** comp.
For consolation: [poems]. *Home Words.* 1915. 32p. il.

C.A. Alington, J.E.M. Barlow, L. Binyon, C.E.C.H. Burton,
Civis, pseud., D. Clark, E. Dart, W. De La Mare, H.R.
Freston, H.C. Gardner, H.E. Goad, E. Gosse, J.M.A.
Hawksley, F.E. Maitland, H. Newbolt, C. Norwood, H.D.
Rawnsley, R.E. Vernède.   BPL

114 **TWELVE** poets: a miscellany of new verse. Selwyn &
Blount. 1918. 128p.

V.L. Ellis, R. Flower, J. Freeman.   MPL

115 **WALLACE, P., & others**
The little peacemaker: hymns and poems written during
the Great European War. [Tottington]: [Wallace]. [1918?].
8p. 2 por.

P.S. Beales, J.S. Chatterton, P. Wallace.   MPL

116 **WARD-JACKSON, Cyril Henry,** ed.
Airman's song book: an anthology of squadron, concert
party, training and camp songs and song-parodies, written
by and for officers, airmen and airwomen mainly of the
Royal Air Force, its auxiliaries and its predecessors, the Royal
Flying Corps and the Royal Naval Air Service: the whole
set out in chronological order to present a historical
picture of the R.A.F. through its own songs. With an
intro. and explanatory notes. Sylvan P. 1945. xiv, 190p.
il. (by Biro).

Section *From 1914 to the armistice in 1918.*
All anon. With music where appropriate.   MPL

117 **WARD-JACKSON, Cyril Henry,** ed.
Airman's song book: an anthology of squadron, concert
party, training and camp songs and song-parodies, written
by and for officers, airmen and airwomen mainly of the

Royal Air Force, its auxiliaries and its predecessors, the
Royal Flying Corps and the Royal Naval Air Service: the
whole set out in chronological order to present a
historical picture of the R.A.F. through its own songs.
With an intro. and explanatory notes. 2nd ed. Blackwood.
1967. xxii, 265p. il. (by Biro).

Section *From 1914 to the armistice in 1918*.
All anon. With music where appropriate.   MPL

18 **WELLESLEY, Dorothy, Duchess of Wellington,** ed.
A broadcast anthology of modern poetry. Hogarth P.
1930. 239p. (Hogarth living poets).

Section *War*: E.C. Blunden, R. Brooke, J. Grenfell,
W. Owen, S. Sassoon, J.C. Squire.   MPL

19 **WETHERELL, James Elgin,** ed.
The Great War in verse and prose. With an intro. by Hon.
H.J. Cody. Toronto: Legislative Assembly of Ontario.
1919. xiv, 160p.
    Recommended for use in schools.

H. Asquith, H. Begbie, L. Binyon, F.W. Bourdillon,
J.G. Bower, R. Brooke, C.E.C.H. Burton, P.R. Chalmers,
A.C. Doyle, R. Duffin, J.M. Edmonds, W.C. Galbraith,
E. Gosse, J. Grenfell, P. Haselden, M. Huxley, R. Kipling,
W.M. Letts, H. Lulham, H. Newbolt, A. Noyes, J. Oxenham,
O. Seaman, C.F. Smith, R.E. Vernède, L. Whitmell.   BM

20 **WETHERELL, James Elgin,** ed.
Later English poems, 1901-1922. Toronto: McClelland &
Stewart. 1922. 208p. por.

M. Baring, L. Binyon, J.G. Bower, R. Bridges, R. Brooke,
P.R. Chalmers, T.W.H. Crosland, G. Dearmer, A.C. Doyle,
J. Freeman, E. Gosse, J. Grenfell, T. Hardy, L. Housman,
R. Kipling, W.M. Letts, P.H.B. Lyon, R.C. Macfie, H. Newbolt,
R. Nichols, W. Owen, J. Oxenham, E. Phillpotts, S. Sassoon,
O. Seaman, C.F. Smith, H. Trench, K. Tynan, R.E.
Vernède, W. Watson, F.B. Young.   BPL

21 **WHEELER, William Reginald,** ed.
A book of verse of the Great War. With a foreword by
Charlton M. Lewis. New Haven: Yale U.P. 1917. xxxii,
184p.

L. Binyon, R. Brooke, C.E. Chesterton, G.H. Crow,

Damon, pseud., W.N. Ewer, J.B. Fagan, G. Frankau,
J. Freeman, J. Galsworthy, W.W. Gibson, J. Grenfell,
M.C.D. Hamilton, T. Hardy, M. Hewlett, Humbert, pseud.,
J.H. Knight-Adkin, J. Lee, W.M. Letts, A. Meynell,
H. Newbolt, F. Niven, A. Noyes, E. Owen, W.S. Pakenham-
Walsh, S. Phillips, E. Phillpotts, C. Roberts, G.C. Siordet,
C.F. Smith, K. Tynan, R.E. Vernède.   BPL

122 **WHEELS**: an anthology of verse. Oxford: Blackwell. 1916.
     84p.

     N. Cunard, O. Sitwell, E.W. Tennant, I. Tree.   BM

123 **WHEELS**, 1916: an anthology of verse. 2nd ed. Oxford:
     Blackwell. 1917. 96p.

     N. Cunard, H. Rootham, O. Sitwell, E.W. Tennant,
     I. Tree.   MPL

124 **WHEELS**, 1917: a second cycle. Oxford: Blackwell. 1917.
     118p.
         Bibliog. 2p.

     H. Rootham, O. Sitwell, E.W. Tennant, I. Tree, S. Vines. MPL

125 **WHEELS**, 1918: a third cycle. Oxford: Blackwell. 1918.
     104p.
         Bibliog. 3p.

     O. Sitwell, S. Vines.   MPL

126 **WHEELS**, 1919: fourth cycle. Oxford: Blackwell. 1919.
     103p.
         Bibliog. 5p.
         'Dedicated to the memory of Wilfred Owen, M.C.'

     W. Owen, O. Sitwell, S. Vines.   MPL

127 **WILKINSON, Marguerite,** ed.
     New voices: an introduction to contemporary poetry.
     New York: Macmillan. 1919. xxiv, 409p. por.

     Section *Patriotism and the Great War:* R. Aldington,
     R. Brooke, F.M. Ford, W.W. Gibson, R. Graves, R. Kipling,
     J. Masefield, R. Nichols, S. Sassoon.   MPL

128 **WILLIAMS, Oscar,** ed.
     The war poets: an anthology of the war poetry of the 20th

century. With an intro. New York: Day. 1945. [x], 485p.
por.

Section *The poetry of World War I:* R. Brooke, R. Graves,
T. Hardy, W. Owen, H. Read, I. Rosenberg, S. Sassoon,
W.B. Yeats. BPL

29 **WRIGHT, S. Fowler, ed.**
Contemporary Devonshire and Cornwall poetry.
Fowler Wright. [1930?]. 198p.

L.M. Anderson, G.M.L. Reade, L. Steevens. MPL

30 **YORK, Dorothea, ed.**
Mud and stars: an anthology of World War songs and
poetry. New York: Holt. [1931]. xxvi, 301p.

British section: Marching songs and trench ballads. IWM

31 **ZIV, Frederic W., ed.**
The valiant muse: an anthology of poems by poets killed
in the World War. New York: Putnam. [1936]. xx, 160p.

B. Brooke, R. Brooke, I. Campbell, L.N. Cook, L. Coulson,
J.E. Crombie, M.J.G. Day, R.M. Dennys, H.L. Field,
C. Flower, H.R. Freston, G.W. Grenfell, J. Grenfell, W.R.
Hamilton, W.N. Hodgson, C.M. Horne, H.W. Hutchinson,
A.L. Jenkins, D.F.G. Johnson, T.M. Kettle, F. Ledwidge,
F.C. Lewis, W.H. Littlejohn, E.A. Mackintosh, W.S.
Manning, R.B. Marriott-Watson, C.J.B. Masefield, F.St.V.
Morris, W. Owen, N. Oxland, R. Palmer, C.E.A. Philipps,
A.V. Ratcliffe, A. Robertson, I. Rosenberg, H.L. Simpson,
G.C. Siordet, G.B. Smith, C.H. Sorley, R.W. Sterling,
J.E. Stewart, J.W. Streets, A.J. Stuart, E.W. Tennant,
E. Thomas, B.F. Trotter, R.E. Vernède, G. Waterhouse,
E.F. Wilkinson, W.L. Wilkinson, T.P.C. Wilson, C.W.
Winterbotham. MPL

SECTION B: INDIVIDUAL AUTHORS

A.B. see B., A.

A.B.L. see (63)

A., C.A. see (51)

A.E., pseud. see RUSSELL, George William, (A.E., pseud.)

A.E.G. see GRANTHAM, Alexandra Ethelreda, (A.E.G.)

A.E. McC. see McC., A.E.

A.E.P. see P., A.E.

A.G. see G., A.

A., H. see (2) (24) (47) (48) (49)

A.J. see (72)

A.J.B. see (31) (32)

A., J.C.
The last of four: a poem of the Federated Malay States and
the war, August, 1915, founded on fact. Lincoln: Hedley
Slack. 1916. 39p.   BPL

A., J.W. see (31) (32)

A.L.O.P. see (23)

35

A.M. see (5)

A.N.D. see DAVIES, A.N., (A.N.D.)

A.P.H. see HERBERT, Sir Alan Patrick, (A.P.H.)

A.R.P. see P., A.R.

AARONSON, Abel see (27)

ABBOTT, Claude Colleer, (Claude Colleer, pseud.)
(Private, Artists Rifles)

Collected poems, 1918-1958. Sidgwick & Jackson. 1963.
viii, 168p.   MPL

Poems. Blackwell. 1921. 69p.   BM

The sand castle, and other poems. Cape. 1946. 54p.   MPL

Youth and age: [poems]; by Claude Colleer. Sidgwick &
Jackson. 1918. 28p.   BPL

ABBOTT, W.H.
The unknown warrior, and other poems. Erskine Macdonald.
[1929]. 46p.   IWM

ABEL, George
Wylins fae my wallet: [poems]. Biographical sketch by
Alexander Gammie. 2nd ed. Paisley: Gardner. 1916. xxiv,
8-151p. por.
    In Scots dialect, with a glossary.   MPL

[No copy of 1st ed. 1915 traced].

See also (27)

ABERCROMBIE, Lascelles (Unfit for active service, worked in
a Liverpool shell factory)

Lyrics and unfinished poems. Gregynog P. 1940. xii, 83p.
    A limited ed. of 155 copies.   MPL

ABERCROMBY, Helen see (28)

ABLE SEAMAN, pseud. see BERNARD, W.V., (Able
Seaman, pseud).

ABRAHAM, Nellie see (29)

36

ADAIR, Ivan
Songs from Dublin City: [poems]. Dublin: Talbot P.
1918. 29p.   BM

See also (31) (32) (63)

ADAMSON, Margot Robert
The desert and the sown, and other poems. Selwyn &
Blount. 1921. 84p.   BPL

A year of war, and other poems. Nutt. 1917. [viii], 80p.   BPL

**ADCOCK, Arthur St. John, (Lance-Corporal Cobber,
pseud.)**
The Anzac pilgrim's progress: ballads of Australia's army;
by Cobber. Ed. [or rather written] by A. St. John Adcock.
Simpkin, Marshall. [1918]. 116p.   MPL

City songs: [poems]. Selwyn & Blount. 1926. viii, 79p.   MPL

Collected poems. Hodder & Stoughton. 1929. 303p.   MPL

Exit homo. Selwyn & Blount. 1921. xiv, 47p.   BM

Exit homo. Cheap ed. Selwyn & Blount. 1924. xiv, 47p.   BM

Songs of the World War: [poems]. Palmer & Hayward.
1916. xxiv, 80p.   MPL

Tod MacMammon sees his soul, and other satires for the
new democracy: [poems]. Swarthmore P. [1921]. 83p.   BM

See also (99) (100) (101)

**ADKIN, James Harry Knight- see KNIGHT-ADKIN, James
Harry**

ADLINGTON, A.
Britain's might. 1914. il.
   A postcard.   BM

AGIUS, Ambrose
Winged chariots: [poems]. Printed Welwyn: Broadwater P.
1937. viii, 120p.   BM

AGNEW, Georgette
Songs of love and grief: [poems]. Constable. 1922. viii, 91p.   BPL

Sonnets. Elkin Mathews. 1916. 32p.   BM

37

AINGER, A.
Duty: for the benefit of Tommy and Jack. Leeds: Author.
1916. col. il.
    A postcard.   BM

Gems of my native land: to the heroes of the Jutland
fight, May 31st, 1916, for the benefit of Tommy and Jack.
Leeds: Author. 1916. col. il.
    A postcard.   BM

Men of my kin: to the heroes of the great drive, July 1st,
1916, for the benefit of Tommy and Jack. Leeds: Author.
1916. col. il.
    A postcard.   BM

Recitations and poems. Leeds: Ambler. 1922. 48p. por.   BM

Wishes from home, for Tommy and Jack. Leeds: Author.
1916.
    A postcard.   BM

**AITCH, Auntie, pseud. see HAYWARD, Mrs., (Auntie
Aitch, pseud.)**

AKERMAN, William see (65)

**ALCHIN, Gordon, (Observer, R.F.C., pseud.) (Captain,
Royal Flying Corps.)**

Oxford and Flanders: [poems] ; by Observer, R.F.C.
Oxford: Blackwell. 1916. 40p.   MPL

See also (2) (19) (72)

ALDINGTON, May
Roll of honour, and other poems. Printed Rye: Adams.
[1917]. 32p.   BPL

**ALDINGTON, Richard (Served on the Western Front,
1916-18. Was severely gassed)**

Collected poems. New York: Covici Friede. 1928. xiv, 234p.
    Bibliog. note (author's works) 1p.   BPL

Collected poems. Allen & Unwin. 1929. xiv, 234p.
    Bibliog. note (author's works) 1p.   BM

Collected poems, 1915-1923. New ed. Allen & Unwin.
1933. xiv, 176p.
    Bibliog. note (author's works) 1p.   BPL

Complete poems. Wingate. 1948. 366p.   LPL

The eaten heart. France: Chapelle-Réanville: Hours P.
1929. [vi], 19p.
> A limited ed. of 200 copies, signed by the author.   MPL

The eaten heart, [and other poems]. Chatto & Windus.
1933. [viii], 50p.   MPL

Exile, and other poems. Allen & Unwin. 1923. 62p.
> A limited ed. of 750 copies.   BM

A fool i' the forest: a phantasmagoria. Allen & Unwin.
1925. 63p.   BM

Images, [and other poems], (1910-1915). Poetry Bookshop.
[1915]. 32p.   BM

Images, [and other poems]. *The Egoist.* [1919]. 60p.
> Taken from "Images" publ. 1915, with additional poems.   BM

Images of desire: [poems]. Elkin Mathews. 1919. 39p.   BM

Images of war: [poems]. Allen & Unwin. 1919. 64p.   BPL

Images of war: a book of poems. Beaumont P. 1919. 47p.
col. il. (by Paul Nash).
> A limited ed. of 200 copies.   BM

See also (4) (19) (33) (50) (59) (60) (80) (96) (97) (98) (103)
(112) (127)

ALEXANDER, Eleanor see (19) (47) (48) (49) (55)
(111) (112)

ALINGTON, Cyril Argentine (Headmaster of Eton)
Eton faces, old and young: [poems]. Murray. 1933.
xx, 199p.   MPL

Eton lyrics. Clement Ingleby. [1925]. xvi, 101p.   BM

In shabby streets, and other verses. Eton: Spottiswoode,
Ballantyne. 1942. 63p.   MPL
See also (111) (112) (113)

ALLAN, John
Poems of consolation. Glasgow: Allan. [1916]. 32p.   BPL

ALLEN, Albert
Labour war chants: [poems]. Manchester: National
Labour P. 1914. 16p.

Reprinted from the *Labour Leader,* 24th December 1914.   IWM

ALLEN, Alice Maud, (Allen Havens, pseud.)
The upland field, [and other poems] ; by Allen Havens.
Cambridge: Fraser. 1937. 80p.   MPL

ALLEN, J.W. see (26)

ALLEN, Marian
The wind on the downs, [and other poems]. Humphreys.
1918. 64p.   BM

See also (31)

ALLHUSEN, Beatrice
April moods, and later verses. Humphreys. 1917. viii,
177p.   BM

See also (31) (32)

The **ALLIES'** appeal! Printed Birmingham: Economic
Printing Co. [1914].
   A postcard.   BM

**ALLPASS, Harry Blythe King, ("Rex" Allpass) (2nd
Lieutenant, Essex Regiment)**

Oxford, St. Bees and the front, 1911-1916. Werner
Laurie. [1920]. xii, 80p. por.
   Verse and prose, including some letters.   BPL

ALLSOPP, Henry
Plummets: selected poems. With an intro. by A.St. John
Adcock. Nisbet. 1923. xvi, 107p.   BM

Songs from a dale in war time: [poems]. Bell. 1915.
vi, 32p.   BPL

See also (19) (25)

ALPHA, pseud. see **MACKERETH, Annie, (Alpha pseud.)**

AMBROSE, Robert see (29)

AMCOTTS, John Cracroft
The poems of a patient. Valletta: *Daily Malta Chronicle.*
[1919?]. 26p.
   Written during convalescence in naval hospitals.   BPL

40

AMSTUTZ, Eveline
A book of verse. Zurich: Amstutz, Herdeg. 1943. 85p.
  A limited ed. of 500 copies.
  Includes several war poems written when author was 14-18
years.   MPL

ANDERSON, David
Edith Cavell, and other poems. Longmans, Green. 1918.
vi, 82p.   BPL

ANDERSON, Frederick see (27)

ANDERSON, Jessie Annie see (5)

ANDERSON, Lilian M. see (129)

ANDREWS, Daniel James
The passing of Kitchener of Khartoum. [1916].
  A broadside.   BM

ANDREWS, Francis
Poems. Bristol: Goulding. 1921. [viii], 52p.   BPL

Poems and songs. Bristol: Goulding. 1915. viii,
100p.   BPL

ANGLIN, Norman (Able-Bodied Seaman, Royal Navy)
1919, [and other poems]. Manchester: Sherratt & Hughes.
1919. 79p.   MPL

The wandering wind, [and other poems]. Erskine
Macdonald. 1916. 52p. por.   MPL

ANGLO-AMERICAN, pseud.
The ballad of Kaiser Willhelm; or, the invasion of
Belgium. St. Catherine P. [1915]. 29p.   BPL

ANGUS, Marion E.
The lilt, and other verses. Aberdeen: Wyllie. 1922. [16]p.   BM

Selected poems. Ed. with an intro. by Maurice Lindsay,
and a personal memoir by Helen B. Cruickshank.
Edinburgh: Serif Books. 1950. xxii, 67p. por.   BM

The tinker's road, and other verses. Gowans & Gray.
1924. 54p.   BM

The turn of the day, [and other poems]. Edinburgh:
Porpoise P. 1931. 48p.   MPL

ANSELL, N. see (29)

ARCHER, William see (26) (65) (99) (100) (101)

ARGYLL-DUNN, F.J.
Thistles and gorse: poems. Stockwell. 1923. 20p.   BM

ARKELL, Reginald
All the rumours; rhymed by Reginald Arkell.
Duckworth. 1916. 48p. il. (by Alfred Leete).   BM

The Bosch book: 80 drawings by Alfred Leete. Verses by
Reginald Arkell. Duckworth. 1916. 48p. il.
   Cartoons, with captions and humorous verses.   BM

A children's painting book, in aid of the Belgian Relief
Fund. Jingles by Reginald Arkell. Odhams. 1914.
[64] p. il. (by John Hassall), por.   BM

ARKWRIGHT, Sir John Stanhope
The supreme sacrifice, and other poems in time of war.
Skeffington. 1919. 79p. il. (by Bruce Bairnsfather and others).   BPL

ARMSTRONG, Martin (Served in ranks in Artists Rifles,
1914-15. Commissioned in 8th Middlesex Regiment,
1915-19. Served in France on the Western Front)

The bird-catcher, and other poems. Martin Secker. 1929.
87p.
   A limited ed. of 500 copies.   BM

The buzzards, and other poems. Martin Secker. 1921. 77p.   MPL

Collected poems. Martin Secker. 1931. 191p.   MPL

Thirty new poems. Chapman & Hall. 1918. viii, 77p.   MPL

See also (33) (54) (112)

ARMSTRONG, Nelly M. see (5)

ARMSTRONG, T.H.W. see (77)

ARNELL, Charles John
Love in a mist, and kindred verse. Newport, I.O.W.:
County P. [1920]. [ii], 50p.   BPL

42

On divers strings: selected poems. Exeter: Poetry Publ.
Co. 1927. 24p.   BM

ARNOLD, A.V. see (31) (32)

ARNOLD, Mrs. J.O. see ARNOLD, A.V. (31) (32)

ARTHUR, Frederick, pseud. see LAMBERT, Frederick
Arthur Heygate, (Frederick Arthur, pseud.)

ASCHER, Lily Gordon see (64)

ASHMORE, Dorothy Emily Augusta, Lady
Songs of Glenshee, and other poems. Foulis. 1924. 83p.   EDR

Song of the Camerons, and other poems. Hodder &
Stoughton. 1927. 90p.   BM

ASHMORE, Raymond (Sergeant, Highland Light
Infantry)

Lift high the flag, and other verses. Printed Glasgow:
Crawford. [1918]. [12]p.   IWM

ASKEW, Martha see (29)

ASQUITH, Hon. Herbert (Son of the Prime Minister.
Captain, Royal Field Artillery. Served on the Western Front)

Poems, 1912-1933. Sidgwick & Jackson. 1934. xii, 89p.   MPL

A village sermon, and other poems. Sidgwick & Jackson.
1920. 56p.   BM

The volunteer, and other poems. Sidgwick & Jackson.
1915. 24p.   MPL

The volunteer, and other poems. 2nd ed., with new poems
added. Sidgwick & Jackson. 1917. 48p.   MPL

Youth in the skies, and other poems. Sidgwick & Jackson.
1940. viii, 97p.   BM

See also (2) (4) (16) (17) (18) (19) (31) (32) (33) (35)
(46) (47) (48) (49) (59) (72) (80) (95) (111) (112) (119)

ASTON, Millicent
The Kaiser's ambition. Printed Birmingham: Bentley.
[1917]. [3]p.   BM

43

ATHERTON, Robert, pseud. see BANKS, Robert
Hesketh, (Robert Atherton, pseud.), (Robin O'Bobs, pseud.)

AUMONIER, Henry Francis Butler see (29)

AUNTIE AITCH, pseud. see HAYWARD, Mrs., (Auntie
Aitch, pseud).

AUSTRALIS, pseud. see CORLETTE, Hubert Christian,
(Australis, pseud.)

AYLING, Alan, & CLIFT, Rupert
Poems. Cambridge: Perkin Warbeck. 1921. 28p. (Florin
series, 7).
    Not joint authorship. Some war poetry by Clift, none
by Ayling.   BPL

B., A.
The golden archer: a book of sonnets. Erskine
Macdonald. 1920. 62p.   BM

His coming. Theosophical Publ. Co. [1916].
    A broadside.   BM

B.A.B., pseud. see BABINGTON, T.M., (B.A.B., pseud.)

B., A.J. see (31) (32)

B., C.E. see BURTON, Claude Edward Cole Hamilton,
(C.E.B.), (Touchstone, pseud.)

B., E.S. see BUCHANAN, Edgar Simmons, (E.S.B.)

B., G.M. see BONUS, Gladys M., (G.M.B.)

B., H. see (5)

B., H.D'A. (Major, 55th Division. Served with British
Expeditionary Force in France) see (56) (57) (96)

B.H.W. see (31) (32)

B., J.
The Kaiser's dream: sequel to "The day". Brighton:
Southern Publ. Co. [1918].
    A postcard.   BM

B., M. see (63)

B., M.E. see BONUS, M.E., (M.E.B.)

B., O.
Three poems: "The Dover Patrol"; "The lifeboat crew";
"I stand at the door". St. Catherine P. [1920]. [8]p.   BM

B., P.
Verses. Bristol: Arrowsmith. 1916. 32p.   BM

See also (31) (32)

B., W.E. see BERRIDGE, William Eric, (W.E.B.)

BABINGTON, T.M., (B.A.B., pseud).
The war in verse. Printed Madras: Higginbotham. 1917.
vi, 90p.   BM

BADMINTON, Albert S.B. see (29)

BAERLEIN, Henry (Was attached to an ambulance convoy
of the British Ambulance Committee, serving with the
Chasseurs Alpins)

Rimes of the Diables Bleus. Selwyn & Blount. 1917. 64p.   MPL

Windrush and evenlode: poems. Methuen. 1915.
xii, 60p.   MPL

BAGENAL, Hope
Sonnets in war and peace, and other verses. Oxford U.P.
1940. viii, 54p.   BPL

BAGOTT, Eugene
The genesis of the Great War. Stockwell. [1918]. 16p.   MPL

BAGSHAW, William
"In memoriam: E.M." Manchester: Sherratt & Hughes.
1918.
    A broadside.
    Reprinted from the *Manchester Quarterly*, April 1918.   MPL

BAILEY, H.
Revised lines on our soldiers and the war, fate so
determined by their talents. Leeds: Author. 1916.

A broadside.   BM

Verses on our soldiers and the war. Leeds: Author. 1916.
   A broadside.   BM

Verses on the war, and a peace versus war method. Leeds:
Author. 1916.
   A broadside.   BM

BAILEY, James Signa
Flame-tears and heart-joy: [poems]. Northampton:
Mercury P. [1921]. 48p. por.   BPL

The muse in blue: poems. Stockwell. [1934]. 64p. por.   BM

Soul of mine: a selection of poems. Stockwell. [1929].
16p.   BM

BAILY, Bertha Blacker
Berries on a wayside hedge: [poems]. Printed Douglas:
Fleming. 1923. 24p.
   A limited ed. of 150 copies.   BM

See also (29) (65)

BAIN, Gilbert (Lieutenant, Gloucestershire Regiment)
"The Slashers": a ballad of "The Old Braggs" or "The
Fore & Aft". Bristol: Arrowsmith. 1918. 16p.   BPL

BAIN, Robert
The town on the hill, [and other poems]. Glasgow:
Wylie. 1941. 47p.   BPL

BAINBRIDGE, Stella M. see (49)

BAKER, A.E. Whiting- see **WHITING-BAKER, A.E.**

BAKER, Jack (Signaller, 7th London Regiment. Killed
at Morlancourt, 8th August 1918, aged 21)

"Memories of the line": [poems]. Printed A.J. Wilson.
[1917?]. [16]p.   IWM

BAKER, James
Good Lord! what fools we be! : a satire (with apologies
to Queen Elizabeth). [1918].
   A broadside.   IWM

See also (27)

BAKER, Madeleine Stuart (Honorary Major in Royal
Air Force medical service)

Collected poems. Mitre P. 1961. 35p.   MPL

BAKER, Olaf
The questing heart, [and other poems]. Erskine
Macdonald. 1917. 59p.   BPL

Tramp of eternity, [and other poems]. Allen & Unwin.
1919. 61p.   BM

See also (61) (104)

BALFOUR, John (Prisoner of war)
Ruhleben poems. *Esthonian Review.* 1919. [vi], 45p.
col. il.   BPL

BALLARD, Edwin see (29)

BANKS, Robert Hesketh, (Robert Atherton, pseud.),
(Robin O'Bobs, pseud.)
War songs: songs and recitations on war and patriotism;
by Robert Atherton. Manchester: Author. [1914]. 16p.
facsim.
   Includes one verse in Lancashire dialect.   MPL

When the robin sings, and other verses; by Robin O'Bob's.
Stockwell. [1924]. 24p.   MPL

See also (27)

BANNARD, Henry E. see (27)

BANZIE, Eric De see **DE BANZIE, Eric**

BARBER, Cecil
Sandbag ballads and snow-water songs. Elkin Mathews.
1919. 64p.   MPL

BARD OF SANDHURST, pseud. see **SAUNDERS, T.B.,**
(Bard of Sandhurst, pseud.)

BARGERY, William see (27) (29)

BARING, Hon. Maurice, (M.B.) (Commissioned in
Intelligence Corps. Later transferred to Royal Flying Corps)

Cecil Spencer. Privately printed. 1928. [9]p.
    A limited ed. of 250 copies, printed for private circulation.
    Written on the death, in 1928, of Lieutenant-Commander the Hon. Cecil E.R. Spencer, who gained the D.S.C. and Bar and Legion of Honour for gallantry in action at Zeebrugge and Ostend, 1918.   BM

Cecil Spencer. Heinemann. 1929. [vi], 5p.
    A limited ed. of 525 copies.   BPL

Collected poems. Heinemann. 1925. viii, 359p.   MPL

Fifty sonnets. Printed Ballantyne P. 1915. 59p.
    For private circulation.   BM

In memoriam Auberon Herbert, Captain Lord Lucas, killed November 3, 1916. Oxford: Blackwell. 1917. 14p.
    Cover-title is "In memoriam A.H.".
    Reprinted from *The New Statesman.*   BM

Poems, 1892-1929. Fanfare P. 1929. 129p.
    A limited ed. of 50 copies, privately printed.   BM

Poems: 1914-1917. Martin Secker. 1918. 40p.   MPL

Poems: 1914-1919. Martin Secker. 1920. 60p.   BPL

Poems: 1914-1919. New ed. Martin Secker. 1923. 60p.   LPL

The R.F.C. alphabet; by M.B. Printed Ballantyne, Hanson. 1915. [56]p. il. (by R.C.).
    Printed on one side of leaf only.
    Cartoon drawings with rhyming captions.   BM

[Selected poems]. Benn [1926]. 32p. (Augustan books of modern poetry).
    Bibliog. (author's works) 1p.   BM

Selected poems. Heinemann. 1930. [x], 100p.   MPL

Sonnets. Chiswick P. 1914. [iv], 56p.   BM

See also (18) (33) (35) (46) (66) (102) (111) (112) (120)

BARLOW, J.E.M. see (113)

BARLOW, Jane
Between doubting and daring: verses. Oxford: Blackwell. 1916. [iv], 35p.   BM

BARLOW, John
Poems of peace and progress: an anthology of selected
stanzas, chiefly from "Poems for patriots on the Great
World War". Printed Manchester: Falkner. 1930.
16p.
    Cover-title is "Peace and progress".   MPL

["Poems for patriots on the Great World War" not
traced].

BARNARD, A.S. see **THOMAS, W.G., & BARNARD, A.S.**

BARNARD, William E.
Post-meridian: [poems]. Erskine Macdonald. [1916].
48p. (Little books of Georgian verse).   BM

BARNES, Frederick (Major)
Some verses. Privately printed. [1924?]. [iv], 45p. por.
   Printed for private circulation.   EDR

BARNES, Leonard (Served on the Western Front)
Youth at arms: [poems]. Davies. 1933. [vi], 71p.   BPL

See also (33)

BARNES, Ronald Gorell, Lord Gorell (Colonel, Rifle
Brigade)

Days of destiny: war poems at home and abroad. Longmans,
Green. 1917. x, 36p.   MPL

Many mansions: [poems]. Murray. 1926. viii, 112p.   BM

1904-1936 poems. Murray. 1937. xvi, 592p. por.   MPL

Pilgrimage, [and other poems]. Longmans, Green.
1920. xii, 136p.   BPL

Unheard melodies: [poems]. Murray. 1934. viii, 111p.   BPL

Wings of the morning, and other new poems of peace
and war. Murray. 1948. viii, 71p.   BM

See also (17) (18) (99) (100) (101) (111) (112)

BARNETT, George Lawrence
The hand: recitation. [Cardiff?]: Author. [1915]. [3]p.
   Proceeds to war relief funds.   BM

BARRINGTON, Pauline see (61)

BARRON, David
A book of remembrance. Kingsgate P. [192-]. 280p. por.
   Poetry and prose.   IWM

BARRY, Armstrong
Laurel and myrtle: poems. Glasgow: Hodge. [1918].
78p. il.   BPL

See also (23)

BARRY, John Arthur, (L.L., pseud.)
The sacrament; by L.L. Hodder & Stoughton. 1916.
x, 115p.
   Poems and stories.   BM

BARTHOLEYNS, A.
Chimes for the times: or, light, love and liberty:
a modern pean. McBride, Nast. [1919]. 32p.   BPL

BARTLETT, Brenda Shreeve (Queen Mary's Army
Auxiliary Corps)

Songs of the younger-born: [poems]. Erskine
Macdonald. 1919. 88p.   BPL

BARTLETT, Vernon (Commissioned in 1915. Spent five
months at the front. Sustained a slight wound, and was
invalided home)

Leaves in the wind: [poems]. Amersham: Morland. 1916.
24p.   BM

Songs of the winds and seas: [poems]. Elkin Mathews.
1920. 59p.   BM

BARY, Anna Bunston De see **DE BARY, Anna Bunston**

BASHFORD, Sir Henry Howarth
Songs out of school : [poems]. Constable. 1916. x, 47p.   BPL

See also (17) (18)

BATE, Pauline see (28) (29)

BATEMAN, John
The passing of youth: a volume of poems. Erskine
Macdonald. 1922. 68p.   BM

BATEMAN, Robert
War poems, etc. 1915. 16p.   IWM

BATTERSBY, Henry Francis Prevost
Ash of roses, [and other poems]. Erskine Macdonald.
1920. 50p.   BPL

BATTESON, John see (27)

BAX, Clifford
Farewell my muse: [poems]. Lovat Dickson. 1932. [iv],
204p. por.   MPL

See also (103)

BAYNES, Dorothy Julia, (Dormer Creston, pseud.)
The clown of paradise, [and other poems]; by Dormer
Creston. Heath, Cranton. [1919]. 46p.   BPL

BEALES, P.S. see (115)

BEAZLEY, Mary see (64)

BECKETT, Arthur
Sussex at war: and, Poems of peace. *Sussex County
Herald.* 1916. 36p. por.   BPL

BECKH, Robert Harold (2nd Lieutenant, East Yorkshire
Regiment. Killed in action in France, 15th August 1916)

Swallows in storm and sunlight: [poems]. Chapman
& Hall. 1917. 108p. por.   MPL

BEDFORD, Madeline Ida
The young captain, [and other poems]: fragments of
war and love. Erskine Macdonald. [1917]. [vi], 16p.   BM

BEEK, Theo Van see **VAN BEEK, Theo** (60)

BEGBIE, Alfred J. see (29)

BEGBIE, Harold
Fighting lines and various reinforcements: [poems].
Constable. 1914. vi, 96p.   BPL

See also (19) (23) (31) (32) (45) (47) (48) (49) (55)
(82) (83) (84) (99) (100) (101) (119)

BEGBIE, Janet
Morning mist: [poems]. Mills & Boon. 1916. 106p.   MPL

BELL, Dobrée
Praise of life: [poems]. St. Catherine P. 1916.
[viii], 88p.
Poems written 1907-1915.   BPL

BELL, Sir Harold Idris see (85)

BELL, Henry Thomas Mackenzie
Poetical pictures of the Great War, suitable for
recitation. Series 1-4. Kingsgate P. 1915-18. 4v. il.   BPL

Selected poems. Harrap. 1921. 93p. il.   BM

See also (5) (27) (45) (50)

BELL, Irene Brittain
Homeward, and other verse. Erskine Macdonald. 1917.
46p. (Little books of Georgian verse: second series).   BM

BELL, John Herbert
Poems; and, The gold of Lestelle: a tragedy. Jenkins.
[1929]. 319p.   BM

BELL, Mackenzie see BELL, Henry Thomas Mackenzie

BELL, Maud
London songs and others: [poems]. Bristol: Horseshoe
Publ. Co. 1924. 30p.   BPL

BELL, Maud Anna see (17) (18)

BELL, Neil, pseud. see SOUTHWOLD, Stephen,
(Neil Bell, pseud.)

BELL, Richard G. see (27)

BELLETTI, Lilian M. see (64)

BELLHOUSE, S. see (20)

BENDALL, Frederic William Duffield (Lieutenant-
Colonel, London Regiment)
Front line lyrics. Elkin Mathews. 1918. 52p.   MPL

BENINGTON, Wilson
Love in London; and, The tidal town: [poems].
Scholartis P. 1931. viii, 100p.   BM

See also (65)

BENJAMIN, Joseph
A dog hero, founded on fact: recitation. Mayfair
Publ. Co. [1918?]. [4]p. (Benjamin's penny
recitations and dialogues).
    'Exploits of a soldier dog on the Somme'.   BM

The exploit of the Clan MacTavish: how a British cargo
ship fought a German cruiser: an episode in the war:
recitation. Mayfair Publ. Co. [1917]. [4]p. (Benjamin's
penny recitations and dialogues).   BM

The final message: a true incident of the war: recitation.
Unwin. [1914]. [4]p. (Benjamin's penny recitations
and dialogues).   BM

The gunner's sacrifice, founded on fact: recitation.
Simpkin, Marshall, Hamilton, Kent. [1914]. [4]p.
(Benjamin's penny recitations and dialogues).   BM

A hero's son: the story of a medal: recitation. Mayfair
Publ. Co. [1918]. [4]p. (Benjamin's penny recitations
and dialogues).   BM

His soldier daddy: a story of the war: recitation. Mayfair
Publ. Co. [1916]. [4]p. (Benjamin's penny recitations and
dialogues).   BM

BENNETT, Arthur
The last chance. Warrington: Sunrise Publ. Co. 1916.
(Sunrise leaflets, 7).
    A broadside.   BM

Songs in the darkness: [poems]. Warrington: Sunrise Publ.
Co. 1927. xiv, 214p. por.   BPL

Songs of a chartered accountant: [poems]. Gee. 1930.
129p. por.
    Includes author's "Songs in the darkness".   MPL

See also (27) (29)

BENSON, J.M.
Poems. Daniel. 1919. 32p.   BPL

BENSON, Stella
Poems. Macmillan. 1935. viii, 79p.
  Contains all the poems publ. in author's "Twenty".   MPL

Twenty: [poems]. Macmillan. 1918. viii, 53p.   BPL

BENT, Louisa E. see (29)

BENT, Morris
Mulvaney's gun: a ballad of the trenches, 1915:
recitation for improvised musical accompaniment.
Paignton: Author. [1915]. [3]p.   BM

BERNARD, W.V., (Able Seaman, pseud.)
Poems; by an Able Seaman. Westminster P. 1918. 72p.   BM

Poems; by an Able Seaman. 2nd ed. Westminster P.
1918. 72p.   BPL

BERRIDGE, William Eric, (W.E.B.) (Somerset Light
Infantry. Fell in battle, 20th August 1916)

Verses; [by] W.E.B. Printed Chichester P. [1916?].
61p.   EDR

BERRILL, Roland (Lieutenant, Royal Field Artillery)
Inspirations of Armageddon: [poems]. St. Catherine P.
[1918]. 30p.   BPL

BERT, George A. Le see **LE BERT, George A.** (29)

BERTOUCH, Beatrice De, Baroness see **DE BERTOUCH,
Beatrice, Baroness** (64)

BETHAM-EDWARDS, Matilda
War poems. Bristol: Arrowsmith. [1917]. 24p.   MPL

BETTS, Frank
The iron age: [poems]. Oxford: Blackwell. 1916. 80p.
("Adventurers all" series, 5).   MPL

The new and delectable ballad of King Richard called
Lionheart, and his good cheer for the noble gestes of his
Englishmen, in their great faring overseas. Oxford:
Blackwell. 1918. il.
  A broadside.
  Compares the war with the Crusades.   BM

BEWSHER, Paul (D.S.C. Captain, Royal Naval Air Service)

The bombing of Bruges, [and other poems]. Hodder & Stoughton. 1918. 82p.   MPL

The dawn patrol, and other poems of an aviator. Erskine Macdonald. 1917. 40p.   MPL

See also (11) (16) (17) (18) (33) (46) (50) (52) (58) (60) (96) (111) (112)

BICKLEY, Francis see (16) (18)

BINNS, Henry Bryan
April nineteen-fifteen; with, Six preludes in winter. Fifield. 1915. 31p.   BPL

November: poems in war time. Fifield. 1917. 93p.   MPL

BINYON, Laurence (In 1916 went to the front line as a Red Cross orderly)

The anvil, [and other poems]. Elkin Mathews. 1916. 43p.   MPL

The cause: poems of war. Boston (Mass.): Houghton Mifflin. 1917. viii, 116p.
    Contains "The anvil" and "The winnowing fan".   BPL

The cause: poems of war. Elkin Mathews. [1918]. viii, 115p.   JRL

For the fallen, and other poems. Hodder & Stoughton. [1917]. [55]p. col. il.
    Selected from "The winnowing-fan".   BPL

The four years: war poems collected and newly augmented. Elkin Mathews. 1919. [xii], 170p. por.   MPL

A Laurence Binyon anthology. Collins. 1927. 250p.
    Bibiog. (author's works) 2p.   MPL

Lyrical poems. Macmillan. 1931. xvi, 388p. (Collected poems, v.1).
    "Collected poems" v.2 contains no war poetry.   MPL

The new world: poems. Elkin Mathews. 1918. 39p.   MPL

The new world: poems. 2nd ed. Elkin Mathews. 1919. 39p.   BPL

The north star, and other poems. Macmillan. 1914. viii, 60p.   MPL

The secret: sixty poems. Elkin Mathews. 1920. 96p.   MPL

[Selected poems]. Benn. [1926]. 32p. (Augustan books
of modern poetry).
   Bibliog. (author's works) 1p.   BM

The winnowing-fan: poems on the Great War.
Elkin Mathews. 1914. 38p.   MPL

The winnowing-fan: poems on the Great War. 2nd ed.
Elkin Mathews. 1915. 37p.   UD

The winnowing-fan: poems on the Great War. 3rd ed.
Elkin Mathews. 1915. 37p.   BPL

See also (4) (12) (16) (17) (18) (19) (25) (26) (31)
(32) (33) (37) (46) (47) (48) (49) (50) (51) (53) (55)
(59) (61) (63) (65) (66) (80) (82) (83) (84) (88) (96)
(99) (100) (101) (105) (108) (109) (111) (112) (113)
(119) (120) (121)

BIRCH, William Thomas
Armageddon, and other poems. Manchester:
Heywood. 1918. 256p. por.   ·MPL

BIRD, Geoffrey Paul
Poems. Selwyn & Blount. 1920. 92p.   BPL

BIRKHEAD, Henry see (65)

BIRRELL, William Dunbar
War and patriotic poems. 2nd ed. Dundee: Thomson.
[1918]. 64p. por.   BPL

[No copy of 1st ed. traced].

BLACK, A.W.
Pilau: lays of East and West. Stockwell. [1924]. 106p.   BM

BLACK, John
"Britain's flag", and other poems. West Hartlepool:
Garbutt. 1916. 41p.   BPL

"The flag of the free", and other poems. West
Hartlepool: Garbutt. 1917. 42p.   BPL

"Under one flag", and other poems. Printed West
Hartlepool: Martin. [1922]. 80p.   BPL

See also (29)

BLACKALL, Charles W. (Captain)
Songs from the trenches: [poems]. Bodley Head. 1915.
59p.   MPL

See also (2)

BLAIR, Wilfrid
For Belgium: poems on behalf of the *Daily Telegraph*
Christmas Shilling Fund. Oxford: Blackwell. 1914.
31p. il.   MPL

1915, and other poems. Oxford: Blackwell. 1915. 40p.   BPL

"'Tis simple mirth", [and other poems]. Oxford:
Blackwell. 1915. 40p.   BPL

See also (19) (65)

BLAKE, Corrie see (51)

BLAKEMORE, Trevor
The flagship, and other poems. Erskine Macdonald. 1915.
100p.   MPL

Moonset, and other poems. Elkin Mathews. 1924. 93p.   BM

Poems. Foreword by Sir Compton Mackenzie. Spearman.
1955. 159p. por., facsim.   BM

Star-dust, [and other poems]. St. Catherine P. [1920].
108p.   BPL

BLAKENEY, Edward Henry
Collected war poems. Ely: Author. 1915. [vi], [25]p.
   Printed on one side of leaf only.
   Cover-title is "War poems".
   Printed by author at his private press, King's
School, Ely.   JRL

Falling leaves: or, wayside musings in verse. Winchester:
Author. 1933. [61]p.
   Printed on one side of leaf only.
   A limited ed. of 50 copies.
   Printed by author at his private press.   MPL

In the vale of years: verses on various occasions.
Winchester: Author. 1926. [99]p.
   Printed on one side of leaf only.
   Printed by author at his private press.   BM

Poems in peace and war: 1912-1918. Ely: Author.
1918. [x], [61]p.
    Printed on one side of leaf only.
    A limited ed. of 65 copies.
    Printed by author at his private press, King's
School, Ely.   JRL

To the day: a poem. Ely: Author. 1914. [5]p.
    Printed by the author at his private press, King's
School, Ely.   BM

BLAKER, Hugh
The ballad of disdain. Erskine Macdonald. 1919. [iv], 30p.
    Printed on one side of leaf only.   BPL

BLAKER, Walter Campbell see (27)

BLAND, Robert Henderson- see **HENDERSON-BLAND, Robert**

BLANDFORD, E.S.
"For Dorset's sake", [and other poems]. Printed
Dorchester. 1919. 24p.   IWM

BLANE, William
Verse: a selection. Oxford: Blackwell. 1937. [viii],
118p.   MPL

BLATHWAYT, William
Collected poems. Pitman. 1932. 312p. il., por.   BM

From the twilight: [poems]. Printed Bath: Lewis.
[1920]. 47p. il.   BM

The garden of sleep, and other verses original and
translated. Pitman. 1924. x, 65p. il.   WPL

Love and the stars: verses original and translated. Pitman.
1926. viii, 60p. il.   MPL

Sixty sonnets, with a brief intro. on the sonnet-
structure. Pitman. 1934. 84p. il.   BM

BLISS, H.W. see (19) (40) (41) (65)

BLOOD, M.E.
When good men meet as foe to foe: [poems] written
in Germany. Boston: Southgate P. [1916]. [iv], 29p.   IWM

BLOOM, Ursula
Lyrics of life: [poems]. Galashiels: Walker. 1918. 24p.   BPL

BLOYE, Herbert
The church militant. Fellowship of Reconciliation.
[191-]. 2p.   MPL

BLUNDELL, Agnes see (32)

**BLUNDEN, Edmund Charles, (Fellow of Merton
College, pseud.)** (M.C. Lieutenant, Royal Sussex Regiment.
Fought at the Somme and Ypres)

Choice or chance: new poems. Cobden-Sanderson. 1934.
viii, 60p.   MPL

An elegy, and other poems. Cobden-Sanderson. 1937. 96p.   MPL

English poems. Cobden-Sanderson. 1925. 127p.   WPL

English poems. New York: Knopf. 1926. 127p.   BM

English poems. Duckworth. 1929. 144p. (New readers
library).   WPL

Halfway house: a miscellany of new poems. Cobden-
Sanderson. 1932. xii, 95p.   MPL

Masks of time: a new collection of poems principally
meditative. Beaumont P. 1925. [xvi], 60p. il. (by
Randolph Schwabe).
    A limited ed. of 390 copies.   MPL

Near and far: new poems. Cobden-Sanderson. 1929. 67p.   WPL

Near and far: new poems. New York: Golden Hind P.
1930. x, 65p. col il.
    A limited ed. of 105 copies signed by the author.   BM

On several occasions: [poems]; by a Fellow of
Merton College. Corvinus P. 1938. [57]p.
    Printed on one side of leaf only.
    A limited ed. of 60 copies.   MPL

Pastorals: a book of verses. Erskine Macdonald. 1916.
42p. (Little books of Georgian verse).   MPL

Poems: 1913 and 1914. Printed Horsham: Price.
1914. 41p.   BM

Poems, 1914-30. Cobden-Sanderson. 1930. xviii, 336p.   MPL

Poems, 1930-1940. Macmillan. 1940. xiv, 264p. BPL

Poems of many years. Collins. 1957. 312p. MPL

Retreat: [poems]. Cobden-Sanderson. 1928. 70p. WPL

Retreat: [poems]. New York: Doubleday, Doran.
1928. [x], 60p. BM

[Selected poems]. Benn. [1925]. 32p. (Augustan books
of modern poetry). BM

The shepherd, and other poems of peace and war. Cobden-
Sanderson. 1922. 86p. MPL

The shepherd, and other poems of peace and war. 2nd ed.
Cobden-Sanderson. 1922. 88p. BPL

The shepherd, and other poems of peace and war.
Duckworth. 1922. (New readers library) Not seen

The shepherd, and other poems of peace and war. New York:
Knopf. 1922. 88p. BM

The shepherd, and other poems of peace and war. [New
ed.]. Duckworth.1928. 101p. (New readers library). MPL

A summer's fancy. Beaumont P. 1930. 56p. il.
(by Randolph Schwabe).
    'Written in 1922, when the war had only just receded
from our daily lives' — preface. MPL

To nature: new poems. Beaumont P. 1923. [xii],
50p.
    A limited ed. of 390 copies. UN

The waggoner, and other poems. Sidgwick & Jackson.
1920. viii, 71p. MPL

See also (4) (22) (33) (50) (70) (80) (89) (96)
(103) (112) (118)

BOAS, Frederick Samuel
Songs of Ulster and Balliol: [poems]. Constable. 1917.
44p. BPL

BODY, G.E.
"The evening hour", and other poems. Book 1.
Stockwell. [1927]. 20p. MPL

BOLLAND, Hannah see (28) (29)

60

BOLTON, Lord see ORDE-POWLETT, Nigel, Lord Bolton

BOMFORD, Nora
Poems of a pantheist. Chatto & Windus. 1918. iv, 44p.　　　BPL

BONAVIA, pseud.
Britain's defeat. Heath, Cranton. 1918. [7]p.　　　BPL

BONNYMAN, Jessie see (28) (29)

BONUS, Gladys M., (G.M.B.)
"Be comforted"; by G.M.B. Exeter: Author. [1916]. [4]p.　　　BM

BONUS, M.E., (M.E.B.)
To a soldier or sailor; [by] M.E.B. Exeter: Author. [1916].
[4]p.　　　BM

The BOOK of William, with apologies to Edward Lear.
Warne. [1914]. [43]p. il.
　　　Printed on one side of leaf only.
　　　Limericks referring to the Kaiser.　　　BM

BOOTH, Eva Gore- see GORE-BOOTH, Eva

BOOTH, Mary see (25) (26) (47) (48) (49)

BOOTH, William
Gentlemen all! and other poems of the war. Printed
Salford: Padfield. 1915. 32p.　　　MPL

The songs of a year: [poems]. Nutt. 1914. 52p.　　　MPL

BORASTON, John Maclair
The seal-maid, and other poems. Simpkin, Marshall,
Hamilton, Kent. 1923. 121p.　　　MPL

The shining trail, and other poems. Manchester:
Sherratt & Hughes. 1918. [viii], 165p.　　　MPL

BORDEN, Mary (b. Chicago, but settled in England.
Directed a mobile hospital at the front, 1915 to 1918.
Was made a member of the Legion of Honour and
received the Croix de Guerre)

The forbidden zone. Heinemann. 1929. [x], 199p. il.
　　　Stories, sketches and poems. Poems written between

61

1914 and 1918, during four years of hospital work with
the French army.   MPL

BOSANQUET, Bernard see **BOSANQUET, Helen,
& BOSANQUET, Bernard**

BOSANQUET, Helen, & BOSANQUET, Bernard
Zoar: a book of verse. Oxford: Blackwell. [1919].
60p.   BPL

BOTTOMLEY, Horatio
Songs of the cell: [poems]. Southern. 1928. 113p.   MPL

Why is the red blood flowing? [New] ed. Odhams. [1916].
[3]p. por.   BM

[No copy of 1st ed. traced].

BOUCH, Thomas
Coat of many colours: [poems]. Caraval P. 1953. xii,
132p.   MPL

Sentimentalities: [poems]. Duckworth. 1927. 72p.   BM

Storms in teacups: [poems]. Duckworth. 1922. vi, 56p.   BM

BOULTING, E. Frances
Eight sonnets. Printed Hazell, Watson & Viney.
[1923]. 8p.   BPL

Thoughts and dreams: [poems]. Kegan Paul, Trench,
Trubner. 1917. 31p.   BM

BOULTON, Oscar
The luck of the Navy. Printed Hazell, Watson & Viney.
1926. 15p.   BM

Poems. Kegan Paul, Trench, Trubner. 1916. 156p.   BPL

BOURDILLON, Francis William
Christmas roses, [and other poems] for nineteen
hundred and fourteen. Humphreys. [1914].
[vi], 25p.   BPL

Easter lilies, [and other poems] for nineteen hundred
and fifteen. Humphreys. [1915]. vi, 25p.   BPL

A hymn of hope for the League of Nations. S.P.C.K.
[1919]. [4]p.   BPL

Russia re-born, [and other poems]. Humphreys. 1917.
30p.   BPL

See also (16) (17) (18) (19) (25) (26) (31) (32) (40)
(41) (44) (59) (65) (111) (112) (119)

BOWEN-COLTHURST, Georgina de Bellasis, (G.B.C.)
It is for man to choose: [poems]. Elkin Mathews.
1920. [iv], 12p.   BM

It is for man to choose: [poems]; [by] G.B.C.
Elkin Mathews. 1921. 16p.
   Dedicated 'To my grandson, Patrick, in memory of his
dearly-loved father, killed at St. Eloi, 15th March 1915,
in the World War'.   BPL

BOWER, John Graham, (Klaxon, pseud.)
H.M.S.; by Klaxon. Blackwood. 1918. viii,
328p.
   Stories and verse.   BM

On patrol: [poems]; by Klaxon. Blackwood. 1919.
x, 236p.   BPL

Songs of the submarine: [poems]; by Klaxon. McBride,
Nast. 1917. 48p.
   Publ. for the funds of the Union Jack Club extension.   MPL

See also (24) (31) (32) (111) (112) (119) (120)

**BOWMAN, Archibald Allan (Was a prisoner of
war in Germany)**

Sonnets from a prison camp. Bodley Head. 1919.
xii, 152p.   BPL

BOWMAN, F. (Gunner)
Play the game; by a demobbed and unemployed
soldier. [1919].
   A broadside.   BM

BOX, William
Forty poems. Chester & Lang. 1944. [vi], 50p.   MPL

BOYD, Halbert Johnston
Shreds and patches: [poems]. Foreword by F.
Frankfort Moore. Stockwell. [1926]. 32p.   BM

63

Verses and ballads of north and south. Elkin
Mathews. 1921. 60p.   MPL

BOYD, W.A. see (27)

BOYD-SHANNON, William (D.S.O. Major, Yorkshire
Regiment, Green Howards)

Mars and Eros: poems. Stockwell. [1921]. 32p.   BM

Ranelagh rhymes. Stockwell. [1921]. 32p. il.   BPL

BOYLE, Mary Elizabeth
Aftermath: [poems]. Cambridge: Heffer. 1916. [36]p.
   Dedicated to the author's brother, David Boyle, killed in
action at Le Cateau, 1914.   BPL

BOYLE, W.S. see (25)

BRADBY, Godfrey Fox
Fireside, countryside, and other poems. Oxford U.P.
1923. 70p.   BPL

BRADBY, Henry Christopher
Poems. Printed Plymouth: Latimer, Trend. [1925?]. 60p.
   For private circulation.   BM

Sonnets. [Rugby]: [Author?]. 1918. 16p.   BPL

BRADBY, Mary Katherine
The angels, and other verse. Birmingham: Cornish.
1927. [vi], 138p.   BM

The professor and other verse. Birmingham: Cornish.
1927. [vi], 69p.   BM

BRADSHAW, J.
Loss of the "Royal Edward" troopship, outward bound
to the Dardanelles, torpedoed by German submarine.
[1916].
   A broadside.   BM

Loss of the S.S. "Lusitania", torpedoed by German
pirates off Kinsale, 7th May, 1915. Printed Padiham:
Spencer. [1915]. [2]p. il., por.   BM

BRAIMBRIDGE, Kathleen A.
Dream-songs: [poems]. Erskine Macdonald. 1916. 41p.

(Little books of Georgian verse: second series). BPL

BRAME, J.E.
Mothers of England! have ye mothered a man?;
by an old steward, an Alton Abbey pensioner.
Printed Alton: Moody. [191-].
  A broadside. BM

BRAMMAN, Arthur J. see (29)

BRAMSTON, F.T. see (27) (29)

BRAND, Charles Neville (Lieutenant, Royal Naval
Volunteer Reserve)

The house of time, and other poems. Elkin
Mathews. 1918. 48p. BPL

Perspective: poems. Wilson. 1921. 54p. BM

BRANFORD, Frederick Victor
Titans and gods: [poems]. Christophers. [1922]. 76p. MPL

See also (66) (94) (96) (103)

BRANSON, H.
The Kaiser's dream of heaven. [1917].
  A broadside. BM

"Our dad". [1917].
  A broadside. BM

"The war—and after". [1917].
  A broadside. BM

BRANTON, William, (W.B.L., pseud.)
Our brave boys, and other poems; by W.B.L. Leighton
Buzzard: Rush and Warwick. 1923. [iv], 46p. BM

Our brave boys, and other poems. [New] ed. Merton P.
1923. [iv], 48p.
  'Dedicated to the memory of my only son'. BPL

Remembrance, and various verses; by W.B.L. Leighton
Buzzard: [Author]. [1933?]. 16p. BM

War no more, and various verses. Printed Leighton Buzzard:
Leadbeater. 1936. 16p.
  Dedicated to the memory of an only son. MPL

BRAYE, Lord see VERNEY-CAVE, Alfred Thomas
Townshend, Lord Braye

BRERETON, Cloudesley
Mystica et lyrica: [poems]. Elkin Mathews. 1919. 128p.   BM

Mystica et lyrica: [poems]. 2nd ed. Elkin Mathews.
1919. 128p.   BPL

The Norfolk recruit's farewell: a ballad. Norwich:
Jarrold. [1917]. [4]p.   BM

BRETHERTON, Cyril Herbert see (87)

BREY, Dennis
The Empire our boys built: an illustrated war
epitome and chronique scandaleuse, instructive and
entertaining. Eastbourne: Pucka Poppets. 1918. 31p.
col. il., mps.
     'Set up for printing by a discharged wounded soldier'.
     A parody on "The house that Jack built".   BM

Strays: a little collection of scribbles made during three
years of voluntary war work: [poems]. Eastbourne:
Pucka Poppets. 1918. 24p.   BM

BRICE, Beatrix, pseud. see BRICE-MILLER,
Beatrix, (Beatrix Brice, pseud.)

BRICE-MILLER, Beatrix, (Beatrix Brice, pseud.)
All souls: to the first seven divisions, the fallen, the
prisoners, the disabled, and those still fighting. 1916.
     A Christmas card.   BM

To the vanguard, and other songs to the seven divisions:
[poems]. Bickers. [1917?]. 16p.   IWM

See also (51) (111) (112)

BRIDGES, Elizabeth
Sonnets from Hafez, and other verses. Oxford U.P.
1921. 48p.   BM

Verses. Oxford: Blackwell. 1916. 31p.   BM

See also (111) (112)

BRIDGES, Robert (Poet Laureate, 1913-30)
Britannia victrix. Oxford U.P. 1918. [4]p.   BPL

66

Lord Kitchener. Printed Shorter. 1916. [3] p.
A limited ed. of 20 copies privately printed by
Clement Shorter.   BM

New verse written in 1921, with the other poems of
that year, and a few earlier pieces. Oxford:
Clarendon P. 1925. x, 89p. por.   BM

October, and other poems, with occasional verses on
the war. Heinemann. 1920. xii, 64p.   BPL

Poetical works, excluding the eight dramas. [2nd ed.].
Oxford U.P. 1936. [viii], 576p. por.
1st ed. publ. 1912.   BM

Poetical works, with, The testament of beauty,
but excluding the eight dramas. Oxford U.P. 1953.
viii, 714p.   BM

Poetry and prose. With appreciations by G.M. Hopkins
and others. With an intro. and notes by John Sparrow.
Oxford: Clarendon P. 1955. xliv, 167p. por.   MPL

Selected poems. Faber. 1941. 79p.
Bibliog. (author's works) 2p.   BM

Shorter poems. Enlarged ed. Oxford U.P. 1931.
[viii], 235p. por.
1st ed. publ. 1890.   BM

The tapestry: poems. Privately printed. 1925. [ii],
43p.
A limited ed. of 250 copies.   BM

See also (12) (16) (17) (18) (19) (29) (30) (31)
(32) (45) (46) (54) (82) (83) (84) (108) (109)
(112) (120)

BRIGGS, Edith Maria see (28)

BRINE, Everard Lindesay (Lieutenant, 4th Battalion,
Hampshire Regiment. Served in Mesopotamia. Died of
illness in Kasvin, 1917)

Poems. Oxford: Blackwell. 1920. 40p. por.   BPL

BRISCOE, Walter Alwyn see (24)

BRISTOW, H.F.
A man: in memoriam of the H.M.S. Good Hope and

H.M.S. Monmouth, under the command of Rear-Admiral
Sir C. Cradock; lost with all hands in the battle off
the Chilean coast on Sunday, November 1st, 1914.
2nd ed. [191-]. [4] p.   IWM

[No copy of 1st ed. traced].

BRISTOWE, Sybil
Provocations: [poems]. With an intro. by G.K.
Chesterton. Erskine Macdonald. 1918. 78p.   BM

See also (64)

BRITANNIA, pseud.
The conflict of the nations. 1914.
   A broadside.   IWM

BRITON, A.
Autumn leaves from my soul's garden: [poems].
Amersham: Morland. 1917. 32p.   BM

BRITON, pseud.
A talk with Kaiser-Bill: a recitation. [1916].
   A broadside.   BM

BRITTAIN, John C. see (27) (29)

BRITTAIN, Vera Mary (Served with the Voluntary
Aid Detachment in army hospitals in London, Malta,
and France)

Poems of the war and after. Gollancz. 1934. 94p.   MPL

Verses of a V.A.D. Foreword by Marie Connor
Leighton. Erskine Macdonald. 1918. 46p.   MPL

See also (13) (14) (77) (78)

BRITTON, Herbert Eyres
Diane, and other poems. Stockwell. [1920]. 80p.   BPL

BROCK, Blanche Adelaide
Flights at twilight: [poems]. Long. [1916]. 79p.   BM

Remembrance, and other poems. Amersham:
Mascot P. [1928]. 13p.   IWM

See also (28) (29)

68

BROCK, Robert see (29)

BRODIE, Charles L.
The outcast, and other poems. Oliver & Boyd.
1919. 212p. il. (by Herbert J. Gunn).   BPL

BRODIE, Meg see (28)

BRODRIBB, Charles William
Poems. With an intro. by Edmund Blunden.
Macmillan. 1946. xviii, 102p. por.   MPL

See also (12) (17) (18) (54) (108) (109)

BROGAN, Thomas
The queen of the ward: in memoriam; composed for
the benefit of the *Daily Mirror* Edith Cavell Memorial
Fund. Keithley: Author. [1915].
   A broadside.   BM

BROMLEY, Leonard Courtney
The picture, and other poems. Elkin Mathews. 1920.
62p.   BPL

BROOK, Kenneth (Lieutenant, Royal Naval
Voluntary Reserve)
Poems. Stockwell. [1919]. 20p.   BPL

BROOKE, Brian, (Korongo, pseud.) (Captain, 2nd
Battalion, Gordon Highlanders. Died of wounds 25th
July 1916)

Poems. With a foreword by M.P. Willcocks. Bodley
Head. 1917. 183p. il., por.   MPL

Poems. With a foreword by M.P. Willcocks. 2nd ed.
Bodley Head. 1918. 183p. il., por.   BPL

See also (131)

BROOKE, John Arthur see (27) (29) (63)

BROOKE, Rupert (Sub-Lieutenant, Royal Naval Division.
Died on active service in the Aegean, 23rd April 1915)

Collected poems. With an intro. by George Edward

Woodberry and a biographical note by Margaret
Lavington. New York: Lane. 1915. 168p. por.   BM

Collected poems. With a memoir [by Edward Marsh].
Sidgwick & Jackson. 1918. clx, 160p. por.   MPL

Collected poems. Lee Warner. 1919. x, 159p. por.
(Medici Society).
   One of the Riccardi P. books.   BM

Collected poems. With a memoir [by Edward Marsh].
2nd ed. Sidgwick & Jackson. 1928. clviii, 162p. por.   Not seen

Collected poems. With a memoir by Edward Marsh.
3rd ed. Sidgwick & Jackson. 1942. clvi, 167p. por.   BUPL

Complete poems. Sidgwick & Jackson. 1932. x, 166p.
por., facsim.   BPL

Complete poems. 2nd ed. Sidgwick & Jackson. 1942. x,
167p. por., facsim.   MPL

"1914": five sonnets. Sidgwick & Jackson. 1915. ii, 5p.   BM

1914, and other poems. Sidgwick & Jackson. 1915. 64p.
por.   MPL

1914, and other poems. Faber. 1941. 64p.   MPL

Poems. Folio Society. 1948. xii, 164p. il.
(by John Buckland-Wright).   BM

Poems. Ed. with an intro. by Geoffrey Keynes. Nelson.
[1952]. xxviii, 164p. (Nelson classics, 401).   BM

Poetical works. Ed. by Geoffrey Keynes. Faber. 1946.
208p. por.   MPL

Poetical works. Ed. by Geoffrey Keynes. 2nd ed.
Faber. 1970. 216p. por.   MPL

Selected poems. Sidgwick & Jackson. 1917. 80p.   BM

[Selected poems]. Benn. [1925]. 32p. (Augustan
books of modern poetry).   BM

[Selected poems]. Eyre & Spottiswoode. [1943]. 28p.
(Augustan poets).
   Bibliog. (author's works) 1p.
   Same selection as Benn ed. of 1925.   BM

Twenty poems. Sidgwick & Jackson. 1935. 48p. por.   MPL

Two sonnets. With a memoir of Winston S. Churchill.

Holland: J. van Krimpen. 1945. [8]p.
A limited ed. of 100 numbered copies. BM

War poems. Privately printed. [1915]. [13]p.
Printed on one side of leaf only.
One of a few copies printed for Lady Desborough. BM

See also (2) (4) (12) (16) (17) (18) (19) (20) (21) (24)
(25) (31) (32) (33) (34) (37) (44) (47) (48) (49) (50)
(51) (53) (59) (66) (70) (72) (80) (88) (89) (95) (96)
(102) (105) (106) (111) (112) (118) (119) (120) (121)
(127) (128) (131)

BROOKS, Collin (Sergeant, Machine Gun Corps)
Echoes and evasions: [poems]. Lovat Dickson. 1934.
xii, 162p. MPL

Poems. Nutt. 1914. 126p. BM

See also (58)

BROWN, Cecil Leonard Morley
Rhymes of the R.A.F. Methuen. 1925. [viii], 40p.
Reprinted from *Punch*. BM

BROWN, Charles Hilton
The second lustre: a miscellany of verse. Oxford:
Blackwell. 1923. [viii], 96p. MPL

See also (87)

BROWN, Charles J. (Instructor at classes for discharged
and disabled ex-servicemen)

Will you forget? A plea on behalf of our discharged
and disabled service men. New Malden: Coombe P.
[1920].
A broadside. BM

BROWN, Edgar Rogers
War Office rhymes. Printed Forest Gate P. 1921.
20p. BM

BROWN, Harold
The shades of evening are falling: in memory of the
brave lads who have given their lives for their king and
country. Middlesbrough: Author. [191-].
A card. BM

BROWN, J.J. see (27)

BROWN, John (M.C. Served with 9th Seaforths, Royal
Scottish Regiment. Killed in action, 1918)

Letters, essays and verses. Edinburgh: Elliot. 1921.
280p. por.   BPL

BROWN, John Lewis Crommelin (Lieutenant, Royal
Garrison Artillery. A Cambridge contemporary of
Rupert Brooke)

Dies heroica: war poems: 1914-1918. Hodder &
Stoughton. 1918. 93p.   MPL

BROWN, R.H.
Poems. Rich & Cowan. 1934. 86p.   BPL

BROWNE, K.M. (Voluntary Aid Detachment. Served
with the Egypt Expeditionary Force)

"Pot luck" (with the E.E.F.). Stockwell. 1920.
96p. il.
    Stories and verses.   BPL

BROWNING, George A.
In memoriam Montague T.S. Browning, Corpl. of
the Royal Horse Guards (Blue), 7th Cavalry Division,
killed in action at Zandvoorde, near Ypres, October
29, 1914. Oxford: Blackwell. 1915. 12p.   BM

BROWNSWORD, Bertha see (28)

BROXBOURNE, Einna
Kitchener calls you! Printed Carlisle: Thurnam.
[191-].
    A broadside.   BM

BRUCE, Sir Michael William Selby (2nd Lieutenant,
Royal Field Artillery)

Songs from the saddle: a collection of rhymes and
songs. Dublin: Hodges, Figgis. 1917. 48p.   MPL

BRUMM, Charles
In quest of the Holy Grail: a hermit's war lyrics.
Manchester: Percy. 1919. 120p.   MPL

In quest of the Holy Grail: a hermit's war lyrics,
selected from his diary. [New] ed. Daniel. 1921. 208p.   MPL

BRUNDRIT, Daniel Fernley
Gleanings: [poems]. Grant Richards. 1919. 60p.   BPL

BRYAN, Daniel
The Derbyshire Christian rhymes upon the present
sinful times: another message from God. Printed Matlock
Bath: Hodgkinson. 1918-22. 3v.   BM

The mind of God with regard to the Great War — its
causes and consequences. Printed Derby. [1918]. 42p.   BM

BRYDEN, W.M. (Sergeant) see (27)

BUCHAN, John, Lord Tweedsmuir (Lieutenant-
Colonel. Went to France in 1915 as a war correspondent.
Later had charge of news services at General Headquarters.
In 1917 was brought home as Director of Information)

Meditations of a country chiel: a collection of
verse. Printed Edinburgh: Bishop. 1918. 32p.
    Some poems in Scots dialect.   BPL

Poems: Scots and English. Jack. 1917. 106p.
    The Scots poems are in dialect.   MPL

Poems: Scots and English. [New] ed. Nelson.
1936. 141p.
    The Scots poems are in dialect.   BM

See also (71) (91)

BUCHANAN, Edgar Simmons, (E.S.B.)
Edith Cavell, shot October 12, 1915; by E.S.B. [1917].
[3]p.   BM

Ronald W. Hoskier, of South Orange, N.J. and
Harvard, who fell in aerial combat near St. Quentin,
aged 20, April 23rd 1917; by E.S.B. [1917]. [3]p.   BM

BUCHANAN-DUNLOP, Archibald (Lieutenant-
Colonel, 1st Battalion, Leicestershire Regiment) see
**WARDLE, Mark Kingsley, & BUCHANAN-DUNLOP,
Archibald**

BUCKINGHAM & CHANDOS, Alice Anne,

Duchess of see GRENVILLE, Alice Anne, Duchess
of Buckingham & Chandos

BUCKLEY, Reginald Ramsden see (99) (100) (101)

BUCKTON, Alice Mary
Daybreak, and other poems. Methuen. 1918.
xii, 148p.   MPL

BUDGEN, Eliza see (28)

BUGLER OF THE LEGION, pseud. see FRASER,
Alexander George, (Bugler of the Legion, pseud.)

BUIST, Alexander
Poems, 1915-1937. Oxford: Blackwell. 1938. viii, 80p.   MPL

BULKELEY, Henry John
With courage: some sonnets of William Wordsworth
written during and after the Napoleonic crisis; and,
Sonnets and other verses, mostly written during the
present war; by Henry John Bulkeley. Routledge. 1914. 96p.   BPL

With courage: [poems]. Second supplement. Routledge.
1918. 58p.   BPL

See also (29)

BULLEN, Arthur Henry
Weeping-Cross, and other rimes [sic]. Sidgwick &
Jackson. 1921. 56p.   MPL

BULLETT, Gerald (Served with the Royal Flying Corps
in France)
Mice, and other poems. Cambridge: Perkin Warbeck.
1921. 28p.   BM

See also (20)

BULLOCK, Llewellyn
In lonely walks: a collection of verse. Methuen. 1916.
x, 68p.   BM

BUNSTON, Anna see DE BARY, Anna Bunston

BUNTING, Beatrice see (28)

74

BURDETT, Leonard (5th Battalion, Leicestershire
Regiment)

Reward, and other poems of war. Chorley: Universal
Publ. Co. [1918]. 28p.   BM

BURDETT, Osbert, (Leon M. Lion, pseud.)
The importance of art in war time: notes for an address;
by Leon M. Lion, together with, The resurrection of
Rheims: a poem; by Osbert Burdett. Henderson. 1920. 24p.   BM

Songs of exhuberance; together with, The trenches.
Op. 1. Fifield. 1915. 160p.   BPL

**BURGHCLERE, Lord see GARDNER, Herbert
Coulston, Lord Burghclere (19) (113)**

BURGOYNE, Sir Alan Hughes
As the spirit moved me: [poems]. Humphreys. 1918.
[viii], 60p. por.   BM

BURKE, Louie Davoren
Poems in peace and war. Printed Halifax: Shibden
Industrial School. [1915]. [viii], 80p.   BPL

See also (28)

BURNHAM, Ralph
To the fallen. Winchester: Burnell Day. [1916].
  A postcard.   BM

BURNS, A.
The Gretna girls. Carlisle: Author. [1917].
  A postcard.
  Refers to girls on war work.   BM

BURROW, Charles Kennett
Poems: in time of war, in time of peace. Collins.
1919. 101p.   BPL

See also (87)

BURROW, F. Russell see (29)

BURT, H.I. see (77)

**BURTON, Claude Edward Cole Hamilton, (C.E.B.),
(Touchstone, pseud.)**

Fife and drum: [poems] ; by Touchstone of *The Daily Mail*
and C.E.B. of *The Evening News*. Simpkin, Marshall,
Hamilton, Kent. 1915. [viii], 134p.   BPL

Fife and drum: [poems] ; by Touchstone and C.E.B. 2nd ed.
Simpkin, Marshall, Hamilton, Kent. 1915. [iv], 134p.   IWM

See also (51) (113) (119)

BURTON, Henry
Britain to America: a war poem. Kelly. [1918]. 28p.   BPL

Killed in action, and other war poems. Kelly. [1918].
26p.   BPL

Songs of the highway: [poems]. Morgan & Scott. 1924.
xii, 268p. por.   BM

BURTON, Henry Bindon
Der Kaiser von Potsdam. Dublin: Hodges, Figgis. 1915.
42p.   BPL

BURTON, John Francis
The quest of new life: sonnets, lyrics and ballads of
war and peace, 1914-1917. Printed Wilkinson. [1917]. 56p.   BPL

BUSBRIDGE, Benjamin C. see (29)

BUSHNELL, George H.
Emptyings of my ash-tray: miscellaneous poems.
Stoke-on-Trent: Hughes and Harber. [1918?]. 27p.   BPL

BUSKIN, Elizabeth Maud see (28) (29)

BUSSY, Philip see (99) (100) (101)

BUSTRIDGE, A.W. see (26)

BUTCHER, W.
Poems. [Luton?]. [1918?]. [8]p.   BPL

BUTT, Henry
William in the looking glass. Privately printed.
[1915]. 7p.
    Refers to the Kaiser.   BM

76

BYERLEY, Hubert Frank
Songs of the war and faith and hope: [poems].
Printed Portsmouth: Barrell. [1918]. 30p.   BPL

BYLES, Charles Edward
Rupert Brooke's grave, and other poems. Erskine Macdonald.
1919. 58p. il.   BPL

BYRDE, Margaretta see (17) (31) (32)

C.A.A. see (51)

C.C. see **CHAPIN, Christina, (C.C.)**

C.C. see **CLIFFORD, C.H., (C.C.), (C.H.C.)**

C., C.H. see **CLIFFORD, C.H., (C.C.), (C.H.C.)**

C., de see **DE C.**

C., E. see **CARPENTER, Edward, (E.C.)**

C., E. see **CARTER, E., (E.C.)**

C.E.B. see **BURTON, Claude Edward Cole Hamilton,
(C.E.B.), (Touchstone, pseud.)**

C., G. see (99) (100) (101)

C., G.A.J. see (19)

C., G.B. see **BOWEN-COLTHURST, Georgina de
Bellasis, (G.B.C.)**

C.H.C. see **CLIFFORD, C.H., (C.C.), (C.H.C.)**

C., J.
Poems. Stockwell. 1923. 64p.   BM

Recruiting poems, published during the progress of the
Great War, 1914-1918. Printed Dungannon: Tyrone
Printing Co. 1919. 14p.   IWM

C.J.O'S. see **O'SHAUGHNESSY, C.J., (C.J.O'S.)**

77

C.J.R. see R., C.J.

C., J.W. see CHEETHAM, John W., (J.W.C.)

C.L. see L., C.

C., M.A., pseud. see MACFADYEN, Dugald, (M.A.C., pseud.)

C.M.R. see (110)

C.M.W. see W., C.M.

C., R.F. see (110)

C.T. see HARVEY, John G. Russell, (J.G.R.H.), & THOMAS, Charles, (C.T.)

C.W. see WALSTON, Sir Charles, (C.W.)

C., W.A. see (110)

CADELL, Henry Mowbray
Rhymes for the times: Kaiser William the Hun and his place in the sun. 2nd ed. Edinburgh: Constable. 1917. viii, 24p.   BM

[No copy of 1st ed. traced].

CALDWELL, Ella Stewart
Ah me! When one loves, and other poems that well up from the human heart. Stockwell. [1926]. 48p.   BM

CALDWELL, Gerald see SIORDET, Gerald Caldwell

CAMERON, Mary
Lochaber's day. Kibble. [1918]. 22p.
   Dedicated 'To the brave sons of Lochaber who have fought the great fight'.   BM

CAMERON, Mercy see (29)

CAMERON, W.J.
War and life: poems. Chapman & Hall. 1916. 48p.   BPL

78

CAMMELL, Charles Richard
Casus belli: a satire, with other poems. Humphreys.
1915. 31p. BPL

Ecrasez l'infâme!: a satire on war. Bern: Wyss.
1918. 18p. BM

Poems, 1911-1929. Grant Richards. 1930. xii, 268p. MPL

Poems: satirical and miscellaneous. Selwyn & Blount.
1923. [ii], 71p.
    A limited ed. of 500 copies. MPL

CAMPBELL, Archibald Young
Poems. Longmans, Green. 1926. xii, 120p. MPL

CAMPBELL, Hon. Ivar (Captain, Argyll & Sutherland
Highlanders. Died of wounds 8th January 1916, at
Sheikh Saad, Mesopotamia) see (131)

CAMPBELL, John, of Birmingham
Patriotic rhymes suited to the times: Birmingham,
1914-15. Birmingham: [Author?]. 1915. 16p.
    Title from cover. BPL

Scotland for ever! and other poems. Birmingham:
Cornish. 1937. [viii], 80p. BM

CAMPBELL, John, of Clapham
Poems. Privately printed. 1924. 87p. por. BM

Verse or reverse?: poems. Stockwell. [1928]. 24p. BM

CAMPBELL, Joseph
Poems. Ed. with an intro. by Austin Clarke. Dublin:
Figgis. 1963. [xii], 273p. (Chomhairle Ealaion series of
Irish authors, 1). BM

CAMPBELL, R.W. (Captain)
The making of Micky McGhee, and other stories in
verse. Allen & Unwin. 1916. 100p. il. (by H.K. Elcock). MPL

See also (110)

CAMPBELL-STRICKLAND, Amy
A call to our men, and other poems. Stockwell. [1915].
32p. BM

CANDOLE, Alec de see DE CANDOLE, Alec

CANN, Charles Garfield Lott Du see DU CANN, Charles Garfield Lott

CANNAN, Gilbert
Adventurous love, and other verses. Methuen. 1915.
vi, 84p.   MPL

Noel: an epic in seven cantos. Martin Secker.
1922. [ii], 371p.
    A limited ed. of 500 copies signed by the author.   BM

Noel: an epic in ten cantos. Grant Richards. [1917-18]. 3v.
    v.1 Introductory. v.2 Cantos I and II. v.3 Cantos III
and IV.
    Only Cantos I-IV publ. — BM.   BM

See also (45) (99) (100) (101)

CANNAN, May Wedderburn (Voluntary Aid Detachment)
The house of hope: poems. Milford. 1923. 64p. il.
(by Phyllis Gardner).   BM

In war time: poems. Oxford: Blackwell. 1917. 80p.   BPL

The splendid days: poems. Oxford: Blackwell. 1919.
80p.   BPL

See also (111) (112)

CANNING, Robert Gordon- see GORDON-CANNING,
Robert

CANTON, S. Ruth see (64)

CAPELL, Richard (Lance-Corporal) see (32)

CAPPER, John Brainerd
Twenty-five trifles in verse. Chatto & Windus.
1918. 54p.   MPL

CAPTAIN WIDEAWAKE, pseud. see WIDEAWAKE,
Captain, pseud.

CARLYON, Edward Henry
Changing chimes: [poems]. Printed Birmingham:
Colmore P. 1921. [31]p.   BPL

CARMICHAEL, Amy Wilson
Made in the pans: [poems]. With foreword by the
Bishop of Durham. Edinburgh: Oliphants. [1918].
144p.   BPL

CARPENTER, Edward, (E.C.)
Three ballads: (an intermezzo in war time): The nonsensical
conjectors; Lieutenant Tattoon, M.C.; Ballad of the bodkin
and the musket; [by] E.C. Printed Manchester: Clarke.
1917. 15p.   JRL

CARPENTER, William Boyd, Bishop of Ripon
see (54)

CARR, Ellen Ada
The union jack. [1914]. [4]p. col. il.
     Cover-title is "With the season's greetings".   BM

CARROLL, John Smyth, & CARROLL, Kathleen Mary
Heroes all: war and other verses. Glasgow: Gibson.
1915. 64p. por.   BPL

"Or sing a sang [sic] at least": war and other verses.
Glasgow: Gibson. [1915]. 48p.
     Profits to the Belgian Relief Fund.   BPL

CARROLL, Kathleen Mary see **CARROLL, John
Smyth, & CARROLL, Kathleen Mary**

CARSTAIRS, Carroll (Lieutenant, Grenadier Guards.
Fought in France. Was wounded 4th November 1918)

My window sill, [and other poems]. Heinemann. 1930.
[47]p.   BM

See also (58)

CARTER, E., (E.C.)
The greater love: a true incident of the war. Weybridge:
Author. [1915?].
     A broadside.   BM

Hymn for our soldiers, sailors, airmen and allied armies;
[by] E.C. Weybridge: Author. [1915].
     A card.   BM

What the British Navy is doing: a reply to the

pessimist. Weybridge: Author. [1915]. col. il.
A postcard.   BM

CARTON, Ronald Lewis (Lieutenant, Duke of Cornwall's
Light Infantry)

Steel and flowers: [poems]. Elkin Mathews. 1917. 48p.
(Vigo cabinet series, 41).   BPL

See also (17) (18)

CASH, Helen, pseud. see STOCKER, Helen, (Helen Cash,
pseud.)

CAVE, Alfred Thomas Townshend Verney-, Lord Braye
see VERNEY-CAVE, Alfred Thomas Townshend, Lord Braye

CAVE, Charles
Poems. Humphreys. 1917. 51p.   BM

CHADWICK, Hugh Brailsford
How war visited earth and what came of it: a poem.
[Hillborne] : [Author?]. 1933. [3] p.   BM

The origin of war verses: sonnets and other verses.
[Poole] : [Looker]. [1934]. 55p.   BM

Safety green: selected poems and verses. Poole:
Wessex P. 1935. [ii], 49p.   BM

CHADWICK, John Hampton
War time poems. Printed Liverpool: Wormald. 1919. 64p.   EDR

CHALLENGER, Ernest K. (Corporal, Royal Engineers)
see (58)

CHALLONER, Alan Crowhall (6th Battalion, Duke of
Cornwall's Light Infantry)

In a rest-camp (near Ypres), [and other poems]. 1915. [2] p.   IWM

CHALMERS, Patrick Reginald see (12) (16) (17) (18) (19)
(44) (46) (87) (96) (119) (120)

CHAMBERS, Amy
Thought blossoms, [and other poems]. With an appendix
"Play-hour lyrics"; by members of the Play-Hour
Comradeship. Aberdeen: Milne & Stephen. 1922. 72p.   BPL

82

CHAPIN, Christina, (C.C.) (A schoolgirl during the war)
Triumph, and other poems: by C.C. Chapman & Hall.
1916. 23p.   BPL

CHAPMAN, Florence see (64)

CHAPMAN, Violet Dorothy see (28) (29) (31) (32)

CHAPPELL, Henry (A railway porter at Bath)
The day, and other poems. With an intro. by Sir
Herbert Warren. Bodley Head. 1918. 80p. por.   MPL

The day. Printed Glasgow: Campbell. [191-].
   A broadside.   IWM

The day. [191-].
   A broadside.
   Reprinted from the *Daily Express.*   BPL

See also (23) (25) (27) (28) (30) (47) (48) (49)

CHARTRES, Annie Vivanti see (19) (26) (40) (41)

CHATTERTON, J.S. see (115)

CHEETHAM, John W., (J.W.C.)
Fate of the Lusitania, who fell a war victim, 7th May,
1915: song or recitation; by J.W.C. Printed Oldham:
Parker. [1915?].
   A broadside.   BM

The Oldham flag song and recitation; [by] J.W.C.
[191-].
   A broadside.   BM

CHERRY, Mary G. (Quartermaster of a Red Cross Hospital)
Hill and heather; or, England's heart: [poems]. Erskine
Macdonald. 1915. 46p. (Little books of Georgian verse).
   Two poems in Scots dialect.   BPL

CHESTERTON, Cecil Edward (Served as a private in France)
see (16) (18) (26) (31) (32) (82) (83) (84) (99)
(100) (101) (121)

CHESTERTON, Frances see (26)

CHESTERTON, Gilbert Keith
The ballad of St. Barbara, and other verses. Cecil
Palmer. 1922. x, 84p.   BPL

Collected poems. Burns, Oates and Washbourne. 1927.
[viii], 364p.   BM

Collected poems. Cecil Palmer. 1927. [viii], 366p.   BM

Collected poems. 3rd ed. Methuen. 1933. viii, 404p.
  Designated 3rd ed. but is in fact 1st Methuen ed.
Reprinted many times.   BM

Poems. Burns & Oates. 1915. viii, 157p. por.   MPL

See also (4) (16) (17) (18) (19) (22) (25) (26) (31)
(32) (49) (53) (65) (66) (80) (82) (83) (84) (94)
(99) (100) (101) (105) (106) (112)

CHILDE, Wilfred Rowland
The golden thurible: poems. Cecil Palmer. 1931. 79p.   MPL

CHILMAN, Eric (Private, East Yorkshire Regiment)
see (31) (32) (58)

CHOYCE, Arthur Newberry (Lieutenant, Leicestershire
Regiment)
Crimson stains: poems of war and love. Erskine
Macdonald. 1917. 56p.   MPL

Memory: poems of war and love. New York: Lane.
1918. 68p. por.   BPL

See also (58)

CHURCH, Richard
Collected poems. Dent. 1948, xii, 291p.   BM

Hurricane, and other poems. Selwyn & Blount.
1919. 48p.   BPL

Twelve noon, [and other poems]. Dent. 1936. x, 67p.   MPL

Twentieth-century psalter: [poems]. Dent. 1943.
[vi], 74p.   MPL

See also (22)

CHURT, J.C., pseud. see COHEN, J.C., (J.C. Churt, pseud.)

CIVIS, pseud. see (113)

CLARK, Cumberland
The Empire song book. Mitre P. [1924]. [viii],
132p. col. il.   BM

Songs and poems. Bournemouth: [Author]. 1936.
[iii], 161p.   SOPL

The sonnet song book :250 sonnets. Shrewsbury:
Wilding. 1935. [x], 254p.   BM

CLARK, Dudley see (25) (47) (48) (49) (87)
(108) (199) (111) (113)

CLARK, Henry William
Collected poems: new and old. Williams & Norgate.
1941. 191p.   MPL

Pilate, and other poems. Chapman & Hall. 1922. 72p.   BM

The watch-tower: poems. Chapman & Hall. 1920. 95p.   BM

CLARK, T.B. (Rifleman, King's Royal Rifles. Served in
France and Salonika)

Captain Dimmer, V.C. [1917?].
    A broadside.   BM

Commentary on rations (with some exaggeration);
composed in the trenches at Armentiers, July, 1915.
[1917?].
    A broadside.   IWM

Eggs "eggs"traordinary; composed at No. 9
Convalescent Camp, Salonika, August, 1918.
Wakefield: Rushfirth. 1918. (Rhymes of a rifleman, 3).
    A broadside.   BM

The grand Stonewall Brigade. [1917]. il.
    A broadside.   BM

A hero of Erin: the story of Private W.F. McFadzean, V.C.,
of the Royal Irish Rifles, who gave his life for his
comrades. [1917?].
    A broadside.   BM

Heroes in khaki: or, tales from the trenches: [poems].
Leeds :Arnold. [1917]. [ii], 62p. il., por.
    'Written in the trenches during the short intervals
of a soldier's leisure' — author's note.   BM

Heroes of Neuve Chapelle: the story of Coy. Sergt.
Major Daniels and Corpl. Noble, 2nd Battn. Rifle
Brigade, V.C. heroes of Neuve Chapelle. [1917?].
A broadside.   BM

Honour to the brave. [1917].
A broadside.   BM

The K.R.R.E.s, with apologies to Sergt. Burley and
Corpl. Lovell; composed in the trenches at
Armentiers, July 1915. [1917].
A broadside.   BM

"K.S.L.I." [King's Shropshire Light Infantry]. [1917?].
A broadside.   BM

The Khud; composed in the trenches in Macedonia.
Wakefield: Rushfirth. 1918. (Rhymes of a rifleman, 8).
A broadside.   BM

The King's Royal Rifle Corps. [1917?].
A broadside.   BM

Matters in Macedonia. Wakefield: Rushfirth. [1918].
(Rhymes of a rifleman, 12).
A broadside.   BM

Once through the alphabet: Tommy's version;
composed in the trenches in Macedonia, October, 1917.
Wakefield: Rushfirth. [1918]. (Rhymes of a rifleman, 13).
A broadside.   BM

The pick and shovel brigade; composed at Salonika,
January, 1916. [1917?].
A broadside.   BM

The pick and shovel division. [1917?].
A broadside.   BM

The pilgrims of the night. [1917?].
A broadside.   BM

Poems of a private: a souvenir of France and Salonika.
Nicholson. [191-]. 64p. por.
    Part of profit to St. Dunstan's Hostel for Blinded Soldiers
and Sailors.   IWM

The Rifle Brigade; composed in the trenches in France,
October 1915. Wakefield: Rushfirth. [1918]. (Rhymes of a
rifleman, 16).
A broadside.   BM

86

Rifleman Mariner, V.C. [1917?].
A broadside.   BM

The Stonewall Brigade. [1917]. il.
A broadside.   BM

The strafing section. [1917].
A broadside.   BM

Tales of a "Tommy": some pieces from abroad. Printed
Peachey. [1943]. [12]p.
'Composed, published and sold in the trenches by a
"Tommy" during the first Great War' — author's note.   BM

Tommy's troubles: rhyme. [1917?].
A broadside.   BM

Tommy's vocabulary; composed in the trenches in
Macedonia, January, 1918. Wakefield: Rushfirth. 1918.
2p. (Rhymes of a rifleman, 23).   BM

The Twenty Seventh Division; composed in the
trenches in Macedonia, October, 1917. Wakefield:
Rushfirth. [1918]. (Rhymes of a rifleman, 24).
A broadside.   BM

CLARKE, Amy Key
Poems. Oxford: Blackwell. 1922. 72p.   BM

See also (55)

CLARKE, D.C. (Private, Honourable Artillery Company)
The taking of Bullecourt: a poem based on actual fact after
the event. [1917].
A card.   BM

CLARKE, Frank W. Grayson see (29)

CLARKE, G. Taverner see (28)

CLARKE, Isabel Constance
The pathway of dreams, and other poems.
Sands. [1919]. 56p.
In memory of author's brother.   BPL

CLARKE, Joseph Ignatius Constantine see (43)

CLARKE, May Herschel- see HERSCHEL-CLARKE, May

87

CLATWORTHY, Mrs. T. Turner
To the memory of Nurse Edith Cavell. [1915].
  A broadside.
  'In aid of our prisoners in Germany'.   BM

Victory of the Great War, 1914-18. [1918?].
  A broadside.   BM

CLAYTON, Philip Byard (Founder of Toc H) see (19) (26)

CLEE, Florence see (28) (29) (65)

CLEMENTS, Reginald F. (2nd Lieutenant, Royal
Sussex Regiment)

Salisbury Plain, and other poems. Salisbury: Bennett.
1917. 19p.   BPL

See also (58)

CLEPHANE, Mary see (28)

CLERK, E.G.
Rhymes of times and climes. Blackpool: Palatine Books.
1929. [vi], 51p.   BPL

CLEWORTH, Ralph
Leaves, and other poems. Cambridge: Perkin Warbeck.
1921. 28p. (Florin series, 6).   BPL

CLIFFORD, C.H., (C.C.), (C.H.C.)
In loving memory of our fallen heroes who lost their
lives in the Great War, Aug. 4th, 1914, to Nov. 11th,
1918; [by] C.H.C. [1919].
  A postcard.   BM

In memory of Kaiser Bill (The Butcher), who lost his
crown, November 9th, 1918, aged 59 years; [by] C.C. [1918].
  A postcard.   BM

CLIFFORD, E.
Tommy Atkins, don't cher know (founded on an
incident in the war). [191-].
  A broadside.   BM

CLIFFORD, Florence
"Look up!" and other poems. Stockwell. [1918]. 12p.   BM

CLIFT, Rupert see AYLING, Alan, & CLIFT, Rupert

CLORISTON, Henry
Sonnets and semblances, chiefly relating to the war.
v.1. London Literary Alliance. 1919. [iv], 51p.
   v. 2 not publ. — BM.   BPL

CLOSE, Evelyne
The tide at night, [and other poems]. Erskine Macdonald.
1918. 68p.   BM

CLOSE, Florence M. see (64)

CLYNE, H. Ross
"Come now!" the appeal from the trenches in
France. Recited by Mr. Clunne-Lees, the celebrated
Manchester elocutionist, at the great recruiting
meetings. [1914].
   A broadside.   MPL

COATES, Kathleen Montgomery
Unreturning. Cambridge: Heffer. 1916. [3]p.
(Cambridge Magazine reprints, 1).   BM

See also (28)

COATES, W.H.
Beating shoes: poems. Heath, Cranton. 1939. 40p.   BM

Tapping the "War Lord's" claret: a set-to at Ilfracombe
in 1878: why Kaiser Bill hates England; or, what happened
at Rapparee. Ilfracombe: Author. [1916].
   A broadside.   BM

Tapping the "War Lord's" claret: a set-to at Ilfracombe
in 1878: why Kaiser Bill hates England; or, what happened
at Rapparee. [New ed.]. Ilfracombe:Author. [1916]. [8]p.   BM

COATS, Victoria Taylor
Things new and old: [poems]. Stockwell. [1919]. 32p.   BPL

To-day and yesterday, [and other poems]. Erskine
Macdonald. [1915]. 88p.   BPL

COBBER, Lance-Corporal, pseud. see ADCOCK,
Arthur St. John, (Lance-Corporal Cobber, pseud.)

COBBOLD, W.N.
De bello, et aliis rebus (About the war, etc.): [poems].
[Cambridge?]. [1981?]. xii, 224p.
    Latin and English text.   BPL

COCHRANE, Alfred
Later verses. Longmans, Green. 1918. viii, 111p. il.
(by H.J. Ford).   BM

See also (31) (32)

COCK, Albert Arthur, & LODGE, John
Songs from camp and college: [poems]. Erskine
Macdonald. 1916. 60p. (Little books of Georgian
verse: second series).
    Not joint authorship.   BPL

COCKER, William Dixon (Prisoner of war)
The dreamer, and other poems. Gowans & Gray. 1920.
40p.   BPL

Further poems, Scots and English. Brown, Son &
Ferguson. 1935. 102p.   BM

Poems: Scots and English. Complete ed. Glasgow: Brown,
Son & Ferguson. 1932. 220p.   BM

COHEN, Mrs. Herbert see **COHEN J.C., (J.C. Churt, pseud.)**

COHEN, J.C., (J.C. Churt, pseud.)
Rhythmic waves: [poems]; by J.C. Churt. Elkin
Mathews. 1916. 88p.   BM

See also (64)

COLDICOTT, Rowlands (Served in the Middle East)
Farewell to Egypt, and other wartime verses.
Middleton, Sussex: [Author?]. 1933. [viii], 84p.   BM

COLE, George Douglas Howard (Head of the research
department of the Amalgamated Society of Engineers,
1914-18. Adviser to the trades unions on war-time
economic problems)

The crooked world: [poems]. Gollancz. 1933. 135p.   BM

**COLE, George Douglas Howard, & COLE, Margaret
Postgate**
The Bolo book. Ed. [or rather written] by G.D.H. Cole

and Margaret Cole. Labour Publ. Co.; Allen & Unwin. 1921. viii, 64p. BPL

COLE, Herbert (Secretary of the Patriots' League)
"Britain's debt to Belgium". Portsmouth: Author. [1915?].
[4] p. por. (Patriots' League. Recitations, 4). BM

"An Englishman's reply": a Briton's answer to the German attack on our glorious Empire in Recitation no. 1, entitled "To der day!" Portsmouth: Author. [1915?].
[4] p. por. (Patriots' League. Recitations, 2). BM

In memoriam 'Lieut. Warneford, V.C., R.N.'. Portsmouth: Author. [1915?]. [4] p. il. (Patriots' League. Recitations, 10). BM

"John Bull's Christmas party". Portsmouth: Author. [1915?]. [4] p. por. (Patriots' League. Recitations, 5). BM

John Bull's game of cards. Portsmouth: Author. [1915?].
[4] p. il (Patriots' League. Recitations, 3). BM

"The Kaiser's dream". Portsmouth: Author. [1915?].
[4] p. il. (Patriots' League. Recitations, 8). BM

"King Albert the brave". Portsmouth: Author. [1915?].
[4] p. il. (Patriots' League. Recitations, 6). BM

"Our boys in brown and blue". Portsmouth: Author. [1915?]. [4] p. il. (Patriots' League. Recitations, 7). BM

"To der day!": a German's ideas on the European situation. Portsmouth: Author. [1915?]. [4] p. il. (Patriots' League. Recitations, 1). BM

COLE, Hylda Constance
Heather ways: [poems]. Erskine Macdonald. 1915.
43p. (Little books of Georgian verse). BM

COLE, Margaret Postgate
Poems; by Margaret Postgate. Allen & Unwin. 1918.
[vi], 38p. BPL

See also (96)

See also **COLE, George Douglas Howard, & COLE, Margaret Postgate**

COLE, Thomas E.
Bronsil Castle: a love story of 1646; also, Patriotic war songs, and miscellaneous pieces . . . Printed Smith. 1920.

[iv], 254p. il., por. BPL

"The call". Birmingham: [Author]. [1917?].
A broadside. BPL

Call not the laggard, but the brave. Birmingham: [Author].
[1917?].
A broadside. BPL

Khaki and blue. [Birmingham] : [Author]. [1917?].
A broadside. BPL

"The parade". Birmingham: [Author]. [1917?].
A broadside. BPL

Retribution. Birmingham: [Author]. [1917?].
A broadside. BPL

The ship "Vindictive". Birmingham: [Author]. [1918?].
A broadside. BPL

Slow and sure. Birmingham: [Author]. [1918?].
A broadside. BPL

Wooden crosses. Birmingham: [Author]. [1919?].
A broadside. BPL

The Worcesters at Gheluvelt. Birmingham: [Author].
[1918?].
A broadside. BPL

COLEMAN, Ellen
Beyond the war zone, and other poems. Routledge.
[1919]. 95p. BPL

There are no dead, and other poems. Kegan Paul, Trench,
Trubner. [1917]. 62p. BPL

**COLLEER, Claude, pseud. see ABBOTT, Claude Colleer,
(Claude Colleer, pseud.)**

COLLIER, Madeleine
Fragments: [poems]. Amersham: Morland. 1918. 32p. BPL

COLLIGAN, A.M.
Hazel leaves: a selection of poems. Mitre P. [1929]. 48p. BPL

COLLINS, Gilbert
Sidelights of song: [poems]. Long. 1920. 62p. BPL

COLLINS, Mary Gabrielle
"Branches unto the sea": [poems]. Erskine Macdonald.
1916. 42p.   BPL

COLLINSON, Thomas Harrison
Poems of life. Daniel. 1930. 295p.   BM

COLLY, Alice
A book of verse. Birmingham: Cornish. 1916. 47p.   BPL

COLONIAL, pseud.
Kitchener's army: an acrostic: [poems]. Edinburgh:
Green. 1916. 20p.   BPL

COLTHURST, Georgina de Bellasis Bowen- see
BOWEN-COLTHURST, Georgina de Bellasis, (G.B.C.)

COLVILL, Helen Hester see (28) (31) (32)

COMPTON-RICKETT, Leonard Allen
The divine drama: [a play]; and, Poems. Kegan Paul,
Trench, Trubner. 1916. [viii], 276p.   BM

The human touch: [a play], with fantasy and poems.
With a foreword by Katharine Tynan. Routledge. 1921.
xii, 228p.
    Poems are entitled "Prismatic glass: verses and sonnets". BM

See also (27)

CONGREVE, Celia, Lady
The castle, and other verses. Humphreys. 1920. 49p.   BPL

See also (25)

CONGREVE, G.A. see (5)

CONNOLLY, Michael Eugene
Through the window, and other poems. Stockwell. [1930?].
16p.   BM

CONSTABLE, M., & WHITNEY, T.
Dies Dei. Dobson. [1919]. 32p.   BPL

CONSTANTINE, H.F. (Major) see (60)

93

COOK, Augustus Henry (Surgeon-Major, Royal Fusiliers)
The happy warrior, and other poems. Bell. 1917.
viii, 86p. por.   BPL

Sapphire wings: [poems]. Printed Hampstead:
Hewetson. [1920?]. 67p.   BM

COOK, Jane Elizabeth see (29)

COOK, Leonard Niell (M.C. 2nd Lieutenant, Royal
Lancashire Regiment. Killed in action 7th July 1917)
see (58) (131)

COOK, Winifred A. see (32)

COOKE, Alice M. Peppard
Irish heroes in red war: [poems]. Dublin: Maunsel.
1915. 31p.   BPL

The pipe of peace: a book of verse. Stockwell. [1926]. 56p.   BM

COOKE, Greville
Poems. Oxford: Blackwell. 1933. viii, 75p.   BM

COOKSON, Geoffrey Montagu
Poems. Elkin Mathews & Marrot. 1932. viii, 215p.   MPL

COOPER, Alfred
The blind soldier. Printed Chapeltown: Parkin. [1918?].
[4]p.
   In aid of St. Dunstan's Home for Blinded Soldiers and
Sailors.   BM

The last message. Printed Chapeltown: Parkin.
[1914]. [4]p.   BM

The shamrock, rose and thistle. Printed Chapeltown:
Parkin. [1914]. [4]p.   BM

War; and, Peace: [poems]. Printed Chapeltown: Parkin
[1919]. 8p.   BM

COOPER, Allan
Come, ye sons of Britain's glory. Printed Southampton:
Wilson. [191-].
   A broadside.   BM

15 patriotic songs: new words to old tunes for camp, recruiting, marching, or the concert room. Printed Southampton: Wilson. 1915. 16p.
    Title from cover.   BM

The world's new birth: an ode to liberty and peace, and other poems. Erskine Macdonald. 1919. 80p.   BPL

COOPER, E.
The German bomb: how it came; and what it did: lines on the air raid of Whit Sunday — Monday, May 19-20, 1918. Printed Moon. [1918]. [4]p. (Wolkern postcard-album poems, for reading or for reciting, 1).   BM

COOPER, Eric Thirkell (Major, London Regiment, Royal Fusiliers)

Soliloquies of a subaltern, somewhere in France. Burns & Oates. 1915. 52p.
    Written in the trenches.   MPL

Tommies of the line, and other poems. Jenkins. 1918. 126p.   MPL

See also (2)

COOPER, Gerald M. (2nd Lieutenant, Scots Guards)
see (58)

COPE, Michael see (30)

COPPARD, Alfred Edgar
Collected poems. Cape. 1928. 109p.   BM

Hips and haws: poems. Waltham Saint Lawrence: Golden Cockerel P. 1922. 45p.
    A limited ed. of 500 copies.   MPL

COPY of the Kaiser's will, issued to the Allied Nations.
Printed Birmingham: Economic Printing Co. [1914].
    A postcard.   BM

CORAH, William
War ditties. Printed [Birmingham?]. [1915]. 10p.
    Title from cover.   BPL

The Worcestershire Hussars. Printed [Birmingham?]. [1915?]. por.
    A broadside.   BPL

CORBETT, E.J.
Vesper, for time of war. [191-].
A broadside.   BM

CORBETT, Frederick St. John see (27)

CORBETT, Noel Marcus Francis (Lieutenant-Commander, Royal Navy)

A naval motley: verses written at sea during the war
and before it. Methuen. 1916. xii, 52p.   BM

A naval motley: verses written at sea during the war
and before it. 4th ed. Methuen. 1916. x, 52p.   MPL

[No copies of 2nd and 3rd eds traced].

See also (2) (17) (18) (72)

CORKERY, Daniel
I Bhreasail: a book of lyrics. Elkin Mathews. 1921.
viii, 76p.   MPL

CORLETTE, Hubert Christian, (Australis, pseud.) (Major)
The rivals, the swords and the signs, and other
recruiting rhymes; by Australis. Printed Norwich:
Soman. 1917. 67p.   BPL

A song of life in sonnets and other verses; by
Australis. Printed Norwich: Soman. 1917. 60p.   BPL

CORNWALL, Isabel J. see (51)

CORSER, Helen A. see (29)

COTTON, John
Gleanings: some gathered verses; and, Wildings from
my field of thought. Bromsgrove: Messenger Co.
1922. 2v. in 1.   BPL

Verses pertaining to the Great War. [Bromsgrove]:
Messenger Co. [1922?]. [10]p.
    Extracted from author's "Gleanings".   BPL

COUCH, Sir Arthur Quiller- see **QUILLER-COUCH,
Sir Arthur**

COULSON, F. Raymond see (25)

COULSON, Leslie (Sergeant, 12th London Battalion, Royal Fusiliers. Died of wounds 7th October 1916, near Lesboeufs, Somme valley)

From an outpost, and other poems. Erskine Macdonald. 1917. 42p.   BM

From an outpost, and other poems. 2nd ed. Erskine Macdonald. 1917. 48p.   MPL

From an outpost, and other poems. 3rd ed. Erskine Macdonald. 1918. 56p.   BPL

See also (2) (16) (18) (24) (31) (32) (33) (50) (52) (58) (66) (72) (96) (111) (112) (131)

COURTHOPE, William John
Country town, and other poems. With a memoir by A.O. Prickard. Oxford U.P. 1920. 106p. por.   MPL

See also (65)

COURTNEY, Joseph Monlas (Captain, Royal Army Medical Corps)

As the leaves fall, and other poems. Printed Wantage: Convent of S. Mary. 1917. 26p.   BM

As the leaves fall, and other poems written in France. Erskine Macdonald. 1918. 62p.   MPL

See also (52) (56) (57)

COURTNEY, William Leonard see (17) (18) (19) (25) (26) (45) (54) (99) (100) (101)

COUTTS, Francis, Lord Latymer
A ballad of the war. Humphreys. 1915. [iv], 15p. Reprinted from the *English Review,* June 1915.   BM

The spacious times, and others: [poems]. Bodley Head. 1920. 134p.   BPL

See also (12) (31) (32) (99) (100) (101)

COUTTS, Jessie see (29)

COVENTRY, Richard George Temple see (42) (112)

COWLES, Frederick Ignatius see (29)

COX, Herbert J. see (27)

COX, S. Donald (Rifleman, London Rifle Brigade)
see (31) (32) (52) (56) (57) (58)

COXWELL, Charles Fillingham
Chronicles of man: [poems]. Watts. 1915. xvi, 656p.   MPL

CRABTREE, Ethel see (29)

CRAIG, L.
"A glad, glad time in England", and other verse.
Stockwell. [1918]. 15p.   BPL

CRAIG, Thomas Forrest (Temporary Captain, Royal
Army Medical Corps. Died 2nd February 1918, as
result of wounds received in action)
Poems. Printed Liverpool: Tinling. [192-?]. 36p.
por.   CWR

CRAMPTON, Arthur Wesley
War poems. Cursitor Publ. Co. 1919. 48p.   BPL

CRANMER, Elsie Paterson
The spring, and other poems. Teddington: Poetry P.
[1931]. 32p.
    'In memory of the author's husband, her two brothers
and her sister's betrothed, all of whom gave their lives
in the Great War'.   BM
To the living dead, and other poems. Daniel. [1920]. 52p.   BPL

CRAVEN, Edith A.
Poems in wartime. Amersham: Morland; Foyle.
1919. 36p.   BPL

CRAWFORD, Ethel Marion see (28) (29)

CRAWFORD, Norah Mary see (28) (29)

CRAWSHAY-WILLIAMS, Eliot (Captain, Leicestershire
Royal Horse Artillery)
Clouds and the sun: [poems]. Allen & Unwin.
1919. 52p.   BM

98

Flak: a collection of poems. Long. [1944]. 56p. il.
(by Sybil C. Williams).
    Poems written 1919-1943.
    'The feelings of a soldier who fought the last war and
is too old to fight in this' — foreword.   BM

The gutter and the stars: [poems]. Erskine Macdonald.
1918. 86p.   MPL

No one wants poetry, [and other poems]. Newtown: Welsh
Outlook P. [1938]. 67p. il.   BM

Songs on service. Oxford: Blackwell. 1917. xii, 104p.   MPL

See also (59) (60) (61)

CREGAN, Beatrice see (31) (32)

CRESTON, Dormer, pseud. see **BAYNES, Dorothy
Julia, (Dormer Creston, pseud.)**

CREWE, Lord see **CREWE-MILNES, Robert Offley
Ashburton, Lord Crewe**

**CREWE-MILNES, Robert Offley Ashburton,
Lord Crewe** see (17) (18) (19) (25) (31) (32) (47) (48)
(49) (52) (55) (63) (65) (111) (112)

CRIPPS, Arthur Shearly (b. England. After some time as an
army chaplain and a vicar in Sussex, went to Rhodesia as
a missionary)

Lake and war: African land and water verses. Oxford:
Blackwell. 1917. xii, 120p.   MPL

Pilgrim's joy: verses. Oxford: Blackwell. 1916. viii,
87p.   BM

CRITTEN, Julie
Topical Tommy's book o' the words. Simpkin, Marshall,
Hamilton, Kent. [1914]. [32]p.
    Printed on one side of leaf only.
    'Rhymes to sing to favourite marching tunes' — author.   BPL

CROCKET, Andrew see (27) (29)

CROFT, Frederic see (29)

CROMBIE, John Eugene (Captain, 4th Gordon Highlanders.
Killed in action, 23rd April 1917, at Roeux on the Somme)
see (52) (58) (131)

CRON, Alice R. see (28)

CROSBIE, Marjorie
Love's melodies: [poems]. Printed Wolverhampton:
Hinde. [1915]. [viii], 87p.   BPL

The things that count, [and other poems]. With a foreword
by Russell Markland. Birmingham: Cornish. 1930.
viii, 64p. por.   BM

See also (5)

CROSFIELD, Sir Arthur
A pilgrimage of the Empire. Eyre & Spottiswoode.
1916. 56p. il.
    Dedicated to those fighting the 'Battle of the Empire'.   BPL

CROSLAND, Thomas William Hodgson, ("X" pseud.)
A chant of affection, and other verses. Printed
Lakeman & Tucker. 1915. 24p.   MPL

Collected poems. Martin Secker. 1917. x, 206p. por.   MPL

Last poems. Fortune P. 1928. [iv], 116p.
    A limited ed. of 325 copies.   BM

War poems; by "X". Martin Secker. 1916. viii, 96p.   MPL

See also (19) (25) (111) (112) (120)

CROSS, Albert Francis
Charnwood poems. Nuneaton: Chronicle P.
1928. viii, 66p.   BPL

The tower of harmony. Nuneaton: Chronicle P.
[1925]. [33]p.
    Printed on one side of leaf only.
    A limited ed. of 250 copies.
    'Dedicated to the brave men of Loughborough who fell
in the Great War, 1914-1918'.   BM

CROSS, H.H.V. (Rifleman, 1st London Rifle Brigade.
Severely wounded at the Somme, 9th September 1916)

A young soldier's "De profundis": [poems]. Erskine
Macdonald. [1916]. 16p. (Malory booklets).   MPL

CROSS, Norman
Collected poems. Favil P. 1938. 120p. BM

The red planet, and other poems. Fifield. 1917. 63p. BM

Songs after sunset: [poems]. Oxford: Blackwell. [1921].
[iv], 80p. BM

CROSS FLEURY, pseud. see RIGBYE, R.E.K.,
(Cross Fleury, pseud.)

CROUCH, Richard A. see (31) (32)

CROW, Gerald Henry see (19) (121)

CROZIER, Phyllis see (5)

CRUMP, Geoffrey Herbert (Major, Essex Regiment)
Mattins, and other poems. Erskine Macdonald.
1918. 58p. BPL

See also (52) (58)

CRUTTWELL, Edith Mary
New poems. Amersham: Morland. 1920. 23p. BM

See also (28)

CRYER, James Wilfred
A vision of hope: [poems]. Manchester: Pearce &
Gardner. [1917]. 52p. col. il. MPL

CRYER, William see (27)

CUMBER, Q., pseud.
The king's "Contemptibles": an epic of the men of
Mons: [poems]. Henderson. 1918. 32p. BPL

CUMBERLAND, Gerald, pseud. see KENYON,
Charles Frederick, (Gerald Cumberland, pseud.)

CUNARD, Nancy
Outlaws, [and other poems]. Elkin Mathews. 1921. 64p. BM

Parallax. Hogarth P. 1925. 64p. BM

Relève into Maquis. Derby: Grasshopper P.
1944. [4]p. BM
See also (122) (123)

CURCHOD, Mary M.
Sprigs of lavender from Algiers: [poems]. Elkin Mathews.
1929. 152p.   BM

The union jack, and other battle songs and poems on
incidents connected with the war of the nations. Paisley:
Gardner. 1915. 76p.
   Proceeds of sales for benefit of the wounded British
and French soldiers.   MPL

See also (29)

CURTOIS, Dering see (64)

CURWEN, Annie Isabel see (28) (29)

CUST, Henry
Occasional poems. Chosen by N.C. and R.S. Jerusalem.
1918. 31p. por.   BM

CUTHBERT, V.I., & E., H.
Evening reflections, and other poems. Stockwell.
[1922]. 32p.   BPL

D., A.N. see **DAVIES, A.N., (A.N.D.)**

D.C.S. see **S., D.C., & S., P.C.**

D., D. see **DAWSON, D., (D.D.)**

D.L.I. see **I., D.L.**

D.M. see **M., D.**

D., M.J., & D., W.G.M.
Border songs, and other verse. Printed Dumfries: Maxwell.
1914. 22p.
   Publ. on behalf of war relief funds.   BPL

D., N. see (51)

D.O.L. see **LUMLEY, Sir Dudley Owen, (D.O.L.)**

D., R. (Interned at Groningen, Holland)
Poems; by R.D. (interned). Printed Groningen:
Werkman. 1915. 16p.

Enclosed in wrapper on which is printed 'With the sincerest wishes for a Merry Christmas and a Happy New Year from A[?] Werkman, Printer of the Camp Magazine'.

IWM

D.S.M. see MacCOLL, Dugald Sutherland, (D.S.M.)

D., T.B., pseud. see JAMES, Sir William Milburne, (T.B.D., pseud.)

D., W.G.M. see D.M.J., & D., W.G.M.

DACOMB, Alfred C.
Our bit. [191-].
    A postcard.

BM

Some Sergeant-Major. [191-].
    A postcard.

BM

Union is strength. [191-].
    A postcard.

BM

DAINOW, Morley (Served with the 9th Middlesex Regiment)
An ode to Sergeant Samuel Meek, Platoon Sergeant, 13 Platoon, "D" Company, 9th Middlesex (D.C.O.) Regiment, who died in Dum Dum, Bengal, India, on October 6th, 1915. Printed Bengal: [Middlesex Regiment?]. 1915. 3p.
    Proceeds of sale devoted to Meek's widow and children.

BPL

DALMON, Charles
A poor man's riches: a bundle of lyrics. Methuen. 1922. xvi, 118p.

BPL

Singing as I go: poems, lyrics and Romany songs. Constable. 1927. xii, 94p.

MPL

DALSTON, D.F.
Songs and shadows: [poems]. Erskine Macdonald. 1919. 66p.

BPL

DALTON, Moray see (16) (17) (18) (51)

DALTON, R.F. (Corporal, 186 Co., Royal Engineers)
Diverse verse. Privately printed. [1940?]. 15p.
    Title from cover.

IWM

DALZIEL, H.A.
The tower, and other poems. Oxford: Blackwell. 1927. 114p.   EDR

DAMON, pseud. see (121)

DANBY, Frank, pseud. see FRANKAU, Julia, (Frank
Danby, pseud.) (26)

DARBYSHIRE, J.R.
A thanksgiving hymn for peace. 1919.
   A broadside.   BM

DAREING, Jane, pseud.
Maid, mother — and widow: poems of peace and war.
Stockwell. [1918]. 13p.   BPL

DARLING, Charles, Lord Darling of Langham
On the Oxford circuit, and other verses. 3rd ed.
Murray. 1924. 143p.
   1st and 2nd eds publ. 1909. This ed. contains a
section *In war time,* comprising 10 poems.   BPL

Reconsidered rimes [sic]. Hodder & Stoughton. 1930.
105p. por.   BM

See also (51)

DARLING, W. Rus
The elf, and other poems on love and war. Edinburgh:
Hodge. 1918. 64p. il.   BPL

DART, Edith see (113)

DARTER, B.
Poems and lyrics. Stockwell. [1930?]. 48p.   BM

DARTFORD, R.C.G. (Captain, attached to the Portuguese
Expeditionary Force in France) see (58)

DARYUSH,Elizabeth
Verses. Oxford U.P. 1930. 44p.   BM

Verses: second book. Oxford U.P. 1932. 72p.   BM

Verses: third book. Oxford U.P. 1933. 62p.   BM

Verses: fourth book. Oxford U.P. 1934. 72p.   BM
See also (11)

DAVENPORT, David
Richard Plantagenet, and other poems. Kegan Paul,
Trench, Trubner. 1920. 48p.   BM

DAVEY, Norman
Desiderium, MCMXV-MCMXVIII: [poems]. Cambridge:
Heffer. 1920. 106p.   BM

See also (87)

DAVIDSON, Nelly
Charitas (a royal bull fight); Vaincre ou mourir, and
other poems. Eugène. [1916]. 40p.   BPL

Charitas (a royal bull fight); Vaincre ou mourir, and
other poems. 2nd ed. Eugène. 1917. [32] p.
   Cover-title is "The Kaiser's ordeal".   BM

"The contest", and other poems. Printed Willesden:
Morton & Burt. 1915. 19p.
   Cover title is ' "The contest", "The martyrs",
"Conscription", etc.'   BM

"The judgment", [and other poems]. Printed Kilburn:
Hunt & Clark. 1915. 26p.   BM

The Kaiser's ordeal, and other poems. Eugène. 1916.
40p.   BM

See also (28)

DAVIES, A.N., (A.N.D.)
Our khaki boys; [by] A.N.D. [Birmingham?]. [1916].
   A postcard.   BM

DAVIES, Oliver
Songs and signs: [poems]. Oxford: Blackwell.
1920. viii, 63p.   BM

DAVIES, Wallace (Private, 4th Monmouth Regiment)
Lyrics and parables. Erskine Macdonald. 1917. 84p.
   Poetry and prose.   BPL

DAVIES, William Henry
The captive lion, and other poems. New Haven: Yale
U.P. 1921. viii, 100p.   BM

Collected poems: second series. Cape. 1923. 157p. por.

First series publ. 1916 does not contain war poetry.   MPL

Collected poems, 1928. Cape. 1928. xx, 399p. por.   MPL

Collected poems. Intro. by Osbert Sitwell. Cape.
1942. 525p. por.   MPL

Complete poems. With an intro. by Osbert Sitwell.
Cape. 1963. 616p.   BPL

Forty new poems. Fifield. 1918. 54p.   MPL

Poems. Cape. 1934. 474p.   MPL

Poems, 1940. Cape. 1940. 525p. por.   MPL

Raptures: a book of poems. Beaumont P. 1918. 39p.
    A limited ed. of 272 copies.   BM

Selected poems. Arranged by Edward Garnett. With
a foreword by the author. Gregynog P. 1928. viii,
92p. por.
    A limited ed. of 310 copies.   BM

See also (111) (112)

DAVIS, Cyril S.
An appeal: an original poem. Liverpool: Davis.
[1914]. [3]p.   BM

DAVIS, L.
A call to arms. Pangbourne: Author. [191-].
    A broadside.
    For benefit of Belgian Relief Fund.   BM

DAVISON, Edward Lewis
Harvest of youth: [poems]. New York: Harper.
1926. xii, 115p.   BM

The heart's unreason: [poems]. Gollancz. 1931. 111p.   BM

Poems. Bell. 1920. x, 65p.   IWM

See also (22)

DAVISON, Henry (Driver, Army Service Corps. Served with
British Expeditionary Force)

Eld, etc.: [poems] ; by the author of "Other poems"
[sic]. Reeves. [1937]. [vi], 45p.   BM

In the infirmary; Our Lady of Boulogne, and other poems;

by the author of "Dovo sono", [etc.]. Reeves. [1932].
[vi], 40p.   BM

"Ward 8": humorous sketch of wounded soldier's
doings in a military hospital. [Swansea?]. 1916. [4]p.
   Written in Bagthorpe Military Hospital.   BM

DAWNAY, Guy
Nigella: [poems]. Methuen. 1919. [viii], 40p. il.   BPL

DAWSON, Arthur John Eardley (2nd Lieutenant, Indian
Army. Served in Middle East)

Children of circumstance, [and other poems]. Grant
Richards. 1921. 94p.   BPL

Night winds of Araby: [poems]. Grant Richards. 1920.
47p.   BPL

DAWSON, D., (D.D.)
War! War! Bellona, the hell-sprite of war; and, The
would that didn't do: [poems]; by D.D. [Fenton, Staffs].
[1917]. [6]p.   BM

DAWSON, May M.
Tinkers twa in peace and war: [poems]. Paisley:
Gardner. [1920]. 107p.
   In Scots dialect.   BPL

DAY, Jeffery see **DAY, Miles Jeffery Game**

DAY, Miles Jeffery Game (D.S.C. Flight-Commander,
Royal Naval Air Service. Shot down in air fight, 27th
February 1918)

Poems and rhymes. Sidgwick & Jackson. 1919.
66p. por.
   With a memoir by E.H.Y. [Edward Hilton Young]
reprinted from the *Cornhill Magazine*, October 1918.   MPL
See also (17) (18) (33) (46) (50) (96) (111)
(112) (131)

DAYNE, Hubert see (65)

DAYSON, Philip, pseud. see **MILLS, Edward, (Philip
Dayson, pseud.)**

DEAN, E.G. (Lance-Corporal, Hampshire Regiment)
A selection of original parodies taken from popular
songs sung by Tommy Atkins: words. [191-]. [4]p.   IWM

DEANE, Mary
A book of verse. Elkin Mathews. 1921. 44p.   BM

DEARMER, Geoffrey (Lieutenant, Royal Army
Service Corps. Fought at Gallipoli and on the Somme)
The day's delight: [poems]. Murray. 1923. viii, 56p.   BM

Poems. Heinemann. 1918. viii, 88p.   MPL

See also (33) (60) (94) (96) (103) (104) (111)
(112) (120)

DEAS, Christie see (28)

DE BANZIE, Eric (Sapper, Royal Engineers) see (58)

DE BARY, Anna Bunston
Collected poems. Mitre P. [1947]. 236p.   BM

New and selected lyrics. O'Connor. [1923]. xii, 156p.
   Cover-title is "Lyrics".   BM

DE BERTOUCH, Beatrice, Baroness see (64)

DE C.
A rubáiyát of the trenches. Fawcett. 1917. 64p.   MPL

DE CANDOLE, Alec (Commissioned in Wiltshire Regiment.
Served in Machine Gun Corps. Killed in France, 3rd
September 1918)

Poems. Cambridge U.P. 1920. viii, 87p. por.   BPL

DEE, E.C.
The unknown warrior, and other poems. Stockwell.
[1926]. 16p.   BM

DEFAULTER, pseud.
"Outpost", and other verses. McBride Nast.
[1916]. 48p. il.   MPL

DELAHUNTY, Paul V.
[Verses written for] a dinner given by Mr. Sam
Meadowcroft at the Reform Club, Manchester, on
March 9th, 1920, to commemorate his rescue from
the S.S. "Arabic", torpedoed on August 19th, 1915,
and to celebrate the thirtieth anniversary of his entering
the service of Levinstein Limited, March 9th 1890-
March 9th 1920. Medici Society. 1920. [i], 13p.
    A limited ed. of 16 copies, printed at the Riccardi P.   MPL

DE LA MARE, Walter
Collected poems. Faber. 1942. xvi, 334p. il. (by
Berthold Wolpe).   MPL

Complete poems. Faber. 1969. xvi, 948p. por.
    Bibliog. note (auhtor's works) 11p.   MPL

The fleeting, and other poems. Constable. 1933. xii,
179p.   WPL

Motley, and other poems. Constable. 1918. viii, 75p.   MPL

Motley, and other poems. New ed. Constable. 1927.
viii, 70p. il. (by Bold).   BM

Motley, and other poems. Constable. 1931. viii, 70p. il.
(by Bold). (Miscellany of original and selected publications
in literature).   MPL

Poems, 1901 to 1918. v.1. Constable. 1920. x, 251p.
    v.2 contains no war poetry.   MPL

Poems, 1919 to 1934. Constable. 1935. xvi, 379p.   BM

Selected poems. Chosen by R.N. Green-Armytage.
Faber. 1954. 208p.   BM

The sunken garden, and other poems. Beaumont P.
1917. 40p.
    A limited ed. of 270 copies.   BM

See also (16) (18) (19) (22) (30) (35) (60) (80)
(108) (109) (111) (112) (113)

**D'ELBOUX, Raymond Herbert see HASELER, Digby
Bertram, (Spring Poet, pseud.), & D'ELBOUX, Raymond
Herbert**

DENBY, Emily see (29)

DENEY, Mary Du see **DU DENEY, Mary**

DENNYS, Richard Molesworth (Captain, Loyal North Lancashire Regiment. Wounded in the Somme advance, 12th July 1916. Died twelve days later)

There is no death: poems. With a foreword by Desmond Coke. Bodley Head. 1917. 110p. por.　　　　　　　MPL

There is no death: poems. With a foreword by Desmond Coke. 2nd ed. Bodley Head. 1918. 110p. por.　　　　　IWM

There is no death. Bodley Head. 1919. [4]p. col. il.
　This single poem is reprinted from author's "There is no death: poems", and illuminated in colour.　　　　BPL

See also (72) (131)

DE S., E. see **DE STEIN, Sir Edward, (E.D.S.), (E. De S.)**

DE ST. OUEN, G.
"Lest we forget": a note addressed to H.I.M. Wilhelm II, Emperor of Germany, on behalf of the British volunteers from the republics of the River Plate. Buenos Aires: British Printery. 1916. 16p.　　　　　　　　　　BPL

DESMOND, Harry
The broken melody, and other poems. Stockwell. [1941]. 80p. por.　　　　　　　　　　　　　　　　BM

Golden orchids: [poems]. Ilfracombe: Stockwell. 1946. 79p.　　　　　　　　　　　　　　　　　BM

The sands are sinking on the desert waste, and other poetical works. Ilfracombe: Stockwell. [1943]. 216p. por.　　　　　　　　　　　　　　　　　BM

The voice of to-morrow, and other poems. Ilfracombe: Stockwell. [1942]. 88p. por.　　　　　　　　　BM

DE STEIN, Sir Edward, (E.D.S.), (E.De S.) (Major, King's Royal Rifles. Served in France, 1916-18)

The poets in Picardy, and other poems. Murray. 1919. 92p.　　　　　　　　　　　　　　　　　MPL

See also (17) (18) (31) (32) (33) (47) (48) (49) (111) (112)

DEVERELL, Gladys
A few little verses about the war. Sharpe & Gibson.
[1918]. [iv], 8p.   BPL

DIBBEN, George (Special Constabulary)
"The indictment of 1914"; by a London Special
Constable. [1914]. [4] p.
'Written in the early hours of the morning while
watching for Zeppelins on the Thames Embankment'.   BM

DICKINSON, Frank B.
"Hands off!" Printed Peterborough: Caster. [1916].
[3] p.   BM

DICKSON, Mona
A miscellany of verse. Merton P. 1922. 40p.   BM

DILLON, Doreen Mollie see (29)

DIRCKS, Helen
Finding, [and other poems]. Chatto & Windus. 1918.
96p.   BPL

Passenger: [poems]. Chatto & Windus. 1920. viii, 72p.   BPL

DIXEY, Giles see **DIXEY, Harold Giles**

DIXEY, Harold Giles
Darien: poems. Oxford: Blackwell. 1923. [viii], 121p. BPL

Fūrin: collected verses. Oxford: Blackwell. 1948.
[4], viii, 394p.   WPL

Hymns without faith: [poems]. Oxford: Dixey. 1946. 16p.
    A limited ed. of 83 copies, hand-printed by the author.   BM

Ourselves a dream: verses. Oxford: Dixey. 1947. 24p.
    A limited ed. of 83 copies, hand-printed by the author.   BM

Sonnets in sand. Oxford: Dixey. 1946. 16p.
    A limited ed. of 83 copies, hand-printed by the author.   BM

Soundings: [poems]. Simpkin, Marshall, Hamilton, Kent.
1919. [iv], 128, iv p.   BM

Versions; and, Afterthoughts: [poems]. Oxford: Dixey.
1934. [vi], 54p. il.
    A limited ed. of 100 copies, hand-printed by the author. BM

DIXON, Edwin M. see (29)

DIXON, William Macneile
In Arcadia: [poems]. Blackie. 1933. x, 84p.   MPL
See also (16) (18)

DOAK, Hugo L.
The three-rock road, [and other poems]. Dublin: Talbot P.;
Fisher Unwin. 1919. 62p.   BM

Verdun, and other poems. Dublin: Maunsel. 1917. 46p.   MPL

DOBELL, Bertram
Sonnets and lyrics: a little book of verse on the
present war. Dobell. 1915. xvi, 71p.   BPL
See also (55)

DOBELL, Mrs. C. Oliver
"Son of mine": a poem. Daniel. [1917]. 30p.
   Written by the mother of a conscientious objector.   BM

DOBELL, Eva
A bunch of Cotswold grasses: [poems]. Stockwell.
[1919]. 64p.   BPL

Verses new and old. Favil P. 1959. [viii], 66p.   CPL

DOBSON, Austin
Complete poetical works. Oxford U.P. 1923. xxiv,
526p. por.   MPL

Poems on the war. Printed Shorter. [1915]. [8]p. facsim.
   A limited ed. of 20 copies, privately printed by Clement
Shorter.   BM

Selected poems. Revised and enlarged ed. Oxford U.P.
1924. xii, 247p. il. (World's classics).
   Forerunner of this ed. publ. 1905.   BM

See also (12) (16) (17) (18) (25) (31) (32) (54) (59)

DOBSON, James W. see (29)

DODD, Alfred
The ballad of the iron cross, [and other poems].
Erskine Macdonald. 1918. 62p.   BM

The ballad of the iron cross, [and other poems]. 2nd ed.
Erskine Macdonald. 1918. 62p.   BPL

See also (52)

DODDERIDGE, George Victor
War poems. Hereford: Herefordshire P. & Printing Co.
1915. [12]p.
    'Gross proceeds will be devoted to the War Funds'.   BM

DODDS, Andrew (Worked for the Young Men's Christian
Association in France)

The Lothian land: poems. 2nd ed. Aberdeen: *Scottish
Farm Servant*. 1918. 84p.
    Some in Lothian dialect.   BM

The Lothian land: poems. 3rd ed. Aberdeen: *Scottish
Farm Servant*. 1918. 88p.
    Some in Lothian dialect.   SCL

[No copy of 1st ed. traced].

Songs of the fields: [poems]. Stirling: *Scottish
Farm Servant*. 1920. 32p.   BM

See also (91)

DODSLEY, S. Gresham see (27)

DOLDEN, Arthur George
Kilmore: the medicine man: a legend of the Great War.
Leytonstone: Author. [1915]. [3]p.   BM

Soldier lad!: addressed to a soldier about to leave for
the front. [Leytonstone?]: Author. [1915].
    A card.   BM

DOLPHIN, May I.E.
More songs from the moorland: [poems]. Oxford:
Blackwell. 1924. 99p.   BM

Songs from the moorland: [poems]. Oxford: Blackwell.
1922. 83p.   BM

Swords and ploughshares: [poems]. Durham:Bailes.
[1947]. 35p.   BM

DOMLEO, Constance M.
Lost or won, and other poems. Stockwell. [1920]. 16p.   BM

DON, pseud.
Memories of Peeko: poems. Printed Ripon: Taylor.
1916. 24p.   IWM

DONEY, May
The way of wonder: [poems]. With an intro. by Sir Arthur
Quiller-Couch. Methuen. 1917. xvi, 118p.   MPL

DONNAN, Jeanie
The hills o' hame: poems. Newton Stewart: *Galloway
Gazette*. 1930. [v], 135p.   BM

War poems. Newton Stewart: *Galloway Gazette.*
1915. 32p.
   Some in Scots dialect.   WCL

War poems. [New] ed. Newton Stewart: *Galloway
Gazette.* [1919]. [viii], 72p.
   Some in Scots dialect.
   Proceeds given to the Fund for Disabled Soldiers and
Sailors.   BPL

See also (28) (29) (65)

DONNER, C. see (27)

DOOUSS, F.j. (Lieutenant, Suffolk Regiment)
Poems of war. Erskine Macdonald. 1918. 30p. (Little
books of Georgian verse: war time series).   MPL

DORMER, Dent, pseud. see **SLEEP, Frederick, (Dent
Dormer, pseud.)**

DOWDALL, Launcelot see (27)

DOWN, Oliphant (M.C. Captain, 4th Battalion, Royal
Berkshire Regiment. Killed on the Somme, May 1917)

Poems. Gowans & Gray. 1921. viii, 79p.   BPL

DOWNES, Olive Primrose
The bridge of memory: [poems]. Stockwell. [1921]. 32p.   BM

See also (5)

DOWSING, William
War cartoon sonnets; based on Louis Raemaeker's war

cartoons. Printed Sheffield: Northend. 1918. 6v. por.
A limited ed. of 475 copies.   BPL

DOYLE, Sir Arthur Conan
The Guards came through, and other poems. Murray.
1919. 78p.   MPL

The Guards came through. [1917?]. [2]p.   IWM

Poems. Collected ed. Murray. 1922. xii, 242p.
Cover-title is "Collected poems".   MPL

See also (12) (16) (17) (18) (30) (31) (32) (43)
(51) (107) (119) (120)

DOYLE, Lily
Bound in khaki, [and other poems]. Intro. by Sir Ignatius
O'Brien. Elliot Stock. 1916. 63p.   BPL

DRANE, Henry J., (Indignant Englishman, pseud.)
The mailed fist, based upon a true incident of the war in
Belgium, October 7, 1914, and addressed to His Imperial
Majesty the German Emperor; by an indignant Englishman.
Drane. [1919]. [4]p.   BPL

DRAPER, William Henry (Lost three sons in the war)
Poems of the love of England. Chatto & Windus.
1914. viii, 80p.   BPL

See also (17) (18)

DREW, Annie
Poems. Taunton: Barnicott & Pearce. 1928. iv, 40p.   EDR

DREW, Edwin
We fight or fall: the song of Empire. [1914].
A postcard.   BM

DREWETT, A.W. see (5) (29)

DRINKWATER, John
Collected poems. v.1. 1908-1917. Sidgwick & Jackson.
1923. xiv, 234p. il.   MPL

Collected poems. v.2. 1917-1922. Sidgwick & Jackson.
1923. xii, 240p. il.   MPL

From an unknown isle: [poems]. Sidgwick & Jackson.
1924. 46p.   WPL

Loyalties: [poems]. Sidgwick & Jackson. 1919. 64p.   MPL

New poems. Boston: Houghton Mifflin. 1925. viii, 64p.   BM

Olton pools, [and other poems]. Sidgwick & Jackson.
1916. 48p.   MPL

Seeds of time: [poems]. Sidgwick & Jackson. 1921. 74p.   MPL

Summer harvest: poems, 1924-1933. Sidgwick & Jackson.
1933. xii, 175p.   WPL

Swords and ploughshares: [poems]. Sidgwick & Jackson.
1915. 57p.   MPL

Tides: [poems]. Sidwick & Jackson. 1917. 56p.   MPL

See also (16) (17) (18) (19) (31) (32) (33) (34) (42)
(46) (65) (81) (82) (83) (84) (95) (111) (112)

DRUCE, Clifford J. (2nd Lieutenant, Gloucestershire
Regiment) see (58)

DU CANN, Charles Garfield Lott (Lieutenant, Army
Cyclist Corps.)

'Prentice poems. Erskine Macdonald. 1917. 54p.   BPL

Triolets from the trenches: [poems]. Erskine Macdonald.
1917. 40p.   MPL

See also (2)

DUCLAUX, Agnes Mary Frances Robinson
Images and meditations: a book of poems. Fisher Unwin.
1923. [x], 67p.   BPL

See also (19) (42) (59) (65)

DU DENEY, Mary
War-time verses. Channing P. 1934. 30p. il. (by E.M.
Channing-Renton). (Channing poets' library, 6).   BM

See also (28) (29)

DUDLEY, Anita
Songs of deliverance: [poems]. Methuen. 1933. 68p.   IWM

Valediction: sonnets to Kitchener. Humphreys. 1916. 29p.   BPL

Vision valley, [and other poems]. Humphreys. 1916. viii,
62p.   BM

DUFF, Sylvia see (64)

DUFFIN, Celia see DUFFIN, Ruth, & DUFFIN, Celia

DUFFIN, Ruth see (31) (32) (47) (48) (49) (63) (119)

DUFFIN, Ruth, & DUFFIN, Celia
Escape: poems. Dent. 1929. xii, 130p.
    Not joint authorship. No war poetry by Celia Duffin.   BM

DUGGAN, George Chester
The watchers on Gallipoli. Dublin: Hodges, Figgis.
1921. 43p.
    Dedicated to author's two dead brothers, killed at
Suvla.   BPL

DUMAR, Claud
Picturesque poems of the war. Stockwell. [1916]. 31p.   BPL

DUMARTIN, Hart, pseud. see TIDMAN, Arthur, (Hart
Dumartin, pseud.)

DUMBRELL, J.H. (Lieutenant, Royal Sussex
Regiment)
Bosh ballads. Stockwell. [1918]. 16p.
    Dedicated to the men of the Royal Sussex Regiment.   MPL

DUNKERLEY, William Arthur see OXENHAM, John,
(b. William Arthur Dunkerley)

DUNLOP, Archibald Buchanan- see WARDLE, Mark
Kingsley, & BUCHANAN-DUNLOP, Archibald

DUNLOP, W. Cathcart
Pro patria: verses on occasions connected with the war.
Bridgetown, Barbados: Advocate Co. 1918. [16]p.
    Profits for Red Cross Fund.   BPL

Undersongs: translations and other verses. Erskine
Macdonald. 1916. 84p.   BM

DUNN, F.J. Argyll- see ARGYLL-DUNN, F.J.

DUNN, George W.M.
Poems — group one. Cape. 1934. 78p.   BM

DUNSANY, Lord see PLUNKETT, Edward John Moreton
Drax, Lord Dunsany

DUXBURY, Ada see (28)

DYNES, Eric see (27)

E., A., pseud. see RUSSELL, George William,
(A.E., pseud.)

E.C. see CARPENTER, Edward, (E.C.)

E.C. see CARTER, E., (E.C.)

E.D.S. see DE STEIN, Sir Edward, (E.D.S.), (E.De S.)

E. DE S. see DE STEIN, Sir Edward, (E.D.S.), (E. De S.)

E.E. see EMMONS, Elise, (E.E.)

E.G. see G., E.

E., H. see CUTHBERT, V.I., & E., H.

E.H.W.M. see MEYERSTEIN, Edward Harry William,
(E.H.W.M.)

E.J. see (51)

E.L.S. see S., E.L.

E.M.T. see (63)

E., N.R. see EDWARDS, N.R., (N.R.E.)

E.S. see STRICKLAND, Eugene, (E.S.) (5)

E.S.B. see BUCHANAN, Edgar Simmons, (E.S.B.)

E.S.S.W. see WALLINGTON, Emma S.S., (E.S.S.W.)

E.T. see T., E.

E.W.H. see HAMILTON, Eric William, (E.W.H.)

EAGAR, Aimée E.
Our heroes, (1914-1916). Erskine Macdonald. 1916. 45p.   BPL

EARP, T.W. see (60)

EAST, Neil
A talent of silver: poems. Humphreys. 1917. 72p.   BPL

EASTAWAY, Edward, pseud. see THOMAS, Edward, (Edward
Eastaway, pseud.)

EASTER, Norris
Khaki characters and mufti monologues. [Leeds?] :
[Author?]. 1916. 95p.   BPL

EDE, J.P. (Private, Royal Army Medical Corps.) see (110)

EDEN, Helen Parry
Coal and candlelight, and other verses. Bodley Head.
1918. 84p.   BPL

See also (25) (63) (111) (112)

EDIS, Emily see (28)

EDITH Cavell: inspiration words before her doom,
in front of the firing squad, and in the sight of God;
[and], In memory. [1916]. [2]p.   BM

EDMEADES, Edith E.
Fragments of fact and fancy: [poems]. Stockwell. [1918].
16p.   BM

EDMONDS, John Maxwell
Twelve war epitaphs. [Chelsea] : [Ashendene P.]. [1920].
    A broadside.   BM

See also (51) (119)

EDWARDS, Matilda Betham- see BETHAM-EDWARDS,
Matilda

EDWARDS, N.R., (N.R.E.)
Opals: [poems] ;by N.R.E. Liverpool: Philip. 1918. 49p.   LPL

Opals: [poems] ; by N.R.E. 2nd ed. Liverpool: Philip.
1918. 49p.   BPL

ELBOUX, Raymond Herbert D' see HASELER, Digby
Bertram, & D'ELBOUX, Raymond Herbert

ELDRIDGE, Robey Frank
Our padre. S.P.C.K. 1918. 8p.   BPL

See also (29)

ELLIOT, Alice
"The sparrow hath found her an house", [and other poems].
Bristol: Arrowsmith. 1924. 61p.   BM

ELLIS, Eric Kent
St. Patrick, and other poems. Cambridge: Heffer. 1931.
54p.   BPL

ELLIS, Frank
"Somewhere in France", and other poems. Frings. 1918.
88p.   BPL

ELLIS, Vivian Locke
Collected lyrical poems. With an intro. by Walter De La
Mare. Faber. 1946. [ii], 136p.   MPL

See also (114)

ELTON, Godfrey, Lord Elton
Schoolboys and exiles: [poems]. Allen & Unwin.
1919. 46p.   BPL

Years of peace: poems. Allen & Unwin. 1925. 48p.   BM

See also (73) (74)

ELYOTT, John
The one voice, and other verses, national and
historical. Dorchester: Friary P. 1932. 63p.   BPL

EMMONS, Elise, (E.E.)
Autumn songs among the leaves: [poems]. Watkins.
1921. 112p.   BPL

The crystal sea, and other poems. Stockwell. [1925].
112p. il., por.   BM

Spring songs among the flowers: [poems]. Leamington Spa:
Tomes. [1920?]. 80p.   BM

Summer songs among the birds, [and other poems] ; by
E.E. Watkins. 1918. il.   BPL

Winter songs among the snows: [poems]. Watkins. 1919.
108p.   BPL

ENGLAND, M.
The story and glory of Ze[e]brugge. Revised by a friend —
Mr. Russell. Printed Dover: Newing & Gibbons.[1918?].
[2]p.
    On behalf of the Dover Patrol Fund.   BM

ENSOR, Sir Robert Charles Kirkwood
Odes and other poems. Sidgwick & Jackson. 1917. 102p.   MPL

EQUITES, pseud. see (5)

ESSON, Valerie L. see (64)

ETESON, Ada M.
"The monsoon", and other poems. Amersham: Morland;
Foyle. 1919. 80p. il.   BPL

ETIENNE, pseud. see KING-HALL, Stephen, Lord King-
Hall, (Etienne, pseud.)

ETON, pseud. see (63)

EVANS, William (Vicar of St. Peter's, North London)
Killed in action: (poems of consolation). Erskine
Macdonald. 1916. 32p.   BPL

EVANS, William, (Wil Ifan, pseud.)
Songs of the heather heights: [poems] ; by Wil Ifan.
Hodder & Stoughton. [1921]. viii, 80p.   BPL

EVEREST, Kate
The dreaming antinous, and other poems. Richmond.
[1919]. 81p. por.   BM

See also (28)

EVOE, pseud. see KNOX, George Valpy, (Evoe, pseud.)

EWER, William Norman
Five souls, and other war-time verses. *The Herald.*
[1917]. 47p.   MPL

Satire and sentiment: [poems]. *The Herald.* 1918.
[vi], 42p.   BM

See also (4) (12) (38) (39) (47) (48) (49) (50)
(59) (61) (66) (96) (121)

EWING, John Orr (M.C. Major)
Hoofmarks, and other impressions: [poems]. Witherby.
1934. 96p. il. (by G.H.S. Dixon).   BPL

EWING, O.H.
Dunstanburgh: a metrical history, (1313-1919) : [poems].
Newcastle-upon-Tyne: Reid. [1920]. 77p.   BM

EYRE, Beatrice A. see (29)

F., H.C. see (51)

F., J.
Verses. Humphreys. 1917. 32p.   BPL

F.L. see **LUDLOW, Frederick, (F.L.)**

F., P.E.T.
Two friends, and other poems. Cornish. 1916. 24p.   BPL

F.S. see **SIDGWICK, Frank, (F.S.)**

F.W.M. see **M., F.W.**

FABER, Sir Geoffrey (Captain)
The buried stream: collected poems, 1908 to 1940.
Faber. 1941. 256p.   MPL

In the valley of vision: poems written in time of war.
Oxford: Blackwell. 1918. viii, 67p. (Initiates series of
poetry by proved hands, 1).   MPL

Interflow: poems, chiefly lyrical. Constable. 1915. xvi,
112p. (New poetry series).   MPL

See also (19)

FAE, Jyos
Love blossoms from my garden of dreams: [poems].

Humphreys. 1915. 52p.
  Printed on one side of leaf only.   BM

FAGAN, James Bernard see (19) (25) (40) (41) (47) (48)
(49) (82) (83) (84) (121)

FAIRFAX, James Griffyth (b. Australia. Educated at
Winchester and New College, Oxford. Captain, Royal
Army Service Corps. Attached to 15th Indian Division,
1914-19. Mentioned in dispatches).

Mesopotamia: sonnets and lyrics at home and
abroad, 1914-1919. Murray. 1919. viii, 80p.   MPL

The temple of Janus: a sonnet-sequence. Smith, Elder.
1917. [103]p. il. (by F.M. McArthur).
  Printed on one side of leaf only.
  A limited ed. of 500 copies.   BPL

See also (33) (111) (112)

FALCONER, Agnes S. see (19) (25) (42)

FANSHAWE, Reginald
By Yser banks: an elegy on a young officer. Oxford:
Blackwell. 1915. 15p.   BPL

FARJEON, Eleanor
A collection of poems. Collins. 1929. xiv, 242p.   WPL

First and second love: sonnets. Joseph. 1947. 56p.   BM

First and second love: sonnets. Oxford U.P. 1959.
[vi], 52p.   BM

Sonnets and poems. Oxford: Blackwell. 1918. 50p.
(Initiates series of poetry by proved hands, 2).   MPL

See also (60)

FARRANTS, F.W.
But for the men. Printed Poplar: Wilson. [1919?].
  A broadside.   BM

FARRAR, Thomas see (29)

FARRER, A. Muriel
In loving memory. Fellowes. 1916.
  A broadside.   BM

FARRER, Alice S.E. Downing
A war prayer. Boscombe: Author. [1915].
A card. BM

FARRINGTON, Anthony Charles
All the way in his life: varied phases and experiences
in the life of Anthony Charles Farrington; by Evelyn
C. Farrington. With appendix of his "Occasional poetic
thoughts". Norwich: Jarrold. 1932. xii, 308p. il., por. MPL

See also (27) (29)

FATHER, pseud.
In honour: an elegy; by a father. Constable. 1915.
[viii], 63p.
To G.M.J.S., killed in action near Ypres, 9th February
1915. BPL

FAY, Stanley J.
The allies' alphabet. *Daily Chronicle.* 1914. 24p. col.il.
(by Norman Morrow).
Illustrations with humorous rhymes. Not seen

See also (87)

FEASEY, E.
The written lie: a thrilling episode of the war.
Kibble. [1918]. 4p. BM

FEATHERED HEELS, pseud.
A song of war, and other poems. Elliot Stock. 1917.
vi, 58p. BPL

FELLOW OF MERTON COLLEGE, pseud. see **BLUNDEN,
Edmund Charles, (Fellow of Merton College, pseud.)**

FENTON, Frederick B. (Was wounded in France)
Poems of peace and war. Heath, Cranton. [1916]. 28p. BPL

FERGUS, John
The sodger, and other verses. Glasgow: Gowans & Gray.
1916. 31p.
In Scots dialect. EPL

The sodger, and other verses. 2nd ed. Glasgow: Gowans
& Gray. 1916. 32p.
In Scots dialect. BM

FERGUS, John Freeland
Fancies of a physician: verses, medical and otherwise in
Scots and English. Glasgow: Brown, Son & Ferguson.
1938. xiv, 209p.   BM

FERGUSON, John Alexander
On Vimy Ridge, and other poems. Gowans & Gray.
1917. 43p.   BPL

FERGUSSON, D. Fergus (Gunner, Royal Garrison Artillery)
War verses. Paisley: Gardner. 1917. 33p.   BPL

FERRAR, William John
The little brothers, and other poems chiefly of the
war. Erskine Macdonald. [1918]. 60p.   BPL

Three faces in a hood: poems of peace and war. Pitman.
1916. viii, 56p.   BPL

FETHERSTON, Sir George Ralph see (27)

FEW, Marguerite
Laughing gas, and other poems. Cambridge: Perkin
Warbeck. 1921. 28p.   BPL

See also (32) (52)

FIELD, A.N. (Private) see (16) (18)

FIELD, Henry Lionel (Lieutenant, Royal Warwickshire
Regiment. Killed in action 1st July 1916)

Poems and drawings. Birmingham: Cornish. 1917.
43p. il., por.   MPL

See also (131)

FIELD, M.G. (Captain)
Ambush and song: [poems]. Heath, Cranton. [1920]. 36p.   BPL

FIELD, Parnell (Royal Warwickshire Regiment)
Comrades: [poems]. Stratford-on-Avon: Author.
[1918?]. [3]p.   BM

Consider this!: [poems]. [Stratford-on-Avon]:
[Author?]. [1929]. [4]p.
    Title from cover.   BM

Empire, [and other poems]. Stratford-on-Avon: [Author?].
[1923]. [8]p.
    Bibliog. (author's works) 1p.   BM

Genesis till to-morrow. [Stratford-on-Avon?] : [Author?].
[1920]. 12p.   BM

Jerusalem, and other pieces. Stratford-on-Avon: Author.
[1918?]. [4]p.   BM

Princess and peace: [poems]. Stratford-on-Avon: Author.
[1923]. [4]p.   BM

Self-sacrifice: [poems]. [1928]. [4]p.   BM

Souvenir: the 61st Division: [poems]. Stratford-on-Avon:
[Author]. 1929. [11]p. il.
    Description of the Divisional War Memorial, 61st South-
Midland Division, Royal Warwickshire Regiment.   BPL

An unknown British soldier. Stratford-on-Avon. [1917].
    A postcard.   BM

Victory; and, Peace: [poems]. Stratford-on-Avon:
Author. [1918]. [3]p.   BM

The war: [poems]. Stratford-on-Avon: Author.
[1914-18].
    7 parts, printed on card (each 3 or 4 pages), marked
The war, card 1, The war, card 2, etc.   BM

FIELD, Samuel G.
The world's greatest war: a poem. Stratford-on-Avon:
Shakespeare P. [1914]. 8p.   MPL

FIELD OFFICER, pseud.
A soldier's sonnets: verses grave and gay. Northampton:
Birdsall. [1916]. 74p. il., por.   BPL

A soldier's sonnets: verses grave and gay. 2nd ed.
Northampton: Birdsall. [1916]. 74p. il., por.   BM

FIELDHOUSE, Edith A.
A call from the trenches: London's great recruiting
rally, October 2nd, 1915. Printed Camberwell: Haycock-
Cadle. 1915.
    A broadside.   BM

FIELDHOUSE, Lily see (5)

FIELDING, Esmé
A little . . . wooden cross, and other poems. Stockwell.
[1919]. 16p.   BPL

FIELDING-HALL, Harold
For England. Constable. 1916. 144p.
  Poems and stories.   BPL

For England. Boston: Houghton Mifflin. 1916. 144p.
  Poems and stories.   BPL

FINDLAY, George Paxton see (29)

FIRTH, Ivan (2nd Lieutenant, Royal Field Artillery)
Bellicosities in prose and verse, written under active
service conditions. Printed Gravesend: Reporter Office.
1915. [vi], 78p.   BPL

FISHER, Philip John (Chaplain to the Forces. Served in
England and France) see (31) (32)

FISON, Louis George
In pastime wrought: poems. Drane. [1915]. 158p.   BM

The village green, and other poems. Elliot Stock. 1922.
[vi], 165p.   BM

FITZGERALD, Colin
The rubáiyát of Omarred Wilhelm. Edwards. 1916.
[i], 57p.
  A parody of Edward Fitzgerald's version of the "Rubáiyát"
of Omar Khayyam.   BPL

FITZGERALD, Martin (Lieutenant, Machine Gun Corps)
Shambles: [poems]. Amersham: Morland. 1917. 32p.   MPL

FLECKER, James Elroy
The burial in England. Printed Shorter. 1915. [8]p.
  A limited ed. of 20 copies printed by Clement Shorter for
distribution among his friends.
    Reprinted from *The Sphere*, 27th February 1915.   BM

Collected poems. Ed. with an intro. by J.C. Squire.
Martin Secker. 1916. xxxii, 250p. por.   MPL

Collected poems. Martin Secker. 1923. 262p.
  A limited ed. of 500 copies.   BM

127

Collected poems. Ed. with an intro. by Sir John Squire.
[2nd] ed. Martin Secker. 1935. xxxviii, 250p. por.   MPL

Collected poems. Ed. with an intro. by Sir John Squire.
3rd ed. Secker & Warburg. 1946. xxx, 162p.   MPL

God save the king. Printed Shorter. 1915. [10]p. facsim.
   Bibliog. (author's works) 1p.
   A limited ed. of 20 copies printed by Clement Shorter
for distribution among his friends.
   Reprinted from *The Sphere*, 16th January 1916.   BM

The old ships, [and other poems]. Poetry Bookshop.
[1915]. 32p.   MPL

Selected poems. Martin Secker. 1918. [viii], 104p. por.   BM

See also (26) (70) (104) (111) (112)

FLEMING, Noel see (27) (29)

FLETCHER, Joseph Smith
Collected verse, (1881-1931). Harrap. 1931. 210p.   BM

FLETT, John G.S. see (27) (29)

FLEURY, Cross, pseud. see Rigbye, R.E.K., (Cross
Fleury, pseud.)

FLINT, Frank Stewart (Served in the Army for eleven months,
based in England)

Otherworld: cadences. Poetry Bookshop. 1920. xiv, 66p.   MPL

See also (97) (98)

FLOWER, Clifford (Driver, Royal Field Artillery. Killed
in action 20th April 1917)

Memoir and poems. Printed Stockport: Hurst. [1917?].
32p. por.   BPL

See also (131)

FLOWER, Robin
Hymenaea, and other poems. Selwyn & Blount.
1918. 48p.   MPL

Poems and translations. Constable. 1931. xii, 176p.   MPL

See also (114)

FOLLETT, Frederick Vernon
Flowers of fate, and other poems. Stockwell. [1917]. 44p.   BM

FORBES, Lady Helen Emily
The saga of the Seventh Division. Bodley Head. 1920.
74p.   BPL

FORD, Ford Madox, (b. Hueffer) (Lieutenant, Welch Regiment)
Antwerp. Poetry Bookshop. 1914. 8p.
   Title from cover.   BM

The good soldier; Selected memoires; Poems. Bodley
Head. 1962. 380p. (Bodley Head Ford Madox Ford, v.1).   MPL

On heaven, and poems written on active service. Bodley
Head. 1918. 128p.   MPL

See also (50) (96) (104) (106) (112) (127)

FORD, S. Gertrude
The England of my dream, and other poems. Daniel.
1928. 56p.   MPL

"A fight to a finish", and other songs of peace
sung in war time. Daniel. 1917. 22p.   MPL

Poems of war and peace. Erskine Macdonald. [1915].
38p.
   Profits to the British Red Cross Society.   BPL

See also (65)

FORDHAM, Edward Wilfrid (Special Constabulary)
Songs of the Specials, and other verses. With an intro.
by G.K. Chesterton. Palmer & Hayward. 1916. [viii],
64p. il. (by Hugh G. Riviere)   MPL

FORDHAM, Sir Herbert George (2nd Lieutenant, 1st
Volunteer Battalion, Cambridgeshire Regiment)
Scraps from the School of Musketry, Hythe, March-
April, 1918: [poems]. Hythe: [Author?]. 1918. 15p.
   Title-page has 'by Sir G.H. Fordham' (probably
typographical error).   BM

FORMAN, Elizabeth Chandler see (31) (32)

FORSHAW, Charles Frederick see (29)

FORSTER, Robert Henry
War poems of a Northumbrian. Newcastle-on-Tyne:
Noble. 1914. 32p.   MPL

War poems of a Northumbrian. (Second series).
Newcastle-on-Tyne: Noble. 1915. 39p.   MPL

See also (29) (54) (99) (100) (101)

FORT, James Alfred
Sonnets and other verses. Chapman & Hall. 1916. 72p.   BM

See also (55)

FOSTER, A. Austin see (29)

FOSTER, John M. see (27) (29)

FOSTER-MELLIAR, Robert Aubrey
I take the road: poems. Humphreys. 1917. 60p.   BM

Poems, (1916). Humphreys. 1916. [x], 61p.   BM

Poems: selected. Humphreys. 1921. [x], 108p.   BM

FOWLER, Henry Watson
Rhymes of Darby to Joan: flotsam from the good
ship Felicity, launched 1908, foundered 1930.
Dent. 1931. 96p. por.   MPL

FOXCROFT, Charles Talbot (Captain)
The night sister, and other poems. Methuen. 1918. 96p.   MPL

FOXCROFT, Helen Charlotte
Verses appropriate to the war. Printed Frome:
St. Aldhelm's Home for Boys. [1918]. 17p.   BPL

FRAMPTON, William
Britain's glory! The homeland's pride. Cowes: [Author?].
[191-].
   A broadside.   BM

British boys. Cowes: [Author?]. [191-].
   A broadside.   BM

The conscientious objector. Cowes: [Author?]. [191-].
   A broadside.   BM

Corduroys or reefer jacket. Cowes: [Author?]. [1918].
   A broadside.   BM

Coupon mad. Cowes: [Author?]. [191-].
A broadside. BM

The Empire's watchword not in vain. Cowes: [Author?].
[191-].
A broadside. BM

Join the R.F.C's. Cowes: [Author?]. [191-].
A broadside. BM

Lieut. Guynemer, Viking of the air. Cowes: Author.
[1916].
A broadside. BM

The munition worker. Cowes:[Author?]. [1916?].
A broadside. BM

The munitions brigade. Cowes: [Author?]. [191-].
A broadside. BM

The old home's calling me! Cowes:[Author?]. [191-].
A broadside. BM

The white ribbon of honour: don't forget the
Lusitania. [Cowes]: [Author?]. [191-].
A broadside. BM

Yankee boys. Cowes: [Author?]. [191-].
A broadside. BM

FRANCIS, Alfred Ernest F.
Shocks of corn: poems. Stockwell. 1917. 71p. por. MPL

FRANKAU, Gilbert (Commissioned with 9th East Surrey
Regiment in October 1914. Transferred to Royal Field
Artillery in March 1915. Fought at Loos, Ypres and the
Somme. Invalided out in February 1918, with rank
of captain)

The city of fear, and other poems. Chatto & Windus. 1917.
[viii], 48p. MPL

The guns: [poems]. Chatto & Windus. 1916. [viii], 35p. MPL

The judgement of Valhalla: [poems]. Chatto & Windus.
1918. viii, 52p. MPL

One of them: a novelette in verse. Hutchinson.
1918. 264p. BM

One of them: a novelette in verse. 2nd ed. Hutchinson.
1918. 264p. WPL

The other side, and other poems. New York: Knopf.
1918. [vi], 74p.   BPL

Poetical works. v. 1. 1901-1916. Chatto & Windus. 1923.
[viii], 244p. por.   BPL

Poetical works. v.2. 1916-1920. Chatto & Windus. 1923.
[vi], 220p.   BPL

Selected verses. Macdonald. 1943. 32p.   BM

A song of the guns. Boston: Houghton Mifflin. 1916.
[viii], [47]p.
    Printed on one side of leaf only.   BPL

See also (2) (11) (16) (17) (18) (19) (33) (47) (48)
(49) (50) (59) (72) (111) (121)

FRANKAU, Julia, (Frank Danby, pseud.) see (26)

FRASER, Alexander George, (Bugler of the Legion, pseud.)
(Medical Officer with the British Expeditionary Force)

Idylls of life and love: [poems]. Manchester: Sherratt
& Hughes. 1916. xii, 170p. por.   MPL

Idylls of life and love: [poems]. Second series. Manchester:
Sherratt & Hughes. 1919. xii, 132p. por.   MPL

Pour passer le temps: random rhymes; by "The Bugler
of the Legion". Manchester: Sherratt & Hughes. 1923. 61p.
    'Dedicated to my brother officers of the 57th General
Hospital, B.E.F.'   BM

FREELAND, Alonzo J. see (27) (29)

FREEMAN, John
Collected poems. Macmillan. 1928. x, 227p. por.
(by Dame Laura Knight).   MPL

Last poems. Ed. with an intro. by J.C. Squire. Macmillan.
1930. xxxiv, 185p.   MPL

Memories of childhood, and other poems. Selwyn &
Blount. 1919. 128p.   MPL

Poems new and old. Selwyn & Blount. 1920. 318p.   BPL

Presage of victory, and other poems of the time.
Selwyn & Blount. 1916. 30p.   MPL

Stone trees, and other poems. Selwyn & Blount.
1916. 60p.   MPL

See also (16) (17) (18) (19) (26) (33) (35) (36) (46)
(50) (80) (82) (83) (84) (96) (102) (104) (111) (112)
(114) (120) (121)

FREEMAN, R.M. see (99) (100) (101)

FRENCH, Cecil
Between sun and moon: poems. Favil P. 1922.
48p. il. (by the author).
    A limited ed. of 350 copies.   BM

With the years, [and other poems]. Richards P. 1927.
viii, 60p. il.
    A limited ed. of 500 copies.   BM

FRENCH, Fred H.
ANZAC!! (its meaning): Australian, New Zealand Army
Corps. 1916.
    A postcard.   BM

The robin's-son: Win Leefe Robinson — "the air bird".
[1916].
    A postcard.   BM

"Victory assured!" (Prime Minister at the Guildhall).
[1917].
    A postcard.   BM

FRENCH, R.W.
War echoes: [poems]. Bristol: Arrowsmith. 1916. 88p.   IWM

FRESTON, Hugh Reginald, ("Rex" Freston) (2nd
Lieutenant, Royal Berkshire Regiment. Killed in action in
France, 24th January 1916)

Collected poems. Oxford: Blackwell. 1916. viii, 154p.
por.   MPL

The quest of beauty, and other poems. Oxford: Blackwell.
1915. 52p.   BM

The quest of truth, and other poems. Oxford: Blackwell.
1916. 92p. por.   MPL

See also (19) (46) (47) (48) (49) (113) (131)

133

FRIEDLAENDER, V.H.
A friendship, and other poems. *Country Life.* 1919.
72p.   BM

Mirrors and angles: [poems]. *Country Life.* 1931. x, 78p.
il. (by Margaret Dobson).   BM

See also (19) (42)

FRIEDLANDER, Melville
Why war? Turner. [1916].
   A card.   BM

FRITH, James Cartwright
The verge of victory, and other verses written
during the war. Allen & Unwin. 1916. 45p.   BPL

FRY, Agnes
Winter sunshine, and other verses. Leominster:
Orphans' Printing P. [1929]. [ii], 63p.   BM

FULLER, George see (5)

FULLER-MAITLAND, Ella
To a nursing-sister, and other verses. Chiswick P.
1916. 12p.   EDR

A vision, and other verses, 1915-16. Chiswick P.
[1916]. 8p.   EDR

See also (31) (32)

FURSE, Margaret Cecilia
The gift: [poems]. Constable. 1919. vi, 42p.   BPL

FYSON, Geoffrey Ford (Was gassed and wounded)
Here comes she home: poems. Parthian P. 1949. 61p. por. EDR

Island lights: poems. Elkin Mathews. 1925. 40p.   BM

The survivors, and other poems. Erskine Macdonald.
1919. 60p.   BPL

See also (20)

G., A.
Verses. Printed Tiverton: Gregory. 1920. [ii], 26p.
   Publ. for the benefit of the Tiverton War Memorial Fund.   EDR

G., A.E. see GRANTHAM, Alexandra Ethelreda, (A.E.G.)

G.A.J.C. see (19)

G.A.M. see M., G.A.

G.B.C. see BOWEN-COLTHURST, Georgina de Bellasis,
(G.B.C.)

G.C. see (99) (100) (101)

G., E.
The song of the gay light cruisers, and other verses.
Weymouth: Sherren. [1918]. 28p.   BPL

G.E.R. see (24)

G.G.N. see NAPIER, George Glen, (G.G.N.)

G.H. see H., G.

G., J. see GEE, Jesse, (J.G.)

G., J. see GRENFELL, Hon. Julian, (J.G.)

G., J.G. see (110)

G.M.B. see BONUS, Gladys M., (G.M.B.)

G.M.L.R. see READE, Gerald M'Carthy Lewin,
(G.M.L.R.)

GADSDON, W.H. see (31) (32)

GALBRAITH, W. Campbell (Lieutenant-Colonel)
see (17) (18) (31) (32) (119)

GALES, Richard Lawson
Ballads and carols. Simpkin, Marshall. 1916. 69p.   MPL

Poems. Selected, with an intro., by Anthony C.
Deane. Brentano's. 1930. xvi, 66p. (Alcuin P.).
    Cover-title is "Selected poems".   BM

Skylark and swallow: [poems]. Erskine Macdonald.
1920. [viii], 78p.   BPL

See also (26)

135

GALLETLEY, Leonard
The call of the miles, [and other poems]. Erskine
Macdonald. 1916. 42p. (Little books of Georgian verse:
second series). BM

Evening on the Mawddach Estuary, [and other poems].
Benn. [1929]. 32p. (Shilling books of new poetry, 9). BM

GALLIENNE, Richard Le see LE GALLIENNE, Richard

GALSWORTHY, John
The bells of peace. Cambridge: Heffer. 1920. [4] p. BPL

Collected poems. Heinemann. 1934. xvi, 137p. por. MPL

The Inn of Tranquility, and other impressions;
[and], Poems. Heinemann. 1923. xviii, 386p. il.
(Works. Manaton ed., v. XV).
    A limited ed. of 530 copies. JRL

[Selected poems]. Benn. [1932]. 32p. (Augustan
books of poetry).
    Bibliog. (author's works) 1p. BM

Verses new and old. Heinemann. 1926. xii, 60p. por. MPL

See also (16) (17) (18) (59) (96) (121)

GANDY, A. Violet see (28)

GAPE, Herbert (Attached to 9th Middlesex Regiment and afterwards transferred to the Royal Defence Corps)

"Guarding the line", and 50 other original poems. Lewes:
Lewes P. 1918. 44p. BM

"Guarding the line", and original poems. [New] ed.
Lewes: Lewes P. 1919. [ii], 46p. BPL

Guarding the line, and other poems. Stockwell. [1920].
74p. BM

GARD, Lillian see (19) (26) (42)

GARDINER, Dorothy Kempe
Mary in the wood, with other lyric poems. Erskine
Macdonald. 1917. 48p. (Little books of Georgian
verse). BM
See also (52)

GARDNER, Herbert Coulston, Lord Burghclere
see (19) (113)

GARROD, Heathcote William
Epigrams: [poems]. Oxford: Blackwell. 1946. 31p.
  Includes poems first publ. in 1919.   BM
Worms and epitaphs: [poems]. Oxford: Blackwell. 1919.
[iv], 55p.   BPL

GARSTANG, Walter (2nd Lieutenant, West Yorkshire
Regiment)
The return to Oxford: a memorial lay. Oxford:
Blackwell. 1919. 14p.   BPL

GARSTIN, Crosbie (Joined 1st King Edward's Horse.
Commissioned in the field, 1915)
The ballad of the Royal Ann, [and other poems]. Heinemann.
1922. [x], 90p.   MPL
Vagabond verses. Sidgwick & Jackson. 1917. x, 70p.   MPL
See also (33) (87) (111) (112)

GARSTIN, Denis see (87)

GARSTIN, E.J. Langford (Lieutenant, 12th Battalion,
Middlesex Regiment. Served with British Expeditionary Force)
see (56) (57) (96)

GASKING, Samuel see (27) (29)

GATES, S. Barrington
Cargo: [poems]. Oxford: Blackwell. 1918. 68p.
("Adventurers all" series, XX).   BPL

GEDDES, D.
1914 and now. [Falkirk?]: Scottish Federation of
Discharged and Demobilised Sailors and Soldiers.
1918.
  A postcard.   BM

GEE, Jesse, (J.G.)
Braggart of Braggadocia; by J.G. [191-].
  A broadside.   BM

GEEVES, Harry J. (Private, Royal Army Service Corps)
"Shrapnel": poetic fragments on the present European War.
Printed Luton: *Luton News.* [1915?]. 20p. por.   BPL

"Shrapnel": twenty-five poems on the Great European
War. 2nd ed. Luton: Author. [1920?]. 28p. por.   BPL

GELL, William see (29)

GEORGE, Hugh Allen
The grand reveille. Birmingham: Author. 1917. [4]p.   BM

The shield of liberty. Birmingham: Author. 1919. [3]p.   BM

GERMAN Emperor's will. Printed Birmingham: Economic
Printing Co. [1914].
      A postcard.   BM

GERRARD, Edith C. see (28) (29)

GERY, Henry Theodore Wade- see WADE-GERY,
Henry Theodore

GIBBON, Monk (Served in Army)
For daws to peck at: [poems]. Gollancz. 1929. 96p.   BM

This insubstantial pageant: [poems]. Phoenix House.
1951. 190p.   MPL

GIBBS, J. Melton
A modern Horatius: an incident of the Battle on the
Aisne, September, 1914, with acknowledgements
to Macauley's [sic] "Lay of Ancient Rome": verses.
[Privately printed]. [1914]. [3]p.
      Proceeds to Red Cross Society, towards the
equipment of a motor ambulance.   BM

GIBSON, Amy Mends- see MENDS-GIBSON, Amy (64)

GIBSON, J.G. see (27)

GIBSON, M.E. see (28)

GIBSON, Reginald D.
Nothing but eyes to weep with, and other poems
of the war. Simpkin, Marshall, Hamilton, Kent.
1916. [vii], 43p.   BPL

GIBSON, Rowland Routledge (Lieutenant-Colonel, Royal Fusiliers)

The lamp of freedom: a ballad for the English-speaking peoples. Skeffington. [1919]. 32p.　　　　BPL

GIBSON, Sydney R. see (5)

GIBSON, Wilfrid Wilson (Served as a private on the Western Front)

Battle: [poems]. Elkin Mathews. 1915. 46p.　　　　MPL

Collected poems, 1905-1925. Macmillan. 1926.
xxiv, 792p. por.　　　　MPL

Friends: [poems]. Elkin Mathews. 1916. 38p.　　　　MPL

Fuel, [and other poems]. Macmillan. 1934. vi, 150p.　　　　MPL

Hazards, [and other poems]. Macmillan. 1930. xii, 99p.　　　　MPL

Home: a book of poems. Beaumont P. 1920. 43p.
　　A limited ed. of 295 copies.　　　　BPL

Livelihood: dramatic reveries: [poems]. Macmillan.
1917. xii, 135p.　　　　MPL

Neighbours: [poems]. Macmillan. 1920. xii, 170p.
　　Written in memory of friends killed in the war.　　　　MPL

[Selected poems]. Benn. [1931]. 32p. (Augustan books of poetry).
　　Bibliog. (author's works) 1p.　　　　BM

Sixty-three poems. Selected for use in schools and colleges by E.A. Parker, with a critical intro.
Macmillan. 1926. viii, 147p.　　　　MPL

Solway Ford, and other poems: a selection made by Charles Williams. Faber. 1945. 74p.　　　　MPL

Thoroughfares: [poems]. Elkin Mathews. 1914. 48p.　　　　MPL

Twenty-three selected poems. Athenaeum Literature Department. [1919]. 48p. (Westminster classics, II).　　　　BPL

Whin: [poems]. Macmillan. 1918. viii, 59p.　　　　MPL

See also (4) (12) (13) (14) (16) (17) (18) (19)
(31) (32) (33) (34) (35) (38) (39) (46) (47) (48)
(49) (50) (59) (60) (61) (80) (81) (94) (96) (105)
(111) (112) (121) (127)

GIBSON, William K.
For God, king, and fatherland: [poems]. Printed Belfast:
Brown. 1931. 62p.
  For private circulation, to commemorate British
Legion Cregagh and District Branch Armistice night
dinner, 11th November 1931.   BM

GILBERT, Bernard
Back to the land, [and other poems]. Oxford:
Blackwell. 1919. viii, 68p.
  Some in Lincolnshire dialect.   MPL

Gone to the war, and other poems in the Lincolnshire
dialect. Lincoln: Ruddock. 1915. 88p.   MPL

Rebel verses. Oxford: Blackwell. 1918. viii, 64p.
  Some in Lincolnshire dialect.   MPL

War workers, and other verses. With an intro. by Redfearn
Williamson. Erskine Macdonald. 1916. 68p.
  In Lincolnshire dialect.
  'Dedicated to my friends in the Ministry of Munitions' —
author's note.   MPL

See also (19)

GILHAM, J.
A Christmas card to the Kaiser. [1914].
  A postcard.   BM

The Kaiser's Christmas dinner. [1914].
  A postcard.   BM

GILL, Anthony Kirby see (65) (99) (100) (101)

GILL, Emily P.
War and victory: [poems]. Elliot Stock. 1918. 60p.   BPL

GILLESPIE, A.B. see (87) (96)

GILLESPIE, Violet
Poems of 1915, and other verses. Erskine Macdonald.
1915. 83p.   BM

See also (19) (52) (63) (65)

GILMORE, Alfred J.
Patriotic poems on the Great War, 1914-15-16.
Printed Birmingham: Victoria Printing Co. 1916. 46p.   BPL

GILSON, E.B.
Hilltops and song: [poems]. Erskine Macdonald.
1916. 68p.   MPL

GINGOLD, Hélène
Visions of mine head: [poems]. Stockwell. [1918].
84p. por.   BM

GIRDLESTONE, Frederick Stanley (D.S.O. Senior
Chaplain to 56th London Division)
The ponderin's of Peter, and other ballads. Stockwell.
[1922]. 64p.
   In Cockney dialect.   BM

GIRLING, Frank B. see (29)

GITTINGS, Robert
Matters of love and death: [poems]. Heinemann.
1968. vi, 72p.   MPL

GLADWELL, Miriam E.
In war-time: poems. Ramsgate: *Thanet Advertiser.*
[1916]. 66p. por.   IWM

GLASGOW, Geraldine Robertson- see **ROBERTSON-
GLASGOW, Geraldine**

GLAZEBROOK, Ethel
Lyrics of life and thought: [poems]. Macmillan.
1925. viii, 53p.   BM

GLEN-WORPLE, pseud. see **TOVEY, Duncan, (Glen-
Worple, pseud.)**

GOAD, Harold Elsdale see (99) (100) (101) (113)

GODDARD, Gregg see (19)

GODFREY, Walter Scott
At odd moments: [poems]. Grant Richards. 1917. 86p.   BPL

GOFF, Charles see (27)

GOLDEN, Grace Mary
Backgrounds: [poems]. Oxford: Blackwell. 1917. 24p.   BPL

GOLDING, Louis
Shepherd singing ragtime, and other poems.
Christophers. [1921]. 56p.   MPL

Sorrow of war: poems. Methuen. 1919. xii, 116p.   MPL

See also (60) (94) (104)

GOLDRING, Douglas
In the town: a book of London verses. Selwyn & Blount.
1916. 64p.   BM

Streets, and other verses. Selwyn & Blount. [1921].
108p. por.   MPL

GOLDRING, Maude
The country of the young: [poems]. Elkin Mathews.
1914. xii, 100p.   BM .

See also (30)

GOMERSALL, W.J. see (29)

GOMME, Laurence see (26)

GOODRICKE, Mary
The charge of the "London Scottish", Messines, October
31st, 1914: poem. Printed Hove: Cliftonville P. [1914].
(Soldiers' stories told in verse, III).
    A broadside.   BM

The charge of the Ninth Lancers, August 24th, 1914:
poem. Printed Hove: Cliftonville P. [1914]. (Soldiers'
stories told in verse, I).
    A broadside.   BM

God's bugle-call, Marne, September, 1914: poem.
Printed Hove: Cliftonville P. [1914]. (Soldiers' stories
told in verse, VI).
    A broadside.   BM

How "B11" raided the Dardanelles, December 13th, 1914:
poem. Printed Hove: Cliftonville P. [1915]. (Sailors' stories
told in verse, 1).
    A broadside.   BM

How the dispatch went through: an incident of the
retreat from Mons, Aug. 1914: poem. Printed Hove:
Cliftonville P. [1914]. (Soldiers' stories told in verse, II).
    A broadside.   BM

142

How the Ninth Lancers spiked the guns: a survivor's
tale, Aug. 1914: poem. Printed Hove: Cliftonville P.
[1914].
    A broadside.   BM

How the Victoria Cross was won: Private George Wilson,
V.C., Highland Light Infantry, Sept. 14th, 1914: poem.
Printed Hove: Cliftonville P. [1914]. (Soldiers' stories told
in verse, V).
    A broadside.   BM

"Three crosses", Ypres, November, 1914: poem. Printed
Hove: Cliftonville P. [1914]. (Soldiers' stories told in
verse, IV).
    A broadside.   BM

GORDON, Angela, pseud. see **SMITH, Alice Mary, (Angela
Gordon, pseud.)**

GORDON, Hampden
Fighting types: verses. Bodley Head. 1919. [69]p. il.
(by W. Otway Cannell).   BM

Our girls in wartime: rhymes. Bodley Head. [1917].
[60]p. col. il. (by Joyce Dennys).   BM

Rhymes of the red triangle [Young Men's Christian
Association]. Bodley Head. [1918]. [60]p. col. il.
(by Joyce Dennys).   MPL

GORDON, Hampden, & TINDALL, M.C.
Our hospital Anzac, British, Canadian: verses. 4th ed.
Bodley Head. [1916]. [60]p. col. il. (by Joyce Dennys).
    Cover-title is "Our hospital ABC".   BPL

[No copies of other eds traced].

GORDON-CANNING, Robert
Bodabil: or, the twilight of Granada, and other poems.
Hodgson. [1930?]. xii, 151p.   BM

Flashlights from afar: [poems]. Elkin Mathews. 1920.
viii, 72p.   IWM

A pagan shrine: [poems]. Erskine Macdonald. 1922. 78p.   BM

GORE, Reginald
Poems. Humphreys. 1916. [vi], 44p.   BM

GORE-BOOTH, Eva
Broken glory: [poems]. Dublin: Maunsel. 1918. 30p.   MPL

Poems. Complete ed., with, The inner life of a child;
and, Letters, and a biographical intro. by Esther Roper.
Longmans, Green. 1929. xx, 655p. por.   MPL

See also (60) (61) (112)

GORELL, Lord see BARNES, Ronald Gorell, Lord Gorell

GORST, Hester Gaskell see (29)

GOSSE, Sir Edmund see (113) (119) (120)

GOSSELIN, Gerald (Lieutenant, Royal West Kent Regiment)
Bits and pieces: grave and gay: [poems]. Hodder &
Stoughton. 1918. 36p.   MPL

GOULD, Gerald (Fellow of Merton College, Oxford,
1909-16)

Collected poems. Gollancz. 1929. 256p.   MPL

The happy tree, and other poems. Oxford: Blackwell.
1919. [vi], 51p.   BPL

[Selected poems]. Benn [1928?]. 32p. (Augustan books
of English poetry: second series, 20).
    Bibliog. (author's works) 1p.   BM

GOWER, Charles
Cordis flamma: [poems]. Watts. 1933. viii, 71p.   BPL

GOWER, Millicent, Duchess of Sutherland see (25) (26) (29)

GRAHAM, H.S. (Captain, Royal Engineers) see (58) (72)

GRAHAM, Muriel Elsie
Collected poems. Williams & Norgate. 1930. 133p.   BPL

Vibrations, [and other poems]. Erskine Macdonald.
1918. 62p.   MPL

See also (52)

GRAHAM, Nathan Percy (Commissioned in Royal Garrison
Artillery. Fought at Battles of Ypres, Passchendaele and
Messines. Sustained shell-shock. Invalided out)

144

Poems. Bristol: Arrowsmith. 1921. lxxiip. il., por.
(by Estella B. Graham). IWM

GRANT, Peggy see (28)

GRANT, Lady Sybil
The end of the day: [poems]. Hodder & Stoughton.
[1922]. 94p. BM

The end of the day: [poems]. 2nd ed. Hodder & Stoughton.
[1922?]. 94p. BPL

The unseen presence. Erskine Macdonald. 1918. [4] p.
Reprinted from *The Poetry Review*, March-April 1918. BPL

GRANTHAM, Alexandra Ethelreda, (A.E.G.)
Mater dolorosa; by A.E.G. Heinemann. 1915. 56p. por.
Dedicated to author's son, Hugo Frederick Grantham,
killed in the Gallipoli Peninsula, 28th June 1915. BPL

GRANTHAM, Sybil
Silent songs: [poems]. Gay & Hancock. 1915. viii, 120p. BPL

Through tears to triumph: [poems]. Gay & Hancock.
1914. viii, 120p. BM

GRANVILLE, Charles
A medley of humours: [poems]. Richmond: Parkshot P.
[1922]. 36p. BM

Poems of nature and war. Dryden Publ. Co. [1918]. 80p. BPL

Soldier moods: [poems]; by the author of "A soldier son".
Dryden Publ. Co. 1916. 31p. MPL

A soldier son, [and other poems]. Dryden Publ. Co. [1915].
[ii], 14p. IWM

GRATEFUL YORKSHIREMAN, pseud.
"The Norfolks": a rhyming record of the Regiment; by
a grateful Yorkshireman. Allen Taylor. 1917. [26] p. IWM

GRAVES, Alfred Perceval see (19) (26) (65)

GRAVES, Arnold F. (Served as a soldier at Mons)
The long retreat, and other doggerel. Murray. 1915.
viii, 50p. BPL

145

The turn of the tide: [poems]. Murray. 1916. viii, 46p.   BPL

See also (2)

GRAVES, Charles Larcom
Lauds and libels: [poems]. Sidgwick & Jackson.
1918. 96p.   MPL

New times and old rhymes. Oxford: Blackwell. 1921. 128p.   BPL

War's surprises, and other verses. Sidgwick & Jackson.
1917. viii, 128p.   MPL

See also (25)

GRAVES, Frank H.B. see (27) (29)

GRAVES, Philip Percival
The pursuit: Hauran, autumn 1918. Faber. 1930. 31p.
Dedicated 'To my old friends of the Arab Bureau'.   BPL

GRAVES, Robert (Captain, Royal Welch Fusiliers. Fought
at Loos and on the Somme, where he was seriously wounded)

Collected poems. Cassell. 1938. xxiv, 190p.   MPL

Collected poems (1914-1947). Cassell. 1948. xii, 240p.   MPL

Collected poems 1959. Cassell. 1959. xviii, 320p. por.   MPL

Collected poems. New York: Doubleday. 1961. 358p.   BM

Collected poems 1965. Cassell. 1965. xx, 450p.   MPL

Country sentiment: [poems]. Martin Secker. 1920.
81p.   MPL

Fairies and fusiliers: [poems]. Heinemann. 1917. x, 84p.
Dedicated to the Royal Welch Fusiliers.   MPL

Fairies and fusiliers: [poems]. New York: Knopf. 1919. 97p.
Dedicated to the Royal Welch Fusiliers.   BM

Goliath and David, [and other poems]. Chiswick P.
[1916]. 18p.
A limited ed. of 200 copies printed for private
circulation.   BM

No more ghosts: selected poems. Faber. 1940. 79p.   MPL

Over the brazier, [and other poems]. Poetry Bookshop.
1916. 32p.   MPL

146

Over the brazier, [and other poems]. New ed. Poetry
Bookshop. 1920. 32p.   BPL

Poems (1914-26). Heinemann. 1927. xii, 218p.
   Bibliog. (author's works) 1p.   MPL

Poems (1914-1927). Heinemann. 1927. xii, 230p.
   Bibliog. (author's works) 1p.
   A limited ed. of 115 copies.   BM

Poems, 1926-1930. Heinemann. 1931. [xii], 89p.   BM

Poems, 1938-1945. Cassell. 1946. [viii], 40p.   MPL

Poems, 1968-1970. Cassell. 1970. x, 90p.   MPL

Poems and satires, 1951. Cassell. 1951. xii, 40p.   MPL

Poems chosen by himself. New York: Doubleday. 1958.
xviii, 302p. (Doubleday anchor books).   BM

Poems selected by himself. Harmondsworth: Penguin
Books. 1957. 204p. (Penguin poets).   MPL

[Selected poems]. Benn. [1925]. 32p. (Augustan books
of modern poetry).
   Bibliog. (author's works) 1p.   BM

Welchman's hose: [poems]. Fleuron P. 1925.
x, 61p. il. (by Paul Nash).
   A limited ed. of 525 copies.   BM

See also (4) (17) (18) (33) (35) (50) (59) (66) (70)
(72) (80) (81) (89) (96) (102) (106) (111) (112) (127)
(128)

GRAY, Claribel
Albert on the Somme, and other poems. Stockwell.
[1920?]. 24p.   BPL

GRAY, Eleanor
Alfieri, and other poems. Kegan Paul, Trench, Trubner.
1927. [viii], 105p.   BM

The poet wanderer, and other poems. Daniel. 1932. 56p. BM

See also (28)

GRAY, J.A. (Lieutenant, 2nd Royal Berkshires. Killed
in action 4th March 1917)

A souvenir of the war: four poems. High Wycombe: Beal.
1917. 8p.   IWM

GREAVES, David W. see (65)

GREAVES, Robert Bond
Lays by the way. Erskine Macdonald. 1920. 72p.   BPL

GREEN, A.E.
Fragments: [poems]. Dublin: Talbot P.; Fisher
Unwin. 1920. 63p.   BPL

GREEN, Arthur Romney
Peace and war: a verse pamphlet. Poetry Bookshop.
1915. 12p.   MPL

GREEN, Bassett
The dawn, and other poems. Elliot Stock. 1918. 119p.   BPL

GREEN, Margaret Tyrrell- see TYRRELL-GREEN,
Margaret

GREENAWAY, Harvey J. (Driver, Royal Field Artillery)
see (5)

GREENLAND, George see (31) (32)

GREENWAY, J.D. (2nd Lieutenant, Rifle Brigade)
Moods: [poems]. Erskine Macdonald. 1917. 54p.   MPL

GREENWOOD, Frank Gardner see (27) (29)

GREGORY, Hugh
August 1914: a poem. Fifield. 1916. 29p.   BPL

GREGORY, Padraic
Complete collected ballads (1912-1932).
Burns, Oates & Washbourne. 1935. x, 166p. por.
    Cover-title is "Collected ballads".   MPL

GRENFELL, Hon. Gerald William (Lieutenant, Rifle
Brigade. Killed in action 30th July 1915) see (72) (131)

GRENFELL, Hon. Julian, (J.G.) (D.S.O., mentioned
twice in dispatches. Captain, Royal Dragoons.

148

Wounded 12th May 1915 near Ypres-Menin road.
Died 26th May)
Into battle; [by] J.G. [Medici Society]. [1915].

Purports to be a single copy of a broadside printed for
presentation to Lady Desborough, mother of the author.
BM copy was presented by the Medici Society, with a
covering letter. There are possibly other copies.   BM

See also (4) (16) (18) (19) (21) (31) (32) (33) (44)
(48) (49) (50) (51) (52) (55) (56) (57) (59) (63)
(70) (72) (80) (81) (88) (96) (102) (108) (111)
(112) (118) (119) (120) (121) (131)

GRENSIDE, Dorothy
Green ways: [poems]. Elkin Mathews. 1919. 56p.   BM
Open eyes: [poems]. Elkin Mathews. 1917. 48p. il.
(by Bessie Fyfe).   BM

**GRENVILLE, Alice Anne, Duchess of Buckingham
& Chandos**
The assault on Zeebrugge. Printed Women's Printing
Society. 1918. [4]p.   IWM

War-time ditties. Truslove & Hanson. 1917. 40p.   BPL

GREY, Thomas see (27)

GRICE, T. see (27)

GRIEVE, Christopher Murray, (Hugh MacDiarmid, pseud).
Collected poems. Oliver & Boyd. 1962. xiv, 498p. por.   MPL

Collected poems; by Hugh MacDiarmid. New York:
Macmillan. 1962. xiv, 498p.por.   BM

First hymn to Lenin, and other poems; by Hugh MacDiarmid.
With an introductory essay by 'AE' (George William
Russell). Unicorn P. 1931. [viii], 44p. por. (by 'AE').
A limited ed. of 500 copies.   BM

Second hymn to Lenin, and other poems; [by] Hugh
MacDiarmid. Nott. 1935. 77p. il.   MPL

Stony limits; and, Scots unbound, and other poems; by
Hugh MacDiarmid. Combined ed. Printed Edinburgh:
Castle Wynd Printers. 1956. viii, 156p.
Some poems in Scots dialect.   MPL

See also (71)

GRIFFITH, Llewelyn Wyn (Commissioned. Fought at the Somme)

The barren tree, and other poems. Cardiff: Penmark P. [1947]. 79p.

BM

See also (13) (14) (33)

GRIFFITH, Wyn see **GRIFFITH, Llewelyn Wyn**

GRIFFITHS, David A. see (27) (29)

GRIFFITHS, Nora see (19) (42)

GRINDLAY, I. (Queen Mary's Army Auxilliary Corps)
Ripples from the ranks of the Q.M.A.A.C.: [poems].
Erskine Macdonald. 1918. 63p.

MPL

GRINLING, Charles Herbert
Strays in war-time and before the war: [poems]. Woolwich:
Pioneer P. 1915. 24p. ("Pioneer" reprints, 1).

BPL

See also (29)

GROGAN, Walter E. see (40) (41)

GROVE, J. Hulbert see (29)

GROWLER, pseud. see (12)

GRUFFYDD, William John see (3)

GUNSTON, E. Leslie
The nymph, and other poems. Stockwell. [1917]. 55p.
    Dedicated to Wilfred Owen.

BM

GURDON, John see (52) (63)

GURNER, Ronald
War's echo: [poems]. Fisher Unwin. 1917. 80p.
    'Written, with very few exceptions, during spare
moments at the front' — preface.

MPL

See also (2)

GURNEY, Diana
The poppied dream: poems. Humphreys. 1921. [viii],
56p.

BM

150

Verses. Cayme P. 1926. 41p. il. BM

GURNEY, Dorothy Frances
A little book of quiet: [poems]. *Country Life.*
1915. 61p. BPL

See also (25)

GURNEY, Ivor (Private, Gloucestershire Regiment.
Suffered from shell-shock after his experiences on the
Somme)

Poems, principally selected from unpubl. manuscripts.
With a memoir by Edmund Blunden. Hutchinson.
1954. 104p. MPL

Severn and Somme: [poems]. Sidgwick & Jackson.
1917. 70p. MPL

War's embers, and other verses. Sidgwick & Jackson.
1919. 94p. MPL

See also (4) (50) (72) (80) (89) (96) (102) (105)

GUTHRIE, George C.
In days of peace, in times of war: [poems]. Ardrossan:
Guthrie. 1928. 107p. BPL

GUTHRIE, James
To the memory of Edward Thomas. Bognor Regis: Pear
Tree P. 1937. 34p. il.
    A limited ed. of 250 copies.
    Personal reminiscences of Edward Thomas. Includes
verses of lament by author. BM

GUY, E. see (28)

GWATKIN, Frank Trelawny Arthur Ashton, (John Paris, pseud.)
A Japanese Don Juan, and other poems; by John Paris.
Collins. 1926. 127p. BPL

GWILI, pseud. see JENKINS, John, (Gwili, pseud.)

GWYNN, Stephen (Captain, 6th Connaught Rangers.
Went to France in December 1915 with the 16th Irish
Division. Invalided home with trench fever in 1917.
Subsequently received the Legion of Honour)

Collected poems. Blackwood. 1923. vii, 110p.   MPL
See also (43)

GYLES, Althea see (30)

H.A. see (2) (24) (47) (48) (49)

H., A.P. see HERBERT, Sir Alan Patrick, (A.P.H.)

H.B. see (5)

H.C.F. see (51)

H. D'A. B. see (56) (57) (96)

H.D.C.P. see PEPLER, Hilary Douglas Clerk,
(H.D.C.P.)

H.E. see CUTHBERT, V.I., & E., H.

H.E.J. see J., H.E.

H., E.W. see HAMILTON, Eric William, (E.W.H.)

H.F.W. see (5)

H., G.
The Kaiser's favourite song: he is constantly singing it
upon the battlefield. Printed Birmingham: Economic
Printing Co. [1914].
    A postcard.   BM

What will the harvest be: dedicated to the Kaiser.
Printed Birmingham: Economic Printing Co.
[1914].
    A postcard.   BM

H., J.E. see HODGSON, J.E., (J.E.H.)

H., J.G.R. see HARVEY, John G. Russell, (J.G.R.H.)

H.J.M. see (24)

H., M. see (99) (100) (101)

H., M.B. see (24) (49)

H., M.C.D. see (12)

H., N.G. see (31) (32)

H., N.M. see (19)

H.P.H. see HAWKINS, Hester Periam, (H.P.H.)

H.S. see (63)

H., S.C. see HANNING, S.C., (S.C.H.)

H., S.L.
The Red Cross bloke. [191-]. [3]p.
   Sold in aid of the Pavilion Hospital, Lancashire
County Cricket Ground, Old Trafford.   MPL

H.S.S. see SMITH, Hugh Stewart, (H.S.S.)

H.T. see (5)

H.V.P. see (51)

H.W.B.W. see W., H.W.B.

HACKLEPLUME, pseud.
The Black Watch bouquet; and, The hackle and
plume, [and other poems]. Watts. 1919. [xii], 68p.
col. il.   BPL

My lady's garden, planted and grown: [poems]. Watts.
1921. xiv, 219p. col. il.
   Poems 'to give pleasure to all who have suffered, or
are suffering, through the war.'   BPL

HADGRAFT, Genevieve
The green copse: [poems]. Erskine Macdonald. 1927.
68p.   BM

See also (29)

HADLEY, A.H. (Private, South Wales Borderers.
Wounded at the Dardanelles, 6th August 1915)

Charles and Harry Bell. [Liverpool]. [1916].
A broadside. BM

The Kaiser's sin. [1916]. [3]p. BM

What is life? [1916].
A broadside. BM

"Worthy of his name". Hightown: Author.
[1916]. [2]p. BM

HALDANE, John Burdon Sanderson see (77)

HALIBURTON, Hugh, pseud. see **ROBERTSON, James Logie, (Hugh Haliburton, pseud.)**

HALL, David
If only! [and other poems]. Paisley: Gardner. 1920.
87p. PPL

HALL, Edgar Vine
In full flight, [and other poems]. Denny. 1921.
[x], 48p. BM

The last line, and other poems. Fisher Unwin. 1916.
112p. BPL

See also (11)

HALL, Harold Fielding- see **FIELDING-HALL, Harold**

HALL, Horace S. (7th Battalion, Essex Regiment)
A poem of the Great War; by an ex-soldier. Walthamstowe:
Author. 1920.
A broadside. BM

HALL, Isaac M.
The Kaiser and the Bradda (Bradwell) lads; composed and
recited by Isaac M. Hall at the War Concert, Bradwell, Oct.
17th, 1914. [Bradwell?]: [Author?]. 1914. [4]p.
In dialect verse. BM

The soldiers of the Peak. Bradwell: Author.
[1918?]. [4]p. BM

HALL, Martha see (28) (29)

HALL, Mary E. see (28) (29)

154

HALL, Stapleford
The Devil's visit to the Kaiser. Patriotic Publ. Co.
1914. [2]p.   BM

German dogs, and other poems. Savoy Publ. Co.
[1915]. 8p. il., col. il.   BM

Hell let loose by the fiend of Potsdam-nation: [poems].
Savoy Publ. Co. [1915]. 8p.   BM

The iron cross. 1914. [2]p.   BM

The Kaiser's doom, [and other poems]. Rea & Inchbould.
[1916]. [4]p. il.   BM

**HALL, Stephen King-, Lord King-Hall see KING-HALL,
Stephen, Lord King-Hall, (Etienne, pseud.)**

HALL, W. Robert
Towards freedom: poems. Chorley: Universal Publ. Co.
[1918]. [iv], 28p.   MPL

HALLIDAY, Wilfrid Joseph (Lieutenant, West Yorkshire
Regiment)

Refining fires: [poems]. Erskine Macdonald. 1917. 80p.   MPL

See also (56) (57) (58)

HALLOWES, Kenneth Knight
Poetical works. v.1. 1896-1934. Methuen. 1934. xvi,
212p. por.   BM

Songs of war and patriotism: [poems]. Longmans,
Green. 1919. xiv, 57p.   BPL

Songs of war and patriotism: [poems]. 2nd ed. Longmans,
Green. 1920. xiv, 62p.   EDR

HALSALL, Francis P. see (27)

HAMILTON, A.R. see (65)

HAMILTON, Cicely see (19) (26) (47) (48) (49)

HAMILTON, Clive, pseud. see **LEWIS, Clive Staples,
(Clive Hamilton, pseud.)**

HAMILTON, Eric William, (E.W.H.)
Gas attacks. Printed Hong Kong: *South China Morning Post.*
155

[1917]. [ii], 24p.
'Doggerel verse' — author. BM

The poets in camp, and other verses; by E.W.H.
Printed Hong Kong: Kelly & Walsh. [1918]. 35p. BM

HAMILTON, F. de C., & STEPHENS, Bessie May
The eternal quest: a scroll of empires: [poems].
Simpkin, Marshall, Hamilton, Kent. 1924. 125p. il. MPL

HAMILTON, Sir George Rostrevor, (George Rostrevor, pseud.)
Collected poems and epigrams. Heinemann. 1958.
356p. MPL

The making: poems. Heinemann. 1926. xii, 112p. MPL

Memoir, 1887-1937, and other poems. Heinemann.
1938. viii, 51p. BM

Stars and fishes, and other poems. Bodley Head.
1917. 90p. BPL

See also (12) (16) (31) (32) (46) (48) (49) (59)

HAMILTON, Helen
Hope, and other poems. Bristol: Horseshoe Publ. Co.
1924. 55p. BM

Napoo!: a book of war bêtes-noires: [poems]. Oxford:
Blackwell. 1918. [vi], 102p. MPL

The vision of Fra Bartolo: sonnets and lyrics. Aberdeen:
Wyllie. 1932. x, 80p. BM

HAMILTON, Sir Ian Standish Monteith
Now and then: [poems]. Methuen. 1926. xii, 122p. il.
(by William Strang). MPL

HAMILTON, Mary C.D. see (121)

HAMILTON, William Hamilton
Desire of the moth: [poems]. Selwyn & Blount. 1925.
[viii], 71p. BM

HAMILTON, William R. (South African, enlisted in United
Kingdom. Lieutenant, Machine Gun Corps. Killed in action,
1917)

Modern poems. Oxford: Blackwell. 1917. [viii], 60p.

'Written in barracks between parades' — preface. BPL

See also (131)

HAMMOND, C.R.A. see HAMMOND, Charles Edward,
& HAMMOND, C.R.A.

HAMMOND, Charles Edward, & HAMMOND, C.R.A.
Norge, and others, 1908-1921: [poems]. Ely: Tyndall.
1921. [iv], 79p. il., por. EDR

HAMMOND, Irene
The hundred steps, and other verses. St. Catherine P.
1916. 51p. BPL

War verses, and others. St. Catherine P. 1915. 30p. BPL

HAMUND, St. John
The rubáiyát of William the war lord. Grant Richards.
1915. [40]p. il.
    A parody of Edward Fitzgerald's version of the "Rubáiyát"
of Omar Khayyam. BPL

The war men-agerie. Grant Richards. 1915. [vi],
40p. il. (by Walter H. Cobb).
    Limerick-type verses. BM

HANBURY, Robert see (27)

HANCOCK, Clarice Laurence, (Clarice Laurence, pseud.)
"When the trumpet is calling", and other poems; by
Clarice Laurence. Amersham: Morland; Foyle. 1919.
[ii], 23p. BPL

HANCOCK, Sardius
King Alfred, and other poems. Philip Allan. 1919.
[vi], 188p. BM

HANNAH, Percy
Poems. Stockwell. [1920]. 44p. BPL

HANNING, S.C., (S.C.H.)
When heaven was dark: [poems]; by S.C.H. [Privately
printed]. [1918?]. 19p. MPL

HARDEN, Florence see (28) (29)

HARDING, William D. see (27) (29)

HARDY, Blanche C.
The buried city: poems, 1914-1920. Heath, Cranton.
[1920]. 43p.   BPL

HARDY, Thomas
And there was a great calm. Chiswick P. 1920. 8p.
  A limited ed. of 25 copies printed for Florence Emily
Hardy.   BM

Before marching and after: in memoriam F.W.G. Printed
[Shorter]. 1915. [8]p. por.
  A limited ed. of 25 copies.
  In memory of the author's cousin, Frank William George,
2nd Lieutenant, 5th Dorset Regiment, killed at Gallipoli,
21st August 1915.   BM

A call to national service; An appeal to America; Cry
of the homeless. Chiswick P. 1917. 8p.
  A limited ed. of 20 copies printed for Florence Emily
Hardy.   BM

A choice of poems. Made by Geoffrey Grigson. Macmillan.
1969. 95p. il. (by Glynn Thomas).   MPL

Chosen poems. School ed. Macmillan. 1929. xii, 277p.
  First publ. as "Selected poems" 1916.   BM

Collected poems. Macmillan. 1919. xx, 521p. por.
(Poetical works, v.1).
  Poetical works, v.2 is "The dynasts".   MPL

Collected poems. 2nd ed. Macmillan. 1923. xxiv, 676p.
por. (Poetical works, v.1).   BM

Collected poems. 3rd ed. Macmillan. 1928. xxviii, 809p.
por. (Poetical works, v.1).   BPL

Collected poems. 4th ed. Macmillan. 1930. xxxii, 917p.   MPL

England to Germany; The pity of it; I met a man;
A New Year's eve in war time. Chiswick P. 1917. 10p.
  A limited ed. of 25 copies printed for Florence Emily
Hardy.   BM

The fiddler's story; [and], A jingle on the times. Chiswick P.
1917. [ii], 8p.
  A limited ed. of 25 copies, printed for Florence Emily
Hardy.   BM

Human shows, far phantasies: songs, and trifles.
Macmillan. 1925. x, 280p.   BM

In time of "the breaking of nations". Printed Shorter.
1916. [4] p.
   A limited ed. of 25 copies printed by Clement Shorter for
private circulation.   BM

Late lyrics and earlier, with many other verses. Macmillan.
1922. xxiv, 288p.   BM

Moments of vision, and miscellaneous verses. Macmillan.
1917. xii, 256p.   MPL

Moments of vision, and miscellaneous verses. Pocket ed.
Macmillan. 1919. xii, 256p.   BPL

Satires of circumstances; Lyrics and reveries; with
Miscellaneous pieces. Macmillan. 1914. x, 230p.   BM

Satires of circumstances; Lyrics and reveries; [and]
Moments of vision, and miscellaneous verses. Macmillan.
1919. xvi, 410p. il. mp. (Wessex ed. Verse, v.4).   JRL

Selected poems. Macmillan. 1916. x, 214p. por.
(Golden treasury series).   MPL

Selected poems. Lee Warner. 1921. x, 147p. il.
(by William Nicholson), por. (Medici Society).
   One of the Riccardi P. books.   BM

Selected poems. Ed. with an intro. by G.M. Young.
Macmillan. 1940. xxxiv, 204p.   MPL

Selected poems. Ed. with an intro. by G.M. Young.
Macmillan. 1950. xxxiv, 204p. (Golden treasury
series).   BM

Selected poems. Ed. with an intro. by John Crewe
Ransom. New York: Macmillan. 1961. xxxvi, 134p.   BM

Selected poems. Ed. with an intro. and notes by P.N.
Furbank. Macmillan. 1964. xxii, 122p. mps. (English
classics — new series).
   Bibliog. 1p.   BM

Selected poems. Ed. with an intro. and notes by P.N.
Furbank. 2nd ed. Macmillan. 1966. xxii, 122p. mps.
(English classics — new series).
   Bibliog. 1p.   MPL

A selection of poems. Chosen and ed. by W.E. Williams. Harmondsworth: Penguin Books. 1960. 220p. (Penguin poets). BM

Song of the soldiers.Shorter. 1914. [8]p.facsim.
A limited ed. of 12 copies printed by Clement Shorter for private circulation. BM

Song of the soldiers. Printed Hove. 1915. [5]p.
Printed on one side of leaf only.
Reprinted from *The Times* of 9th September 1914. BM

Stories and poems. Ed. by N.V. Meeres. Macmillan. 1934. xx, 252p. por., mp. (Scholar's library). BM

Winter words, in various moods and metres: [poems]. Macmillan. 1928. xii, 203p. BM

See also (4) (16) (17) (18) (19) (22) (23) (25) (26) (30) (31) (32) (33) (37) (40) (41) (45) (46) (50) (53) (54) (66) (80) (81) (88) (96) (99) (100) (101) (105) (106) (107) (108) (109) (111) (112) (120) (121) (128)

HARDYMAN, Maitland (D.S.O., M.C. Lieutenant-Colonel, Somerset Light Infantry. Killed in action, 24th August 1918, aged 23)

A challenge: [poems]. Allen & Unwin. 1919. 32p. 1 por. MPL

HARE, Kenneth (2nd Lieutenant. Served in the trenches)
New poems. With an intro. by Douglas Jerrold. Benn. 1923. 102p. MPL

HARKER, W.E. (4th Battalion, Royal Sussex Regiment)
Sussex at peace and war: [poems]. Brighton: Southern Publ. Co. 1918. 44p. IWM

HARLEY, G.W. (Private, Lincolnshire Regiment)
Thoughts of home, written in the trenches. [191-].
A broadside. IWM

HA ROLLO, pseud. see ROLLO, Ha, pseud.

HARPER, Isabel Westcott see (18)

HARRIS, Dudley H. (Cadet, Tank Corps) see (58)

HARRIS, Mrs. Ellis
Some thoughts in verse. Stockwell. [1919]. 20p. il. BM

The Taj Mahal, and other poems. Stockwell. [1922]. 83p. BM

HARRISON, Ada May see (20)

HARRISON, Frank Inigo
"Killed in action": Philip George Holmes, 2/7th
Manchester Regiment, killed in action July 23rd, 1917, aged
19 years, interred at Coxyde Military Cemetry, near
Nieuport, Belgium. [1918]. [3]p. por. BM

HARRISON, L. Nield
War, 1914, and other poems. Erskine Macdonald. 1916.
48p. BPL

HART, Edith Tudor- see **TUDOR-HART, Edith**

HARTLEY, Annie see (28) (29)

HARTLEY, John see (27)

HARVEY, Frederick William (D.C.M. Lieutenant,
Gloucestershire Regiment. Was prisoner of war in several
camps, including Gutersloh and Crefeld)

Ducks, and other verses. Sidgwick & Jackson. 1919. 90p. BPL

Farewell: [poems]. Sidgwick & Jackson. 1921. 80p. BPL

Gloucestershire: a selection from the poems. Oliver
& Boyd. 1947. xiv, 77p. MPL

Gloucestershire friends: poems from a German prison
camp. Intro. by Bishop Frodsham. Sidgwick & Jackson.
1917. 72p. MPL

A Gloucestershire lad at home and abroad: [poems].
Sidgwick & Jackson. 1916. xvi, 64p. MPL

[Selected poems]. Benn. [1926]. 32p. (Augustan books
of modern poetry).
 Bibliog. (author's works) 1p. BM

September and other poems. Sidgwick & Jackson. 1925.
xii, 66p. BM

See also (17) (18) (33) (50) (59) (72) (80) (95) (96)
(111) (112)

HARVEY, George Rowntree (Royal Flying Corps)
Comrades! My comrades!: verses in war time. Aberdeen:
Milne & Stephen. 1919. 24p.   BPL

See also (56) (57)

HARVEY, James
Sussex, and other rhymes. Heath, Cranton. [1924]. 222p.   BM

HARVEY, John
Poems. Oxford: Blackwell. 1924. [viii], 48p.   BM

HARVEY, John G. Russell, (J.G.R.H.)
Tommy's ABC: [by] J.G.R.H. 3rd ed. Bristol: British
Red Cross Society. Bristol Branch. 1916. [32]p. col. il.
  Illustrations with rhyming captions.
  Title from cover.
  Dedicated to the soldiers of the king.
  'Every copy sold at 1/- will yield six-pence profit for the
funds of the Red Cross Society (Bristol Branch)'.   BM

[No copies of 1st and 2nd eds traced].

**HARVEY, John G. Russell, (J.G.R.H.), & THOMAS,
Charles, (C.T.)**
Allies in a Wilhelmsland, (with apologies to "Alice in
Wonderland"). Printed Bristol: Ford. 1914. [12]p. il.
  Sold for the benefit of the Belgian Refugees' Relief Fund.   IWM

Rhymes of the times, for war babies of all ages. Bristol.
1918.   Not seen

HARWOOD, H.C. see (19) (61) (73) (74)

HARWOOD, M.A.
Poems. Epworth P. 1939. 48p.   BM

HASELDEN, Percy
In the wake of the sword: [poems]. Erskine Macdonald.
1917. 48p.
                                                              MPL
See also (25) (119)

HASELER, Digby Bertram, (Spring Poet, pseud.)
(Lieutenant, King's Shropshire Light Infantry)
Patriotic and war rhymes. 2nd ed. Shrewsbury:
Shrewsbury Chronicle. [1915?]. [16]p.

Total profits for Prince of Wales Relief Fund.   MPL

[No copy of 1st ed. 1914 traced].

Verses from France to the family. Erskine Macdonald.
1918. 62p.   MPL

See also (20)

**HASELER, Digby Bertram, (Spring Poet, pseud.), &
D'ELBOUX, Raymond Herbert**
Home-made verses. Cambridge: Perkin Warbeck. 1921.
28p.   BPL

HASKINS, Minnie Louise
The gate of the year: [poems]. Hodder & Stoughton.
1940. 90p.   MPL

The potter, [and other poems]. Erskine Macdonald. 1918.
30p. (Little books of Georgian verse).   BPL

See also (47) (48) (49)

HASTINGS, Harold
The heavenly tavern, and other poems. Erskine Macdonald.
1917. 48p.   BPL

Myrrh, and other poems. Stockwell. [1919]. 32p.   BPL

**HAVENS, Allen, pseud. see ALLEN, Alice Maud,
(Allen Havens, pseud.)**

HAWARD, Edwin
The last rebellion [a verse play], and other poems.
Shanghai: *North-China Daily News & Herald*. 1935. 54p.   BM

HAWKINS, Hester Periam, (H.P.H.)
Verses; by H.P.H. Printed Bedford: Sidney P.
[1928?]. 67p. por.   IWM

HAWKSLEY, Julia M.A. see (113)

HAWORTH-BOOTH, Benjamin
Collected poems. Nisbet. 1931. xii, 228p.   BPL

HAWTHORN, F. Horderne
Abiding memories: [poems]. Rees. [1920]. xii, 164p.   BM

When her soul awoke, [and other poems]. Elliot Stock.
1916. [iv], 112p.   BM

HAY, Arthur C.
Ignatius: a lay of modern Russia. Aberdeen U.P.; Keith:
Mitchell. 1916. 16p.
   Based on an article entitled "Guerilla bands in the
Poliesie", which appeared in *The Scotsman,* 18th
December 1915.   BPL

HAY, Auriol
Images: [poems]. Oxford: Blackwell. 1920. [iv], 35p.   BM

HAY, John Macdougall
Their dead sons: [poems]. Erskine Macdonald. 1918.
88p.   BPL

HAY-DRUMMOND, [Florence Mary?], Countess Kinnoull
Our own men. Printed Perth: Hay. 1915. [4]p.
   Cover-title is "Patriotic verses".   BM

HAYDEN, Rosa Ayscoughe
The graves of France. [1919?].
   A card.
   Sold for the benefit of the Graves' Photographic Fund.   BPL

This for remembrance: war poems. Galashiels: Walker.
1917. 32p.
   Sold for the benefit of the Prisoners of War Fund.   BPL

See also (28)

HAYES, Herbert Edward Elton
Ultimate values, crudely expressed in verse: written on the
fields of France and Flanders, 1914-1918. Stockwell.
[1920]. 31p. il.   BPL

HAYWARD, Charles William
Policies in poems and parody. Daniel. 1916. 61p.   BPL

HAYWARD, Mrs, (Auntie Aitch, pseud.)
In memoriam of the "Empress of Ireland"; [by] Auntie
Aitch. Folkstone: Author. [191-]. il.
   A card.   BM

HEAD, Sir Henry
Destroyers, and other verses. Milford. 1919. 88p.   BPL

See also (17) (18)

HEARN, Ila
Dust, [and other poems]. Erskine Macdonald. 1918.
30p. (Little books of Georgian verse).   BPL

HEATH, Effie Margaret, (E.M. Holden, pseud.)
A peal of bells: [poems]; by E.M. Holden. Brighton:
Dolphin P. 1916. 16p.   BM

Veil and vista, [and other poems]. Guildford: Author.
1930. 24p.   BM

See also (52)

HEATHCOTE, I.B.
"You mothers of England!" and other poems. Stockwell.
[1918]. 24p.   BPL

HELSTON, John
Broken shade: poems. Chapman & Hall. 1922. 93p.   MPL

Lyric earth: [poems]. Allan. 1920. 30p.   MPL

See also (16) (17) (18) (63)

HEMPHREY, Malcolm (Corporal, Army Ordnance Corps.
Served with British Expeditionary Force in Nairobi,
East Africa) see (16) (52) (56) (57) (58)

HENDERSON, Bernard William
At Cambridge, and other poems. Methuen. 1919. viii,
48p.   BM

HENDERSON, Henry see (27) (29)

HENDERSON, J.T. (Gunner, Royal Garrison Artillery)
see (110)

HENDERSON, Mary H.J.
In war and peace: songs of a Scotswoman. Erskine Macdonald.
1918. 62p.   BPL

See also (64)

HENDERSON-BLAND, Robert (Captain, Gloucestershire
Regiment)

Actor-soldier-poet: [autobiography]. With an appreciation
by General Sir Hubert Gough. Heath, Cranton. 1939.
327p. il., por.
   Includes "A sheaf of poems".   MPL

HENKEL, Dorothy see (29)

HENLEY-WHITE, Lucie
'Twixt dusk and dawn: [poems]. Ed. by Chas. F. Forshaw.
Bradford: Institute of British Poetry. 1917. 94p.
(Parnassian series, 4).   BM

'Twixt dusk and dawn: [poems]. Ed. by Chas. F. Forshaw.
Elliot Stock. 1917. 94p. (Parnassian series, 4).   BPL

See also (28) (29)

HENNESLEY, Edmund (Sergeant, Honourable
Artillery Co.)

Erotia: [poems]. Erskine Macdonald. 1917. 62p.   MPL

Love songs of a soldier: [poems]. Nisbet. [1918]. 42p.   MPL

HENREY, R.S. see (5)

HENRY, Leigh
Poems. Glyn P. 1944. 62p. (Poet musician series).   EDR

HENSLOW, Thomas Geoffrey Wall (2nd Lieutenant, 4th
Battalion, Argyll & Sutherland Highlanders)

Early poems. *The Gentlewoman.* [1917]. 196p. il., por.   BM

Toasts: [poems]. Electrical P. 1920. 50p. por.   BM

War poems. Bridge. [1919]. [ii], 50p. il.
(by J. Dalgleish), por.   MPL

War poems. 2nd ed. Bridge. [1920]. [ii], 50p. il.
(by J. Dalgleish), por.   BM

HERBERT, Sir Alan Patrick (A.P.H.) (Lieutenant, Royal
Naval Division. Fought at Gallipoli and on the Somme.
Mentioned in dispatches. Wounded and invalided out)

The bomber gypsy, and other poems. Methuen.
xii, 84p.   BM

The bomber gipsy, and other poems. 2nd ed. Methuen.
1919. xii, 100p.   MPL

Half-hours at Helles: [poems]. Oxford: Blackwell.
1916. viii, 63p.   MPL

"The likes of they". St. George's P. 1918. [3] p.
    Cover-title is "The seamen's boycott song".   IWM

See also (2) (4) (32) (33) (51) (80) (87) (96) (111) (112)

HERBERT, Hon. Aubrey (Captain, Irish Guards. Served
as an interpreter) see (72)

HERBERTSON, Agnes Grozier
The quiet heart, and other poems. Elkin Mathews.
1919. 48p.   BPL

This is the hour: poems. Fortune P. [1942]. [ii], 30p.   BM

See also (63)

HERFORD, Charles Harold see (47) (48) (49)

HERSCHEL-CLARKE, May
Behind the firing line, and other poems of the war.
Erskine Macdonald. 1917. 16p. (Malory booklets).   BPL

HETHERINGTON, B.H.M. see (24) (31) (32) (63)

HEWETT, Osborne
Heroes from the seething fight! To our wounded soldiers.
[1914].
    A postcard.   BM

Right welcome, luckless Belgians! To the Belgian
refugees. [1914].
    A postcard.   BM

"A soldier of the king!": the recruit's message. [1914].
    A postcard.   BM

HEWITT, Ethel May see (17) (18)

HEWLETT, Maurice
A ballad of "The Gloster" and "The Goeben". Poetry
Bookshop. [1914]. [4] p. col. il.   MPL

Flowers in the grass (Wiltshire plainsong). Constable.
1920. viii, 71p.   MPL

Gai saber: tales and songs. Elkin Mathews. 1916. 176p.　　BPL

Singsongs of the war: [poems]. Poetry Bookshop.
1914. 24p.　　MPL

Singsongs of the war: [poems]. New ed. Poetry
Bookshop. 1914. 24p.　　IWM

The song of the plow [sic] : being the English
chronicle. Heinemann. 1916. xii, 244p.
　'A long, narrative poem on English history, written in
1913' — preface. "Envoy: New Domesday", p. 206-222,
written 1916.　　MPL

The village wife's lament. Martin Secker. 1918. 64p.　　MPL

See also (12) (16) (17) (18) (19) (26) (45) (47) (48)
(49) (82) (83) (84) (99) (100) (101) (121)

HEYWOOD, Raymond (Lieutenant, Devon Regiment)
The greater love: poems of remembrance. Elkin Mathews.
1919. 40p.　　MPL

The greater love: poems of remembrance. 2nd ed. Elkin
Mathews. 1919. 40p.　　BPL

Roses, pearls and tears: [poems]. Erskine Macdonald.
1918. 46p.　　MPL

HIBBS, Reginald R.
Ballade of night — murder done! Nurse Edith Cavell
condemned to death by German court martial and
executed at 2 a.m. Printed Fulham: Acme P. [1915].
　A postcard.　　BM

Denunciation: an English reply to the German "Hymn of
hate". Printed Fulham: Acme P. [191-].
　A broadside.　　BM

To V.C.'s and British soldiers and sailors all. Printed Fulham:
Acme P. 1915.
　A broadside.　　BM

HICKS, Edward Lee, Bishop of Lincoln see (99)
(100) (101)

HIGGS, Mary
An octave of song, a rainbow of hope: poems concerning
the Lord's Prayer, Easter, 1917. Headley. [1917]. 48p.　　MPL

HIGHET, Campbell
Berks 13, V.A.D. and the Great War. [191-].
  A broadside.   IWM

HILL, Brian (2nd Lieutenant, Durham Light Infantry)
Youth's heritage: [poems]. Erskine Macdonald.
[1917]. 45p.   MPL
See also (31) (32) (58) (96)

HILL, Harold George (2nd Lieutenant, Royal Garrison
Artillery)
Songs of the highlands and islands, and other poems.
Erskine Macdonald. 1920. 136p.
  'Dedicated to my brother Alfred S. Hill, M.A., B.Sc.,
2nd Lieutenant, R.G.A., who was killed in action on Nov.
20th 1917'.   BM

HILL, Martin see (58)

HILL, Norman (51st Highland Division)
The ballad of Beaumont-Hamel. Stockwell. [1927]. 16p.   IWM

HILL, Roland
Poems of peace. Ouseley. [1921]. 64p.   BPL

HILLCOAT, Arthur
"Woman, clever woman"; (recited by the Great Mac
(Major Mac), amid deafening applause at the London Halls).
Privately publ. [1918].
  A broadside.
  Refers to the nurses' work in the war.   BM

HIND, Emily see (28) (29)

HINTON, Archibald Campbell, (Spotter, pseud.)
The discharged soldier's appeal; by "The Spotter".
1917.
  A broadside.
  Reprinted from the *Hackney Spectator,* 7th May 1917.
  In aid of the Discharged Sailors and Soldiers Fund.   BM

HITCHINGS, J.L. see (11)

HOARE, Edward Godfrey (Lieutenant-Colonel, King's Own
Royal Lancaster Regiment)

Dawn, and other poems. Erskine Macdonald. [1920].
vi, 104p.   MPL

One hour together: [poems]. Muller. 1945. 80p.   BM

HOARE, Louise see (28)

HOBBS, L.J. see (29)

HOBDAY, Charles F. see (27)

HOBSON, John Collinson (Lieutenant, 116th Machine Gun
Company. Killed in action 31st July 1917).

Poems, etc. With biographical note. Memoir by John Murray.
Oxford: Blackwell. 1920. xvi, 87p. il., por.   IWM

HOCKLIFFE, Ernest see (90)

HOCKLIFFE, Marion see (90)

HODGE, Hugh Sydenham Vere
Half-way: [poems]. Selwyn & Blount. 1920. 76p.   IWM

HODGSON, J.E., (J.E.H.)
Lines on the Fleet: [poems] ; by J.E.H. Chiswick P.
1915. [4]p.   BM

HODGSON, Ralph
Collected poems. Macmillan. 1961. x, 186p. por.   MPL

Poems. Macmillan. 1917. viii, 70p.   MPL

HODGSON, William Noel, (Edward Melbourne, pseud.)
(M.C. Lieutenant, Devon Regiment. Killed in the Somme
advance, 1st July 1916. A contemporary of Rupert
Brooke at Cambridge)

Verse and prose in peace and war. Smith, Elder.
1916. 8, 100p. por.   MPL

Verse and prose in peace and war. 2nd ed. Smith, Elder.
1917. [8], 104p. por.   BPL

Verse and prose in peace and war. 3rd ed. Murray, 1917.
118p. por.   IWM

See also (2) (4) (16) (17) (18) (26) (31) (32) (33) (46)
(50) (51) (56) (57) (70) (72) (96) (111) (112) (131)

HOGBEN, John
The highway of Hades: war verses, with some prose.
Edinburgh: Olivier & Boyd. 1919. xii, 100p.
   A limited ed . of 200 copies.   BPL

See also (17) (18) (31) (32)

HOLBORN, Ian Bernard Stoughton
Children of fancy: poems. Edinburgh: Elliot.
1915. x, 256p.   MPL

HOLBROOKE, C.
The German eagle, with acknowledgments to Poe's
"Raven". [1916]. 4p.   BM

HOLDEN, E.M. pseud. see HEATH, Effie Margaret,
(E.M. Holden, pseud.)

HOLDSWORTH, Alfred see (27)

HOLDSWORTH, Edwin (27) (29)

HOLE, W.G. see (31) (32) (65)

HOLLAND, E.F. see (5)

HOLLAND, Madeleine (b. Rhodesia. Studied at Oxford)
Collected poems. Merton P. [1923]. [iv], 50p.   BM

HOLLAND, Michael J.
Verse. Boar's Head P. [1937?]. 45p.   BM

HOLMES, A.L.
The great sacrifice. [1918]. [4]p. por.
   Written by the mother of Private Philip George Holmes,
2/7th Manchester Regiment, killed in action July 23rd,
1917, at Petit Synthe, France.   BM

HOLMES, Alec, pseud. see SCOTT, Aimée Byng, Lady,
(Alec Holmes, pseud.)

HOLMES, Edmond Gore Alexander
Sonnets and poems: an anthology selected and arranged
by T.J. Cobden-Sanderson. Cobden-Sanderson. 1920.
127p.   BM

See also (40) (41) (107)

HOLMES, George S. (Private, 5th Royal Dublin Fusiliers)
Two Irish Fusiliers. Dublin: Author. [1917].
A postcard. BM

HOLMES, Ward
War verse and more verse. Stamford: Dolby. [1918].
56p. MPL

HOLMES, William Kersley (Captain)
Ballads of field and billet. Paisley: Gardner. 1915.
112p. BM

Ballads of field and billet. 4th ed. Paisley: Gardner.
1916. 112p. MPL

[No copies of 2nd and 3rd eds traced].

In the open: verses. Gowans & Gray. 1925. 67p. BM

The life I love: verses. Blackie. 1958. [viii], 56p. BM

More ballads of field and billet, and other verses.
Paisley: Gardner. 1915. 159p. MPL

See also (2) (17) (18) (87)

HOLTHUSEN, Mr.
"Ze[e]brugge", April 23rd, 1918: dedicated to Francis
Robert Butler, Royal Marine Light Infantry. Printed
Finsbury: Cooper, Scannell. 1918.
A broadside. BM

HONER, A.J. (Signaller, Scottish Rifles)
Brother o'mine. [1916].
A broadside. BM

HOOD, Arthur, pseud. see MENDS-GIBSON, Amy,
(Arthur Hood, pseud.) (64)

HOOD, Francis see (27) (29)

HOOKHAM, Paul
Two kings, and other poems. Oxford: Blackwell.
1917. x, 120p. BM

HOOLEY, Teresa
Collected poems. Cape. 1926. 128p. MPL

The singing heart: poems. Muller. 1944. 87p. WPL

Songs of all seasons: [poems]. Cape. 1927. 48p.   MPL

Songs of the open: [poems]. Cape. 1921. 64p.   BM

Twenty-nine lyrics: [poems]. Cape. 1924. 32p.   BM

HOPE, H.J. see (77)

HOPE, John Maurice Vaizey
"Greater love hath no man than this that a man lay down
his life for his friends": a poem which obtained the
Seatonian prize for 1917 in the University of Cambridge.
Cambridge: Deighton, Bell. 1917. [16]p.   BPL

HOPE, Richard (Lieutenant, Royal Navy. Served on H.M.S.
Dreadnought) see (31) (32)

HOPPER, Amy A. see (29)

HOPWOOD, Ronald Arthur (Rear-Admiral, Royal Navy)
The laws of the Navy, and other poems. Murray. 1951.
viii, 71p.   WPL

The new Navy, and other poems. Murray. 1919. 96p.   MPL

The old way, and other poems. Murray. 1916. 63p.   BPL

The secret of the ships, [and other poems]. Murray.
1918. 64p.   MPL

See also (72) (111) (112)

HORNE, Cyril Morton (Captain, 7th Battalion, King's Own
Scottish Borderers. Killed in action in France, 27th
January 1916)

Songs of the shrapnel shell, and other verse. New York:
Harper. 1918. [viii], 99p. por.   BPL

See also (131)

HORNE, John
Mid-way tracks: [poems]. Kirkintilloch: Macleod;
Edinburgh: Menzies. [1918]. [vii], 80p.
    Publ. on behalf of the Fund for Blinded Soldiers.   BPL

HORNUNG, Ernest William (Young Men's Christian
Association worker in France)

173

The ballad of Ensign Joy. New York: Dutton. 1917.
[vi], 55p. BPL

Wooden crosses. Nisbet. [1918]. 8p. il.
First printed in *The Times,* 20th July 1917. MPL

The young guard: [poems]. Constable. 1919. vi, 47p. MPL

HORSNELL, Horace
The horoscope: a biographical poem in three books with
an epilogue. Hamilton. 1934. [vi], 107p.
A limited ed. of 500 numbered copies. BPL

HORSPOOL, Amos, (Ora, pseud.)
William, Kaiser, by the grace of the —; by Ora. Duncon.
[1914]. [3]p. BM

HORSWILL, Lily
Duty's call. Liverpool: Author. 1914. [3]p. BM

HOTBLACK, N.
Stray thoughts, as originally entitled "A few poems".
3rd ed. collected and ed. by Frank A.Hotblack.
Stockwell. [1924]. 52p. BM

[No copies of 1st and 2nd eds traced].

HOUGHTON, Claude, pseud. see OLDFIELD, Claude
Houghton, (Claude Houghton, pseud.)

HOUSMAN, Alfred Edward.
Collected poems. Cape. 1939. 256p. BM

Collected poems. Harmondsworth: Penguin Books.
1956. 256p. (Penguin poets). MPL

Collected poems. New ed. Cape. 1960. 175p. MPL

Complete poems. Centennial ed. With an intro. by
Basil Davenport and a history of the text by Tom Burns
Haber. New York: Holt, Rinehart & Winston. 1959.
[vi], 268p. por. BM

Last poems. Grant Richards. 1922. 79p. MPL

Last poems. Chipping Camden: Alcuin P. 1929. 68p. BM

More poems. Cape. 1936. 71p. por. MPL

174

More poems. New York: Knopf. 1936. xiv, 74p. por.,
facsim.   BM

See also (4) (22) (33) (46) (80) (88) (105) (111) (112)

HOUSMAN, Laurence
Collected poems. Sidgwick & Jackson. 1937. xiv,
368p. por.   MPL

The heart of peace, and other poems. Heinemann. 1918.
vi, 140p.   MPL

The winners. Booklovers' Resort. [1915]. [3] p.   BM

See also (50) (60) (104) (120)

HOUSTON, Andrew see (27)

HOW to cook a German sausage. Printed Birmingham:
Economic Printing Co. [1914].
   A postcard.   BM

HOWARD, Geoffrey (Lieutenant, Royal Fusiliers)
see (16) (52) (56) (57) (96)

HOWCROFT, Jimmy (Sustained a fractured spine while
serving as an airman)

Looking on: [poems]. 2nd ed. Printed Margate:
Bobby. 1922. [ii], 30p. por.   BPL

[No copy of 1st ed. traced].

The songs of a broken airman: [poems]. With an intro.
by John O'London. Hodder & Stoughton. [1923]. xii,
42p. por.   MPL

HOWE, Frank W.
Many moods: a collection of poems. Amersham:
Morland; Foyle. 1919. 56p.   BPL

HOWITT, John Leslie Despard
In a cottage, and other verses. Heath, Cranton. [1917].
32p.   BPL

HUDSON, Herbert Kynaston see (27)

HUDSON, William
Wilhelm and his God, and other war sonnets. Drane.
[1917]. [iv], 91p.   BPL

HUEFFER, Ford Madox see FORD, Ford Madox,
(b. Hueffer)

HUGHES, Ellard
Poems. Bristol: Arrowsmith; Simpkin Marshall.
1917. 76p.   MPL

HULME, Thomas Ernest (Enlisted at the beginning of the
war and was sent to France in 1915. Killed near Nieuport,
Belgium, in 1917)

Complete poetical works, in Ezra Pound's Umbra:
early poems. Elkin Mathews. 1920. p.123-5.
  Six poems in all, the first five publ. 1912. The sixth
"Poem abbreviated from the conversation of Mr. T.E.H."
is 'abbreviation of some of his talk made when he came
home with his first wound in 1915' — Ezra Pound.
Entitled "Trenches: St. Eloi" in (105).   MPL

See also (105)

HUMBERT, pseud. see (121)

HUME, D.C.M. (Major, Royal Air Force)
Nursairy rimes [sic]. *Aeroplane;* General Publ. Co.
1919. 34p. il. (by H.R. Millar).   BPL

The HUN hunters: cautionary tales from the trenches.
Grant Richards. 1916. [48]p. il.
  Humorous verse.   BPL

HUNT, S.S., (Bernard Moore, pseud.) (Sergeant, Middlesex
Regiment)

A Cornish chorus, [and other poems]; by Bernard
Moore. Sidgwick & Jackson. 1919. 108p.
  Some poems in Cornish dialect.   BPL

A Cornish collection: [poems]; by Bernard Moore.
Daniel. 1933. 160p.   BM

Cornish corners, and other verses; by Bernard Moore.
Daniel. 1923. 62p.   BM

A Cornish haul, [and other poems]; by Bernard Moore.
Stockwell. [1917]. 67p.   BM

HUNTER, James see (27)

HUNTER, Jane C. see (29)

HUNTER, Stuart Kerr
Poems. Glasgow: Jackson, Wylie. 1932. xii, 100p.
   Printed for private circulation.   EDR

HURRELL, John Weymouth
Time and place: poems. Elliot Stock. 1921. 96p.   MPL

HURRY, Colin
The last illusion, and other poems. Constable. 1923.
viii, 46p.   BPL

Receding galaxy: a selection of verse, serious, light
and flippant. Nicol Books. 1964. 57p.   BM

HUSSEY, Dyneley (Lieutenant, 13th Battalion,
Lancashire Fusiliers)

Fleur de lys: poems of 1915. Erskine Macdonald. 1916.
54p. (Little books of Georgian verse: second series).   MPL

See also (16) (19) (50) (52) (56) (57) (63) (72) (111)

HUTCHEON, Lessel (Lieutenant, Royal Flying Corps)
see (72)

HUTCHINSON, Henry William (Lieutenant, Middlesex
Regiment. Killed on active service in France, 13th March
1917, aged 19) see (16) (18) (131)

HUTCHINSON, Winifred Margaret Lambart see (99) (100) (101)

HUTCHISON, Isobel Wylie
Lyrics from West Lothian: [poems]. Printed Edinburgh:
Pillans & Wilson. [1916?]. 61p.
   For the Red Cross Fund.   BPL

See also (91)

HUW MENAI, pseud. see WILLIAMS, Huw Menai,
(Huw Menai, pseud.)

HUXLEY, Mildred see (17) (18) (31) (32) (51) (55)
(63) (119)

HYMAN, Dave
The answer: an original summary. Printed Clapham:
Lamb. [191-].
  A broadside.   BM

Gratitude: an original recitation. Privately publ.
[1920?]. [3]p.   BM

HYSLOP, Matthew see (27)

I., D.L.
Sonnets after loss. Dent. 1919. [58]p.   BPL

IDRIS, pseud. see **MEE, Arthur, (Idris, pseud.)**

IFAN, Wil, pseud. see **EVANS, William, (Wil Ifan, pseud.)**

IMTARFA, I.C. see (72)

INCE, Richard Basil
The white roads, and other verses. Erskine Macdonald.
1916. 33p. (Little books of Georgian verse: second
series).   BPL

INDIGNANT ENGLISHMAN, pseud. see **DRANE, Henry J.,**
(Indignant Englishman, pseud.)

INGAMELLS, H. see (12) (51)

INGERSLEY, R.M., pseud. see **MARKLAND, Russell,**
(R.M. Ingersley, pseud.) (65)

INGLEDEW, Claire
Jean, and other poems. Daniel. 1926. 46p.   BPL

Poems. Stockwell. [1935]. 64p.   BM

ISRAELSTAM, Gerald
Idle moments: poems. Routledge. 1917. 63p.   BPL

J., A. see (72)

J.B. see **B., J.**

J.C. see **C., J.**

J.C.A. see A., J.C.

J.C.R. see RICHARDSON, James C., (J.C.R.)

J., E. see (51)

J.E.H. see HODGSON, J.E., (J.E.H.)

J.F. see F., J.

J.G. see GEE, Jesse, (J.G.)

J.G. see GRENFELL, Hon. Julian, (J.G.)

J.G.G. see (110)

J.G.R.H. see HARVEY, John G. Russell, (J.G.R.H.)

J., H.E.
When peace will come. South Shields: Jennings. 1917.
  A broadside.   BM

J.H.S. see (19)

J.H.S. see also SUMS, J.H., (J.H.S.)

J.L.Y. see YATES, John Lygo, (J.L.Y.)

J.M. see MALLETT, John, (J.M.)

J.M.S. see STANIFORTH, Joseph Morewood, (J.M.S.)

J. McD. see McDONALD, John, (J. McD.)

J.W.A. see (31) (32)

J.W.C. see CHEETHAM, John W., (J.W.C.)

JACKSON, Mrs. Clement Nugent
Harry, the hero of the Victoria Cross: the favourite
ballad; by Jim's wife. Skeffington. [1914]. 16p.   BM

Plain speaking; by Jim's wife: fourth series of the Gordon
League ballads. Skeffington. [1932]. 126p.   BM

JACOB, Violet
More songs of Angus and others: [poems]. *Country Life.*
1918. 60p.   BPL

Scottish poems. Edinburgh: Oliver & Boyd. 1944. 96p.
   In dialect.   BM

See also (19) (59) (71)

JACOBS, Muriel Leslie
War poems. [Croydon?]. [1916]. 8p.   BPL

JAMES, G. see (42)

JAMES, T.L.
The beginning and ending of the Great War, as foretold
in II Esdras Chap. II. Printed Dowlais: Cartwright. [191-].
   A broadside.   BM

JAMES, Sir William Milburne, (T.B.D., pseud.)
(Commander, Royal Navy)

Songs of the sailor men: [poems]; by T.B.D. Hodder &
Stoughton. 1916. 128p.   BPL

See also (72)

JAP, pseud. see (110)

JARVIS, Harold John (Corporal, Duke of Cornwall's Light
Infantry) see (58)

JEAVONS, William
The hope beyond, and other verse. Stockwell. [1918].
15p.   BPL

JENKINS, Arthur Lewis (Lieutenant, Royal Flying Corps.
Killed in aeroplane accident, 31st December 1917)

Forlorn adventurers, [and other poems]. Sidgwick &
Jackson. 1918. 58p.   MPL

See also (46) (72) (87) (131)

JENKINS, Elinor
Poems. Sidgwick & Jackson. 1915. 54p.   BPL

Poems, to which are now added, Last poems. Sidgwick

& Jackson. 1921. 80p. por.   BM

See also (19) (95) (112)

JENKINS, Ivor B., (Loot, pseud.)
Poems of peace and war. [1919]. 15p.   BPL

JENKINS, John, (Gwili, pseud.)
Poems; by Gwili. Printed Cardiff: Lewis. [1920].
xii, 104p.   BPL

JENKINSON, Editha see (28) (29) (52)

JENNINGS, Irene see (29)

JERRAM, Charles Samuel
War: verses. Elkin Mathews. 1915. 40p.   BPL

JERROLD, Ianthe (A schoolgirl in 1915)
The road of life, [and other poems]. Erskine Macdonald.
1915. 45p. (Little books of Georgian verse).   BM

JERVIS, H.
When the Kaiser will invade England. [1915].
    A postcard.   BM

JEWITT, Georgiana E.G. see (28) (29)

JOHN, Edmund (Artists Rifles. Discharged with heart disease,
1916. Died 28th February 1917)

Symphonie symbolique, [and other poems]. Erskine
Macdonald. 1919. 80p. il. (by Stella Langdale).   MPL

The wind in the temple: poems. Erskine Macdonald.
1915. 53p. (XXth century poetry series).   BM

See also (19)

JOHN, Mary St. see **ST. JOHN, Mary**

JOHNSON, Donald Fredric Goold (Lieutenant, Manchester
Regiment. Killed while leading an attack)

Poems. With a prefatory note by P. Giles. Cambridge
U.P. 1919. x, 80p. por.   MPL

See also (18) (20) (131)

181

JOHNSON, Lewis
Recreations in verse. Tynemouth: Priory P.
1928. [vi], 35p.
   A limited ed. of 120 copies.   MPL

JOHNSTON-SMITH, Frederick James
The union jack: what is it and what it means, with
twelve lyrics. Portsmouth: Holbrook. [1914]. 38p.
col. il.   BM

The union jack: what it is and what it means, with twelve
lyrics. [2nd] ed. Portsmouth: Barrell. [1915]. 30p.
col. il., por.   BM

Union jack lyrics, and a foreword concerning the
flag. Erskine Macdonald. 1914. 38p. col. il.   BPL

JOHNSTONE, Philip see (4) (13) (14) (33)

JONES, Arthur Glyn Prys- see **PRYS-JONES, Arthur Glyn**

JONES, Claud Whally
Verses. [1922]. 16p.
   Reprinted from *The Cologne Post*.   BPL

JONES, D.T. (2nd Lieutenant, Machine Gun Corps. Served
in France) see (58)

JONES, David (15th Royal Welch Fusiliers. Served in France
and Flanders, 1915-18)

In parenthesis: seinnyessit e gledyf ym penn mameu.
Faber. 1937. xxii, 226p. il., mp.
   A verse and prose account of 'some things I saw, felt, and
was part of ', December 1915 to July 1916.   BM

In parenthesis: seinnyessit e gledyf ym penn mameu.
Faber. 1963. xxii, 226p. (Faber paper covered editions).
   A verse and prose account of 'some things I saw, felt, and
was part of', December 1915 to July 1916.   MPL

See also (33)

JONES, Gwyn see (3)

JONES, Herbert
Finlay, [and other poems]. Bodley Head. 1923. [x], 126p.   BM

See also (16) (18) (99) (100) (101)

JONES, Leslie Phillips (29th Division, Royal Berkshire Regiment. Died of wounds, 7th June 1915, in the Dardanelles)

Youth: a song, [and other poems]. Printed [Nottingham]: [Vice]. [1915]. 51p. por.   BM

See also (73) (74)

JOSEPH, D.L.G. see (62)

JOURDAIN, Margaret see (99) (100) (101)

JOUSIFFE, Louise see (5)

JOYCE, Annette see (5)

JOYCE, James
Critical writings. Ed. by Ellsworth Mason and Richard Ellman. Faber. 1959. 288p.
  Includes "Dooleysprudence", written in 1916 when Joyce was in Switzerland 'offensively neutral'. The poem reflects his pacifist irritation with both sides in the war. Not included in his "Collected poems" 1936.   MPL

See also (50)

JULIUS, Stanley de Vere Alexander (Prisoner of war)
Poems. Longmans, Green. 1928. 132p.   BPL

Verse. Printed [Singapore]: Fraser & Neave. [1924].
[ii], 37p.   BM

JUNIOR SUB, pseud. see **STADDON, C. Eric, (Junior Sub. pseud.)**

JUNIUS REDIVIVUS, pseud.
The holy war; Diabolus; Extremes: generosity and avarice: a satire: [poems]. Bale & Danielsson. 1915. 16p.
  Proceeds to *The Times* Red Cross Fund.   BPL

Munitions: a poem. Birmingham: Cornish. 1915. 6p.   MPL

JUPP, A.S.
Consolation. Amersham: Morland. [1917].
  A card.   BM

War; [and], Until then: [poems]. Amersham: Morland.
[1917?].
A card.   BM

K., W.E. (Served in France with the British Expeditionary
Force) see (31) (32)

The **KAISER'S** dream. Printed Birmingham: Economic
Printing Co. [1916].
A postcard.   BM

Der **KAISER'S** end. [1915].
A postcard.   BM

The **KAISER'S** horoscope. [1914]. [3] p.
Cover-title is "The horoscope of his satanic majesty
Wilhelm II (would-be) emperor of the world".   BM

The **KAISER'S** mistake! "Made in Germany". [1914].
A postcard.   BM

The **KAISER'S** nightmare. Printed Birmingham:
Economic Printing Co. [1914].
A postcard.   BM

The **KAISER'S** request, addressed to Old Nick. Printed
Birmingham: Economic Printing Co. [1914].
A postcard.   BM

The **KAISER'S** telegram. Printed Birmingham: Economic
Printing Co. [1914].
A postcard.   BM

KAY, Thomas
She, or Nan: [poems]. Stockwell. [1930]. 32p.   BM

KEATE, Frederick B. see (29)

KEIGWIN, Richard Prescott
Lyrics for sport: [poems]. Oxford: Blackwell. 1917. 59p.   MPL

KELLETT, Arthur H. (Derbyshire Yeomanry) see (29)

KELLY, George see (63)

184

KEMBLE, Wilfrid
War lyrics and others. Privately publ. [1917?]. 25p.
  Title from cover.
  In aid of funds of the British Red Cross Hospital, Henley-
in-Arden.   IWM

KEMP, William Albert George (Royal Army Medical Corps)
From Kemmel Hill, and other poems. Stockwell. [1919].
23p.   BPL

KEMPE, Dorothy see **GARDINER, Dorothy Kempe**

KENDALL, Guy
The call, and other poems. Chapman & Hall. 1918. 64p.   BPL

The poet's flower, and other verses. Hull: Guild P. 1958.
16p.   BM

See also (17) (18)

KENDALL, Harriet see (64)

KENNEDY, Geoffrey Anketell Studdert, ("Woodbine Willie")
(M.C. Chaplain to the Forces)

Lighten our darkness: some less rough rhymes of a padre.
Hodder & Stoughton. [1925]. 93p.   BM

More rough rhymes of a padre. Hodder & Stoughton.
[1920]. 90p.   MPL

Peace rhymes of a padre. Hodder & Stoughton. [1920].
94p.   BPL

Rhymes. Hodder & Stoughton. 1929. 123p.   BPL

Rhymes. Hodder & Stoughton. 1940. 180p. (Black jacket
books).   BPL

Rough rhymes of a padre; by "Woodbine Willie". Hodder
& Stoughton. [1918]. 95p.   BM

Rough rhymes of a padre; by "Woodbine Willie". Toronto:
Hodder & Stoughton. 1918. 99p.   BM

Rough rhymes of a padre. 3rd ed. Hodder & Stoughton.
1918. 95p.   MPL

Rough rhymes of a padre; by "Woodbine Willie". 5th ed.
Hodder & Stoughton. 1918. 95p.   IWM

Rough rhymes of a padre. 6th ed. Hodder & Stoughton. 1918. 95p.   BPL

[No copies of 2nd and 4th eds traced].

Songs of faith and doubt: [poems]. Hodder & Stoughton. [1922]. 75p.   BM

The sorrows of God, and other poems. Hodder & Stoughton. [1921]. x, 91p.   MPL

The unutterable beauty: collected poetry. Hodder & Stoughton. 1927. viii, 182p.   MPL

The unutterable beauty: [poems]. 14th ed. Hodder & Stoughton. 1947. 180p.   MPL

The unutterable beauty: collected poetry. 16th ed. Hodder & Stoughton. 1961. 180p.   MPL

The unutterable beauty: [poems]. 17th ed. Hodder & Stoughton. 1964. 158p. 1 il.   BM

[No copies of other eds traced. Eds apparently almost identical].

See also (18)

KENNEDY, R.A.
The new benedicite, or songs of nations: the true answer to the "Hymn of hate". Knight. [1915]. 12p.   IWM

The new 'benedicite', or song of nations: the true answer to the "Hymn of hate". 2nd ed. Knight. [1915]. 12p.   BM

KENNET, Lord see **YOUNG, Edward Hilton, Lord Kennet**

KENNETH, F.E. see (63)

KENNEY, Jack (Private, 16th Service Battalion, Highland Light Infantry)

"After the war". [1915].
    A postcard.   BM

KENNY, Muriel
Khaki soldiers, and other poems for children. Cambridge: Heffer. 1915. 20p.   BM

KENWAY, Philip T.
Hits . . . and misses . . .: [poems]. Brenton. 1924. 52p.   BM

KENYON, Charles Frederick, (Gerald Cumberland, pseud.)
Rosalys, and other poems; by Gerald Cumberland. Grant
Richards. 1919. 48p.   MPL

See also (81)

KENYON, Ellen Blackwood
Found by the way: [poems]. Privately printed. 1919. 24p.   BM

KEOWN, Anna Gordon see (31) (32)

KERNAHAN, Coulson see (65) (99) (100) (101)

KERR, Mark (C.B., M.V.O. Rear-Admiral, Royal Navy)
Saga of the drifters, 1917: [poems]. British & Foreign
Sailors' Society. [1917]. [8]p. il.   BPL

KERR, R. Watson (2nd Lieutenant, Tank Corps)
War daubs: poems. Bodley Head. 1919. xii, 56p.   BPL

See also (58) (71)

KERR, Robert J.
The tulip tree, and other poems. 6th ed. Dublin:
Combridge. 1915. 328p.
    Earlier eds are pre-war.   BM

The tulip tree, and other poems. [New] ed. Dublin:
Author. 1918. 362p.   BM

See also (27)

KETTLE, Thomas Michael (Lieutenant, 9th Dublin
Fusiliers. Killed in action, 8th September 1916, at the
Battle of the Somme)

Poems and parodies. Duckworth. 1916. 86p. por.   MPL

Poems and parodies. Dublin: Talbot P. 1916. 86p. por.   EDR

See also (18) (33) (43) (70) (104) (131)

KEY, Helen
Broken music: [poems]. Elkin Mathews. 1916. 68p.
(Vigo cabinet series).   BM

KILLIN, Thomas
Holy Willie's prayer, (with apologies to the shade of Burns).
Printed [Glasgow?]. [1915?].

A broadside, reprinted from *The Evening Times*, 8th
December 1914.   IWM

KING, Baragwanath
Arthur, and others in Cornwall: [poems]. Erskine Macdonald.
1925. 106p.   BM

KING, George (2nd Lieutenant, 9th Suffolk Regiment.
Killed in action on the night of 12th February 1917, aged 20)
Verses: most written in France or Flanders during the
winters of 1915-1917. Printed Derby: Mawbey. [1918?]. 24p.   IWM

KING, K.M. see (62)

KING-HALL, Stephen, Lord King-Hall, (Etienne, pseud.)
(Lieutenant, Royal Navy)
Verses from the Grand Fleet; by Etienne. Erskine
Macdonald. 1917. 46p. (Malory booklets).   MPL

See also (2)

KINGSTON, William A. see (29)

KINNOULL, Countess see **HAY-DRUMMOND, [Florence
Mary?], Countess Kinnoull**

KIPLING, Rudyard
A choice of Kipling's verse; made by T.S. Eliot, with an
essay on Rudyard Kipling. Faber. 1941. 306p.   MPL

A choice of Kipling's verse; made by T.S. Eliot, with an
essay on Rudyard Kipling. Faber. 1963. 306p. (Faber
paper covered editions).   BM

A choice of songs from the verse of Rudyard Kipling.
Methuen. 1925. viii, 66p.   BM

The day of the dead. New York: Doubleday, Doran.
1930. [4]p.   BM

Early verse; The muse among the motors; Miscellaneous.
Macmillan. 1939. vii, 409p. (Sussex ed., v. XXXV).
    A limited ed. of 525 copies.   BM

Early verse; Verses 1889-1896; The five nations; The
years between; Poems from history; If—, and other
poems. Scribners. [1936]. Various paging. il. (Compact
ed., v.6).

Cover-title is "Poems". BM

For all we have and are. Methuen. [1914]. 3p. BPL

"The holy war". New York: Doubleday, Page. 1917. 6p. BM

The holy war. Methuen. [1918]. 4p. BM

The holy war. [New ed.]. Methuen. [1925]. 4p. il. BM

Hymn before action. Methuen. [1914]. [4]p. MPL

Hymn before action. [New ed.]. Methuen. [1915]. [8]p.
Illuminated in colour by Henrietta Wright. BM

The Irish Guards. 1918. [3]p.
A limited ed. of 100 numbered copies. BM

The Irish Guards. New York: Doubleday, Page. 1918. 6p.
A limited ed. of 70 copies. BM

Justice. New York: Doubleday, Page. 1918. [5]p. BM

Justice. Methuen. [1919]. 2p. BPL

A Kipling anthology: verse. Methuen. 1922. xvi, 202p.
Reissued several times, designated as new ed. MPL

A Kipling anthology. Ed. by W.G. Bebbington. Methuen.
1964. 152p. BM

London town, (November 11, 1918-1923). New York:
Doubleday, Page. 1923. 4p.
Kipling's bibliographer, J. McG. Stewart, states there was
an error on cover and title-page. Title should be "London
stone". BM

Mesopotamia. New York: Doubleday, Page. 1917. 6p. BM

The outlaws. 1914.
A broadside. BM

Poems, 1886-1929. v.3. Macmillan. 1929. xxii, 355p.
v. 1 and v. 2 do not contain war poetry. BM

Poems, 1886-1929. v. 3. New York: Doubleday, Doran.
1930. xxii, 354p.
A limited ed. of 537 copies.
v. 1 and v. 2 do not contain war poetry. BM

The scholars. New York: Doubleday, Page. 1919. 6p.
On 'the young naval officers whose education was
interrupted by the war and who are to be sent to various
colleges at Cambridge'. BM

Sea and Sussex from Rudyard Kipling's verse. With an introductory poem. Macmillan. 1926. xvi, 96p. col. il. (by Donald Maxwell).　BM

Selected poems. Methuen. 1931. viii, 64p.　BM

The seven seas; The five nations; The years between. Macmillan. 1938. xii, 467p. (Sussex ed., v. XXXIII).
　A limited ed. of 525 copies.　BM

So shall ye reap: poems for these days. Hodder & Stoughton. 1941. x, 149p.　WPL

The song of the lathes: (words of the tune hummed at her lathe by Mrs. L. Embsay, widow). New York: Doubleday, Page. 1918. 6p.　BM

Songs for youth, from Collected verse. Hodder & Stoughton. [1925?]. 243p. col. il. (by Leo Bates).　WPL

Songs from books; and, Later songs from books: [poems]. Macmillan. 1939. xii, 447p. (Sussex ed., v.XXXIV).
　A limited ed. of 525 copies.　BM

Songs of the sea from Rudyard Kipling's verse. Macmillan. 1927. xii, 100p. col. il. (by Donald Maxwell).　MPL

Twenty poems. Methuen. 1918. vi, 38p.
　Reissued several times, designated as new ed.　IWM

Twenty poems. Special limited ed. Methuen. 1937. vi, 40p.　BM

Verse. Inclusive ed. Hodder & Stoughton. 1919. 3v.　MPL

Verse, 1885-1918. Inclusive ed. New York: Doubleday, Page. 1919. xiv, 784p.　BM

Verse, 1885-1918. Inclusive ed. Hodder & Stoughton. [1921]. xiv, 787p.　BM

Verse, 1885-1918. Inclusive ed. New York: Doubleday, Page. 1923. xii, 787p.
　Smaller format then 1919 ed.　BM

Verse, 1885-1926. Inclusive ed. Hodder & Stoughton. 1927. xiv, 744p.　BM

Verse, 1885-1926. Inclusive ed. New York: Doubleday, Page. 1927. xviii, 862p.　BM

Verse, 1885-1932. Inclusive ed. Hodder & Stoughton. 1933. xviii, 821p. por.　WPL

Verse. Definitive ed. Hodder & Stoughton. 1940. xvi,
845p.   MPL

War writings; and, Poems. New York: Scribners. 1937.
x, 471p. por. (Writings in prose and verse, v. XXXIV).
   Described as 'Outward bound' ed. by BM.   BM

The years between: [poems]. Methuen. 1919. xiv, 160p.   MPL

The years between: [poems]. New York: Doubleday, Page.
1919. xiv, 154p.   BM

The years between; [and], The muse among the motors.
Macmillan. 1919. xvi, 137p. (Bombay ed., v. XXV).   BM

The years between; and, Parodies. New York: Doubleday,
Page. 1919. xviii, 153p. (Seven seas ed., v. XXV).   BM

The years between; and, Poems from history. De luxe
ed. Macmillan. 1919. xviii, 174p. (Writings in prose and
verse, v. XXX).   BM

The years between; and, Poems from history. New York:
Scribners. 1919. xii, 189p. il., por. (Writings in prose
and verse, v. XXVII).
   Described as 'Outward bound' ed. by BM.   BM

See also (4) (16) (18) (22) (33) (46) (48) (49)
(50) (54) (80) (82) (83) (84) (96) (99) (100)
(101) (108) (111) (112) (119) (120) (127)

KITCHIN, Clifford Henry Benn
Curtains: [poems]. Oxford: Blackwell. 1919. 24p.   BPL

Winged victory: [poems]. Oxford: Blackwell. [1921].
64p.   BPL

See also (77)

KITCHING, George
Poems and tales. Spalding: "Spalding Free Press"
Printing and Publ. Co. [1925]. 115p.   BM

Tales and poems. Derby: Author. 1915. [iv], 68p.   BM

See also (29)

KLAXON, pseud. see **BOWER, John Graham, (Klaxon
pseud).**

KLIP-KLIP, pseud. see **RUTTER, Owen, (Klip-Klip, pseud.)**

KNIGHT, Joseph
Died for his enemy: a true story, dedicated to the Lord
Bishop of Hereford: verses. Hereford: *Hereford Journal.*
1916. [3] p.   BM

KNIGHT-ADKIN, James Harry (Captain, Royal Gloucestershire
Regiment. Joined 4th Battalion, City of Bristol, on first day of
war. Sent to the front in March 1915. Was wounded at
Ploegsteert the same year) see (2) (12) (16) (17) (18) (24)
(31) (32) (51) (121)

KNIPPER, pseud. see **SCARR, C.W.**, (Knipper, pseud.),
(Merlin, pseud.)

KNOBLOCK, Edward (b. New York, became British citizen in
1916)

Cot 5: [poems]. Methuen. 1917. viii, 36p.   MPL

Cot 5; and, Rose Vaquette of La Boiselle: [poems].
2nd ed. Methuen. 1918. viii, 44p.   BPL

KNOTT, E. see (5)

KNOX, Edmund George Valpy, (Evoe, pseud.)
(Served in the Lincolnshire Regiment. Was wounded
at Passchendaele)

Poems of impudence. 1926. 128p. il. (by Arthur Watts).   MPL
See also (25)

KNOX, Kathleen see (17) (18)

KORONGO, pseud. see **BROOKE, Brian**, (Korongo, pseud.)

L., A.B. see (63)

L., C.
Avenae: [poems]. Rugby: Over. 1917. [vi], 32p.   MPL

L., D.O. see **LUMLEY, Sir Dudley Owen**, (D.O.L.)

L., F. see **LUDLOW, Frederick**, (F.L.)

L.L., pseud. see **BARRY, John Arthur**, (L.L., pseud.)

L., O.E. see LINDSAY, Olive E., (Leo, pseud), (O.E.L.)

L., P.H.B. see LYON, Percy Hugh Beverley, (P.H.B.L.)

L., R.W.
The fighters and workers. 1917.
  A postcard.   BM

L., S.L. see LLOYD, S.L., (S.L.L.)

L., W. see (31) (32)

L.W. see WHITMELL, Lucy, (L.W.) (17) (18)
(24) (31) (32) (47) (48) (49) (51) (96) (111) (112)
(119)

L., W.B., pseud. see BRANTOM, William, (W.B. L., pseud.)

LA MARE, Walter De see DE LA MARE, Walter

LAMBE, J.F.
Real British grit. Roach. [1916].
  A broadside.   BM

War forced upon us: a poem. Printed Williams &
Strahan. 1914. [4]p.   BM

LAMBERT, Frederick Arthur Heygate, (Frederick
Arthur, pseud.)
Unseen horizons: [poems]; by Frederick Arthur. Elkin
Mathews. 1915. 152p.   BPL

LAMBERT, R.S. see (73) (74)

LANE, Joseph J.
The Belgians' song of hope. Bradford: Thornton & Pearson.
[1915?].
  A broadside.   BPL

Beyond the veil: a war poem. 2nd ed. 1918. 15p.   BPL

[No copy of 1st ed. traced].

The old year and the new, 1916-1917: [poems]. [1917?].
3p.   BPL

Peace at last: hymn written immediately after hearing the

church bells proclaim the welcome news, June 28th, 1919.
Brighouse. [1919].
> A card.   BPL

Peace with honour, 1918. 1917.
> A card.   BPL

Sonnet to the Kaiser. [191-].
> A card.   BPL

The supreme sacrifice. 1918. 3p.   BPL

Victory then peace. [191-]. 3p.   BPL

See also (27) (29)

LANG, H.G. (Major)
Simple lyrics. Elkin Mathews. 1917. 32p.   BPL

LANGBRIDGE, Frederick see (65)

LANYON, Harold C.
Hasty verses of a "temporary". Amersham: Morland.
1920. 33p.   BPL

LARKIN, M.F.
Our ally the war horse. [1916].
> A broadside.
> Proceeds in aid of the Blue Cross Fund.   BM

See also (5)

The **LAST** will and testament of H.I.M. the Kaiser,
Wilhelm the Second (and the last): [poems]. Compact
Publicity Co. [1914]. [2]p.
> Cover-title is "The last will of the past Will, to wit:—
> The Kaiser".   BM

LATYMER, Lord see COUTTS, Francis, Lord Latymer

LAURENCE, Clarice, pseud. see HANCOCK, Clarice
Laurence, (Clarice Laurence, pseud).

LAW, Alice see (64)

LAW, R.H. see (31) (32)

LAWFORD, Peggie
Verses. Cheltenham: Looker-On Printing Co.
194

[1914]. [20]p.
Cover-title is "Inasmuch". BM

LAWRENCE, David Herbert
Bay: a book of poems. Beaumont P. 1919. [ii], 45p.
A limited ed. of 200 copies. BM

Collected poems. v.1. Rhyming poems. Martin Secker.
1928. 232p. JRL

Collected poems. v.2. Unrhyming poems. Martin Secker.
1928. 304p. JRL

Collected poems. Martin Secker. 1932. vi, 530p. por. BM

Complete poems. Heinemann. 1957. 3v. (Phoenix edition). MPL

Complete poems. Collected and ed. with an intro. and
notes by Vivian de Sola Pinto and Warren Roberts. Heinemann.
1964. 2v. por., facsim. MPL

Last poems. Ed. with an intro. by Richard Aldington.
Martin Secker. 1933. 182p. BM

Look! We have come through! :[poems]. Chatto &
Windus. 1917. 164p. BM

Look! We have come through! A cycle of love poems.
With an intro. by Frieda Lawrence. Marazion: Ark P. 1958.
112p. il. (by Michael Adam), facsim. MPL

Look! We have come through!: [poems]. With an intro.
by Frieda Lawrence. 2nd ed. [Marazion]: Ark P. 1959.
112p. il. (by Michael Adam), facsim. BM

Pansies: poems. Martin Secker. 1929. 156p. MPL

Poems. Pocket ed. Heinemann. 1939. 2v. MPL

Selected poems. Chosen with an intro. by W.E. Williams.
Harmondsworth: Penguin Books. 1950. 160p. BM

Selected poems. Ed. with an intro. by Keith Sagar.
Harmondsworth: Penguin Books. 1972. 269p. (Penguin
poets). MPL

See also (50) (80) (97)

LAWRENCE, Lucy see (5) (29)

LAWRENCE, Margery
Fourteen to forty-eight: a diary in verse. Hale. [1950].

84p. por. MPL

See also (64)

LAWSON, James Burnett (Lieutenant, 2nd Cameronians,
Scottish Rifles)

A Cameronian officer: a memoir of Lieutenant James
Burnett Lawson, Second Cameronians (Scottish Rifles);
by James Burnett Lawson, [senior]. Glasgow: Smith. 1921.
viii, 255p.
    Includes Lieutenant Lawson's "Early contributions
in prose and verse". BPL

LAXTON, E. Faulkner
Memories of the Great War, 1914-1918, and other
selected poems. Ipswich: Smith. 1929. 43p. BPL

LAYTON, Margaret E.
Poetic pilgrimage, 1929-1939. [Gateshead]: Northumberland
P. [1940]. 253p. BM

LEADER, Edward (Coldstream Guards)
Songs of life and love: [poems]. Stockwell. 1918. 47p. BPL

LE BERT, George A. see (29)

LEDWIDGE, Francis (Lance-Corporal, 5th Battalion, Royal
Inniskilling Fusiliers. Killed in action in Flanders, 31st July
1917)

Complete poems. With intros by Lord Dunsany. Jenkins.
1919. 291p. por. MPL

Complete poems. With intros by Lord Dunsany. [2nd ed.].
Jenkins. 1944. 191p. por. BM

Complete poems. With intros by Lord Dunsany. 3rd ed.
Jenkins. 1955. 112p. MPL

Last songs: [poems]. Jenkins. 1918. 80p. MPL

Songs of peace: [poems]. With an intro. by Lord Dunsany.
Jenkins. 1917. 110p. QUB

See also (17) (18) (24) (33) (50) (59) (96) (102)
(111) (112) (131)

LEE, Edmund see (27)

LEE, Joseph (Lance-Corporal, Black Watch. Became 2nd
Lieutenant, King's Royal Rifles)

Ballads of battle. Murray. 1916. x, 102p.
il. (by the author).   MPL

Work-a-day warriors: [poems]. Murray. 1917. xii,
111p. il. (by the author).   MPL

See also (2) (12) (16) (17) (18) (31) (32) (59) (66)
(71) (72) (110) (121)

LEE, Sydney
H.M.S. Mystery "Q": her first battle with the "U": (the
ballad of the "V.C." ship). Pain. [1919]. 4p.
    For the benefit of the Dover Patrol memorial.   BM

"Well done, Vindictive!": the great raid on Zeebrugge on
the eve of St. George's day, 1918: poem. Pain. [1918]. [4] p.
    For the benefit of King George's Fund for Sailors.   BPL

LEES, Beatrice Adelaide see (63)

LEESON, Margaret M.
Thank you, from the wives, mothers and sweethearts of
our Empire, to our brave boys who are fighting and who have
fought for us. Wounded Soldiers' Entertainment Association.
1916.
    A broadside.   BM

LEFEVRE, L.A.
A garden by the sea, and other poems. Humphreys.
1921. [viii], 130p.   BPL

LEFTWICH, Joseph (Was a friend of Isaac Rosenberg)
Along the years: poems, 1911-1937. Anscombe. 1937.
148p. por.
    A limited ed. of 750 copies.   BPL

Years following after: poems. Clarke. 1959. 157p. por.   BM

LE GALLIENNE, Richard
The silk-hat soldier, and other poems. Bodley Head.
1915. 48p.   MPL

War. New York: Woolly Whale P. 1929. [10] p.
    A limited ed. of 50 copies.
    Printed for private distribution in commemoration of

Armistice Day, 1929.   BM

See also (17) (18) (47) (48) (49)

LEGGE, Diana see (5)

LEHMANN, Rudolf Chambers
The vagabond, and other poems from *Punch*. Bodley
Head. 1918. x, 115p.   MPL

LEIGH, Mabel see (42)

LEIGH, Margaret
Songs from Tani's garden: [poems]. Stockwell. [1923].
16p.   BM

See also (76)

LEO, pseud. see LINDSAY, Olive E., (Leo, pseud.),
(O.E.L.)

LEONARD, G.H. see (26) (47) (48) (49)

LESLIE, Sir Shane (Cousin of Sir Winston Churchill)
Jutland: a fragment of epic. Benn. 1930. xviii, 203p.   MPL

Poems and ballads. Benn. 1933. [131]p.   MPL

Verses in peace and war. Burns & Oates. 1916. 30p. por.   MPL

LESLIE, Tiny see (28)

LETTS, Winifred M.
Hallow-e'en, and other poems of the war. Smith, Elder. 1916.
viii, 101p.   MPL

The spires of Oxford, and other poems. New York:
Dutton. 1917. x, 105p.   BPL

See also (12) (16) (17) (18) (19) (24) (31) (32) (45)
(47) (48) (49) (51) (59) (99) (100) (101) (104) (119)
(120) (121)

LEVEY, Sivori, (Wounded Warrior, pseud.) (Lieutenant,
West Yorkshire Regiment. Lost a leg).

The air-raiders (twelve German Gothas). Levey. [1919].
    A broadside.   BM

Britishers! And other songs for the war. Levey. 1914.
33p. (Sixpenny booklets of verse, 8).   BM

Flanders to Fowey: ("Ypres" and "après"): verses of
active service, hospital, and convalescence; by a Wounded
Warrior. Levey. 1917. 22p.   BM

"Forty-seven thousand!": (the black book). Levey. 1918.
8p.   BM

The fourth of July (Inter-dependence Day; London, 1918).
Levey. [1918].
   A broadside.   BM

A "Foyen" picture book; by a Wounded Warrior. Fountain
Publ. Co. [1918]. 20p. il., por.
   Poems and photographs illustrating the author's convalescence.   BM

H.M.S. "Vindictive" (the raid on the Mole): a story of the
old Nelson touch. Levey. 1918. 8p. por.   BM

Ils ne passeront pas! (They shall not pass!). Levey. [191-].
   A broadside.   BM

Jazzer's joy!: song souvenirs: [poems]. Fountain Publ.
Co. 1919. [iv], [47]p. il., por.
   Printed on one side of leaf only.   MPL

Keep cool. Levey. 1918. [4]p. (Dramatic series, 6).   BM

Nennette and Rintintin (Paris, 1918), dedicated to the
American Red Cross. Levey. 1918. 8p.
   Nennette and Rintintin were 1 inch high doll mascots.   BM

Radadou, the baby. Fountain Publ. Co. [191-].
   A broadside.
   Radadou was the "offspring" of the mascots, Nennette
and Rintintin.   BPL

The Roehampton reciter: dramatic and humorous
selections. Popular ed. Fountain Publ. Co. [1918]. [viii],
44p. por.   MPL

Roehampton rhymes: selections from a Dover House
revue. Levey. 1918. 24p.   BM

The rose of France (July 14th, 1918): the French
national fete, July 14 — the anniversary of the fall of the
Bastille, 1789. Levey. [1918].
   A broadside.   BM

The second thousand million! (national war bonds): an

up-to-date patriotic recitation. Fountain Publ. Co. 1918.
8p. por.   BM

When the Sammies marched through London (May 11th,
1918). Levey. [1918?].
A broadside.   BM

LEWIN, Richard S.S. Ross- see **ROSS-LEWIN, Richard
S.S., & ROSS-LEWIN, Robert O'D.**

LEWIN, Robert O'D. Ross- *see* **ROSS-LEWIN, Richard
S.S., & ROSS-LEWIN, Robert O'D.**

LEWIS, Agnes Smith
Margaret Atheling, and other poems. Williams & Norgate.
1917. xiv, 384p.   MPL

**LEWIS, Clive Staples, (Clive Hamilton, pseud.) (Lieutenant,
Somerset Light Infantry)**

Spirits in bondage: a cycle of lyrics; by Clive Hamilton.
Heinemann. 1919. 107p.   MPL

LEWIS, Dorothy Perch
Poems. Printed Cardiff: Lewis. [1919]. x, 58p. por.   EDR

LEWIS, Frank C. (Flight Sub-Lieutenant, Royal Naval Air
Service. Killed in air battle, 21st August 1917) see (58)
(131)

LEWIS, George F.
"How Bill Adams settled the Germans": [a monologue]
featured by Wilfrid Liddiatt in the entertainments of the
"Beaux Belles" concert party, etc. [191-]. [2]p. por.   BM

LEWIS, S. (Sergeant, 12th Battalion, West Yorkshire Regiment)
The Battle of Mons: poem. [1914]. [2]p.   BM

LEY, Leonard
A pot pourri of verse. Printed Cambridge: Heffer.
1929. [vi], 68p.   IWM

LIGHT, John
Two gardens, and other poems. Printed Guildford:
Billing. 1921. viii, 69p.   BM

LILL, James see (27)

LILLEY, Harold see (65)

LILLINGSTON, Kathleen M.E. see PAYNE, David Bruce,
& LILLINGSTON, Kathleen M.E.

LINCOLN, Bishop of see HICKS, Edward Lee, Bishop
of Lincoln (99) (100) (101)

LINDGREN, Louis
"Day of honour". 1915.
   A postcard.   BM

The "national" post card. 1917.   BM

LINDSAY, Alison see (31) (32)

LINDSAY, Olive E., (Leo, pseud.), (O.E.L.)
A little rhyme: [poems]. Printed Edinburgh: Oliver &
Boyd. 1925. 126p.   BM

Salutations: [poems]; by Leo. Stockwell. [1919]. 24p.   BPL

"Something": [poems]; by O.E.L. Edinburgh: Oliver &
Boyd. 1916. viii, 87p.
   A limited ed. of 250 copies.   BM

LINEKAR, T.J. see (27)

LING, Ellen
Cloth o'gold for every-day wear, [and other poems].
Printed Blackburn: *The Times* Printing Works. 1931. 95p.   MPL

A prayer for peace, and other poems. Ilfracombe:
Stockwell. 1947. 15p.   BM

See also (28)

LION, Leon M., pseud. see BURDETT, Osbert, (Leon M.
Lion, pseud.)

LISTER, Edward
Memories of 1915, and other verses. Elliot Stock. 1922.
31p.   BPL

War time and peace: sonnets. Stockwell. [1923?]. 56p.   IWM

LITTLE, T.W. see (27)

LITTLEJOHN, W.H. (Company Sergeant-Major, Middlesex Regiment. Killed in action 10th April 1917) see (72) (131)

LLEWELLYN, D.
The noble slackers: appeal to the young manhood of our nation. Swansea: [Author]. [1916]. [3] p.   BM

LLOYD, E. Hardress (Lieutenant, London Irish Rifles) see (56) (57)

LLOYD, S.L., (S.L.L.)
Midnight musings: some impressions in verse of a practical idealist; by S.L.L. Elliot Stock. 1919. 95p.   BPL

LLOYD, William
Morn mist, and other poems. Ilfracombe: Stockwell. 1960. 38p.   BM

Poems. Ingpen & Grant. 1928. viii, 54p.   BPL

LLOYD, William Henry
Humours of the cotton trade: poems; by an old boy. Printed Liverpool: *Daily Post* Printers. 1918. 91p.   MPL

See also (27)

LOCKE, Arthur
The sons of old Surrey. Woking: [Author]. [1918].
  A broadside.
  'Originally written for friends and neighbours in Woking who had lost relatives in the war'.   BM

LOCOCK, Brynhild see (5)

LODGE, J.W.
The Prussian Junker's toast: "Der Tag": an acrostic. [Sowerby Bridge] : *Hebden Bridge Times*. 1915. 12p. il., por.   BPL

LODGE, John (Lieutenant, Bedfordshire Regiment) see (52) (56) (57)

See also **COCK, Albert Arthur, & LODGE, John**

LOMAX, Alfred
The two flags. Blackpool: [Author]. [1915].
  A broadside.   BM

LONG, A.J.
A famous war poem. Redruth: Author. [1919?]. [4]p. por.   BM

Ships. Redruth: Author. 1920. [4]p.   BM

Think of mother. Redruth: Author. 1921. [4]p. por.   BM

The town clock: a peace and war time rhyme. Printed
Redruth: Prater. [1919]. [4]p. por.   BM

LONG, C.
Khaki pal. [1916].
  A postcard.   BM

LONG, Walter
The world's war, and other poems. Headley. [1917]. 90p.   BPL

LONGFIELD, Lewis see (27)

LONGRIGG, George H. see (27)

LOOKER, Samuel Joseph
Green branches: selected poems. Billericay: Grey Walls P.
1941. 48p.   BM

Slaves of the sword, and other verses. Daniel. 1917. 16p.   BPL

Songs of the wayside: lyrics and sonnets, 1913-1916.
Manchester: National Labour P. 1916. [ii], 54p.   BPL

Thorns and sweet briar: love and nature lyrics with
satires. Printed Hackney: Keeley. [1917]. 60p.   BPL

Thorns and sweet briar: [poems]. Stoke Newington:
Author. [1922]. 60p.   BM

LOOT, pseud. see **JENKINS, Ivor B., (Loot, pseud.)**

LOVELACE, W.C.
The Battle of Jutland: a historical poem. Printed
Maidment. 1919. 12p.   BPL

LOVELIT flames, [and other poems]. Stockwell. [1918]. 24p.   BM

LOVETT, J.E.
Patriotic and other verses. Stockwell. [1917]. 32p.   BM

LOW, Mildred
Victory or death, and other poems. Scott. [1916]. 22p.   BPL

LOW, Sidney see (32)

LOWE, Francis J.
"Victory": "The day is done"; [and], Nobody works in
Britain (with apologies to the Bolsheviks): [poems]. [1919].
[2] p.   BM

LOYSON, Paul Hyacinthe see (31) (32)

LUCAS, Edward Verrall
The debt. Methuen. [1914]. 4p.
    Reprinted from *The Sphere.*   MPL

Guillaumism: two aspects. Shorter. [1914]. [8] p.
    A limited ed. of 25 copies printed by Clement Shorter
for private circulation.
    Comprises "The debt" and and an essay "Allies to the end".   BM

Swollen-headed William: painful stories and funny
pictures after the German. Methuen. 1914. [iv], [40] p.
il. (by George Morrow).
    Printed on one side of leaf only.
    Humorous verses.   BM

Swollen-headed William: painful stories and funny
pictures after the German! 5th ed. Methuen. 1914.
[iv], 40p. il. (by George Morrow).
    Printed on one side of leaf only.
    Humorous verses.   BPL

[No copies of 2nd, 3rd and 4th eds traced].

See also (16) (18) (19) (59)

LUDLOW, Frederick, (F.L.)
Gallant sons of Warwickshire!: a tribute to the Royal
Warwicks; by F.L. [West Bromwich]: [Author]. [1917].
    A broadside.   BM

The sinking of "Shark": a ballad of the Fleet. [Privately
printed]. [1918?]. [4] p.   BM

LUFKIN, Marie C. see (28) (29)

LULHAM, Habberton
Kettle-songs: [poems]. Hove: Combridges. 1922. x, 88p. BM

The other side of silence, [and other poems]. Simpkin,
Marshall, Hamilton, Kent. 1915. x, 116p. MPL

The other side of silence, [and other poems]. 2nd ed.
Simpkin, Marshall, Hamilton, Kent. 1915. x, 116p. BPL

See also (19) (31) (32) (47) (48) (49) (51) (65) (119)

LUMLEY, Sir Dudley Owen, (D.O.L.) (Lieutenant)
Songs of a subaltern: [poems]; by D.O.L. Chapman &
Hall. 1915. 28p. MPL

Songs of a subaltern: [poems]; by D.O.L. 2nd ed.
Chapman & Hall. 1915. 28p. IWM

See also (2)

The **"LUSITANIA".** 1915. il.
 A postcard. BM

LUSTED, Charles
The garden of heaven, and other poems. Werner Laurie.
[1926]. 144p. BM

LUXMOORE, F.V.
Beyond the sunset: reflections in verse. Elkin Mathews &
Marrot. 1929. 76p. BM

LYND, Sylvia
Collected poems. Macmillan. 1945. viii, 100p. MPL

The goldfinches: [poems]. Cobden-Sanderson. 1920. 48p. BM

[Selected poems]. Benn. [1928?]. 32p. (Augustan books
of English poetry).
 Bibliog. (author's works) 1p. BM

LYNNFORD-SMITH, Arthur
Harvest home: [poems]. Oxford: Blackwell. 1936.
[vi], 86p. MPL

LYON, Lilian Bowes
Bright feather fading, [and other poems]. Cape. 1936. 60p. BM

Collected poems. Introduced by C. Day Lewis. Cape.
1948. 191p.   MPL

See also (26)

LYON, Percy Hugh Beverley, (P.H.B.L.) (M.C. Captain,
Durham Light Infantry. Served in France and Flanders.
Was wounded in 1918)

France: the Newdigate prize poem, 1919. Oxford:
Blackwell. 1919. 16p.   BPL

[Selected poems]. Benn. [1931]. 32p. (Augustan books
of poetry).
    Bibliog. (author's works) 1p.   IWM

Songs of youth and war: [poems]. Erskine Macdonald.
1918. 64p.   MPL

Turn fortune: [poems]. Constable. 1923. viii, 82p.   MPL

See also (24) (31) (32) (33) (58) (59) (111)
(112) (120)

LYON, Walter Scott Stuart (Lieutenant, Royal Scots)
Easter at Ypres, 1915, and other poems. Glasgow:
Maclehose. 1916. viii, 140p. por.   MPL

See also (2) (17) (18)

LYONS, James (Private, Royal Army Medical Corps)
Gleam o' pearls: [poems]. Manchester: Cornish. 1919.
xxxiv, 169p. por.   MPL

Sons of the Empire, and other poems. Manchester:
Heywood. 1916. ii, [62] p.   MPL

LYSAGHT, Sidney Royse see (49)

M., A. see (5)

M.A.C., pseud. see **MACFADYEN, Dugald, (M.A.C.,
pseud.)**

M.B. see (63)

M.B.H. see (24) (49)

M.C.D.H. see (12)

M., D.
The soldier's farewell to his mother. Printed Birmingham:
Economic Printing Co. [1914].
    A postcard.   BM

M., D.S. see **MacCOLL, Dugald Sutherland, (D.S.M.)**

M.E.B. see **BONUS, M.E., (M.E.B.)**

M., E.H.W. see **MEYERSTEIN, Edward Harry William,
(E.H.W.M.)**

M., F.W.
The railway guard and the German: (a true story). [1914].
    A postcard.   BM

M., G.A.
Six satires: [poems]. Poetry Bookshop. [1919]. 16p.   BPL

M.H. see (99) (100) (101)

M., H.J. see (24)

M., J. see **MALLETT, John, (J.M.)**

M.J.D. see **D., M.J. & D., W.G.M.**

M., N.D. (9th Battalion, Border Regiment)
Salvos from Salonika: [poems]; [by] N.D.M. Printed
Carlisle: Thurnam. [1919]. 32p.
    Dedicated to the 9th Battalion (Pioneers), Border Regiment.   BM

M., O. see (19)

M., P.S. see (31) (32)

M.R.C.S. see **S., M.R.C.**

M.S. see **SYMINGTON, M., (M.S.)**

MA wee bit cot. [191-]. il.
    A broadside.   BM

MACARTNEY, Carlile Aylmer (Lieutenant, Hampshire
Regiment)

Poems. [Ed. by S. Gertrude Ford]. Erskine Macdonald.
1915. 40p.   MPL

See also (2) (32)

MACAULAY, Dame Rose
[Selected poems]. Benn. [1927]. 32p. (Augustan books
of English poetry: second series, 6).
   Bibliog. (author's works) 1p.   BM

Three days: [poems]. Constable. 1919. 68p.   BPL

See also (94) (111) (112)

MACBRIDE, Mackenzie
For those we love at home, and other war songs and
ballads. Newberry & Pickering. [1916]. 29p.
   Includes one poem in Scottish dialect and one poem in
Gaelic.   BPL

McC., A.E.
Thoughts in verse through many years. [1920?]. [ii], 30p.   EDR

McCARTHY, Justin Huntly see (26) (99) (100) (101)

McCLYMONT, Murray (2nd Lieutenant. Served with
British Expeditionary Force in France) see (32) (58)

MacCOLL, Dugald Sutherland, (D.S.M.) (Keeper of the
Wallace Collection, 1911-24)

Another neutral; by D.S.M. Glasgow: Maclehose. 1915. 9p.   BPL

Bull, and other war verses. Constable. 1919. xxii, 84p.   BPL

A German peace, flyting [sic] to Herr Houston Stewart
Chamberlain. Glasgow: Maclehose. 1916. [ii], 7p.   BPL

A merry new ballad of Dr. Woodrow Wilson, President of
the United States in [sic] America. Glasgow: Maclehose.
1915. 32p. il.
   Printed for private circulation.   BM

See also (33)

McCORQUODALE, J.C.
In divers moods: with a motive: a book of verses. Dundee:
Lotus P. 1917. 64p.

A limited ed. of 1,000 copies.
Proceeds to prisoners of war.   BPL

McCURDY, Edward (Worked in the Ministry of Pensions)
The lays of a limpet. Selwyn & Blount. 1920. 64p.   BPL

McCURRY, Samuel S.
The ballads of Ballytumulty. With an intro. in the Ulster
dialect by Sir John Byers. Belfast: Carswell. [1922?]. 138p.   IWM

John the Hermit, and other poems. Stockwell. [1922].
xvi, 132p.   BM

See also (27)

McD., J. see **McDONALD, John, (J. McD.)**

MacDIARMID, Hugh, pseud. see **GRIEVE, Christopher
Murray, (Hugh MacDiarmid, pseud.)**

McDONALD, Hon. Donald (Lived in Antigua, West Indies)
Songs of an islander: [poems]. Elliot Stock. 1918. 48p.   BPL

McDONALD, John, (J. McD.) (Stationmaster at Dalguise,
Perthshire)

Honour "Jack". Dalguise: Author. [191-]. il.
    A postcard.   IWM

Let's not forget them. Dalguise: [Author]. [191-].
    A broadside.
    In aid of Dunkeld and Little Dunkeld Parish Memorial Fund. IWM

Lines in memory of my clansmen who fell in the Great War,
1914-1918. Dalguise: Author. 1919.
    A broadside.   IWM

Poems; by a roadside stationmaster. Printed Coupar
Angus: Culross. 1918. 104p. il., por.
    Some in Scots dialect.   IWM

Poems; by a roadside stationmaster. [New ed.]. Printed
Coupar Angus: Culross. 1925. 76p. il., por.
    This is a different collection from previous entry.   BM

Remember our prisoners; [by] J. McD. Dalguise: Author.
[191-]. il.
    A postcard.   IWM

MACDONALD, Mary Adair see (31) (32) (42)

MACDONALD, Nina
War-time nursery rhymes, dedicated to D.O.R.A.
[Defence of the Realm Act]. Forewords by George R. Sims.
Routledge. [1918]. 80p. il. (by L. Grace Arnold & Irene B.
Arnold).   BM

MACDONALD, William
When England goes to war. Westminster P. 1914. 8p.   MPL

McDONNELL, Randal
Songs of seaside places, and other verses. Dublin:
Talbot P. 1932. 101p.   BM

A study in starlight, and other poems. Dundalk:
Dundalgan P. 1919. 136p. por.   BM

See also (27)

MACDOUGALL, Ian
Brothers: a dramatic sketch; and, Two selected poems.
Stockwell. [1922]. 16p.   BPL

McEWEN, Sir John Helias Finnie (Prisoner of war)
Poems. Elkin Mathews. 1920. 52p.   BM

There is a valley, [and other poems]. Printed Edinburgh:
Cousland. 1950. 106p.   BM

See also (20)

MACFADYEN, Dugald, (M.A.C., pseud.) (Young Men's
Christian Association worker)
The call: verses; by M.A.C. Marshall. [1916]. 35p.
    Bibliog. (author's works) 1p.   MPL

MACFIE, Ronald Campbell
Collected poems. Grant Richards; Humphrey Toulmin.
1929. 270p.   MPL

Complete poems. Humphrey Toulmin. 1937. xiv, 398p.   BM

Odes, and other poems. Murray. 1919. viii, 136p.   BM

Odes. Humphrey Toulmin. 1934. 104p.   BPL

War. Murray. 1918. 72p.   BPL

See also (120)

MacGILL, Patrick (Joined Army at outbreak of war. Sergeant.
London Irish Rifles. Wounded at Loos in 1915)

Soldier songs: [poems]. Jenkins. 1917. 120p.   MPL

See also (2) (12) (17) (18) (33) (51) (72) (104)
(111) (112)

MACGILLIVRAY, Pittendrigh
Bog-myrtle and peat reek: verse mainly in the north and
south country dialects of Scotland. Edinburgh: Author. 1922.
xvi, 142p.
     A limited ed. of 300 copies.   BM

Pro patria: [poems]. Edinburgh: Elliot. 1915. xiv, 80p. il.
A limited ed. of 400 copies.   BPL

McGOWN, George W.T.
Under the red lamp; Songs of Yarrow, etc. Selkirk:
Lewis. 1920. [x], 96p.   BPL

MACGREGOR, John (Lieutenant-Colonel. Surgeon, Indian
Medical Service)

The legend of Alompra, and other poems, (first of the camp
and jungle series). Simpkin, Marshall, Hamilton, Kent. 1924.
160p. por.   BM

Through death to victory, and other poems. Routledge.
1922. 152p. il.   BPL

MACIEL, C.
"Floreat Britannica": the golden crown of peace. Southampton:
Macsim P. [1919?].
     A card.   BM

MACINTIRE, Irene see (28)

McINTOSH, Hugh P.F.
A soldier looks at beauty: [poems]. With a foreword by
Ernest Rhys. Simpkin Marshall. 1928. xiv, 31p.   BPL

MACKAY, Helen
London, one November: [poems]. Melrose. 1915. vi, 106p.   BPL

See also (47) (48) (49)

MACKENZIE, ?
Sound, bugles, "all clear!": the birthday of peace, (Armistice

Day, November 11th, 1918). Riorden. [1918]. ("Souvenir"
post cards, 101). BM

MACKENZIE, Ian H.T. (2nd Lieutenant, Highland
Light Infantry)

The darkened ways, [and other poems]. Chapman & Hall.
1917. 30p. MPL

Forgotten places: [poems]. With an intro. by Arthur
Waugh. Chapman & Hall. 1919. 67p. por. MPL

See also (58)

MACKENZIE, Margaret
The station platform, and other poems. Sands. 1918. 48p. BPL

MACKENZIE, Orgill
Poems and stories. Dent. 1930. viii, 194p. BM

Poems and stories. Cheap ed. Dent. 1933. viii, 194p. MPL

MACKENZIE, Lady Thèrese Muir see (64)

MACKERETH, Annie, (Alpha, pseud.)
Killantringan, and other poems. Selwyn & Blount. 1922. 32p. BPL

Songs of the red rose: [poems]; by Alpha. [Manchester?].
[1915]. 27p.
   Dedicated to the Lancashire Fusiliers.
   Reprinted from the *Manchester Weekly Times.* MPL

MACKERETH, James Allan
Earth, dear earth: [poems]. Bodley Head. 1928. xii, 164p. MPL

The red, red dawn: [poems]. Erskine Macdonald. 1917.
132p. BPL

Song of the young and old men, in years of world-wide
suspicion, fear, and folly; [and, V.C. veteran to his son
armed, 1914-18—1939]. Printed Bradford: Country P. [1939].
[11]p. BM

See also (19) (52)

MACKINTOSH, Ewart Alan (M.C. Lieutenant, Seaforth
Highlanders. Wounded at High Wood during Somme
Battle. Returned to the front and was killed in action
at Cambrai, 21st November 1917)

A highland regiment: [poems]. Bodley Head. 1917.
96p.   MPL

[No copy of 2nd ed. traced].

A highland regiment: [poems]. 3rd ed. Bodley Head.
1918. 96p.   IWM

Miserere Domine. Bodley Head. 1919. [2] p. il.
   Cover-title is "Miserere".
   From author's "A highland regiment".   BPL

War, the liberator, and other pieces. With a memoir;
[by John Murray]. Bodley Head. 1918. iv, 156p. por.   MPL

See also (4) (18) (33) (50) (66) (70) (72) (131)

MACKINTOSH, Hugh Stewart (Fought in Battle of
Passchendaele)

Ballades, and other verse. Hart-Davis. 1953. 92p.   BM

Rhyme and reason: [poems]. Hart-Davis. 1956. 63p.   BM

See also (96) (103)

MACKLIN, Alys Eyre see (64)

MACLAREN, W.F. de Bois
Word pictures of war: [poems]. Methuen. 1917. xii,
78p.   BPL

See also (51)

MACLEAN, Duncan
Poems. Ed. by John Riddell. Manchester: Heywood.
1917. por.   MPL

MACLENNAN, R.J. see (91)

McLEOD, Irene Rutherford
The darkest hour: [poems]. Chatto & Windus. 1918.
viii, 120p.   MPL

One mother. Chatto & Windus. 1916. 7p.
   Reprinted from author's "Swords for life".   BPL

Swords for life: [poems]. Chatto & Windus. 1916. 115p.   MPL

MACLEOD, John Dunning (Captain, Cameron Highlanders)
Macedonian measures, and others: [poems].

213

Cambridge U.P. 1919. viii, 42p.   MPL

See also (20)

MACLEOD, S.B. (2nd Lieutenant)
Poems of love and war. Simpkin, Marshall. 1918. vi, 86p.   MPL

McMASTER, Bryce
Collected poems. Oxford: Blackwell. 1947. [iv], 123p.   MPL

The stranger, and other poems. Arnold. 1923. 79p.   BM

See also (32)

MACMILLAN, Douglas
Poems of war and peace. The Bookroom. 1918. 15p.   BPL

Ultimata, and other questings: [poems]. The Bookroom.
1920. 22p.   BPL

MACNAIR, J.H. see (64) (111) (112)

McNAIR, Marjorie
Poems, 1908-1919. Cambridge: Heffer. 1919. 46p.   BPL

McPHERSON, Robert (16th Northumberland Fusiliers)
Comrades of the Great War. [Newcastle-on-Tyne?]:
Author. [1918].
A broadside.   BM

MACQUAID, L.P. Carolan
Wearing of the green. Cambridge: Heffer. 1917. il.
A broadside.   BM

McQUILLAND, Louis J.
A song of the open road, and other verses. With a proem
[sic] in verse by "G.K.C." [Chesterton]. Heath, Cranton.
[1916]. 72p. il. (by David Wilson).   BM

McWILLIAM, Thomas
Around the fireside: homely sketches in prose and verse.
Aberdeen: Wyllie. 1927. 89p. il., por.   BM

The passing days, and other verses. Aberdeen: Bon-Accord P.
1917. [xii], 51p. il.
'To the memory of Lieut. Charles T. McWilliam, the 5th
Battalion, the Gordon Highlanders'.   BM

See also (91)

MADDEN, William see (65)

MAIL, M.
Our wounded, and other poems. Bristol: Arrowsmith;
Simpkin, Marshall, Hamilton, Kent. 1917. 87p. il.
(by Donald D. Mail).
    'Profits from the sale of this book will be devoted to a
Fund for Disabled Sailors and Soldiers, established by the
Bristol War Pensions Committee'.   BPL

MAIR, Alexander William
Poems. With a preface by H.J.C. Grierson. Edinburgh:
Oliver & Boyd. 1929. [ii], 100p. por.   BM

See also (29)

MAIR, Mary
Gypsy love, and other poems. Merton P. 1924. 24p.   BM

MAITLAND, Ella Fuller- see FULLER-MAITLAND, Ella

MAITLAND, Francis Edward
Poems. Elkin Mathews. 1917. 56p. (Vigo cabinet series:
second century, 40).   BM

See also (31) (32) (47) (48) (49) (55) (108)
(109) (113)

MAJOR, Irene C. see (62)

MALACRIDA, Nadja, Marchioness, (Nadja, pseud.)
For Empire, and other poems; by Nadja. Humphreys.
1916. 39p.
    Profits to the Star and Garter Home for Totally Disabled
Soldiers and Sailors.   BPL

The full heart: poems; by Nadja. Humphreys. 1919. 63p.   BM

Love and war: [poems]; by Nadja. Humphreys. 1915.
[viii], 27p.   BM

MALAHER, Bruce (Served in Mesopotamia)
The wizard's loom, and other poems. Stoneham. 1916. 64p.   BM

MALCOLM, Sir Ian Zachary
Stuff—and nonsense: a book of war verses. Hodder &
Stoughton. 1919. 96p.   BPL

MALLETT, John, (J.M.)
A tribute of love and gratitude to William Victor
Lancelot Mallett and Hubert Mallett, brothers-in-life,
brothers-in-love, brothers-in-arms, and brothers-in-death,
who, honouring their country, and being honoured
through her as officers of the East Surrey Regiment,
wrought for her, fought for her, and died for her during the
Great War; [by] J.M. Privately publ. 1919. [12]p.
   Poems and obituaries.   BM

The writing on the wall: an indictment [of the Emperor
Wilhelm II]. Malley. 1915. 31p.   BM

MALLETT, Louise see (28)

MALLETT, Reddie
Freedom songs: [poems]. Watts. 1916-17. 2v.   BPL

Poems from beyond; by the author of "Nature's way".
Plymouth: Smith. [1916]. viii, 51p.   BPL

Poems from beyond. Watts. 1920. [viii], 124p.   MPL

Poems from beyond, and other verse. Watts. 1927. x,
276p.   BM

See also (29)

MALLOCH, George Reston (Worked in Casualty
Department of the Admiralty)

Poems. Heinemann. 1920. x, 121p.   BM

Poems and lyrics. Heinemann. 1916. xii, 98p.   MPL

Poems and lyrics. New York: Dutton. 1917. xii, 98p.   BM

MANN, Alice see (28) (29)

MANN, Arthur James, ("Hamish" Mann) (2nd Lieutenant,
8th Black Watch. Took part in the battles on the Somme.
Wounded at Arras, 9th April 1917. Died the following day)

Balkan fancies, and other poems. Black. 1919. 80p.
1 col. il.   MPL

A subaltern's musings: [poems]. Long. 1918. 96p. por.
   Includes 10 prose poems.   MPL

MANN, Francis Oscar
Poems. Oxford: Blackwell. 1924. [viii], 77p.   BPL

St James's Park, and other poems. Hogarth P.
1930. 102p.   BM

MANN, Frederic
Poems of hope and vision. Stockwell. [1922]. 112p.   BM

MANNING, Frederic (b. Australia, self-educated in England.
Enlisted in King's Shropshire Light Infantry in October 1915.
Served with the 7th Battalion throughout the Somme
Battle, 1916. Commissioned in Royal Irish Regiment, May
1917)

Eidola: [poems]. Murray. 1917. viii, 88p.   MPL

See also (16) (17) (18) (50)

MANNING, Walter E. see (29)

MANNING, William Sinkler (Killed in action on the Meuse,
6th November 1918) see (131)

MANSFIELD, H.G. (Lieutenant, Essex Regiment)
'By Jaffa way', 'The Judah 'ills', and other poems.
Scott. 1919. 40p.   MPL

MARCUS, Lily
Lyrical links: selections from poems. Londonderry:
Author. 1920. 68p.   BM

War poems. Printed Londonderry: *Derry Standard.*
1916. 80p.
      Proceeds to St. Dunstan's Hostel, N.W.   BM

See also (28) (29)

MARDEL, Nina (Voluntary Aid Detachment)
Plain song: [poems]. Erskine Macdonald. 1917. 32p.   MPL

MARE, Walter De La see **DE LA MARE, Walter**

MARJORIBANKS, Edward
Poems. Chapman & Hall. 1931. 64p.   MPL

MARKLAND, Russell, (R.M. Ingersley, pseud.) see (65)

MARKS, Phyllis see (65)

MARRIOTT, Constance Sutcliffe see (29)

MARRIOTT-WATSON, R.B. (Lieutenant, 2nd Royal Irish
Rifles. Killed in action 24th March 1918) see (33) (111)
(112) (131)

MARSDEN, William Murray
The wine drop, and other poems. Moring. 1922. viii,
52p.   MPL

MARSH, John R.
To Belgium. Privately publ. [1915?].
  A broadside.
  'Proceeds of sale to be devoted to the Friends of Belgium
Society'.   BM

MARSHALL, James W. see (27) (29)

MARSHALL, William Forbes
Verses from Tyrone. Stockwell. [1923]. 44p.   BM

MARTIN, E.M.
Apollo to Christ, and other verses. Chapman & Hall. 1922.
[vij], 57p.   BM

MARTIN, Elsie R.
After death, and varied verses. Stockwell. [1923]. 40p.   BM

MARTIN, Henry
A patriotic appeal "for all our wounded heroes here at
home". Rosyth: Author. [191-].
  A broadside.   BM

MARTINEAU, Mary
Prisoners of hope, and other verses. Birmingham: Cornish.
1916. 22p.
  Sold for the relief of British and allied war prisoners.   BPL

MASEFIELD, Charles John Beech (Cousin of John Masefield.
M.C. Captain, 5th North Staffordshire Regiment. Wounded
in action, 1st July 1917. Died in prison camp the following
day)

218

Dislikes: some modern satires: [poems]. Fifield. 1914.
48p.   NCL

Poems. Oxford: Blackwell. 1919. viii, 130p. por.   MPL

See also (58) (96) (131)

MASEFIELD, John (Served with the Red Cross, first in France
and later on a hospital ship at Gallipoli)

Collected poems. Heinemann. 1923. x, 784p.   BM

Collected poems. New ed. Heinemann. 1932. xiv, 957p.   BM

Collected poems. New ed. Heinemann. 1938. xiv, 1136p.   BM

Lollingdon downs, and other poems, with sonnets.
Heinemann. 1917. [vi], 93p.   MPL

Lollingdon downs, and other poems. New York: Macmillan.
1917. 53p. por.   BM

Philip the King, and other poems. Heinemann. 1914.
viii, 119p.   MPL

Poems. Collected ed. New York: Macmillan. 1918.
xiv, 521p. por. (Poems and plays, v.1).
    v.2 contains plays only.   BM

Poems. Complete in one volume. New York: Macmillan.
1929. xii, 438p.   BM

Poems. Complete ed., with recent poems. New York:
Macmillan. 1935. [xxii], 673p. por.   BM

Poems. Heinemann. 1946. x, 933p.   BM

Selected poems. Heinemann. 1922. x, 224p. por.   BM

Selected poems. Heinemann. 1922. viii, 245p. por.
    A limited ed. of 530 copies.   BM

Selected poems. New ed. Heinemann. 1938. xiv, 271p. por.   BM

Sonnets and poems. Cholsey, Berks. :Author. 1916. 52p.   MPL

Sonnets and poems. Letchworth: Garden City P. 1916.
51p.
    A limited ed. of 200 copies.   BM

See also (16) (17) (18) (19) (46) (127)

MASEFIELD, Susan see (28) (29)

MASON, Gladys M. see (28)

MASON, John (Captain, Royal Scots)
The valley of dreams: [poems]. Erskine Macdonald.
1918. 61p.   MPL

See also (58)

MASSEY, W.
A quiet talk with "Kaiser Bill"; by a West Ham tram
conductor. Printed Plaistow: Goddard. [1914].
    A broadside.   BM

MASTERMAN, Lucy see (31) (32)

MATHAMS, Walter John see (23)

MATHER, Ophelia George see (28)

MATHESON, Annie
Roses, loaves and old rhymes. New ed. Milford. 1918.
xxxviii, 152p. por.
    1st ed. publ. 1900.   MPL

MATTHEWS, J.E.
The dried fount, and other poems. *Kent Guardian*
Printing & Publ. Co. 1929. [vi], 179p.   BM

A garland of sonnets. Stockwell. [1925]. [iv], 20p.   BPL

A garland of verse, culled in and around Herne Bay.
Southern Counties P. [1933]. 55p.   BM

Wild roses, and other verse. Stockwell. [1926]. 20p.   BPL

MAUDSLAY, Walter
Pen pictures: [poems]. Houghton Publ. Co. 1935. 82p.   BM

See also (27)

MAURICE, Charles Edmund
Poems. Ed. by Emily Southwood Maurice. Methuen.
1929. viii, 80p.   BPL

MAXWELL, Gordon Stanley (Lieutenant, Royal Naval
Volunteer Reserve)

The rhymes of a motor launch, and other M.L. odies [sic] and verses. Dent. 1919. 92p. il. IWM

The rhymes of Amot Orlaunch [sic], and other M.L.
odies [sic] and verses. Dent. 1919. 90p. il. BPL

Tommy Atkins' requiem. Brodie. [191-].
  A broadside.
  In Cockney dialect. BM

MAXWELL, William Coghlan
The rhyme of the king's high way, and other verse.
Bale & Danielsson. 1927. viii, 134p. MPL

The sponger of Strand Alley, and other verse. Bale &
Danielsson. 1926. viii, 100p. BM

MAY, Ida see (63)

MAYNARD, Constance Louisa
Watching the war: thoughts for the people: [poems].
Allenson. [1914-15]. 4v. BPL

MAYNARD, Theodore (b. India. Educated in England.
Worked in Ministry of Munitions. Eventually became an
American citizen)

Collected poems. Intro. by Alfred Noyes. New York:
Macmillan. 1946. xviii, 222p. BM

Drums of defeat, and other poems. Erskine Macdonald.
1917. 76p. (Little books of Georgian verse: new series, 1). BM

Folly, and other poems. Erskine Macdonald. 1918. 94p. BPL

The last knight, and other poems. Erskine Macdonald.
1924. xii, 139p. BM

Laughs and whifts of song: [poems]. Erskine Macdonald.
1915. 62p. (XXth century poetry series). MPL

See also (31) (32) (52)

MAYOR, Beatrice
Poems. Allen & Unwin. 1919. 60p. WPL

MEAGHER, J.R. see (27)

MEE, Arthur, (Idris, pseud.)
Orphans in Belgium. Cardiff: *Western Mail.* [1914].
  A broadside. BM

MEGROZ, Rodolphe Louis (Lance-Corporal, West Yorkshire Regiment)

Personal poems. Elkin Mathews. 1919. [ii], 88p.   BPL
See also (58)

MELBOURNE, Editha
A sheaf of songs, and other poems. Stockwell. [1923]. 32p.   BM

MELBOURNE, Edward, pseud. see **HODGSON, William Noel, (Edward Melbourne, pseud.)**

MELDRUM, Helen
The unknown God. Erskine Macdonald. 1917. 14p. (Malory booklets).   BPL

MELLERSH, Kate
The roll of honour and the crown of life: [poems]. Dent. 1917. 48p.   BM

MELLIAR, Robert Aubrey Foster- see **FOSTER-MELLIAR, Robert Aubrey**

MELLOR, H. Christian (Sergeant, Army Service Corps)
Romance, and other poems. Erskine Macdonald. 1918. 62p.   MPL

MELVILLE, Ernest Craigie (b. Scotland, emigrated to Boston (Mass.). Enlisted in Argyll & Sutherland Highlanders in 1915. Commissioned 1917).

Poems from the trenches. Somerville (Mass.): Thistle P. 1918. [viii], [51]p.
    Printed on one side of leaf only.   BPL

MENAI, Huw, pseud. see **WILLIAMS, Huw Menai, (Huw Menai, pseud.)**

MENDS-GIBSON, Amy see (64)

MERCER, T.W.
Harvest, and other poems. Plymouth: Plymouth Printers. 1918. 56p.   BM

MEREWETHER, M.E.A.
Victory day, and other poems. Stockwell. [1920]. 16p.   BPL

MERLIN, pseud. see SCARR, C.W., (Knipper, pseud.),
(Merlin, pseud.)

MEUGENS, M.G. see (19) (25) (42)

MEW, Charlotte
Collected poems. Duckworth. 1953. 80p. por., facsim.   MPL

The farmers' bride, [and other poems]. New ed., with
eleven new poems. Poetry Bookshop. 1921. 59p.
   1st ed. 1916 contains no war poetry.   MPL

The rambling sailor: [poems]. Poetry Bookshop. 1929.
45p. por.   MPL

See also (80)

MEYERSTEIN, Edward Harry William, (E.H.W.M.)
In time of war: poems. Richards P. 1942. 38p.   BPL

Some poems. Selected and ed. by Maurice Wollman.
With an intro. by Nathaniel Micklem. Spearman. 1960. 168p.
   Bibliog. (author's works) 2p.   BM

Symphonies: [poems]; by E.H.W.M. Oxford: Blackwell.
1915. [viii], 80p.   BPL

Symphonies: [poems]. (Second series). Oxford:
Blackwell. 1919. 61p.   BPL

MEYNELL, Alice
A father of women, and other poems. Burns & Oates.
1917. 31p.   MPL

Last poems. Burns, Oates & Washbourne. 1923.[ii], 54p.   BM

Poems. Complete ed. Burns, Oates & Washbourne.
1923. x, 144p. por.   MPL

Poems. Complete ed. Burns, Oates & Washbourne. 1940.
xiv, 222p.   MPL

Poems, 1847-1923. Centenary ed. Hollis & Carter.
1947. 192p.   MPL

Poems on the war. Printed Shorter. [1915]. [8]p. facsim.
   A limited ed. of 20 copies printed by Clement Shorter for
circulation among his friends.   BM

[Selected poems]. Benn. [1926]. 32p. (Augustan books
of modern poetry).   BM

223

Selected poems. With an introductory note by W.M. [Wilfrid
Meynell]. Nonesuch P. 1930. xii, 58p.   MPL

Ten poems, 1913-1915. Romney Street P. 1915. 16p.
   A limited ed. of 50 copies printed by Francis Meynell.   BM

See also (19) (22) (25) (32) (50) (54) (63) (66)
(112) (121)

MEYNELL, Wilfrid
Rhymes with reasons; by the author of "Aunt Sarah and
the war". Burns & Oates. [1918]. 27p.   BPL

See also (63)

MICHAEL, George C. (Lance-Corporal, Royal Engineers)
see (52) (56) (57) (96)

MILES, pseud. see SITWELL, Sir Osbert, (Miles, pseud.)

MILES, Patrick
The victory march, and other poems. Stockwell. [1920].
20p.   BPL

MILES, Susan, pseud. see ROBERTS, Ursula, (Susan Miles,
pseud.)

MILLAR, C.
Thoughts on love, and other poems. Stockwell. [1917].
30p.   BM

MILLAR, James
Clydeside melodies: [poems]. Stockwell. [1921]. 112p.   BM

Etincelles, [and other poems]. Stockwell. [1921]. 106p.   BM

A patriot of Britain, and other poems. Stockwell. [1918].
62p. por.   BPL

Poems, whisperings of love. Stockwell. [1919]. 63p.   BM

Songs of a musician: [poems]. Stockwell. [1918]. 69p.
por.   BPL

Sunshine and shadows: poems. Printed Hamilton: *Hamilton
Advertiser.* 1916. 68p.   BPL

MILLER, A.A. see (29)

224

MILLER, G.M.
South African harvest, and other poems. Oxford: Blackwell.
1939. 87p. BPL

MILLER, Jessie
Duty and ease: poems, to which are added several poems by
her sister Mary H. Miller. Stirling: Jamieson & Munro. [1935].
192p. por. IWM

MILLER, R.G. (Sapper, Royal Engineers)
In the camp fire smoke: songs by a sentimental Tommy:
[poems]. Calcutta: Thacker, Spink. 1917. [18]p.
Includes some poems in Scots dialect. BM

MILLIGAN, Corporal (Corporal, 6th Dorsets) see (110)

MILLIGAN, E.H. Marcus
Songs for the times: [poems]. Erskine Macdonald. [1918].
[4]p. BPL

MILLINGTON, W.T.
Cockney rhymes. Erskine Madonald. 1918. 48p. BPL

MILLS, Angus, pseud. see MILNE, David, (Angus Mills,
pseud.)

MILLS, Edward, (Philip Dayson, pseud.)
The Kitchener men; by Philip Dayson. [1914]. [3]p. BM

MILLS, I.M. see (46)

MILLS, James W.
The labyrinth, and other poems. Foreword by Patrick
Braybrooke. Williams & Norgate. 1930. xvi, 90p. il.
(by Raymond McGrath).
A limited ed. of 50 copies signed by the author. BM

MILLS, John Saxon see (29)

MILLWARD, Duncan
The drummer boy: poem. Printed Birmingham: Economic
Printing Co. [191-]. il.
A broadside.
All profits devoted to Belgian Relief Fund. BM

MILNE, Alan Alexander (Lieutenant, Royal Warwickshire
Regiment. Fought at the Somme)

For the luncheon interval: cricket and other verses.
Methuen. 1925. 64p.   BM

See also (33)

MILNE, David, (Angus Mills, pseud.)
The gamble of war: a record of the outstanding events
of the great conflict, 1914-1918; by Angus Mills. Printed
Forfar: *Forfar Herald.* [1929]. [iv], 352p. il.
   Long narrative poems, with a little prose.   BPL

MILNE, J. Napier see (31) (32) (47) (48) (49)

MILNES, Minnie see (28)

MILNES, Robert Offley Ashburton Crewe- , Lord Crewe
see CREWE-MILNES, Robert Offley Ashburton, Lord Crewe (17)
(18) (19) (25) (31) (32) (47) (48) (49) (52) (55)
(63) (65) (111) (112)

MILSOM, Stanley
To the level of the proud: [poems]. Ilfracombe: Stockwell.
[1938?]. 20p.   EDR

MINOR, pseud.
"The patriot's dream". Printed Watford: King. [1915]. 4p.   BM

See also (5)

MINTER, W.J.
"Our farm": the popular patriotic recitation. McAra &
Whiteman. [1914]. [4]p.   BM

MITCHAM, Helen
Limehouse, and other poems. Erskine Macdonald. 1920.
78p.   BM

MITCHELL, Alexander Gordon
War songs: [poems]. Stirling: Scott, Learmonth &
Allen. 1916. 102p. por.   BPL

See also (29)

MITCHELL, Colin (Sergeant, Rifle Brigade. Killed in

226

action 22nd March 1918)

Trampled clay: [poems]. Erskine Macdonald. 1917. 47p.   MPL

See also (52)

MITCHELL, Frederic L.
Songs of protest: [poems]. With an intro. by R.O. Prowse.
Erskine Macdonald. 1916. 58p. (XXth century poetry series).   BM

MITCHELL, G.M. see (87) (96)

MITCHELL, James
The warning bell, and other war poems. Printed Leith:
Mackay. 1915. 34p.   BPL

The warning bell, and other war poems. 2nd ed. Printed
Leith: Mackay. 1917. 80p. por.   BM

"Yepres"[sic]. Printed Gateshead: Wilson. 1920. [4]p.
    BM

MITCHELL, John
Bydand: poems of war and peace. With an intro. and
notes by J.M. Bulloch. Aberdeen: Bon-Accord P. 1918. x,
82p. il., por.
    Many poems in Scots dialect.   MPL

Jock McCraw: the tale of a Gay Gordon. Aberdeen:
Smith. 1918. 8p.
    In Scots dialect.   BPL

MITTON, Thomas Edward (2nd Lieutenant, Royal
Engineers, Signals. Killed in action 24th December 1917)

[Poems]. Birmingham: Cornish. 1918. 31p. por.
    Printed for private circulation.   BPL

MOBERLY, Lucy Gertrude see (5) (23) (82) (83) (84) (96)

MOGGRIDGE, Harry Weston
The history of England: [poems]. Oxford: Blackwell.
1937. viii, 80p.   BM

MONCRIEFF, Charles Elliott Scott- see SCOTT-
MONCRIEFF, Charles Elliott

MOND, Henry
Poems of dawn and the night. Chapman & Hall. 1919.
59p.   BPL

227

MONRO, Harold (Commissioned in anti-aircraft battery, Royal Artillery. Later posted to War Office)

Children of love, [and other poems]. Poetry Bookshop. 1914. 32p.   BPL

Collected poems. Ed. by Alida Monro, with a biographical sketch by F.S. Flint, and a critical note by T.S. Eliot. Cobden-Sanderson. 1933. xx, 217p. por.
    Bibliog. (author's works) 1p.   MPL

Collected poems. Ed. by Alida Monro. With a preface by Ruth Tomalin. Duckworth. 1970. xxxii, 217p. por.
    Bibliog. (author's works) 1p.   MPL

Strange meetings, [and other poems]. Poetry Bookshop. 1917. 64p.   MPL

Strange meetings: a book of poems. [New ed.]. Poetry Bookshop. 1921. 64p.   MPL

See also (33) (50) (80) (106)

MONTEITH, J.T. see (29)

MONTGOMERIE, Emily J. see (28)

MOOR, Anita
Roundels and rhymes. Simpkin, Marshall, Hamilton, Kent. 1919. [xvi], 179p.   BPL

Roundels and rhymes. Alvechurch: *Poetry*. 1921. xvi, 177p.   BPL

Sonnets. Constable. 1922. xii, 42p.   BM

MOOR, Robert
Hope re-born, and other poems. Stockwell. [1919]. 32p.   BPL

MOORE, Bernard, pseud. see **HUNT, S.S., (Bernard Moore, pseud.)**

MOORE, E. Hamilton
The fountain of ablutions, and other poems. Cambridge: Heffer. 1921. [viii], 65p.   BPL

MOORE, George H. (Chaplain, Queen's Hospital, Birmingham)
Songs and poems. Birmingham: *Midland Counties Herald*. [1914?]. [ii],23p. por.   BPL

MOORE, Harold William, (Holdar Roome, pseud.)
(Joined 6th Battalion, Gloucester Regiment at outbreak of war.
Was wounded in the Battle of the Somme, July 1916. Later
gained a commission in the Royal Artillery, serving with the
Essex Battery at Ypres, where he was again wounded)

The Magians, and other poems; [by] Holdar Roome.
Mitre P. 1964. 68p.   BM

One man's war: 1914-1918: a chapter of autobiography:
[poems]; [by] Holdar Roome. Mitre P. 1968. 157p.   MPL

MOORE, Richard Louis-Bertrand, (Ricardo, pseud)
The warblings of a windy warrior: [poems]. Birmingham:
Cornish. 1923. 47p.   BPL

MOORE, Thomas Sturge
Poems. Collected ed. v. 4. Macmillan. 1933. [viii], 382p.   MPL

Selected poems. Macmillan. 1934. x, 207p.   MPL

MORE, John (Served in Palestine)
Dugout doggerels from Palestine. Heath, Cranton.
[1922]. 52p. il. (by Lunt Roberts).   BPL

MORGAN, Charles Langbridge (Lieutenant, Royal Naval
Division. Served at Antwerp, was taken prisoner and
interned in Holland) see (16) (18)

MORGAN, Constance see (28)

MORGAN, Evan, Lord Tredegar (2nd Lieutenant, Welsh
Guards)

Fragments: [poems]. Erskine Macdonald. 1916. 64p.   MPL

Gold and ochre: [poems]. Erskine Macdonald. 1917. 96p.   BPL

See also (56) (57)

MORGAN, R.R. see (47) (48) (49)

MORGAN, Vaughan
Poems and plays. Abertillery: *South Wales Gazette*.
1917. 92p.   BM

MORLEY, A. see (5)

MORRIS, Alfred see (27)

MORRIS, Francis St. Vincent (Lieutenant, 3rd Battalion,
Sherwood Foresters. Died of wounds 29th April 1917)

Poems. Oxford: Blackwell. 1917. 80p. por.   MPL

See also (75) (131)

MORRIS, Jim (Sapper, Royal Engineers)
Give us our due: a record of a conversation in a train
between a soldier on leave from Macedonia and a
"Cuthbert" who had not been combed out: the words
of the musical monologue. Salonika. 1919. [4]p.   IWM

"Who won the war and why!!", as told by a Cockney
member of the Salonika force to his grandson on his
return to Blighty, year unknown: words of the humorous
musical monologue. Salonika. 1918. 5p.   BM

MORTON, Alfred
Day dawn in rural England, and other poems. Birmingham:
Wakelin. 1923. [viii], 87p. por.   MPL

The footfall of the snowflakes. [Birmingham]: Author.
1920.
    A broadside.   BM

The Kaiser's soliloquy; [and], The political outlook,
past, present and future: [poems]. 1914. [2]p.   BM

A year and a half of war. Printed Birmingham: Wakelin.
1916.
    A broadside.   BM

The Zeebrugge Mole exploit, written at odd moments,
October 13th, 14th, 15th, and 16th, 1918. 1918.
    A broadside.   BM

MOSS, Alfred
War and peace. [Walsall]. [1917].
    A broadside.   BM

MOSTYN, Mary see (28) (29)

MOTHER, pseud.
Poems of a mother, 1914-1916. Erskine Macdonald.
[1916]. 16p. (Malory booklets).   IWM

MOTTRAM, Ralph Hale
Poems new and old. Duckworth. 1930. xii, 107p.   MPL

See also (96) (103)

MOULE, Handley Carr Glyn see (27)

MOULT, Thomas see (36) (66)

MOUNT, Emma H.
Oh Lord, hear our cry. Lowestoft: [Author?]. [1916].
  A card.   BM

MOUNT, Gertrude see (64)

MOUNTAIN, James see (29)

MOZLEY, John Rickards
Seven lyrics, expressive of the heart of those, who when
the throes of war have passed, look for a new birth of time.
Cambridge: Heffer. 1918. 15p.   BPL

MUDGE, E.C. (Sergeant, 7th Battalion, London Regiment)
Songs of a "Shiny" sergeant: [poems]. [1919]. 32p.   BPL

MUIR, A.
The bad boy. [Glasgow] : [Higgins]. [191-].
  A postcard.   BM

Britannia. [Glasgow] : [Higgins]. [191-].
  A postcard.   BM

Don't. [Glasgow] : [Higgins]. [191-].
  A postcard.   BM

Don't worry. [Glasgow] : [Higgins]. [191-].
  A postcard.   BM

"I wish ma man was hame". [Glasgow] : [Higgins].
[191-].
  A postcard.   BM

"Jack" on the German Fleet. [Glasgow] : [Higgins].
[191-].
  A postcard.   BM

"Jock". [Glasgow] : [Higgins]. [191-].
  A postcard.
  In Scots dialect.   BM

Kaiser to Gott. [Glasgow] : [Higgins]. [191-].
A postcard.
In 'broken' English.   BM

Der Kaiser's dream. [Glasgow] : [Higgins]. [191-].
A postcard.
In 'broken' English.   BM

Der Kaiser's dream, and other poems on the war.
Glasgow: Higgins. [1914]. [16]p.   BM

The march of the Kaiser's men. [Glasgow] : [Higgins].
[1915].
A postcard.
In Scots dialect.   BM

Powder and shot: (a collection of topical verses of the
Great War of 1914-15). Printed Glasgow: Higgins. [1915].
[48]p. por.
Some in Scots dialect.   BM

To the footballer at the front. [Glasgow] : [Higgins].
[191-].
A postcard.   BM

The war loan. [Glasgow] : [Higgins]. [191-].
A broadside.
In Scots dialect.   BM

Willie dear. [Glasgow] : [Higgins]. [191-].
A postcard.   BM

MULHALL, Marion, (Tephi, pseud.)
General Allenby's address to his army on the eve before
the taking of Jerusalem: a fantasy. [191-].
A card.   BM

Vision of General von Emmich during the Siege of Liege;
[by] Tephi. [191-].
A card.   BM

MUNRO, Neil
Poetry. With a preface by John Buchan. Blackwood. 1931.
88p.
Some poems in Scots dialect.   MPL

See also (17) (18) (31) (32) (66) (71) (91) (99)
(100) (101) (111) (112)

232

MURCOTT, W.
Topical verses. Long Eaton: Author. 1917.
    A broadside.

BM

MURPHY, William S.
In memoriam: Edith Cavell. Stoneham. 1916. [20] p.
por.
    Printed on one side of leaf only.

BPL

MURRAY, A.E. (Served as a nurse in a military hospital.
Drove cars and motorcycles for the Royal Flying Corps and
Red Cross, the latter in France) see (17) (18) (31) (32)

MURRAY, Charles
Hamewith, and other poems: Hamewith; A sough o'war;
In the country places. Collected ed. Constable. 1927. viii,
180p.
    In Scots dialect. With a glossary.

BM

A sough o'war, [and other poems]. Constable. 1917. 56p.
    In Scots dialect. With a glossary.

MPL

See also (91)

MURRAY, H. Robertson
Kultur and the German blunder (buss): [poems]. Ewart,
Seymour. 1914. 16p. il. (by Charles Grave).
    Title from cover.

MPL

MURRY, John Middleton
Poems: 1916-20. Cobden-Sanderson. 1921. 58p.

MPL

Poems: 1917-18. Heron P. 1918. 39p.
    A limited ed. of 120 copies.

BM

See also (66)

MYERS, S.
Kitchener's call to arms (answered): dedicated to
the troops of Kitchener's army, the Franco-British and
German War. Printed Harpenden: Fisher, Knight. [191-].
    A postcard.

BM

N.D. see (51)

N.D.M. see **M., N.D.**

N.E.Z. see (5)

N., G.G. see NAPIER, George Glen, (G.G.N.)

N.G.H. see (31) (32)

N.M.H. see (19)

N.R. see RICHFIELD, Nathan, (N.R.)

N.R.E. see EDWARDS, N.R., (N.R.E.)

NADJA, pseud. see MALACRIDA, Nadja, Marchioness, (Nadja, pseud.)

NANKIVELL, Austin Threlfall (Captain) see (17) (18) (111)·

NAPIER, George Glen, (G.G.N.)
Sonnet on seeing on a newspaper bill, of 6th June, 1916, the words "Kitchener drowned"; [by] G.G.N. [1930].
  A broadside.

BM

Sonnet on seeing on a newspaper bill, of 6th June, 1916, the words "Kitchener drowned". [1930].
  A broadside.
  Different format from previous entry.

BM

See also (29)

NASH, Geoffrey Dalrymple see (31) (32)

NELSON, Horace
Musings and memories: [poems]. Simpkin, Marshall. 1920. 72p.

BM

NESBIT, Edith
Many voices: poems. Hutchinson. 1922. 94p.

BM

See also (19) (26) (31) (32)

NESBITT, Henry Arthur
Neuve Chapelle, and other poems. Kegan Paul, Trench, Trubner. 1916. 64p.

BPL

See also (2) (51)

NESS, Elizabeth see (29)

NEUMAN, B. Paul see (31) (32)

NEVINSON, Henry Woodd (Helped organize the Friends'
Ambulance Unit between Dunkirk and Ypres. War
correspondent in many battle areas)

Lines of life: [poems]. Allen & Unwin. 1920. 89p.   BPL

[Selected poems]. Benn. [1928?]. 32p. (Augustan books
of modern poetry).
   Bibliog. (author's works) 1p.   BM

NEWBOLT, Sir Francis
The enchanted wood: a little book of etchings, prose and
verse. Philip Allan. 1925. xiv, 81p. il., por.   MPL

NEWBOLT, Sir Henry (Chairman of the departmental
committee on the distribution of books abroad and
Controller of Wireless and Cables)

A perpetual memory, and other poems. With brief memoirs
by Walter De La Mare and Ralph Furse. Murray. 1939. xxii, 40p.
por. (by Sir William Rothenstein).   WPL

Poems: new and old. 2nd ed. Murray. 1919. xvi, 268p.

   1st ed. publ. 1912.   SPL

St. George's Day, and other poems. Murray. 1918. 48p.   MPL

Selected poems. With an intro. by John Betjeman. Nelson.
1940. 160p. (Nelson classics).   BM

See also (16) (17) (18) (22) (25) (31) (32) (33) (47)
(48) (49) (51) (54) (55) (59) (82) (83) (84) (99) (100)
(101) (108) (109) (111) (112) (113) (119) (120) (121)

NEWTON, Eileen
Lamps in the valley: a book of verse. Elkin Mathews &
Marrot. [1927]. 56p.   BM

See also (32)

NEWTON, George R. (Served on Western Front)
Poems of war. Printed Freshwater: Selden. [1918].
[7]p.
   Title from cover.
   'All profits on the sale of this booklet will be given to the

National Association of Discharged Sailors and Soldiers'.   BM

NEWTON, Walter
Poems and sonnets. Manchester: Sherratt & Hughes. 1926.
[xvi], 279p.   MPL

NICHOLL, Theodore
Poems. Ingpen & Grant. 1934. viii, 37p.   BPL

NICHOLS, A.G. see (5)

NICHOLS, Dudley M. (2nd Lieutenant, Royal Air Force)
Lays of stirring days. Faulkner. [1918]. 36p. por.   BPL

NICHOLS , Robert (Lieutenant, Royal Field Artillery. Fought
on the Somme. Was invalided out with shell-shock. Gave
public readings of his war poetry to large audiences)

Ardours and endurances: [poems] ; also, A faun's holiday;
and, Poems and phantasies. Chatto & Windus. 1917.
x, 208p. por.   LPL

Ardours and endurances: [poems] ; also, A faun's holiday;
and, Poems and phantasies. 2nd ed. Chatto & Windus.
1917. x, 208p. por.   MPL

The assault, and other war poems from "Ardours and
endurances". Chatto & Windus. 1918. 78p.   BPL

Aurelia, and other poems. Chatto & Windus. 1920. viii,
98p.   MPL

Invocation: war poems and others. Elkin Mathews.
1915. 44p.   MPL

Invocation and peace celebration: hymn for the British
peoples. Henderson. 1919. 10p.   BM

[Selected poems]. Benn. [1932]. 32p. (Augustan books
of poetry).
    Bibliog. (author's works) 1p.   BM

Such was my singing: a selection from poems written between
the years 1915 and 1940. Collins. 1942. 174p. por.
    Bibliog. (author's works) 1p.   MPL

See also (2) (4) (16) (17) (18) (33) (35) (37) (50) (59)
(66) (70) (72) (80) (81) (102) (104) (105) (108) (109)
(111) (112) (120) (127)

NICHOLS, Wallace Bertram
Selected poems. St. Catherine P. 1943. [ii], 8p.   BM

See also (31) (32)

NICKLIN, John Arnold
"And they went to the war": [poems]. Sidgwick & Jackson.
1914. 16p.   BPL

See also (19)

NICOL, Charles
On the coming of peace: a Christian ode with an evolutionary
setting. Glasgow: Higgins. [1918]. [4]p.   BM

NICOL, James see (27) (29)

NICOLL, David M. see (29)

NIGHT PATROL, pseud.
Silence broken: verses written on the roof during the Zeppelin
raids (1914-1915), and as a record now published for the first
time. Fountain Publ. Co. 1920. 36p.   NCL

NIGHTINGALE, Arthur W. (Corporal)
Windmill Hill. Bedford: Hill. [1915]. 4p.   BM

NIGHTINGALE, Madeleine
Verses wise and otherwise. Oxford: Blackwell. 1918. 63p.
il. (by C.T. Nightingale).   BPL

NIVEN, Frederick (b. Chile of Scottish parents. Educated in
Glasgow. Worked in the Ministry of Food and the Ministry
of Information, 1914-18. Settled in Canada after the war)

A lover of the land, and other poems. New York: Boni
& Liveright. 1925. 72p.   BM

Maple-leaf songs: [poems]. Sidgwick & Jackson. 1917. 45p.   MPL

See also (12) (31) (32) (121)

NOBLE, J.N. see (29)

NORMAN, Alfred Bathurst (Royal Flying Corps)
Ditchling Beacon, [and other poems]. With an introductory
note by E.V. Lucas. Sidgwick & Jackson. 1918. 36p.   MPL

NORMAN, Oswald see (27)

NORRIS, C.G.
Vitem impendere vero. [Privately printed]. [1919].
  A broadside.   BM

NORTH, Harold L. (Private, 1st Garrison Battalion,
Hampshire Regiment)
The night guard. 1917.
  A broadside.   IWM

NORTHCOTE, Hugh, & NORTHCOTE, Marion A.
Edith Cavell's last thoughts, and other poems. Kegan Paul,
Trench, Trubner. [1918]. 79p.   BPL

NORTHCOTE, Marion A. see NORTHCOTE, Hugh, &
NORTHCOTE, Marion A.

NORTHERN CELT, pseud.
1914-1918: the darkness, the dawn and a vision: our
Britain's part in the Great War: a tribute and a call:
[poems]. Simpkin, Marshall, Hamilton, Kent. [1918]. 86p.   BPL

NORTHWOOD, A.M. see (63)

NORTON, Hon. Eleanour
Magic, and other poems. Wilson. 1922. [x], 83p.
  A limited ed. of 500 copies.   BPL

NORTON, Frederick
An elegy on the death of a mad dog, with all due respect
to Dr. Goldsmith and R. Caldecott. Warne. [1914]. 29p. il.
(by Lewis Baumer).
  Cover-title is "The mad dog of Potsdam".
  Brief satirical verses on the Emperor Wilhelm II.   BM

NORTON, J. Smedley
The Kaiser's nightmare: the cinematograph version of
this travesty poem, which has been filmed by the Charing
Cross Film Co., is being shown in all the principal picture
palaces thoughout the United Kingdom. Printed
Marshalsea P. 1914. [4]p. il., por.   BM

NORTON, Robert Douglas
The leaf, and other verses. Lamley. 1918. [ii], 36p.   BPL

NORTON, Smedley
Now's the time. Patriotic Publ. Co. 1914. [2]p.   BM

The roll call: in memory of the British soldiers who have
already fallen during the present European conflict. Patriotic
Publ. Co. 1914. [2]p.   BM

"Sergeant, call the roll!" Edinburgh P. 1918. [2]p.
   Cover-title is "Hands across the sea".   BM

NORWOOD, Sir Cyril see (113)

NOTT, Jane Prothero
A little book of verse. Erskine Macdonald. [1921]. 38p.   BM

NOYES, Alfred (Attached to Foreign Office, 1916-18)
Collected poems. Blackwood. 1914-27. 4v.   JRL

Collected poems. Murray. 1950. 415p.   SPL

Collected poems. 2nd ed. Murray. 1963. [ii], 427p.   MPL

The elfin artist, and other poems. Blackwood. 1920.
x, 196p.   MPL

The lord of misrule, and other poems. New York:Stokes.
1915. [viii], 184p. col. il. (by Spencer Baird Nichols).   BPL

The new morning: poems. New York: Stokes. [1919].
xii, 172p.   BM

Poems: the author's own selection for schools. Collins.
[1935]. 256p.   BM

Rada: a Belgian Christmas Eve. Methuen. 1915. viii,
84p. il.
   A drama in prose and verse. Includes a poem
"Intercession".   MPL

A salute from the Fleet, and other poems. Methuen.
1915. viii, 208p.   MPL

A salute from the Fleet, and other poems. 2nd ed.
Methuen. 1915. viii, 208p.   IWM

A salute from the Fleet, and other poems. 3rd ed.
Methuen. 1916. viii, 208p.   BPL

The searchlights. Methuen. [1914]. [4]p.   BM

[Selected poems]. Benn. [1931]. 32p. (Augustan books
of poetry).

Bibliog. (author's works) 1p. BM

Selected verse, including "A victory dance", and other poems old and new. Blackwood. 1921. vi, 92p. MPL

Shadows on the down, and other poems. Hutchinson. [1945]. 127p. WPL

Songs of shadow-of-a-leaf, and other poems. Blackwood. 1924. viii, 128p. BM

Songs of the trawlers: [poems]. Shorter. 1916. 12p.
    A limited ed. of 25 copies privately printed by Clement Shorter for distribution among his friends. BM

See also (16) (17) (18) (19) (25) (26) (31) (32) (46) (47) (48) (49) (54) (55) (59) (82) (83) (84) (108) (111) (112) (119) (121)

NUTTALL, P.J.
Wycollar Dene, and other poems. Stockwell. [1922]. 24p. BPL

NYREN, Arthur
Prairie flowers, and other poems. Merton P. [1924]. [iv], 49p. BPL

O., pseud. see (72)

O.B. see **B., O.**

O.C. PLATOON, pseud. see (24) (51)

O.E.L. see **LINDSAY, Olive E., (Leo, pseud.), (O.E.L.)**

O.M. see (19)

O., R.L., & another
War-time verses. Dundee: Mathew. 1918. 56p.
    Proceeds of sale to Dundee Branch of British Red Cross Society. BPL

O., W.H. see (31) (32)

OATWAY, H.
Our mother land. 1919. [4]p. BM

OBBARD, Constance Mary
Thoughts: [poems]. Kegan Paul, Trench, Trubner.
1921. 84p.   BPL

O'BOB'S, Robin, pseud. see **BANKS, Robert Hesketh,**
(Robert Atherton, pseud.), (Robin O'Bob's, pseud.)

OBSERVER, R.F.C., pseud. see **ALCHIN, Gordon,**
(Observer, R.F.C., pseud.)

O'CONNOR, Armel (Private, East Anglian Field Ambulance)
The exalted valley: [poems]. Ludlow: Mary's Meadow P.;
Burns & Oates. 1915. 48p. por.   BM

The happy stillness: [poems]. Ludlow: Mary's Meadow P.
1920. 40p.   BM

Lilies of His love: [poems]. Ludlow: Mary's Meadow P.
1920. 40p.   BM

The little company: [poems]. Ludlow: Mary's Meadow P.
1925. 72p. col. il.   MPL

A singer in Palestine: [poems]. Ludlow: Mary's Meadow P.
1919. 40p. por. (Mary's Meadow series, X).   MPL

See also (47) (48) (49) (58)

See also **O'CONNOR, Violet, & O'CONNOR, Armel**

O'CONNOR, Violet, & O'CONNOR, Armel
Peace-makers. With foreword by John Oxenham. Methuen.
1916. [viii], 63p. por.
    'Papers and verses'.   BPL

O'CONOR, Norreys Jephson see (17) (18)

OGILVIE, Juliet
Ad vitam: poems. Cassell. 1923. 56p.   BM

OGILVIE, William Henry
Galloping shoes: verses. Constable. 1922. xii, 94p.
col. il. (by Lionel Edwards).   BPL

See also (16) (17) (18) (19) (31) (32) (42) (51) (54)
(71) (87)

OLD HUNTER, pseud. see (5)

OLD LOOT, pseud.
Barbed wire. Beaumont. 1918. 56p.
Verse and prose.   BPL

OLDFIELD, Claude Houghton, (Claude Houghton, pseud.)
(Rejected for active service on the grounds of poor eyesight.
Obtained a position at the Admiralty)

The phantom host, and other verses; by Claude Houghton.
Elkin Mathews. 1917. 48p. (Vigo cabinet series, 39).   BPL

The tavern of dreams: a volume of verse; by Claude
Houghton. Grant Richards. 1919. 88p.   BM

See also (17) (18)

OLIPHANT, Emily Caroline
Chrysoprase: [poems]. Printed Blairgowrie: *Advertiser.*
1915. 43p.
Sold for the Prince of Wales National Relief Fund.   BM

Socks, [and other poems]. Printed Blairgowrie:
Advertiser. 1915. 34p.
Sold for the Prince of Wales National Relief Fund.   BPL

O'LONGAN, P.C. Stacpoole- see STACPOOLE-O'LONGAN, P.C.

OMAN, Carola (Served with Voluntary Aid Detachment on
the Western Front)

The Menin road, and other poems. Hodder & Stoughton.
1919. 74p.   BPL

ONE OF "OURS", pseud.
A soldier's life at our camp: a little fun. [191-].
A postcard.   IWM

O'NEAL, Robert see (29)

OPENER, T.I.N., pseud.
The rubáiyát of a Maconochie ration. Gay & Hancock.
[1919]. 32p.   BPL

[No copy of 2nd ed. traced].

The rubáiyát of a Maconochie ration. 3rd ed. Gay &
Hancock. 1919. 32p.   IWM

ORA, pseud. see HORSPOOL, Amos, (Ora, pseud.)

The **ORANGE** and the green. Printed Birmingham:
Economic Printing Co. [1914].
   A postcard.   BM

ORD, Hubert
Poems of peace and war. St. Catherine P. [1915]. 31p.
il. (by Cecil Hunt).   BPL

ORDE-POWLETT, Nigel, Lord Bolton (Cadet, Officer
Cadet Battalion, Eton College)

Vale, and other poems. Eton College; Spottiswoode,
Ballantyne. 1918. [vi],38p.   BPL

ORELLIUS, pseud. see (31) (32)

O'ROURKE, May
West wind days: [poems]. Erskine Macdonald. 1918.
62p.   BM

See also (31) (32) (49)

ORR, Emily
A harvester of dreams, [and other poems]. Burns, Oates &
Washbourne. 1922. viii, 103p.   BM

ORR, Robert
Hot reception for the Kaiser. Kilmarnock: Author.
[191-].
   A broadside.   BM

O'S., C.J. see O'SHAUGHNESSY, C.J., (C.J.O'S.)

OSBORNE, Antill H. see (27)

OSBOURNE, David Cox McEwen (Lance-Corporal, 1st
Battalion, Middlesex Regiment) see (58)

O'SHAUGHNESSY, C.J., (C.J.O'S.)
Kitchener; by C.J.O'S. [Dublin?]. [1919?]. 19p.   BPL

O'SULLIVAN, Seumas, pseud. see STARKEY, James
Sullivan, (Seumas O'Sullivan, pseud.)

OSWALD, Justin
The World War: [poems] dedicated to the noble and the
brave. Drane. [1924]. 108p. il. BPL

OSWALD, Sydney (Major, King's Royal Rifle Corps)
see (16) (19) (56) (57) (96)

OTTLEY, Edward
Beside "Himself". Printed Shepherd's Bush: Whittell.
1914.
A broadside.
A limited ed. of 36 copies. BM

OUEN, G. de St. see DE ST. OUEN, G.

OWEN, Alfred H.
The world in travail: a drama of evolution: [poems].
Bale & Danielsson. 1931. [vi], 119p. BPL

OWEN, David, (Eifion Wyn, pseud.) see (3)

OWEN, Everard
Three hills, and other poems. Sidgwick & Jackson.
1916. 11p. BPL

See also (16) (17) (18) (24) (47) (48) (49) (50)
(51) (95) (111) (112) (121)

OWEN, Wilfred (M.C. Captain, Manchester Regiment.
Served in trenches, January - June 1917, when he was
invalided home with shell-shock. Met Siegfried
Sassoon at Craiglockart Hospital, near Edinburgh.
Killed in action 4th November 1918, while leading
his men over the Sambre Canal)

Collected poems. Ed. with an intro. and notes by
C. Day Lewis, and with a memoir by Edmund Blunden.
Chatto & Windus. 1963. 191p. facsim. MPL

Poems. With an intro. by Siegfried Sassoon. Chatto &
Windus. 1920. xii, 34p. por. MPL

Poems. New ed. including many pieces now first published,
and notices of his life and work by Edmund Blunden.
Chatto & Windus. 1931. viii, 135p. por. MPL

Poems. Ed. with a memoir and notes by Edmund Blunden.
Chatto & Windus. 1933. viii, 135p. (Phoenix library). BPL

244

Poems. Ed. with a memoir and notes by Edmund Blunden.
[New] ed. Chatto & Windus. 1946. viii, 135p.   MPL

Poems. Ed. with a memoir and notes by Edmund Blunden.
Chatto & Windus. 1966. viii, 135p. (Queen's classics,
certificate books).   MPL

Thirteen poems. Printed Northampton (Mass.):
Gehenna P. 1956. [35]p. il. (by Ben Shahn), por.
    A limited ed. of 400 copies.   BM

See also (4) (13) (14) (22) (33) (37) (50) (53) (59)
(70) (80) (88) (89) (96) (102) (104) (105) (106)
(112) (118) (120) (126) (128) (131)

OWLETT, Frederick Charles (Royal Air Force)
Kultur and anarchy: [poems]. With an intro. by A. St.
John Adcock. Elkin Mathews. 1917. 46p. il.   BPL

OWLEY, Jacob
"Courage!", and other poems. Stockwell. [1918]. 12p.   BPL

OXENHAM, John, (b. William Arthur Dunkerley)
(Oxenham not used as pseud. Name changed by usage,
possibly by deed-poll)

Ad finem: when will the war end? and how? Methuen.
[1916]. [4]p.   BPL

"All clear!": a book of verse commemorative of the
great peace. Methuen. 1919. [viii], 88p.   BPL

"All's well!": some helpful verse for these dark days.
Methuen. 1915. 80p.   BM

'All's well!'": some helpful verse for these dark days
of war. [2nd] ed. Methuen. 1916. 128p. col. il. (by
Mary Bredall).   BM

"All's well!": some helpful verse for these dark days of war.
19th ed. Methuen. 1918. 80p.   BPL

[Many eds publ. during the war. These were apparently
reprints, apart from the illustrated ed.].

The fiery cross: some verse for to-day and to-morrow.
Methuen. 1917. 96p.   BM

The fiery cross: some verse for to-day and to-morrow.
2nd ed. Methuen. 1917. 96p.   BPL

Hearts courageous: [poems]. Methuen. 1918. [viii],
88p. il.   BPL

The "John Oxenham" book of daily readings. Comp.
by A. Andrews-Dale. Clarke. [1920]. 159p.   BM

The king's high way: some more helpful verse. Methuen.
1916. 94p.   BM

[No copy of 2nd ed. traced].

The king's high way: some more helpful verse. 3rd ed.
Methuen. 1916. 94p.   BPL

The later Te Deums. Methuen. [1916]. 12p.   BPL

A little Te Deum of the commonplace. Methuen. [1915].
12p.   BPL

Policeman X, the man who did not dare; and, After!: [poems].
Methuen. [1914]. 8p.
    "Policeman X", written in 1898, refers to the Kaiser.
    "After!" , an epilogue, was written in November 1914. MPL

Selected poems. Fisher Unwin. 1924. xvi, 302p.   MPL

Selected poems. Ed. by Charles L. Wallis. With a biographical
sketch by Erica Oxenham. New York: Harper. 1948.
xxvi, 178p.   BM

Victory day: an anticipation – written in 1914.
Methuen. [1919?]. [4]p. il.   BM

The vision splendid: some verse for the times and the
times to come. Methuen. 1917. 96p.   BM

[No copy of 2nd ed. traced].

The vision splendid: some verse for the times and
the times to come. 3rd ed. Methuen. 1917. 96p.   BPL

"Vox clamantis": (the song of a munition worker).
Witherby. [1917]. 16p.
    Bound with "The girl he left behind him: the
story of a war-worker", an essay by Hugh Martin.   MPL

Wide horizons: some selected verse for these times.
Methuen. 1940. 64p.   BM

See also (25) (31) (32) (49) (55) (119) (120)

OXLAND, Nowell (Lieutenant, 6th Border Regiment. Killed
in action at Suvla Bay, 9th August 1915) see (17) (18) (33)
(111) (112) (131)

OYLER, Leslie Mary
The children's entente cordiale: [poems]. Jack. [1915]. [44]p.
il. (by George Morrow). BM

P., A.E.
All, all you need can in Jesus be found: a word to the
soldiers. Carter. [1914]. [4]p. BM

P., A.L.O. see (23)

P., A.R.
Poems, grave and gay. Stockwell. [1934]. 119p. BPL

P.B. see **B., P.**

P.C.S. see **S., D.C., & S., P.C.**

P.E.T.F. see **F., P.E.T.**

P.H.B.L. see **LYON, Percy Hugh Beverley, (P.H.B.L.)**

P., H.D.C. see **PEPLER, Hilary Douglas Clerk, (H.D.C.P.)**

P., H.V. see (51)

P.S.M. see (31) (32)

P., W.H.
Uncivilized warfare. [Birmingham] : [Economic Printing
Co.]. [1915]. col. il.
A postcard. BM

PAGET, Georgina B.
Song of the unborn, [and other poems]. Grant Richards.
1916. 64p. BM

PAIN, Barry (Chief Petty Officer, Royal Naval Volunteer
Reserve) see (16) (17) (18) (19) (25) (26) (99) (100)
(101) (107) (111) (112)

PAINTER, Margaret see **PAINTER, Monica, & PAINTER,
Margaret**

PAINTER, Monica see (52)

247

PAINTER, Monica, & PAINTER, Margaret
Reality with faery meets: poems. Erskine Macdonald.
1917. 64p.
    Not joint authorship.   BM

PAKENHAM-WALSH, William Sandford
Chants in war: [poems]. Thacker. 1916. [vi], 42p.   BM

Chants in war: [poems]. Elliot Stock. 1917. viii, 91p.   BPL

Through cloud and sunshine: [poems]. Golden Vista P.
[1932?]. 36p. por.   BM

See also (121)

PALMER, Frederick C.
A legend of liberty, and other verse. Birmingham:
Cornish. 1916. 48p.   BM

PALMER, Harold see (29)

PALMER, Herbert Edward
The armed muse: poems. Hogarth P. 1930. 44p.   MPL

Collected poems. Benn. 1933. xiv, 238p.   MPL

[Selected poems]. Benn. [1931]. 32p. (Augustan books of
poetry).
    Bibliog. (author's works) 1p.   BM

A sword in the desert: a book of poems and verses for
the present time. Harrap. 1946. 95p.   WPL

Two fishers, and other poems. Elkin Mathews. 1918. 32p.   BPL

Two foemen, and other poems. Elkin Mathews. 1920. 63p.   BPL

The unknown warrior, and other poems. Heinemann.
1924. xii, 84p.   BPL

The vampire, and other poems and rimes [sic] of a
pilgrim's progress. Dent. 1936. x, 49p.   BM

See also (50) (81)

PALMER, John Richard see (27) (29) (65)

PALMER, Hon. Robert (Grandson of Lord Salisbury.
Captain, 6th Battalion, Royal Hampshire Regiment. Was
wounded in Battle of Umm-El-Hannal, Mesopotamia, 21st

January 1916. Died in Turkish prison camp) see (33) (72)
(111) (112) (131)

PANTER, L. Lydia Acadia see (28) (29)

PARIS, John, pseud. see GWATKIN, Frank Trelawny
Arthur Ashton, (John Paris, pseud.)

PARISH, Leonard (Lieutenant. Served in Mesopotamia)
Dusk of Avon: [poems]. Erskine Macdonald. 1921. 78p.   BM

PARKER, Eric
Sussex woods, and other verse. Eyre & Spottiswoode.
1936. viii, 54p.   MPL

PARNELL, Mary Teresa
Out of the mists: [poems]. Philip Allan. 1936. 96p.   BM

PARR, Ethel F. see (28)

PARRY, Harold (2nd Lieutenant, King's Royal Rifle Corps.
Killed by a shell in Flanders, 6th May 1917)

In memoriam Harold Parry. Printed W.H. Smith. [1918?].
xiv, 143p. por.
      Parry's poems and letters. With a foreword by G.P.D.
[Geoffrey P. Dennis].   SCO

PARRY, Williams see (3)

PARSONS, Lydia Dorothy
Collected poems. With a foreword by Adam Fox. Abingdon:
Abbey P. 1964. [xii], 266p.   BM

PARTRIDGE, J.H.
Hands up, obey! Burgess Hill: Author. 1916.
      A broadside.   BM

PATERSON, Charlotte E.
From the watch-tower: [poems]. Allenson. [1916]. 75p.   BPL

PATMORE, F.J. (Captain. Hampshire Regiment. Taken
prisoner of war after the capture of Kut El Amara, Asia
Minor) see (111) (112)

PATON, M. Waller see (28) (29)

249

PATRIOTS— and people; by the authors of "The Hun hunters".
Grant Richards. 1917. 45p. il.
    Humorous verse.   BPL

PATTERSON, John Edward
Ballads and addresses. Simpkin, Marshall. 1916. 88p.   MPL

PAUL, Elizabeth
Fragments and fancies: [poems]. Oxford: Blackwell.
[1934]. [viii], 29p.   BM

PAYNE, David Bruce, & LILLINGSTON, Kathleen M.E.
Grant us Thy peace: a war vesper. Novello. [1916].
    A card.   BM

PAYNE, James
Nil desperandum! Inspiriting democratic songs and poems
for upholding the world's freedom contra German
militarism. Printed Aldershot: Hunt. [1916]. 13p.   BPL

PEARCE, Patrick
A Christmas story, and other poems. Printed Margate:
Parrett. 1919. 32p.   BM

Poems. Printed Margate: Parrett. 1918. 31p.   BPL

PECK, Robert Bowman
This land I love, [and other poems]. Selwyn & Blount.
1922. xii, 65p.   BM

PEEL, George (Member of Parliament)
To a fallen friend and poet: [poems]. [14]p.   IWM

PEELER, A., pseud.
Polefield Hall Red Cross Hospital, Prestwich, 1915:
a descriptive poem. Printed Prestwich: Booth. 1915. [4]p.
    'Proceeds will be used for purchase of cigarettes for the
soldiers at Polefield'.   BM

PELLOW, J.D.C.
Parentalia, and other poems. Oxford U.P. 1923. 104p.   BPL

PEMBERTON, Jane E. see (28) (29)

PEMBERTON, V.T. (M.C. Captain, Royal Garrison Artillery.
Killed in action 7th October 1918)

Reflections in verse. Grant Richards. 1919. 46p. por.   MPL

PENROSE, Claude Lewis (b. United States, but brought up in
United Kingdom. Major, Royal Garrison Artillery)

Poems; with a biographical preface. Harrison. 1919. [vi],
274p. il., col. il., por., gen. tab.   MPL

PENTY, James R.
Hail! Union of the brave, [and other poems]. Stockwell.
[1920]. 19p.   BPL

PEPLER, Hilary Douglas Clerk, (H.D.C.P.)
God and the dragon: rhymes; by H.D.C.P. Ditchling:
Douglas Pepler. 1917. [vi], 45p. il. (by A.E.R.G.)   MPL

Pertinent and impertinent: an assortment of verse.
Ditchling: St. Dominic's P. 1926. [vi], 69p. il.
    A limited ed. of 200 copies.   MPL

PEROWNE, Victor (Lieutenant, Scot Guards) see (24) (72)

PERRING, Sir Philip
Air raids from dreamland: [poems]. Bell. 1919. 91p.   BPL

PERRY, Beatrice
The girls' battalion. Birmingham:Author. 1916.
    A postcard.
    Proceeds of sale given to wounded soldiers and sailors funds.   BM

PETERSON, John, (Private Pat) (Private, Seaforth Highlanders)
Roads and ditches: [poems]. Lerwick: Manson. 1920.
[viii], 39p.   IWM

Streets and starlight, [and other poems]. Erskine
Macdonald. 1923. 64p.   BM

See also (58)

PETERSON, Margaret
The women's message. Parliamentary Recruiting Committee.
1914.
    A broadside.   MPL

The women's message, 1915, [and other poems]. Truslove
& Hanson. 1915. [29]p.   BPL

See also (16) (26) (47) (48) (49)

251

PETRE, Enid
Autumn leaves, 1915. 4th ed. Humphreys. 1916.
[vi], 23p.   BM

[No other eds traced].

Fallen petals: [poems]. Humphreys. 1917. 36p.   BPL

PEZARE, C.T. see (87)

PHELPS, Arthur L. see (17)

PHILIP, Terence (Spent four years as a prisoner of war in
Germany)

Poems written at Ruhleben. Grant Richards. 1920. 60p.   BPL

PHILIPPS, Hon. Colwyn Erasmus Arnold (Captain, Royal
Horse Guards. Killed in action near Ypres, 13th May 1915)

[Verses, prose fragments, letters from the front].
Murray. 1916. xiv, 128p. por.   BPL

[Verses, prose fragments, letters from the front]. 2nd ed.
Smith, Elder. 1916. [x], 128p. por.   MPL

See also (72) (131)

PHILLIMORE, John Swinnerton
Things new and old: [poems]. Milford. 1918. viii, 140p.   BPL

See also (46)

PHILLIPS, E.
The Lancashire landing. 1915.
   A broadside.
   Written at request of Lance-Corporal M. Phillips, 1st
Lancashire Fusiliers.   BM

Vengence is mine. [191-].
   A broadside.   BM

PHILLIPS, Stephen
Panama, and other poems, narrative and occasional.
Bodley Head. 1915. 153p. il. (by Joseph Pennell).   MPL

See also (16) (18) (19) (26) (47) (48) (49) (65)
(99) (100) (101) (121)

PHILLIPS, Will
War poems. Manchester:Author. [191-].
  A broadside, poster size.   MPL

PHILLP, Helen E. see (64)

PHILLPOTTS, Eden
As the wind blows: [poems]. Elkin Mathews. 1920. 80p.   BM

Brother man, [and other poems]. Grant Richards. 1926. 62p.   BM

A Dartmoor village: [poems]. Watts. 1937. viii, 114p.   BM

'Delight', [and other poems]. Palmer & Hayward. 1916.
[viii], 52p. il.   MPL

Goodwill: [poems]. Watts. 1928. 62p.   WPL

A hundred sonnets. Benn. 1929. [110]p.   MPL

Plain song, 1914-1916: [poems]. Heinemann. 1917.
viii, 80p.   MPL

See also (12) (16) (17) (18) (26) (31) (32) (46) (50)
(99) (100) (101) (120) (121)

PHILPOT, Max
Many moods: [poems]. Aberdeen: Smith. 1917. xii, 103p.   BPL

PHYSICK, Edward Harold, (Edward Harold Visiak, pseud.)
The battle fiends, [and other poems]; by E.H. Visiak.
Elkin Mathews. 1916. 48p. (Satchel series).   MPL

Brief poems; by E.H. Visiak. Elkin Mathews. 1919. 14p.   BM

[Selected poems]; [by] E.H. Visiak. Richards. [1936].
32p. (Richards' shilling selections).   BM

See also (59) (61)

PICKARD, Kate see (28)

PIGGOT, Arthur (Lieutenant, Northumberland Fusiliers.
Killed in action September 1915)

Poems. Erskine Macdonald. 1920. 77p. por.   BPL

PIGOTT, E.W. see (87)

PIM, Herbert Moore
Songs from an Ulster valley: [poems]. Grant Richards.
1920. 96p. por. MPL

PINNELL, Charles H.
Sun poems, and others. Simpkin, Marshall, Hamilton,
Kent. 1918. 64p. BPL

PINTO, Vivian de Sola
Duality, [and other poems]. Oxford: Blackwell. 1922. 32p. BM

The invisible sun: poems. Bodley Head. 1934. [x], 77p. BM

Spindrift: [poems]. Chapman & Hall. 1918. viii, 48p. BPL

PITT, Bernard (Lieutenant, Border Regiment. Killed in
action 30th April 1916)
Essays, poems, letters. Francis Edwards. 1917. viii,
194p. por. MPL

PITT, F.W.
The human touch: poems. Pickering & Inglis. 1933.
160p. por. BM

PLASTOW, E.C. (Private, Lincolnshire Regiment. Served
in France)
The A.S.C. [Army Service Corps]; composed in France
by the author of "Alphabetical war rhymes" and "The charge
at Loos". [1918?].
A card. BM

Alphabetical war rhymes, [no. 1?]. [1915].
A broadside. BM

Alphabetical war rhymes, (no. 2). [1915].
A broadside.
'Composed in trenches near Ypres' — pencilled note in
BM copy. BM

The charge at Loos of the 1/5 Lincoln Regt. [1916].
A postcard. BM

In memoriam: Kitchener of Khartoum, born June 24th,
1850, drowned June 5th, 1916. [1916].
A postcard. BM

Rhymes of the times. Printed Grimsby: Carr & Forman.
1918. 16p. BM

PLATOON, O.C., pseud. see (24) (51)

PLATTS, Tom
Musings in verse. Printed Blackpool: Union Printers.
[1928]. viii, 71p.   BPL

PLAYER, Arthur Leonard (Private, 16th Service Battalion,
Royal Warwickshire Regiment)
Offered in aid of recruiting. [Birmingham?]. [1915?].
  A broadside.   BM

Our hopes and our aims. [Birmingham]. [1915?].
  A card.
  Subscribed for by the 16th Service Battalion, R.W.R.
(3rd Birmingham), Spring Hill Barracks, Moseley.   BM

PLAYFORD, Charles Arthur
The lion. [191-].
  A card.   BM

PLIMPTON, Dorothy
My dream, 1914. 1914.
  A postcard.   BM

PLOWMAN, Dorothy
Lyrical poems. Oxford: Blackwell. 1916. 64p. ("Adventurers
all" series, 10).   BM

See also (72)

PLOWMAN, Max (Commissioned in West Yorkshire Regiment.
Fought on the Somme. Became a prominent member of anti-
war movements).

A lap full of seed: [poems]. Oxford: Blackwell. 1917.
xii, 79p.   IWM

Shoots in the stubble: [poems]. Daniel. 1920. 95p.   BM

See also (4) (33) (50) (63) (72)

PLUNKETT, Edward John Moreton Drax, Lord Dunsany
(Captain, Royal Inniskilling Fusiliers. Fought and was
wounded on the Western Front, April 1916)

Fifty poems. Putnam. 1929. x, 58p.   MPL

War poems. Hutchinson. [1941]. 102p.   BM

See also (17) (18) (31) (32) (33) (46) (111) (112)

POCOCK, Guy Noel see (81)

POEMS, 1903-1923. Cambridge: Galloway & Porter. 1924. viii,
306p.
    A limited ed. of 250 copies.   BM

POLLARD, Alfred William see (24)

PONSONBY, Moyra (A schoolgirl in 1917) see (5)

POOLE, Florence H. see (28) (29)

POPE, Jessie
Hits and misses: [poems]. Grant Richards. 1920. 64p.   BM

More war poems. Grant Richards. 1915. 48p. il.   BPL

Simple rhymes for stirring times. Pearson. 1916. 46p. il.   BPL

War poems. Grant Richards. 1915. 44p. facsim.   MPL

See also (5) (19) (25)

PORTER, Alan
The signature of pain, and other poems. Cobden-Sanderson.
1930. 88p.   MPL

POSTGATE, Margaret see **COLE, Margaret Postgate**

POSTLETHWAITE, Elinor see (28)

POULTEN, W. Clifford (Able-Bodied Seaman, Hood Battalion,
Royal Naval Division)

The bukshee ration, and other war time sketches: the
souvenir book of the Royal Naval Division. Morland P.
[1919]. 96p.
    Recitations, monologues, and one-act plays.   BPL

POWELL, Charles see (27)

POWELL, Constance
War poems. Dublin: Maunsel. 1915. 16p.   MPL

POWELL, George Herbert
The Crown Prince's first lesson-book: or, nursery
rhymes for the times. Grant Richards. 1914. 48p. il.
(by Scott Calder).
  Refers to 'His Imperial Highness Frederick William'.   BPL

POWELL, Sydney Walter
One-way street, and other poems. Harrap. 1934. 128p.   BPL

POWLETT, Nigel Orde-, Lord Bolton see **ORDE-POWLETT,**
Nigel, Lord Bolton

POWLEY, Edward Barzillai
Poems, 1914-1950. Muller. 1950. x, 67p.
  A limited ed. of 510 copies.   BM

POWYS, John Cowper
Mandragora: poems. New York: Arnold Shaw. 1917.
xii, 140p.   BM

A selection from his poems. Ed. with an intro. by Kenneth
Hopkins. Macdonald. 1964. 224p. por.   BM
Wolf's-bane: rhymes. Rider. 1916. 120p.   BM

PRANGLEY, C.W.
Quis separabit? Who shall separate us?: a meditation:
[poems]. Jarrolds. [1918]. 32p. por.
Dedicated to the author's son, Charles Dean Prangley,
2nd Lieutenant, Lincolnshire Regiment, killed in the
advance on Gueudecourt, 25th September 1916, aged 19
years.
Proceeds to the Old Comrades' Association of the
Lincolnshire Regiment.   BM

PRATT, Marjorie see (28)

PRECIOUS, Joyce see (28)

PRESLAND, John, pseud. see **SKELTON, Gladys, (John**
Presland, pseud.)

PRESSEY, Robert W.
Poems in Hampshire. Stockwell. [1920]. 20p.
  Dedicated 'To the brave men of Sandleheath who fell in
the Great War'.   BPL

PRESSIMER, Ella see (28)

PRESTON, Dorothea see (29)

PRESTON, Jim
Firelight memories. [1916].
 A broadside.   BM

See also (5)

PRESTON, Sarah A. see (29)

PREVOST, C.M.
The roll of honour, and other verses. Winchester: Warren.
1915. 32p.   BM

PREWETT, Frank (b. Canada. Came to England before the First
World War and remained)

Collected poems. Cassell. 1964. viii, 63p. por.   BM

Poems. Richmond: Hogarth P. [1921]. [20]p.   BPL

See also (96)

PRIESTLEY, John Boynton (Served in the Infantry, 1914-19)
The chapman of rhymes: [poems]. Moring. 1918. 44p.   MPL

PRIOR, Louisa see (28)

PRITT, Lillie see (29)

PRIVATE PAT see PETERSON, John, (Private Pat)

PRYS-JONES, Arthur Glyn
Poems of Wales. Oxford: Blackwell. 1923. [viii], 64p.   BM

[No copy of 2nd ed. traced].

Poems of Wales. 3rd ed. Oxford: Blackwell. 1925. [viii],
64p.   BM

See also (31) (32) (52) (103)

PUGHE, A.O.
Cypress and amaranth: war poems. Heath, Cranton.
1916. 33p.   IWM

PURCELL, Victor William Williams Saunders
The dog; and, The dove: [poems]. Printed Singapore:
Ribeiro. [1931?]. [vi], 46p.   EDR

PURDIE, Albert Bertrand
Poems. Washbourne. 1918. 39p.   MPL

PURKIS, Henry S.
Angel spirits, and other poems. Stockwell. [1928]. 24p.   BM

PURSHOUSE, B.
Survival: [poems]. Mitre P. 1961. 52p.   MPL

PURVES, C.S. see (5)

Q. CUMBER, pseud. see **CUMBER, Q., pseud.**

QUICK, George P. see (27)

QUILLER-COUCH, Sir Arthur
The sacred way. Cambridge: Heffer. 1916. [4] p.
(Cambridge Magazine reprints, 3).   BPL

QUILTER, Inez (Aged 11 years in 1917) see (5)

QUIN, Roger
Midnight in Yarrow, and other poems. Gowans & Gray.
1918. 35p.   BPL

QUIZ, pseud.
The rubáiyát of a ranker: [poems]. Glasgow: Clark.
1918. [39] p. il. (by R. Birrell).
      Printed on one side of leaf only.   BPL

QUONDAM CRICKETER, pseud, see **STUDD, Charles
Thomas, (Quondam Cricketer, pseud.)**

R., C.J. (2nd Lieutenant, Labour Corps)
Spring's highway: poems written between the ages of
14 and 19. Erskine Macdonald. [1919]. 56p.   BPL

R., C.M. see (110)

R.D. see **D., R.**

R.F.C. see (110)

R., G.E. see (24)

R., G.M.L. see READE, Gerald M'Carthy Lewin, (G.M.L.R.)

R., J.C. see RICHARDSON, James C., (J.C.R.)

R.L.O. see O., R.L., & another

R., N. see RICHFIELD, Nathan, (N.R.)

R.V. see (31) (32) (47) (48) (49) (63)

R.W.L. see L., R.W.

RADCLIFFE, Frances see (28) (29)

RADFORD, A., & RADFORD, Ernest
Song in the whirlwind: [poems]. Smith's Publ. Co. 1918.
24p.   BM

RADFORD, Ernest see RADFORD, A., & RADFORD,
Ernest

RADFORD, Sir George
Verses and versicles. Fisher Unwin. 1917. 80p.   UE

RAE, Elsie Spence
Private John M'Pherson, and other war poems. Aberdeen:
Wyllie. [1918]. x, 68p.   BPL

RAFFE, Walter George
Poems in black and white. Cecil Palmer. 1922. xvi,
60p. il. (by the author).   BM

RAGG, Frederick William
Poems. Complete ed. Stockwell. 1929. xviii, 488p. por.   BM

RALEIGH, Richard, pseud. (2nd Lieutenant, Oxford &
Buckinghamshire Light Infantry) see (31) (32) (58)

RAMSAY, John see (29)

RAMSAY, N. (Staff-Sergeant, Royal Engineers) see (110)

RANDALL, Sidney see (29)

RATCLIFFE, Alfred Victor (Lieutenant, West Yorkshire
Regiment. Killed in action 1st July 1916) see (16) (56) (57)
(72) (131)

RATCLIFFE, Dorothy Una
The dales of Arcady, [and other poems]. Erskine Macdonald.
1918. 64p.   MPL

Singing rivers: [poems]. Bodley Head. 1922. xiv, 98p. il.   BM

Yorkshire lyrics: [poems]. Selected by Wilfrid J. Halliday.
Nelson. 1960. xii, 176p, col, por.
    Publ. for the Yorkshire Dialect Society.   BM

RAWNSLEY, Hardwicke Drummond
The European War 1914-1915: poems. Bennett. [1915].
219p.   MPL

See also (5) (16) (17) (18) (25) (26) (27) (31) (32)
(47) (48) (49) (54) (55) (65) (99) (100) (101) (113)

RAYNER, Judith see (28)

READ, Francis T. see (27)

READ, Sir Herbert (M.C., D.S.O., mentioned in dispatches.
Captain, Green Howards)

Collected poems, 1913-25. Faber & Gwyer. 1926. 116p.   MPL

Collected poems. [New] ed. Faber. 1946. 201p.   BM

Collected poems. New ed. Faber. 1953. 203p.   MPL

Collected poems. New ed. Faber. 1966. 286p.   MPL

The end of a war. Faber. 1933. 31p.   MPL

Naked warriors: [poems]. *Art & Letters*. 1919. [ii], 60p.
    Concludes with "Killed in action", a chapter from an
unfinished novel.   MPL

Poems, 1914-1934. Faber. 1935. 168p.   MPL

Thirty-five poems. Faber. 1940. 80p.
    Bibliog. (author's works) 1p.   MPL

See also (4) (33) (50) (60) (80) (96) (128)

261

READE, Arthur
Poems of love and war. Allen & Unwin. 1915. 96p.   BPL

READE, Gerald M'Carthy Lewin, (G.M.L.R.) (Of Alfington
Vicarage, Ottery St. Mary, Devon)

Admiral Lord Jellicoe's advice to the Prime Minister
and the War Cabinet; [by] G.M.L.R. Ottery St. Mary: Author.
1918.
A broadside.
Reprinted from the *Devon and Exeter Gazette,* 12th
February 1918.   BPL

Another plea for unity: the alternative; [by] G.M.L.R.
Ottery St. Mary: Author. 1916.
A broadside.
Reprinted from the *Devon and Exeter Gazette,* 8th
April 1916.   BPL

The army's message; [by] G.M.L.R. Ottery St. Mary:
Author. 1918.
A broadside.
Reprinted from the *Devon and Exeter Gazette,* 10th
May 1918.   BPL

August iv, 1914-August iv, 1918; [by] G.M.L.R.
Ottery St. Mary: Author. 1919.
A broadside.
Reprinted from the *Devon and Exeter Gazette,* 19th
July 1919.   BPL

August 4th, 1918: the 4th anniversary of the outbreak
of war between Great Britain and Germany; [by]
G.M.L.R. Ottery St. Mary: Author. 1918.
A broadside.
Reprinted from the *Devon and Exeter Gazette,* 2nd
August 1918.   BPL

The boy hero (under 16½ years), [John Travers Cornwell]
on H.M.S. "Chester" May 31st-June 1st, 1916, in the
Battle of Jutland. Ottery St. Mary: Author. 1916.
A broadside.
Reprinted from the *Western Times,* 29th July 1916.   BPL

The call from the trenches. Ottery St. Mary: Author.
1915.
A broadside.
Reprinted from the *Devon and Exeter Gazette,* 21st May
1915.   BPL

The coming doom of the Hohenzollerns (as foretold by themselves); [by] G.M.L.R. Ottery St. Mary: Author. 1917.
A broadside.
Reprinted from the *Devon and Exeter Gazette,* 16th February 1917.   BPL

Conscientious objectors of the twentieth century; [by] G.M.L.R. Ottery St. Mary: Author. 1916.
A broadside.
Reprinted from the *Devon and Exeter Gazette,* 17th March 1916.   BPL

Disunion spells disaster; [by] G.M.L.R. Ottery St. Mary: Author. 1916.
A broadside.
Reprinted from the *Devon and Exeter Gazette,* 24th April 1916.   BPL

The East Devon route march, June 14-19, 1915. Ottery St. Mary: Author. 1915.
A broadside.
Reprinted from the *Devon and Exeter Daily Gazette,* 22nd June 1915.   BPL

England and her allies invincible: domestic disunion the main danger. Ottery St. Mary: Author. 1916.
A broadside.
Reprinted from the *Western Times,* 25th April 1916.   BPL

England's call, the Empire's response: duty of Devonians. Ottery St. Mary: Author. 1915.
A broadside.
Reprinted from the *Devon and Exeter Gazette.*   BPL

England's greatest national debt. Ottery St. Mary: Author. 1916. [2] p.
Reprinted from the *Devon and Exeter Gazette,* 30th June 1916.   BPL

Futility of premature peace-talk. Ottery St. Mary: Author. 1915.
A broadside.
Reprinted from the *Otter Vale News,* 15th December 1915.   BPL

German "Kultur": its "tigerish" methods, with apologies to tigers! Ottery St. Mary: Author.
A broadside.
Reprinted from the *Devon and Exeter Daily Gazette,* 11th June 1915.   BPL

The great advance to ultimate victory; [by] G.M.L.R.
Ottery St. Mary: Author. 1917.
A broadside.
Reprinted from the *Devon and Exeter Gazette,* 11th May
1917. BPL

Great Britain and her allies unconquerable. Ottery St.Mary:
Author. 1916.
A broadside.
Reprinted from the *Otter Vale News,* May 1916. BPL

The grumbling press. Ottery St. Mary: Author. 1915.
A broadside.
Reprinted from the *Express and Echo,* 13th October 1915. BPL

Hark! the trumpet. Ottery St. Mary: Author. 1915.
A broadside.
Reprinted from the *Devon and Exeter Gazette,* 4th May
1915. BPL

"Hold fast": the premier's message to the British Empire;
[by] G.M.L.R. Ottery St. Mary: Author. 1918.
A broadside.
Reprinted from the *Devon and Exeter Gazette,* 10th August
1918. BPL

An ideal England: let us all at least do our best to aim
at it; [by] G.M.L.R. Ottery St. Mary: Author. 1916.
A broadside.
Reprinted from the *Devon and Exeter Gazette,* 19th May
1916. BPL

In glorious memory of H.M.S. "Vindictive"; [by] G.M.L.R.
Ottery St. Mary:Author. 1918.
A broadside.
Reprinted from the *Devon and Exeter Gazette,* 12th May
1918. BPL

In memory of John Travers Cornwell: "his age was under
16½ years"; [by] G.M.L.R. Ottery St. Mary: Author. 1916.
A broadside.
Reprinted from the *Devon and Exeter Gazette,* 11th July
1916. BPL

July XIX, 1919: Britain's victory and peace celebration
day after the Great War, 1914-1919: the debt we owe to
the soldiers and sailors, etc.; [by] G.M.L.R. Ottery St. Mary:
Author. 1919.
A broadside.

264

Reprinted from the *Devon and Exeter Gazette,* 19th July
1919.   BPL

The Kaiser and the Crown Prince: (a parody): one probable
result of the Great War, with apologies to the author of
"Alice in Wonderland"; by G.M.L.R. Sidmouth: Day & Bath.
1915. [4]p.
   'All profits will be given to the Mayoress of Exeter's
"Hospitality Fund" '.   BPL

"The Kaiser and the Emperor": a prophetic parody, with
apologies to the author of "The walrus and the carpenter"
in "Alice through the looking glass"; by G.M.L.R. 2nd ed.
Sidmouth: Day & Bath. 1915.
   A broadside.
   "All profits will be given to the Belgian Official Relief
Fund".   BPL

[No copy of 1st ed. traced].

Kaiser's peace proposals; [by] G.M.L.R. Ottery St.
Mary: Author. 1916.
   A broadside.
   Reprinted from the *Devon and Exeter Gazette,* 16th
December 1916.   BPL

The Kaiser's terms of friendship; [by] G.M.L.R. Ottery
St. Mary: Author. 1918.
   A broadside.
   Reprinted from the *Devon and Exeter Gazette,* 21st
February 1918.   BPL

Kaiser's wish for peace; [by] G.M.L.R. [Ottery St.
Mary]: Author. [1916].
   A broadside.
   Reprinted from the *Devon and Exeter Gazette,* 15th
September 1916.   BPL

Lord Kitchener; [by] G.M.L.R. Ottery St. Mary: Author.
1916.
   A broadside.
   Reprinted from the *Devon and Exeter Gazette,* 9th June
1916.   BPL

Lord Kitchener and the British heroes of the Battle of
Jutland; [by] G.M.L.R. Ottery St. Mary: Author. 1916.
   A broadside.
   Reprinted from the *Western Times,* 9th June 1916.   BPL

National service: let us all accept it, with good grace,
as loyal Englishmen and Britons! Ottery St. Mary:
Author. 1916.
A broadside.
Reprinted from the *Western Times*, 9th May 1916.   BPL

The nincompoop, or slacker! Ottery St. Mary: Author.
1915.
A broadside.
Reprinted from the *Devon and Exeter Gazette*, 1st
June 1915.   BPL

No peace possible with Hohenzollerns; [by] G.M.L.R.
Ottery St. Mary: Author. 1918.
A broadside.
Reprinted from the *Devon and Exeter Daily Gazette*, 17th
October 1918.   BPL

No talk of peace till Prussian militarism has been crushed.
Ottery St. Mary: Author. 1916.
A broadside.
Reprinted from the *Western Times*, 14th April 1916.   BPL

The only way; [by] G.M.L.R. Ottery St. Mary: Author.
1917.
A broadside.
Reprinted from the *Devon and Exeter Gazette*, 17th August
1917.   BPL

Our glorious dead; [by] G.M.L.R. [Ottery St. Mary] :
Author. 1916.
A broadside.
Reprinted from the *Otter Vale News*, July 1916.   BPL

Peace-talk: sheer waste of time; [by] G.M.L.R.
Ottery St. Mary: Author. 1918.
A broadside.   BPL

Peace! Thank God!; [by] G.M.L.R. Ottery St. Mary:
Author. 1919.
A broadside.
Reprinted from the *Devon and Exeter Gazette*, 30th June
1919.   BPL

Plea for continued unity; [by] G.M.L.R. Ottery St.
Mary: Author. 1918.
A broadside.
Reprinted from the *Devon and Exeter Gazette*, 25th
November 1918.   BPL

Plea for unity: "united we stand, divided we fall"; by
G.M.L.R. Ottery St. Mary: Author. 1915.
A broadside.
Reprinted from the *Devon and Exeter Gazette,* 30th
November 1915. BPL

A premature peace may suit the Germans and pro-
Germans, but not the allies. Ottery St. Mary: Author. 1915.
A broadside.
Reprinted from the *Express and Echo,* 10th December
1915. BPL

Premature peace-talk: an insult. Ottery St. Mary:
Author. 1915.
A broadside.
Reprinted from the *Devon and Exeter Daily Gazette,*
17th December 1915. BPL

Profitless peace-talk. Ottery St. Mary: Author. 1915.
A broadside.
Reprinted from the *Devon and Exeter Gazette,* 10th
December 1915. BPL

Red tape: dedicated to officialdom — everywhere!; [by]
G.M.L.R. Ottery St. Mary: Author. 1916.
A broadside.
Reprinted from the *Devon and Exeter Gazette,* 29th
September 1916. BPL

Self-denial for England's sake ought to be a joy!; [by]
G.M.L.R. Ottery St. Mary: Author. 1917.
A broadside.
Amended reprint from the *Devon and Exeter Gazette,*
24th February 1917. BPL

Shirkers and their excuses. Ottery St. Mary: Author.
1915.
A broadside.
Reprinted from the *Devon and Exeter Daily Gazette,*
30th March 1915. BPL

The summons. Ottery St. Mary: Author. 1915.
A broadside.
Reprinted from the *Western Times,* 21st May 1915. BPL

Support coalition government; [by] G.M.L.R. Ottery St.
Mary: Author. 1918.
A broadside.
Reprinted from the *Devon and Exeter Gazette,* December
1918. BPL

"There must be 'no next time' "; [by] G.M.L.R. Ottery
St. Mary: Author. 1917.
A broadside.
Reprinted from the *Devon and Exeter Gazette*, 18th
September 1917.   BPL

To Britain! Ottery St. Mary: Author. 1915.
A broadside.
Reprinted from the *Western Times*, 3rd January 1916.   BPL

To Ireland and the millions of true Irish patriots
throughout the world, who are loyal as ever to Great Britain.
Ottery St. Mary: Author. 1916.
A broadside.
Reprinted from the *Devon and Exeter Daily Gazette*,
8th May 1916.   BPL

To our brave soldiers now returning wounded from the
great offensive in France; [by] G.M.L.R. Ottery St.
Mary. 1916.
A broadside.
Reprinted from the *Devon and Exeter Gazette*, 18th July
1916.   BPL

To the Duke of Portland, K.G., etc.; [by] G.M.L.R.
Ottery St. Mary: Author. 1918.
A broadside.
Reprinted from the *Devon and Exeter Daily Gazette*, 29th
May 1918.   BPL

To the faint-hearted; [by] G.M.L.R. Ottery St. Mary:
Author. 1918.
A broadside.
Reprinted from the *Devon and Exeter Gazette*, 8th
January 1918.   BPL

To the glorious memory of Gen. French's "contemptible
little army"; [by] G.M.L.R. Ottery St. Mary: Author.
1917.
A broadside.
Reprinted from the *Devon and Exeter Gazette*, 1st January
1918.   BPL

To the United States of America, the "Entente's" latest
ally; [by] G.M.L.R. Ottery St. Mary: Author. 1917.
A broadside.
Reprinted from the *Devon and Exeter Gazette*, 13th
April 1917.   BPL

A tribute to our brave British women, dedicated to the
Mayoress of Exeter and to all brave British women of every
class and creed. Ottery St. Mary: Author. 1916.

A broadside.

Reprinted from the *Western Times*, 14th July 1916.　　　BPL

Trust Lord Kitchener and the government. Ottery St.
Mary: [Author?]. 1915.

A broadside.

Reprinted from the *Western Times* and *Express and
Echo*, 22nd September 1915.　　　BPL

Trust Lord Kitchener and the government. Ottery St.
Mary: [Author?]. 1915.

A card. Different format from previous entry.

Reprinted from the Exeter *Western Times* and *Express
and Echo*, 22nd September 1915.　　　BPL

The two ideals; [by] G.M.L.R. Ottery St. Mary: Author.
1918.

A broadside.

Reprinted from the *Devon and Exeter Gazette*, 7th May
1918.　　　BPL

U-boat warfare: the destruction of hospital ships and
other Hunnish barbarities known to all; [by] G.M.L.R.
Ottery St. Mary: Author. 1918.

A broadside.

Reprinted from the *Devon and Exeter Gazette*, 23rd
April 1918.　　　BPL

A united front; [by] G.M.L.R. Ottery St. Mary: Author.
1918.

A broadside.

Reprinted from the *Devon and Exeter Gazette*, 27th
February 1918.　　　BPL

What can I do? Ottery St. Mary: Author. 1915.

A broadside.

Reprinted from the *Devon and Exeter Gazette*, March
19th 1915.　　　BPL

What we are fighting for: a reply; [by] G.M.L.R. Ottery
St. Mary: Author. 1917.

A broadside.

Reprinted from the *Devon and Exeter Gazette*, 23rd March
1917.　　　BPL

See also (29) (129)

The **RECRUITS**. *The Times*. 1914. [2]p.
Offprint from *The Times*, 14th September, 1914.   EDR

RED BAND, pseud. (A conscientious objector)
A prisoner of Pentonville. Elkin Mathews. 1919. 64p.   MPL

REDIVIVUS, Junius, pseud. see **JUNIUS REDIVIVUS, pseud.**

REEDY, William Curran (Able-Seaman, Royal Navy)
Blue sea ballads and chanties. Erskine Macdonald. 1917.
62p.   MPL

Spindrift and spunyarn: [poems]. Fortune P. [1942]. 64p.   BM

REES, Aubrey
The heroic spirit, and other verses. Walbrook. 1918. 60p.   BM

REES, G.E. see (17) (18)

REEVE, Alfred
The lays of a labourer: [poems]. Erskine Macdonald.
1916. 22p.   BPL

REEVE, Rosaline
Armageddon, 1914. Printed Clowes. [1915]. 28p.   BPL

RENNELL, Lord see **RODD, James Rennell, Lord Rennell**

RENNIE, Peter see (29)

RENNY, Gertrude see (28)

RENSHAW, Constance Ada
Battle and beyond: [poems]. Erskine Macdonald. 1917.
90p.   BPL

England's boys: a woman's war poems. Erskine Macdonald.
1916. 62p. (XXth century poetry series).   BM

England's boys, [and other poems]. 2nd ed. Erskine
Macdonald. 1918. 74p.   BPL

Lest we forget: [poems]. Oxford: Blackwell. 1937. xii,
78p.   BM

Narcotics: [poems]. Merton P. [1924]. [vi], 108p.   BPL

Up to the hills: [poems]. Merton P. [1922]. [viii], 112p.   LPL

See also (47) (48) (49) (52)

RESEIGH, H. see (29)

RESTALRIG, pseud. see SYMONS, J.B., (Restalrig, pseud.)

REYNOLDS, Frank
An appeal to the women of England. Salisbury: Author.
1915.
   A card.   BM

RHOADES, James
Collected poems. Fisher Unwin. 1925. 196p. por.   BPL

Words by the wayside: [poems]. Chapman & Hall. 1915.
viii, 154p.   BM

See also (5) (29) (31) (32) (51) (99) (100) (101) (111)

RHYS, Brian see (85)

RHYS, Ernest
The leaf burners, and other poems. Dent. 1918. x, 147p.   BPL

Rhymes for everyman. Lovat Dickson. 1933. 64p. il.
(by John Nash).   BM

See also (4) (22)

RICARDO, pseud. see MOORE, Richard Louis-Bertrand,
(Ricardo, pseud.)

RICE, Sir Cecil Arthur Spring- see SPRING-RICE, Sir
Cecil Arthur

RICE, Richard Whately
British Boloism. Blackburn: Author. [1917].
   A postcard.   BM

Chamberlain scheme. Blackburn: Author. [1917].
   A card.   BM

Dangerous aliens: or, the hidden hand. Blackburn: Author.
[1917].
   A postcard.   BM

Duty. Blackburn: Author. [1916].
   A postcard.   BM

Duty's call. Blackburn: Author. [1916].
A postcard. BM

"Economy". Blackburn: [Author?]. [1917?].
A postcard. BM

A few thoughts for our over-sea cousins. Blackburn:
Author. [1917?].
A card. BM

Food restriction. Blackburn: Author. [1917].
A card. BM

For honour and right. Blackburn:Author. [1918].
A postcard. BM

Greed and gain: or, the nation's soul. Blackburn: Author.
[1917].
A postcard. BM

In memory of the late Lord Kitchener. Blackburn: Author.
[1917?].
A card. BM

Increased cost of living. Blackburn: Author. [1916].
A postcard. BM

A kind thought for the Army Service Corps. Blackburn:
Author. [1917].
A postcard. BM

Lord Rhonda, our new Food Controller. Blackburn:
Author. [1917].
A postcard. BM

The nation's duty. Blackburn: Author. 1916.
A postcard. BM

"Old England". Blackburn: Author. [1917].
A postcard. BM

Our air service in war. Blackburn: Author. [1917].
A postcard. BM

Our air service value in war. Blackburn: Author. [1917].
A postcard. BM

"Our economic boycott". Blackburn: Author. [1917].
A postcard. BM

"Peace". Blackburn: Author. [1917].
A postcard. BM

272

Peace and unity. Blackburn: Author. [1917].
A postcard. BM

Profiteering. Blackburn: Author. 1917.
A postcard. BM

Rationing. Blackburn: Author. [1917?].
A card. BM

Sailors and mine-sweepers. Blackburn: Author. [1917?].
A card. BM

Season's hymn for sailors and soldiers. Blackburn: Author.
1916.
A postcard. BM

7th Battalion, Loyal North Lancs. Regiment. Blackburn:
Author. [1917].
A card. BM

"Springtime of peace". Blackburn: Author. [1917].
A postcard. BM

The supreme test: or, "do and d ?". Blackburn:
Author. [1918].
A postcard. BM

Uncle Sam's resolve. Blackburn: Author. [1917].
A postcard. BM

Unity: dedicated to the Prime Minister (the right Hon. D.
Lloyd George, M.P.). Blackburn: Author. [1917].
A postcard. BM

RICE, Stanley Pitcairn
War verses and translations. Printed Coconada: Scape.
1918. [iv], 32p. BM

RICH, W.J.
The blinded hero, and other verse. Stockwell. [1921].
24p. por. BPL

RICHARDS, Frederick see (29)

RICHARDSON, Emmeline
Whither goest? Poems. Elliot Stock. 1918. 73p. BM

RICHARDSON, James C., (J.C.R.)
Poems; by J.C.R. Printed Narodiczky. 1929. [ii], 28p. BM

Poems; and, Nations philosophy; by J.C.R. Printed
Wingfield. 1930. 32p.   BM

Poems; and, Nations philosophy; by J.C.R. [New] ed.
Printed Wingfield. 1930. 32p.   BM

RICHARDSON, Norah see (32) (52)

RICHFIELD, Nathan, (N.R.)
A call to arms; by N.R. [1914].
  A broadside.   BM

Facts and fancies: [poems] ; by N.R. Bristol: Horseshoe
Publ.Co. 1925. 46p.   BM

RICKETT, Leonard Allen Compton- see **COMPTON-
RICKETT, Leonard Allen**

RICKWORD, Edgell (Fought on the Western Front)
Behind the eyes: [poems]. Sidgwick & Jackson. 1921.
56p.   BM

Collected poems. Bodley Head. 1947. 92p.   MPL

Fifty poems: a selection. With an intro. by Roy Fuller.
Enitharmon P. 1970. [8], iv, 67p. por.
  A limited ed. of 362 copies.   WPL

Invocations to angels: [poems] ; and, The happy
new year: [a play]. Wishart. 1928. 77p.   BM

Twittingpan, and some others: [poems]. Wishart. 1931.
45p.   BM
See also (4) (33) (50) (70) (78) (79)

RIDDELL-WEBSTER, Letitia see (28) (29)

RIDGWAY, Gladys
Wayside treasure and poems, 1914-1918. Birmingham:
Shakespeare P. [1923]. 72p.   BPL

RIEU, Emile Victor
The tryst, and other poems. Oxford U.P. 1917. 56p.   BPL

RIGBY, F.
His letter home. [1915].
  A card.   BM

RIGBYE, R.E.K., (Cross Fleury, pseud.)
Armageddon: an invocation; by Cross Fleury. Carlisle:
Author. [1914]. [4]p.   BM

RIPON, Bishop of see CARPENTER, William Boyd, Bishop of Ripon (54)

RIPPON-SEYMOUR, H. (Captain)
Songs from the Somme: [poems]. Long. 1918. 61p.   MPL

RISK, Robert K. see (65)

ROBERTS, Cecil (War correspondent, attached in turn to all three services)
Charing Cross, and other poems of the period. Grant
Richards. 1919. 32p.   MPL

Selected poems, 1910-1960. Preface by Lord Birkett.
Hutchinson. 1960. 151p.
   Author's autobiographical notes appended.   MPL

Twenty-six poems. Grant Richards. 1917. 95p.   MPL

War poems. Collected ed. Clarke. 1916. [viii], 42p.
   A limited ed. of 100 hand-printed copies.   MPL

See also (17) (18) (31) (32) (52) (63) (65) (85)
(104) (121)

ROBERTS, Daniel J. (Gloucestershire Regiment)
Poems. Gloucester: Minchin & Gibbs. 1918. 56p.   MPL

ROBERTS, E.L. (2nd Lieutenant, York & Lancaster Regiment)
Frightful crhymes [sic] : [poems]. Erskine Macdonald.
1918. 91p.   MPL

ROBERTS, Gwendoline see (28) (29)

ROBERTS, Morley
War lyrics. Selwyn & Blount. 1918. 48p.   BPL

See also (17) (18)

ROBERTS, Ursula, (Susan Miles, pseud.)
Annotations: [poems] ; by Susan Miles. Oxford U.P.
1922. 56p.   MPL

Dunch, [and other poems]; by Susan Miles. Oxford:
Blackwell. 1918. 72p. ("Adventurers all" series, XVIII).   BM

ROBERTSON, Alexander (Corporal, York & Lancaster
Regiment. Killed in action 1st July 1916)
Comrades: [poems]. Elkin Mathews. 1916. 44p. (Vigo
cabinet series).   BM
Comrades: [poems]. 2nd ed. Elkin Mathews. 1916. 44p.
(Vigo cabinet series, 36).   MPL
Last poems. With a preface by P. Hume Brown. Elkin
Mathews. 1918. 47p. (Vigo cabinet series, 45).   MPL
See also (16) (56) (57) (72) (96) (131)

ROBERTSON, Duncan John
Wraith and wrack: verses. Longmans, Green. 1918.
xii, 103p.   BM

ROBERTSON, Eric Sutherland
From alleys and valleys: verses. Erskine Macdonald.
1918. 78p.   BM

ROBERTSON, James Logie, (Hugh Haliburton, pseud.)
Petition to the deil, and other war verses. Paisley:
Gardner. 1917. 99p.
    Some in Scots dialect. With a glossary.   BPL
See also (23) (54) (91)

ROBERTSON, Peterishea A.
Until the dawn, and other poems. Paisley: Gardner.
1919. 63p.   BPL

ROBERTSON, Stewart Alan
With double tongue: verses in Scots and English. Harrap.
1928. [ii], 188p.   MPL

ROBERTSON-GLASGOW, Geraldine
Poems of the Great War. Printed Frome: St. Aldhelm's
Home for Boys. [1919]. 35p.   BPL
See also (31) (32) (47) (48) (49) (87)

ROBIN O'BOBS, pseud. see BANKS, Robert Hesketh, (Robert
Atherton, pseud.), (Robin O'Bobs, pseud.)

ROBINSON, A.E.
That boy o' mine. Manchester: Carey. [1916].
  A broadside.   BM

ROBINSON, Agnes Mary Frances see DUCLAUX, Agnes Mary Frances Robinson

ROBINSON, Helena (Company Officer, Hertfordshire Women's Defence Relief Corps) see (5)

ROBINSON, William Fothergill
The harvesting, and other poems. With prefatory note by
Selwyn Image. Erskine Macdonald. 1916. 60p.   BM

Twenty poems, 1912-1915. Exeter: Eland. 1915. 20p.   BPL

See also (47) (48) (49)

ROBISON, David A. see (32)

RODD, James Rennell, Lord Rennell
Trentaremi, and other moods: [poems]. Arnold. 1923.
viii, 40p.   MPL

ROE, William James
The house of light, and other poems. Kegan Paul, Trench,
Trubner. [1920]. viii, 110p.   BPL

ROGERS, H.L. (Headmaster, King's College School,
Wimbledon, 1910-34)

Patterns,[and other poems]. With an intro. by Ronald
Mason, and a memoir by T.R. Harley. Printed Oxford:
Holywell P. [1949?]. 184p. por.   EDR

ROGERS, Kenneth
Musings of a medico: [poems]. Erskine Macdonald. 1918.
72p.   BPL

Thoughts of a nature lover: [poems]. Holden &
Hardingham. 1921. 125p.   BM

ROLLO, Ha, pseud.
Soul voices in the vigil. Sach. [1918]. [13]p.
  Cover-title is "The day of national intercession".   BM

ROLLO, W. Forbes (Lance-Corporal)
Stray shots from the Dardanelles: [poems]. Printed
Carlisle: Thurnam. 1915. 31p. il. (by the author).   MPL

ROMANES, Norman Hugh
War-shrine fragments, and other poems. Printed
Ahmednagar: S.P.G. Mission Printing P. [1919]. 105p.
   Dedicated 'To the memory of Lieutenant-Colonel Maitland
Hardyman, D.S.O., M.C., who fell leading his regiment to
victory on August 24th, 1918, aged 23'.   BPL

ROMILLY, Lady Arabella
In time of war, [and other poems]. Murray. 1914. 6p.
   'Profits will be given to Queen Mary's Needlework Guild'.   IWM

RONALD, Frederick (Served with the Hampshire Regiment
in Greece)

Songs of defiance, and other poems. Erskine Macdonald.
1917. 38p. (Malory booklets).   MPL

ROOKER, Anne see (28)

ROOME, Holdar, pseud. see MOORE, Harold William,
(Holdar Roome, pseud.)

ROOTHAM, Helen see (123) (124)

ROPE, Henry Edward George
The hills of home, and other verses. Stockwell. 1925.
20p.   BM

Religionis Ancilla, and other poems. Heath, Cranton.
1916. 84p.   BM

Soul's belfry, and other verses. Church Stretton: Stretton
P. 1919. 64p.   BM

ROSE, Ellen see (28)

ROSE-TROUP, J.M. (Captain, Queen's Regiment. Was a
prisoner of war in Germany) see (72)

ROSENBERG, Isaac (Enlisted with Suffolk Regiment, then
transferred to King's Own Royal Lancaster Regiment. Killed
in action on the Somme, 1st April 1918)

Collected poems. Ed. by Gordon Bottomley and Denys
Harding. With a foreword by Siegfried Sassoon. Chatto &
Windus. 1949. viii, 240p.
　　First publ. in 1937 as part of "The collected works of
Isaac Rosenberg".　　　　　　　　　　　　　　　　　MPL

Collected works: poetry, prose, letters, and some drawings.
Ed. by Gordon Bottomley and Denys Harding. With a
foreword by Siegfried Sassoon. Chatto & Windus. 1937. xvi,
401p. il., por.
　　Cover-title is "The complete works of Isaac Rosenberg".　　ECPL

Moses: a play; [and, Poems]. Printed Stepney: Paragon.
1916. [ii], 26p.　　　　　　　　　　　　　　　　　　　BM

Poems. Selected and ed. by Gordon Bottomley. With an
introductory memoir by Laurence Binyon. Heinemann.
1922. xii, 187p. por.
　　Bibliog. note 2p.　　　　　　　　　　　　　　　　MPL

Poems. Selected and introduced by Denys Harding.
Chatto & Windus. 1972. 64p. (Compact poets).　　　　　MPL

Youth: [poems]. Printed Narodiczky. 1915. 18p.　　　　　BM

See also (4) (13) (14) (33) (50) (80) (96) (105)
(106) (128) (131)

ROSEVEARE, Hilda
Beauty for ashes, and other poems. Epworth P. [1922].
72p.　　　　　　　　　　　　　　　　　　　　　　　　BM

ROSMAN, Alice Mary Bowyer (b. North of England.
Emigrated to Australia)

An enchanted garden, and other verses. *British Australasian.*
1916. [viii], 96p.　　　　　　　　　　　　　　　　　　BM

ROSS, R. see (27)

ROSS, Sir Ronald (Lieutenant-Colonel)
Fables and satires: [poems]. Harrison. [1929]. iv, 72p.　　BM

Poems. Elkin Mathews & Marrot. 1928. 96p.　　　　　　MPL

See also (16) (17) (18) (19)

ROSS-LEWIN, Richard S.S., & ROSS-LEWIN, Robert O'D.
In Britain's need: [poems]; by the brothers Ross-Lewin.
Dublin: Hodges, Figgis; Erskine Macdonald. 1917. 64p.　　BPL

ROSS-LEWIN, Robert O'D. see ROSS-LEWIN, Richard S.S.,
& ROSS-LEWIN, Robert O'D.

See also (31) (32)

ROSTREVOR, George see HAMILTON, Sir George
Rostrevor, (George Rostrevor, pseud.)

ROWE, Alice E. see (28) (29)

ROWE, Edward Henry
Brought home!: a tribute to the memory of "The unknown
warrior", buried in Westminster Abbey, November 11th, 1920.
South Shields: Author. 1920. il.
   A card.   BM

Her last moments: tribute to the memory of Nurse
Edith Cavell. South Shields: Author. 1917. por.
   A broadside.   BM

Tribute to the memory of Lord Kitchener: verses. South
Shields: Author. [1916].
   A broadside.   BM

Waiting and watching. [South Shields?] : [Author?]. 1917.
   A card.   BM

Wake up, England: verses. South Shields: Author. 1916.
   A broadside.   BM

ROWE, Louise Jopling see (64)

ROWLANDS, John see (27) (29)

ROWLANDS, Victor, pseud.
"Particles of war": poems. Stockwell. [1918]. 47p.   MPL

ROWLEY, Richard, pseud. see WILLIAMS, Richard Valentine,
(Richard Rowley, pseud.)

ROYCE, Marjory see (28)

ROYDS, Thomas Fletcher
My fifty versing years: [poems]. Favil P. 1959. 44p.   MPL

RUDLAND, Ernest Marston
Poems old and new. Oxford: Blackwell. 1930. x, 180p.   BM

RUSKIN, Sybil see (64)

RUSSELL, Cecil Henry St. Leger
Poems. Bristol: Arrowsmith. 1937. 128p.   BM

RUSSELL, Charles (Captain, Gurkha Rifles. Served in
Middle East. Killed in action at Nebi Samwil, 22nd
November 1917)

Sonnets, poems, and translations. With eight introductory
sonnets and a memoir by John Alexander Chapman. Thacker,
Spink. 1920. xxxii, 70p.   BM

Sonnets, poems and translations. With eight introductory
sonnets and a memoir by John Alexander Chapman. [2nd ed.].
Thacker, Spink. 1920. xxxii, 88p.   BM

RUSSELL, George William, (A.E., pseud.)
Collected poems; by A.E. Macmillan. 1919. xvi, 303p.   BPL

Collected poems. 2nd ed. Macmillan. 1926. xx, 430p.   MPL

Gods of war, with other poems; by A.E. Printed Dublin:
Sackville P. 1915. 40p.
    Printed for private circulation.   BM

See also (17) (18) (31) (32) (38) (39) (47) (48) (49)
(59) (60) (61) (66) (108) (112)

RUSSELL, John Howard
Poems. Ouseley. [1919]. 48p.   BM

See also (61)

RUSSELL, R.W.
In memory of our beloved ones embalmed by the seas.
Portsmouth: Author. [1914].
    A postcard.   BM

RUSSELL, William W.
The Battles of Loos and Hill Seventy, September 25th and
26th, 1915, founded on facts, [and other poems]. Printed
Southsea: Hawkins. 1915. 8p. por.
    Title from cover.   BPL

RUTTER, Owen, (Klip-Klip, pseud.) (Captain. Served in Salonika)
The song of Tiadatha. British ed. Fisher Unwin. 1920.
144p.   MPL

281

[First publ. Salonika, 1919. No copy of this ed. traced].

Tiadatha: [poems]. Allan. 1935. 238p. il. (by Richard
B. Ogle).
  Contains "The song of Tiadatha" and "The travels of
Tiadatha". Latter does not include war poetry. MPL

S.C.H. see HANNING, S.C., (S.C.H.)

S., D.C., & S., P.C.
Verses: lyrical, satirical and occasional. Lincoln
Williams. [1934]. viii, 70p. BPL

S., E. see STRICKLAND, Eugene, (E.S.) (5)

S., E.D. see DE STEIN, Sir Edward, (E.D.S.), (E. De S.)

S., E. De see DE STEIN, Sir Edward, (E.D.S.), (E. De S.)

S., E.L.
Hymn in time of war. Elliot Stock. [191-].
  A broadside. BM

S., F. see SIDGWICK, Frank, (F.S.)

S., H. see (63)

S., H.S. see SMITH, Hugh Stewart, (H.S.S.)

S., J.H. see (19)

S., J.H. see also SUMS, J.H.

S.L.H. see H., S.L.

S., J.M. see STANIFORTH, Joseph Morewood, (J.M.S.)

S.L.L. see LLOYD, S.L., (S.L.L.)

S., M. see SYMINGTON, M., (M.S.)

S., M.R.C.
In the new world and the old: [poems]. Kegan Paul,
Trench, Trubner. 1918. viii, 56p. BPL

S., P.C. see S., D.C., & S., P.C.

S., W.G. see SHAKESPEARE, William G., (W.G.S.)

SABIN, Arthur Knowles
Christmas 1914. East Sheen: Temple Sheen P. 1914.
19p.
    A limited ed. of 300 copies, hand-printed by the author.   BPL

New poems. East Sheen: Temple Sheen P. 1914. 51p.   MPL

War harvest, 1914: [poems]. East Sheen: Temple
Sheen P. [1914]. 15p.
    Bibliog. (author's works) 1p.
    Printed by the author, at his private press.   BPL

SACKVILLE, Lady Margaret
Collected poems. Martin Secker. 1939. 324p. por.   MPL

The pageant of war, [and other poems]. Simpkin,
Marshall, Hamilton, Kent. [1916]. 61p.   BPL

Poems. Allen & Unwin. 1923. 63p.
    A limited ed. of 750 copies.   BM

Selected poems. Constable. 1919. x, 141p.   MPL

See also (31) (32) (38) (39) (47) (48) (49) (59)
(60) (61) (94)

ST. JOHN, Mary
The loom of life, and other poems. Stockwell. [1935?].
16p.   BM

ST. OUEN, G. De see DE ST. OUEN, G.

SALMON, Arthur Leslie
Songs of wind and wave: a collection of verse. Edinburgh:
Blackwood. 1916. x, 98p.   BPL

SALMOND, Charles Adamson
Echoes of the war: [poems]. Paisley: Gardner. 1916.
96p.   BPL

See also (23)

SALT, Henry Stephens
Homo rapiens [sic], and other verses. Watts. 1926. 70p.   MPL

See also (61)

The **SALT** of sacrifice, [and other poems]. 1914. 20p.
'Profits are devoted to the fund for the relief of Belgian
refugees'. BM

SALWEY, Charlotte, & SALWEY, Reginald E.
Adoration, and other poems. Heath, Cranton & Ouseley.
1915. 64p. il. (by Jasper Salwey). BPL

SALWEY, Reginald E. see **SALWEY, Charlotte, & SALWEY,
Reginald E.**

SAMPSON, Dudley (Ex Lieutenant-Colonel. Too old for
active service)

Songs of love and life: [poems]. Erskine Macdonald.
1918. 70p. BPL

SAMPSON, Harold Fehrsen
Sounds from another valley: [poems]. Elkin Mathews.
1915. 48p. BM

SAMUEL, Gerald George (Lieutenant, Royal West Kent
Regiment. Killed in action leading his company in the
Battle of Messines, 7th June 1917)

Poems. Humphreys. 1917. 44p. por. IWM

SAMWAYS, George R. (Royal Flying Corps)
Ballads of the Flying Corps. McBride, Nast. 1917. 64p. MPL

War lyrics: [poems]. Stockwell. [1916]. 32p. BPL

SANDFORD, Egbert Thomas
Brookdown, and other poems. Erskine Macdonald. 1915.
61p. (Little books of Georgian verse). BPL

Brookdown, and other poems. 2nd ed. with two additional
poems. Erskine Macdonald. 1916. 61p. (Little books of
Georgian verse). MPL

Mad moments: [poems]. Dublin: Maunsel. 1919. vi,
46p. BM

Poems. Burns, Oates & Washbourne. 1927. 108p. BM

See also (19) (47) (48) (49)

SANSOME, Thomas
Moral tales in rhyme. Birmingham: Lawrence. 1914. 44p. BPL

284

SARGENT, Edward George
Greetings: [poems]. Religious Tract Society. [1929].
58p. por.   BM

The western window, [and other poems]. Religious Tract
Society. 1934. 111p. por.   BM

See also (27)

SASSOON, Siegfried (M.C. Captain, Royal Welch
Fusiliers. Enlisted in 1914 with the Sussex Yeomanry.
Spent some time at Craiglockhart Hospital, where he met Wilfred
Owen)

Collected poems. Faber. 1947. xvi, 269p.   LPL

Collected poems, 1908-1956. Faber. 1961. xx, 317p.   MPL

Counter-attack, and other poems. Heinemann. 1918. 64p.   MPL

Four poems: Dreamers; Does it matter?; Base details;
Glory of women. Cambridge: Severs. 1918. [4]p. (*Cambridge
Magazine* reprints, 7).   BM

The heart's journey: [poems]. New York: Crosby Gaige;
London: Heinemann. 1927. [63]p.
    A limited ed. of 599 copies, printed in the U.S.A.   BM

The heart's journey: [poems]. Heinemann. 1928. 48p.   MPL

Morning-glory, [and other poems]. Chiswick P. [1916].
14p.
    A limited ed. of 11 copies.   BM

The old huntsman, and other poems. Heinemann. 1917.
x, 110p.   MPL

Picture show, [and other poems]. Printed Cambridge.
1919. [75]p.
    A limited ed.of 200 copies, printed for the author by
J.B. Peace at the University Press, Cambridge, June, 1919.   BM

Picture show, [and other poems]. New York: Dutton.
[1920]. x, 56p.
    Contains seven poems not in the limited English ed. of
1919.   Not seen

Poems. Selected by Dennis Silk. Printed Marlborough
College P. 1958. xviii, 85p.
    A limited ed. of 150 copies initialled by the author. Not seen

Poems newly selected, 1916-1935. Faber. 1940. 78p.
Bibliog. note (author's works) 1p. MPL

Recreations: [poems]. Chiswick P. 1923. 40p.
A limited ed. of 75 copies, printed for the author. BM

The redeemer. Cambridge: Heffer. 1916. [4]p.
(Cambridge Magazine reprints, 2). BM

The road to ruin: [poems]. Faber. 1933. 23p. BPL

Satirical poems. Heinemann. 1926. 64p. BM

Satirical poems. New ed., with five poems added.
Heinemann. 1933. 72p. BM

Selected poems. Heinemann. 1925. viii, 75p. MPL

[Selected poems]. Benn. [1926]. 32p. (Augustan books
of modern poetry).
Bibliog. (author's works) 1p. LPL

[Selected poems]. Eyre & Spottiswoode. 1943. 32p.
(Augustan poets).
Bibliog. (author's works) 1p.
Not the same selection as Benn ed. of 1926. BM

Selected poems. Faber. 1968. 93p. MPL

A suppressed poem: Saul Kain says . . . Good-bye to
all that . . . gravely. Unknown P. 1919. [4]p.
A limited ed. of 500 copies.
Sassoon's bibliographer, Geoffrey Keynes, states 'In spite
of the date 1919 on the title-page, this pirated edition of
the suppressed verse letter cannot have been printed before
1929, when Graves's book [Goodbye to all that] was
first published'. Not seen

To any dead officer (who left school for the Army
in 1914). Cambridge: Severs. 1917. [4]p. *(Cambridge
Magazine* reprints, 6). Not seen

Vigils, [and other poems]. Bristol: Cleverdon. 1934.
[51]p.
A limited ed. of 303 numbered copies signed by the
author. BM

Vigils, [and other poems]. Heinemann. 1935. [iv], 36p. BPL

War poems. Heinemann. 1919. 96p. MPL

See also (4) (11) (17) (18) (20) (21) (22) (24) (31)

(32) (33) (35) (36) (37) (38) (39) (46) (50) (53) (59)
(60) (61) (66) (70) (72) (80) (81) (88) (89) (96) (102)
(103) (104) (106) (111) (112) (118) (120) (127) (128)

SAUNDERS, A., & WALSH, J. (Both had active service in the war)

    Once a hero. [1920?].
      A card.   BM

SAUNDERS, D. Pitkethly see (65)

SAUNDERS, T.B., (Bard of Sandhurst, pseud.)
Poems of remembrance; by "The Bard of Sandhurst".
Maidstone: British Legion P. [1933?]. [4] p.   BM

SAUTER, R.H. (Was a prisoner of war)
Songs in captivity: [poems]. Heinemann. 1922. viii, 62p.   BPL

See also (33)

SAVAGE, Constance M. see (29)

SAVILL, George
Idylls of the homeland, and other poems. Cambridge:
Heffer. 1920. vi, 37p.   BPL

The sergeant's dream. Elkin Mathews. 1924. 46p.   MPL

SAYLES, J.H.
The European War. Sheffield: Macdougall. [191-].
    A broadside.
    Written as an aid to recruitment.   BPL

Poems on the war. Sheffield: Macdougall. [1914]. 20p.   BPL

SCARISBRICK, Joseph
Rhymes and runes: (original). Trowbridge: Lansdown.
1921. 168p.   BPL

SCARR, C.W., (Knipper, pseud.), (Merlin, pseud.)
Bertha and Edith: or, two postmaids; by Merlin.
1918. [2] p.   BM

The hunter's moon; [by] Knipper. [1917?].
(Ruin'd rimes).
    A broadside.   BM

The hunter's moon; by Knipper. [1917?]. (Ruin'd rimes).
("Reflector" series, lyrical post cards, 10).   BM

A modern nursery tale; [by] Merlin. 1918. il., por. (Ruin'd rimes).
   A card.   BM

Search lights: or, the waning moon; [by] Knipper. [1917?]. 2p.   BM

The siren's serenade, [and other poems]; by Knipper. [1917?]. 2p.   BM

The siren's serenade. [1918]. ("Reflector" series, lyrical post cards, 9).   BM

SCOTLAND, James S.
Poems, secular and sacred: recreations and meditations from a Scottish manse. Edinburgh: Macniven & Wallace. 1925. viii, 148p. por.   BM

See also (29)

SCOTS GREY, pseud. see (5)

SCOTT, Aimée Byng, Lady, (Alec Holmes, pseud.)
The road to Calais, [and other poems]. Thacker. 1919. [vi], 40p.
   Dedication in memory of those who gave their lives for their country, 1914-1918.   BPL

Scattered leaves: [poems]; by Mrs. Arthur Scott. Oxford: Blackwell. 1916. viii, 70p.   BPL

The secret night, and other poems. Medici Society. 1924. [vi], 48p.   BM

SCOTT, Mrs. Arthur see **SCOTT, Aimée Byng, Lady, (Alec Holmes, pseud.)**

SCOTT, David
Poems and songs. Dalkeith: Author. 1920. 103p.
   Some in Scots dialect.   BM

See also (29)

SCOTT, E.P.
For the sake of his lady fair. [1916].
   A broadside.   BM

SCOTT, J. Cuthbert
A thousand strong, and other war verses. Birmingham:
Cornish. 1916. 42p.   BPL

SCOTT, William Henry
The lute of life, [and other poems]. Werner Laurie.
[1928]. 126p.   BM

SCOTT-MONCRIEFF, Charles Elliott (Captain,
King's Own Scottish Borderers)

War thoughts for the Christian year: [poems].
Skeffington. 1915. 124p.   BPL

See also (72)

SCRYMGEOUR, Norval see (29)

SCUDAMORE, Walter King
Impressions and depressions, and other verses.
Heath, Cranton. [1920]. 72p.   BPL

SEAMAN, Sir Owen
From the home front: verses. Constable. 1918. 62p.
    Reprinted from *Punch*.   MPL

Interludes of an editor: [poems]. Constable, 1929. xii,
156p.   BM

Made in England: verses. Constable. 1916. 56p.
    Reprinted from *Punch*.   MPL

A selection: [poems]. With an intro. by C.L. Graves. Methuen.
1937. xxviii, 340p. por.   MPL

War-time: verses. Constable. 1915. 56p.
    Reprinted from *Punch*.   MPL

War-time: verses. 2nd ed. Constable. 1915. 63p.   BPL

See also (16) (17) (18) (19) (23) (25) (26) (29) (31)
(32) (44) (47) (48) (49) (51) (54) (59) (82) (83)
(84) (99) (100) (101) (107) (111) (112) (119) (120)

SEEBY, G.
"Brown studies": [poems]. Amersham: Morland; Foyle.
1919. 44p.   BPL

SEVEREZ, Helen see (51)

SEWELL, Harold Edward Boeda

The Empire "one and all". [Leeds] : Author. [1916]. [3]p. BM

SEWELL, Wynne

Festubert, and other poems. Sampson, Low, Marston. 1916. 41p. BPL

SEYMOUR, H. Rippon- see **RIPPON-SEYMOUR, H.**

SEYMOUR, William Kean

Caesar remembers, and other poems. Gollanz. 1929. 64p. MPL

Collected poems. Hale. 1946. 257p. MPL

Swords and flutes: [poems]. Fisher Unwin. 1919. 96p. BPL

To Verhaeren, and other poems. Wilson. 1917. 47p.
 A limited ed. of 300 copies. BPL

Twenty-four poems. Palmer & Hayward. 1918. 23p. MPL

The **SHADOW**: a pastoral, July 1914. Grant Richards. 1917. 47p. BPL

SHAKESPEARE, William G., (W.G.S.) (Captain, Royal Army Medical Corps)

A winter fragment, and other poems. Mitre P. [1950]. 47p. BM

Ypres, and other poems. Sidgwick & Jackson. 1916. 43p. MPL

See also (2) (17) (18) (24) (47) (48) (49) (51) (59) (95)

SHANKS, Edward (Joined 8th South Lancashire Regiment in 1914. Invalided out in 1915)

Collected poems, 1910-1925. Arranged in six books. Collins. 1926. xii, 254p. MPL

The man from Flanders, and other poems. Printed St. Clements P. 1940. 28p.
 A limited ed. of 250 copies printed for private circulation. BM

Poems. Sidgwick & Jackson. 1916. 75p. MPL

Poems, 1912-1932. Macmillan. 1933. xvi, 512p. MPL

The Queen of China, and other poems. Martin Secker.

1919. [viii], 240p.   MPL

Poems, 1939-1952. Macmillan. 1954. xii, 107p.   BM

Songs: [poems]. Poetry Bookshop. 1915. 32p.   BPL

See also (33) (72) (95) (102) (111) (112)

SHANNON, William Boyd- see BOYD-SHANNON, William

SHARLAND, Rose E.
Maple leaf men, and other war gleanings. Bristol: Arrowsmith.
1916. 89p. il.
    Poetry and prose.   BPL

SHARPLEY, C. Elissa
Good will, and other verses. [Torquay?]: [Author?].
[1918?]. 12p.   BPL

Service: [poems]. [Torquay?]: [Author?]. [1918?]. 15p.   BPL

See also (28) (29)

SHAW-STEWART, Patrick (Lieutenant-Commander,
Royal Naval Division. Fought at Gallipoli. Killed in
action in France, 1917) see (13) (14) (33)

SHEEN, Bert see (5)

SHEPHERD, Eric
Pilgrimage: poems. Longmans, Green. 1916. xii, 100p.   BM

SHERRINGTON, Sir Charles Scott
The assaying of Brabantius, and other verse. Oxford
U.P. 1925. [iv], 67p.   BM

The assaying of Brabantius, and other verse. 2nd ed.
Oxford U.P. 1940. viii, 88p.   BM

SHILLITO, Edward
Jesus of the Scars, and other poems. Hodder & Stoughton.
1919. 74p.   BPL

The omega, and other poems. Oxford: Blackwell. 1916.
[viii], 63p.   BPL

See also (17) (18) (19) (31) (32) (42) (55) (61) (63)
(111) (112)

SHIRREFF, Alexander Grierson
Tales of the sarai, and other verses. Oxford: Blackwell.
1918. xii, 95p. BM

SHORT, William Ambrose (Lieutenant-Colonel, Royal
Field Artillery. Killed in action 21st June 1917)

Poems. Humphreys. 1918. [viii], 80p. MPL

SHORTER, Dora Sigerson
Comfort the women: a prayer in time of war. Printed
Shorter. [1915]. [8]p.
   A limited ed. of 20 copies printed by Clement Shorter
for distribution among his friends.
   Reprinted from the *Daily Telegraph*, 27th February
1915. BM

An old proverb "It will all be the same in a thousand years".
Printed Shorter. 1916. 7p.
   A limited ed. of 25 copies printed by Clement Shorter
for distribution among his friends.
   First publ. in *The Nation*, 20th May 1916. BM

The sad years, [and other poems]. Constable. 1918.
xvi, 88p. por. MPL

The sad years, [and other poems]. Constable. 1918.
xvi, 88p. il., por., facsim.
   A limited ed. of 50 copies printed for private
circulation. BM

The tricolour: poems of the Irish revolution. Dublin:
Maunsel & Roberts. 1922. [viii], 72p. il., por. MPL

See also (60)

SHORTER, L.A. Hurst
Amaranth and gold, [and other poems]. Humphreys. 1919.
viii, 94p. BPL

The forest child, and other poems. Humphreys. 1917.
[viii], 83p. BM

Poems. Hastings: Parsons. 1916. 47p. BM

Visions of chivalry, [and other poems]. Humphreys.
1918. viii, 80p. BM

White horses, and other poems. Humphreys. 1920.
viii, 112p. BM

SHOVE, Fredegond
Dreams and journeys: [poems]. Oxford: Blackwell.
1918. 50p. ("Adventurers all" series, XXI).   BPL

See also (60) (80)

SIBLEY, Norman Wise see (65)

SICHEL, Walter see (31) (32) (99) (100) (101)

SIDGWICK, Arthur Hugh (Captain. Died of wounds in France,
1917)
Jones's wedding, and other poems. Arnold. 1918. 96p.
por.   MPL

SIDGWICK, Frank, (F.S.) (Served in the Army)
More verse; by F.S. Sidgwick & Jackson. 1921. 64p.   MPL

Some verse; by F.S. Sidgwick & Jackson. 1915. 80p.   MPL

See also (19) (26) (59) (80) (111) (112)

SIEVEKING, Lancelot de Giberne
The Cud: experimental poems. Mills & Boon. 1922.
60p.
   A limited ed. of 500 copies.   BM

SIGERSON, Dora see **SHORTER, Dora Sigerson**

SILLITO, Emmie
The great sacrifice: love; dedicated to mothers.
1916. [3]p.   BM

Killed in action: dedicated to the fallen. [1916]. [3]p.   BM

SILVESTER, James
The highlander at the bridge: a story of the war in verse.
Clacton-on-Sea: Author. 1914. [3]p.   BM

Sonnets of many years. Stanley Martin. [1930]. [viii],
156p.   BM

See also (27) (29)

SIMMONDS, Kathleen O. see (28)

SIMMS, Evelyn
The crowning purpose. Martin Secker. 1916. 55p.   BPL

See also (31) (32)

SIMPSON, Harold see (26) (63)

SIMPSON, Henry
The golden rose, and other poems. Sach. 1917. 80p.   BPL

Lauds and loves: [poems]. With a preface by Gilbert
Frankau. Sach. 1930. 135p.   BM

SIMPSON, Henry Lamont (Lieutenant, 1st Lancashire
Fusiliers. Killed in action 29th August 1918)

Moods and tenses: [poems]. Erskine Macdonald. 1919.
120p. por.   BPL

See also (131)

SIMPSON, James see (29)

SINCLAIR, May (Served with the Red Cross in a Field
Ambulance Corps, Belgium) see (19) (59) (112)

SIORDET, Gerald Caldwell (Served with British Expeditionary
Force. Killed in action 9th February 1917)

[Selected poems and drawings]. Privately printed.
[1918?]. ii, [45]p. il., por.
     Printed on one side of leaf only.   BM

See also (44) (63) (121) (131)

SITWELL, Dame Edith
Clowns' houses: [poems]. Oxford: Blackwell. 1918.
37p. (Initiates series of poetry by proved hands, 5).
     "The dancers: during a great battle, 1916" is the only
war poem. Not included in author's "Collected poems" 1930
or "Collected poems" 1957.   MPL

SITWELL, Dame Edith, & SITWELL, Sir Osbert,
(Miles, pseud.)
Twentieth century harlequinade, and other poems. Oxford:
Blackwell. 1916. 27p.
     Not joint authorship. No war poetry by E. Sitwell.   BM

SITWELL, Sir Osbert, (Miles, pseud.) (Grenadier Guards.
Fought at Loos and throughout the war)

Argonaut and juggernaut: [poems]. Chatto & Windus.
1919. xii, 124p.   MPL

Collected satires and poems. Duckworth. 1931. xii,
292p.   MPL

Selected poems: old and new. Duckworth. 1943. 163p.   MPL

The Winstonburg line: 3 satires. Hendersons. [1920].
20p.   BM

See also (4) (33) (50) (60) (61) (72) (80) (112) (122)
(123) (124) (125) (126)

See also **SITWELL, Dame Edith, & SITWELL, Sir
Osbert, (Miles, pseud.)**

SKEAT, Bertha Marian
Vox clamantis: [poems]. Erskine Macdonald. 1918. 65p.   BPL

SKELTON, Gladys, (John Presland, pseud.)
Poems of London, and other verses; by John Presland.
Macmillan. 1918. viii, 125p.   BM

Selected poems of John Presland. Linden P. 1961. 139p.   BM

SKERRET, Frank W.
Poems. Ilfracombe: Stockwell. [1943]. 22p.   BM

Rhymes of the rail. Leeds: Goodall & Suddick. 1920.
79p.   BPL

SLEEP, Frederick, (Dent Dormer, pseud.)
The devil and the Kaiser, with other poems grave and
humorous; by Dent Dormer. Stockwell. [1925]. 94p.   BM

SMALLEY, Marie
Thoughts of mine: [poems]. Blackburn: Toulmin. 1916.
[ii], 79p. por.   BM

SMELLIE, William T. see (29)

SMIRK, Saddler (117th Battery, Royal Garrison Artillery)
Will they never come?: recitation. [Norfolk?]. [191-].
    A broadside.
    Written pre-conscription, aimed at those who did not
volunteer.   BM

SMITH, Alice Mary, (Angela Gordon, pseud.)
Collected poems. Ed. by Margaret Smith. Sheldon P.
1937. 162p. por.   BM

SMITH, Arthur Lynnford- see LYNNFORD-SMITH, Arthur

SMITH, Arthur William
The circling hours, and other poems. Harborne
[Birmingham]: Bradshaw. 1922. [36]p.   BM

SMITH, Cicely Fox
Fighting men: [poems]. Elkin Mathews. 1916. 64p.
(Vigo cabinet series).   MPL

The naval crown: ballads and songs of the war. Elkin Mathews.
1915. 64p. (Vigo cabinet series).   MPL

Rhymes of the red ensign. Hodder & Stoughton. 1919.
72p.   MPL

Sea songs and ballads, 1917-22. Methuen. 1923. viii,
136p. 6 il. (by W. Phil Smith).   MPL

Small craft, [and other poems]. Elkin Mathews. 1917.
78p.   MPL

Songs and chanties, 1914-1916. Elkin Mathews. 1919.
232p.   MPL

See also (12) (16) (17) (18) (31) (32) (46) (47) (48)
(49) (59) (87) (111) (112) (119) (120) (121)

SMITH, Francis W. (M.C. Lieutenant, Leeds Rifles, West
Yorkshire Regiment)

The great sacrifice, and other poems. Erskine Macdonald.
1917. 44p.   MPL

See also (52)

SMITH, Frederick James Johnston- see JOHNSTON-SMITH,
Frederick James

SMITH, Geoffrey Bache (Lieutenant, Lancashire Fusiliers.
Died of wounds at Waslencourt, France, 3rd December
1916)

A spring harvest: [poems]. Erskine Macdonald.
1918. 78p.   MPL

See also (131)

SMITH, Hugh Darnley see (30)

SMITH, Hugh Stewart, (H.S.S.) (Captain, Argyll &
Sutherland Highlanders. Killed in action in France, 18th
August 1916)

Verses; by H.S.S. [1916?]. [vi], 40p. por.   EDR

SMITH, Isaac Gregory see (19) (54)

SMITH, J.E.
Fear not life's voyage, and other poems. Stockwell.
[1922]. 35p.   BPL

SMITH, J.W.N.
Visions: [poems]. Rugby: Over. 1917. [vi], 32p.   BM

SMITH, Margery
Still in my hand: [poems]. Outpost Publications. 1964. 24p.   BM

See also (46)

SMITH, Norman R. Ewart
The arena, and other verses. Printed Bristol: Bristol Printers.
[1920]. 43p.   BM

Crimson skies, and other poems. Printed Cardiff:
Cardiff Printers. [1935]. xii, 163p. il., por.   BM

Lyrics of love, and other poems. Bristol: Haynes & Brewer.
1925. 64p.   BM

Poems of humanity. Exeter: Wheaton. 1937. 36p.   BM

SMITH, Thomas Napoleon, (Tonosa, pseud.)
Belgium's refugees and Britain's open arms. [Leytonstone?]:
[Author?]. 1915. [3]p.   BM

Burnley's war flame [Jennie Jackson]. [Burnley?]: Author.
1918. por.
  A postcard.   BM

Burnley's winning Jennie [Jennie Jackson], alias "Y.K."
[Burnley?]: Author. 1916.
  A postcard.   BM

God bless: or, Tommy's plum-bombs, [and other poems].
Leytonstone: Author. [1917]. [4]p. por.
  Dedicated to the author's son Corpl. Ewart G. Smith, of

the 2nd Infantry Brigade, Canadian B.E.F., killed in a
trench-hole, 27th September, 1916. BM

He fought for me, [and other poems]. Leytonstone:
Author. [1917]. [4]p. por.
Cover-title is "Wavelets of the world-wide war". BM

"K.K." [Lord Kitchener] and the world-wide war.
Leytonstone: Author. 1916.
A broadside. BM

Lusitania! Lo, Satan near; [and], An examination
prayer: [poems]. Leytonstone: Author. [1915]. [2]p. BM

Patriot or paytraitor? [Leytonstone]: Author. 1917.
A broadside. BM

Their eyes off me: or, those khaki chaps from 'cross the sea:
verses; by Tonoso. [Leytonstone?]: Author. [1915].
A broadside.
First publ. in *The Weekly Scotsman*. BM

Trust the Kaiser?!!! : a timely word to the German
Empire. Leytonstone: Author. 1918.
A broadside.
Written in 1915 — author's note. BM

With the organ to the trenches. Leytonstone: Author.
1916.
A broadside. BM

See also (29)

SMYTH, Marjorie Kane
Poems. Amersham: Morland; Foyle. 1919. 32p. BPL

The **SOLDIER'S** farewell to his lady. Printed Birmingham:
Economic Printing Co. [1914].
A postcard. BM

SOLOMON, Jessica see (64)

SOLOMON, Louis B. (Lieutenant, Royal Fusiliers. Killed
in action 12th April 1918, aged 22)
Wooden crosses, and other verses. Roehampton: Fountain
Publ. Co. [1918]. 24p. por. MPL

SOLOMON, William Ewart Gladstone
Rhymes from an Eastern battlefield. Printed Simla:
Thacker, Spink. 1918. [vi], 44p. MPL

SORBY, John see (29)

SORLEY, Charles Hamilton (Captain, Suffolk Regiment.
Killed in action at Loos, 13th October 1915, aged 20)

Marlborough, and other poems. Cambridge U.P. 1916.
x, 107p. por.   MPL

Marlborough, and other poems. 2nd ed. Cambridge U.P.
1916. [x], 108p. por.   BM

Marlborough, and other poems. 3rd ed., with, Illustrations
in prose. Cambridge U.P. 1916. [xii], 144p.   MPL

Marlborough, and other poems. 4th ed. Cambridge U.P.
1919. xii, 134p.   BM

Marlborough, and other poems. 5th ed. Cambridge U.P.
1922. xii, 134p.   BM

Marlborough, and other poems. Cambridge U.P. 1932.
xii,134p. por. (Cambridge miscellanies, II).   MPL

[Selected poems]. Benn. [1931]. 32p. (Augustan books
of poetry).   BM

See also (4) (16) (17) (18) (19) (22) (33) (49) (50)
(56) (57) (59) (70) (72) (80) (89) (96) (102) (104) (111)
(112) (131)

SOUTAR, William (Able-Seaman, Royal Navy. Discharged
on displaying symptoms of the illness from which he later
died)

Brief words: one hundred epigrams. Edinburgh: Moray
P. 1935. 48p.   BM

Collected poems. Ed. with an introductory essay by
Hugh MacDiarmid. Dakers. 1948. 525p. por.   MPL

SOUTH, Marshal see (38) (39)

SOUTHAM, H.C.
The call to arms "Your king and country need you":
patriotic poem or recitation. Manchester: Author.
[1915?].
    A broadside.
    'Sold for the benefit of the author who is blind'.   BM

SOUTHGATE, Henry W.
Oh! Glorious lads! Liverpool: Author. 1914.
A broadside. BM

SOUTHWOLD, Stephen, (Neil Bell, pseud.)
The common day: [poems]. Allen & Unwin. 1915. 112p. BM

SPAFFORD, Fred
Mother Shipton's later prophecies. Hull:Author.
[191-].
A postcard. BM

SPALDING, Henry Norman
In praise of life: [poems]. Oxford: Blackwell. 1952.
x, 290p. MPL

SPAVEN, Elizabeth
Cheer up, brave hearts! Leeds: Author. [191-].
A card. BM

Keep smiling!: (from a soldier's mother to soldiers'
mothers). [Leeds?] : [Author?]. [1915]. [2]p.
A card. BM

SPEAIGHT, Frank
Beyond the dark: poems. Cecil Palmer. 1923. 144p. BM

SPENCER, Ellen
"And the Lord said", [and other poems]. Heath, Cranton &
Ouseley. [1915]. 45p. BPL

SPENCER, Harold Sherwood see (27)

SPENSLEY, Eleanor see (64)

The **SPOT** that wont rub out (real enamel). [1915?].
A card. BM

**SPOTTER, pseud. see HINTON, Archibald Campbell,
(Spotter, pseud.)**

SPRING, Robert Howard (Served with the Army in France
throughout the war, attached for most of the time to the
Intelligence Corps) see (58)

SPRING POET, pseud. see HASELER, Digby Bertram, (Spring Poet, pseud.)

SPRING-RICE, Sir Cecil Arthur
Poems. Longmans, Green. 1920. xxxii, 182p. por.   BM

SPURRIER, H. (Private, Royal Warwickshire Regiment. Wounded at La Bassée) see (56) (57)

SPURWAY, Eva
Woven arras: [poems]. Erskine Macdonald. [1917?].
[vi], 56p.   BM

SQUIRE, Sir John Collings (Unfit for active service because of poor eyesight)

The birds, and other poems. Martin Secker. 1919. 32p.
   Written between April 1918 and April 1919.   MPL

Collected poems. With a preface by John Betjeman.
Macmillan. 1959. xviii, 242p. por.   MPL

The lily of Malud, and other poems. Martin Secker.
1917. 32p.   BM

Poems. First series. Martin Secker. 1918. 116p.
   Poems written 1905-1917.   MPL

Poems in one volume. Heinemann. 1926. xii, 244p.   MPL

Poems of two wars. Hutchinson. 1940. 46p.   MPL

[Selected poems]. Benn. [1925]. 32p. (Augustan
books of modern poetry).
   Bibliog. (author's works) 1p.   BM

Selected poems. Oliver Moxon. 1948. [viii], 148p. por.   BM

The survival of the fittest, and other poems. Allen &
Unwin. 1916. 64p.   UE

The survival of the fittest, and other poems. [New] ed.
Allen & Unwin. 1919. 63p.   BPL

Twelve poems. Morland P. 1916. [vi], 30p. il. (by
A. Spare).   MPL

See also (20) (31) (32) (35) (61) (104) (105) (111)
(112) (118)

SQUIRES, Augusta see (28) (29)

STABLES, J. Howard (Lieutenant, Gurkha Rifles. Served
in Mesopotamia. Wounded and missing, 17th February
1917, later reported killed)

The sorrow that whistled, and other poems. Elkin
Mathews. 1916. 60p.   MPL

STACPOOLE, Henry de Vere
The North Sea, and other poems. Hutchinson. 1915.
viii, 82p.   BPL

See also (99) (100) (101)

STACPOOLE-O'LONGAN, P.C. (Lieutenant, Royal
Irish Regiment)

Last post, and other poems. Kegan Paul, Trench,
Trubner. 1917. 31p. por.   BPL

STADDON, C. Eric, (Junior Sub, pseud.)
Ranikhet War Fund: random rhymes of Ranikhet; by the
Junior Sub. Printed Ranikhet: Rustomjee. [1917?]. 12p.   IWM

STANIFORTH, Joseph Morewood, (J.M.S.)
Rumours of war: [poems]; by J.M.S. Rangoon:
Rangoon Times P. [1915?]. [31]p.
   Printed on one side of leaf only.
   'Author's profits will be given to the Belgian Relief Fund'.   BPL

STANLEY, Edgar see (29)

STANLEY, Gertrude P. see (28) (29)

STANLEY-WRENCH, Mollie see (64)

STANTON, F.H.
"Arm, arm, ye brave!" : [poems]. [1914].
   A broadside.
   Reprinted from the *Norwood Review* and the *Sydenham
Review,* 5th December 1914.   BM

STARKEY, James Sullivan, (Seumas O'Sullivan, pseud.)
Collected poems: by Seumas O'Sullivan. Dublin:
Orwell P. 1940. 227p.
   A limited ed. of 300 copies.   MPL

Requiem, and other poems; by Seumas O'Sullivan.

Privately printed Dublin. 1917. 23p.
    A limited ed. of 100 copies.   BM

The Rosses, and other poems; by Seumas O'Sullivan.
Dublin: Maunsel. 1918. 39p.   MPL

STAUNTON, Harry
The battle of freedom: Great War poem. [Privately
printed]. [1915]. [3]p.   BM

STAVELEY, Tom
Empty day: verses. Elkin Mathews. 1915. 72p.   BM

STEAD, Henry
Duty or regret. [Doncaster?] : Author. [1915].
    A broadside.   BM

STEDMAN, William Nathan
Thomas Atkins, Esquire, writes home from the front:
a new recitation for every audience, dedicated to the heroes
of Belgium; [and, The God-grit hearts of Belgium]. Printed
Finchley: Simpson. 1914. [4]p.   IWM

With the eagles: Armageddon: or the last great war:
a poem on the fulfilment of history. Printed Finchley:
Simpson. 1914. [4]p. il.   BM

STEEL, Frances Coen see (28)

STEELE, Howard (M.C. Captain)
Cleared for action: [poems]. Fisher Unwin. 1914. 167p.   BPL

See also (2)

STEEVENS, Louise see (129)

STEIN, Sir Edward De see **DE STEIN, Sir Edward, (E.D.S.),**
(E.De S.)

STEPHENS, Bessie May
"Clouds with silver linings": thoughts for war-time and
peace: [poems]. Cardiff: *Western Mail.* 1916. [ii], 46p.   BPL

See also **HAMILTON, F. de C., & STEPHENS, Bessie May**

STEPHENS, Florence see (29)

STEPHENS, James
Collected poems. Macmillan. 1926. xxii, 260p.   MPL

Collected poems. 2nd ed. Macmillan. 1954. xxvi, 390p.   MPL

Green branches: [poems]. Dublin: Maunsel. 1916. 20p.
   A limited ed. of 500 copies.   BM

Green branches: [poems]. New ed. Dublin: Maunsel.
1917. 16p.   BPL

See also (19)

STEPHENSON, Elizabeth Margaret see (28) (29)

STERLING, Robert William (Lieutenant, Royal Scots
Fusiliers. Killed in action 23rd April 1915)

Poems. Oxford U.P. 1915. xvi, 69p. por.   MPL

See also (72) (131)

STEUART, Douglas Stuart Spens see (26)

STEVENSON, Charles Preston see (27)

STEVENSON, Dorothy Emily see (28)

STEVENSON, Francis Seymour
Conflict and quest. Longmans, Green. 1926. x, 300p.
col. il.
   Long narrative poem 'arising out of the Great War, and
more particularly, out of the campaigns in Palestine and
Syria'.   BM

November sunsets, and other poems. Jarrolds. [1919]. 62p.   BM

See also (27)

STEWART, David
Soldiers' songs; and, Poems of love and loss. Stockwell.
1919. 64p.   BPL

STEWART, Edith Anne
Pilgrimage and battle: [poems]. Headley. [1917]. 94p.   BPL

Poems: second book. Swarthmore P. 1919. 43p.   BPL

STEWART, John E. (M.C. Major, Staffordshire Regiment.
Killed in action 26th April 1918)

Grapes of thorns: [poems]. Erskine Macdonald. 1917.
48p.   MPL

See also (2) (16) (58) (96) (131)

STEWART, Patrick Shaw- see **SHAW-STEWART, Patrick**

STEWART, Wynne see (63)

STILL, John (Lieutenant, East Yorkshire Regiment. 3 years
prisoner of war in Turkey)

Poems in captivity. Bodley Head. 1919. xii, 306p. facsim.   BPL

STITT, Innes (Queen's Westminster Rifles) see **STITT,
Innes, & WARD, Leo**

STITT, Innes, & WARD, Leo
To-morrow, and other poems. With a foreword by H.
Scott Holland. Longmans, Green. 1917. 59p.   MPL

STOCKER, Helen, (Helen Cash, pseud.)
The dreamer, and other poems; by Helen Cash. Palmer
& Hayward. 1918. 64p.   BPL

Machines and men, and other new poems. Selwyn & Blount.
1923. 48p.   BM

STODART-WALKER, Archibald
Occasional verse. Glasgow: Maclehose, Jackson. 1920. 141p.   BM

Verses of consolation, and other lines written in war time.
Glasgow: Maclehose. 1915. 46p.   BPL

See also (19)

STONE, Eric
The raving: a ballad of Berlin. Sidgwick & Jackson.
1915. 48p. il.
    A parody of Poe's "The raven", satirizing the German
Emperor, Wilhelm II.   MPL

STONE, James
A black outlook. Fleetwood: Author. 1915.
    A postcard.   BM

Lest we forget, U.B., 1914. Fleetwood: Author. 1918.
    A postcard.   BM

STOPES, Marie Carmichael see (64)

STORRIE, James see (27)

STORY, Alfred Thomas
Songs of a new age: [poems]. Allen & Unwin. 1918. 109p.   BPL

STRACHEY, Constance, Lady see (64)

STRATTON, Ella M. see (28) (29)

STREAKS, John
In memoriam: Miss Cavell, murdered at Brussells, October
12, 1915. Oxford: Author. [1915].
   A card.   BM

The Kaiser's dream. Oxford: Author. 1918.
   A card.   BM

STREETS, John William (Sergeant, 12th York & Lancaster
Regiment. Mortally wounded in the Somme advance, 1st July
1916)

The undying splendour, [and other poems]. Erskine
Macdonald. 1917. xii, 71p.   MPL

See also (2) (52) (56) (57) (63) (72) (96) (110) (131)

STRICKLAND, Amy Campbell- see CAMPBELL-STRICKLAND,
Amy

STRICKLAND, Eugene, (E.S.) see (5)

STRONACH, E.M.
The soldier's grave, and other poems. Stockwell.
[1925]. 16p.   BM

STRONG, Leonard Alfred George (Exempted from military
service because of spinal complaint)

The body's imperfection: collected poems. Methuen.
1957. 164p.   MPL

Call to the swan: [poems]. Hamish Hamilton. 1936. 74p.   BM

March evening, and other verses. Favil P. 1932. [7]p.
   A limited ed. of 100 numbered copies.   BM

306

STROZZI, pseud. see (110)

STUART, Andrew John (Killed in action 26th September 1915) see (19) (131)

STUART, Dorothy Margaret
Beasts royal, and other poems. Clement Ingleby. 1923.
x, 60p.   BM

See also (26) (55) (99) (100) (101) (111) (112)

STUART, Muriel
The cockpit of idols: [poems]. Methuen. 1918. x, 46p.   MPL

Poems. Heinemann. 1922. [viii], 72p.   MPL

See also (112)

STUART, S. see (64)

STUDD, Charles Thomas, (Quondam Cricketer, pseud.)
Quaint rhymes for the battlefield. Clarke. 1914. 88p.   BPL

SUFFOLK, Silly, pseud.
Prose and poetry. Ipswich: Harrison. 1925. 117p.   BM

SULLIVAN, Mary
The song of the road: stray verses. Stockwell. 1924.
24p.   BM

SUMMERS, Elijah see (29)

SUMMERS, Knight see (5)

SUMS, J.H., (J.H.S.)
"It's a tough job to beat the allies": a song for our
soldiers and sailors: verses; by J.H.S. Hazell, Watson &
Viney. [1914].
  A broadside.   BM

SUTCLIFFE, J. Charles see (29)

SUTHERLAND, Millicent, Duchess of see **GOWER,
Millicent, Duchess of Sutherland** (25) (26) (29)

SWAINE, James Edward
Ode on the death of Lord Kitchener of Khartoum.
Stockwell. 1916. 8p.   BPL

SWALLOW, James Edward
My quota: [poems]. Cambridge: Heffer. 1931. [iv], 106p.   BM

SWINGLEHURST, Henry Edward (Lived in Valparaiso, Chile)
Patriotic poems. Unwin. [1915]. 64p. por.   BPL

Patriotic poems. Valparaiso: Author. 1924. viii, 96p.
por.   BM

SYMINGTON, M., (M.S.)
The "lamplighters", and other verses; by M.S. Paisley:
Gardner. [1919]. 51p.   BPL

SYMON, Mary
Deveron days: [poems]. Aberdeen: Wyllie. 1933. [vi], 60p.
   In Scots dialect. With a glossary.   BM

See also (91)

SYMONS, Annie Colenso see (29)

SYMONS, J.B., (Restalrig, pseud.)
War blasts, and other poems. Leith: Leith Printing and
Publ. Co. 1915. xii, 100p. por.
   Some in Scots dialect.   BPL

T.B.D., pseud. see JAMES, Sir William Milburne, (T.B.D.,
pseud.)

T., C. see HARVEY, John G. Russell, (J.G.R.H.), &
THOMAS, Charles, (C.T.)

T., E.
The war alphabet. [1915].
   A postcard.   BM

T., E.M. see (63)

T., H. see (5)

T.I.N. OPENER, pseud. see OPENER, T.I.N., pseud.

TALLENTS, Sir Stephen George see (47) (48) (49)

TATHAM, C.M.
The airman, [and other poems]. Oxford U.P. 1917. 16p.   BPL

TAYLOR, Cyril Gordon
The phantom fiddler, and other poems. Daniel. [1920].
64p.   BM

TAYLOR, F.C.
The Dover Patrol, and other verses. Stockwell. [1919].
16p.   BPL

TAYLOR, Frank see (19)

TAYLOR, Frederic Irving see (63)

TAYLOR, Hope Fairfax
Poems. Methuen. 1916. xii, 356p.   BPL

Songs: [poems]. Oxford: Blackwell. 1919. 56p.   BM

TAYLOR, J. see (27)

TAYLOR, Leonard
Night flight, and other verse. *Air Review.* 1939. 48p. il.   BM

The trackless way: poems. Air League of the British
Empire. [1941]. 32p. il.   BM

Wings of youth: poems. Rolls House Publ. Co. 1957.
112p.   BM

TEE, Eleanor
On the edge of the earth: [poems]. St. Catherine P.
1916. 52p.   BM

TELFORD, Thomas see (27) (29)

TEMPERLEY, Rogerson
"Belgium's loss and Britain's gain": a poetic appeal on
behalf of the Belgian refugees. [1914]. [4]p. il., por.   BM

TEMPLE, Sir Richard
Edith Cavell in 1915 and 1919: [poems]. [1919?]. [4]p.   IWM

TEMPLER, Claude (Captain, Gloucestershire Regiment)
Poems and imaginings. Paris: Bossard. 1920. [ii], 88p. por.　　BPL

TEMPLETON, W.F. (Captain, Royal Scots Fusiliers)
Songs of the Ayrshire Regiment, and other verses.
Paisley: Gardner. 1917. 79p.　　MPL

TENISON, Julian (Lieutenant-Commander, Royal Navy.
Killed in command of his submarine, 15th August 1916)
see (32)

TENNANT, Hon. Edward Wyndham (Lieutenant, 4th Battalion
Grenadier Guards. Killed on the Somme, 22nd September 1916)

[Poems, letters, etc.]. Memoir by his mother Pamela
Glenconnor. Bodley Head. 1919. [xii], 334p. por., facsim.　　BPL

Worple flit, and other poems. Oxford: Blackwell. 1916.
40p.　　BM

See also (16) (17) (18) (33) (49) (50) (51) (59) (72)
(96) (102) (104) (111) (112) (122) (123) (124) (131)

TEPHI, pseud. see **MULHALL, Marion, (Tephi, pseud.)**

TERRY, E. Blanche
The broken promise, and other war poems. Stockwell.
[1915]. 24p.
　　Profits given to the Blue Cross Fund for wounded horses.　　BPL

The roll of honour, and other war poems. Stockwell.
[1916]. 20p.　　BPL

THANET, Lesbia see (31) (32)

THIRLMERE, Rowland, pseud. see **WALKER, John,**
(Rowland Thirlmere, pseud.)

THOMAS, Charles, (C.T.) see **HARVEY, John G. Russell,**
(J.G.R.H.), & THOMAS, Charles, (C.T.)

THOMAS, Edgar Lang (Captain)
Fairyland in 1918, and other poems. Werner Laurie.
1919. 64p.
　　A limited ed. of 500 copies.　　BPL

THOMAS, Edward, (Edward Eastaway, pseud.) (Joined Artists

310

Rifles, then transferred to the Royal Garrison Artillery. Killed
in action at Arras, 9th April 1917)

Collected poems. With a foreword by Walter de la Mare.
Selwyn & Blount. 1920. xx, 190p. por.
   A limited ed. of 100 copies.   MPL

Collected poems. With a foreword by Walter de la Mare.
Ingpen & Grant. 1928. xx, 195p. por.   BM

Collected poems. With a foreword by Walter de la Mare.
Faber. 1936. 208p. (Faber library, 31).   BPL

Collected poems. With a foreword by Walter de la Mare.
New ed. Faber. 1944. 190p.   BM

The green roads: poems for young readers, chosen and
introduced by Eleanor Farjeon. Bodley Head. 1965. 94p. il.
(by Bernard Brett).   MPL

Last poems. Selwyn & Blount. 1918. 96p.   MPL

Poems. Selwyn & Blount. 1917. 64p. por.   MPL

[Selected poems]. Benn . [1926]. 32p. (Augustan books
of modern poetry).
   Bibliog. (author's works) 1p.   BM

Selected poems. With an intro. by Edward Garnett.
Newtown: Gregynog P. 1927. xx, 96p.
   A limited ed. of 275 copies.   MPL

Selected poems. Ed. with an intro. and notes by Robin
Skelton. Hutchinson. 1962. 140p. facsim. (Hutchinson English
texts).   MPL

Selected poems. Selected and introduced by R.S. Thomas.
Faber. 1964. 63p. (Faber paper covered editions).   BM

Six poems; by Edward Eastaway. Printed Pear Tree P.
[1927]. [19]p. il.
   A limited ed. of 100 hand-printed copies.   BM

The trumpet, and other poems. Faber. 1940. 80p.
   Bibliog. 2p.   BM

See also (4) (22) (33) (50) (53) (66) (80) (96) (105)
(106) (111) (112) (131)

THOMAS, Gilbert (Imprisoned as a pacifist)
Collected poems. Newton Abbot: David & Charles;
Allen & Unwin. 1969. 206p.   MPL

The further goal, and other poems. With an intro. by
Arthur Waugh. Erskine Macdonald. 1915. 53p. (20th
century poetry series).   BPL

Poems, 1912-1919. Swarthmore P. 1920. 112p.   MPL

Selected poems, old and new. Allen & Unwin. 1951. 112p.   MPL

Towards the dawn, and other poems. Headley. [1918].
43p.   MPL

The voice of peace, [and other poems]. Chapman & Hall.
1914. [vi], 56p.   BPL

See also (19) (52) (85)

THOMAS, Julian (Brother of Edward Thomas) see (111)

THOMAS, Pardoe
H.M.S. "Téméraire": sailor's song and chanty. Printed
Newport: Sims. 1914. [8]p.   BM

"Mr. Private Khaki": a letter from the front. Printed
Newport: Sims. 1914. [8]p.   BM

"Reveille". Printed Newport: Sims. 1914. [4]p.   BM

Some verse! Printed Newport: Sims. [1915]. 28p.   BM

Three war songs. Printed Newport: Sims. 1914. [8]p.   BM

THOMAS, Philip Edward see THOMAS, Edward, (Edward
Eastaway, pseud.)

THOMAS, W.G.
Amateur soldiers, [and other poems]. Old Royalty Book
Publ. 1928. 60p.   BPL

THOMAS, W.G., & BARNARD, A.S.
The song of the Lewis gun. Prestwich:Authors. 1917.
[2]p.   BM

THOMPSON, Edward John (M.C., mentioned in dispatches.
Chaplain to the Forces, 7th Division, Mesopotamia)

Collected poems. Benn. 1930. xvi, 238p.   MPL

100 poems. Oxford U.P. 1944. x, 101p.   BM

Mesopotamian verses. Epworth P. [1919]. 63p.   MPL

Poems, 1902-1925. Selwyn & Blount. 1926. x, 52p.   MPL

312

[Selected poems]. Benn. [1931]. 32p. (Augustan books of poetry).
    Bibliog. (author's works) 1p.   BM

The Thracian stranger, [and other poems]. Benn. 1929.
112p.   MPL

Vae victis: [poems]. Epworth P. 1919. 32p.   BPL

Waltham thickets, and other poems. Kelly. 1917. 80p.   BM

See also (33)

THOMPSON, Joan (Red Cross worker in France)
Waifs: [poems]. Elkin Mathews. 1917. 48p. (Vigo cabinet
series: second century).   BM

THOMPSON, Mary
The poppies of Flanders, and other thoughts in prose and
verse. Stockwell. [1933]. 20p.   MPL

THOMSON, Clara Pease see (28)

THORLEY, Wilfrid
The Londoner's chariot, [and other poems]. Cape. [1925].
[xi], 84p.
    A limited ed. of 750 copies.   BM

See also (47) (48) (49)

THORNE, Ada
A summer day, and other poems. Stockwell. [1918]. 15p.   BPL

THORNELY, Thomas
Collected verse. Cambridge: Heffer. 1939. x, 231p.   MPL

Verses from fen and fell. Cambridge U.P. 1919. x, 98p.
    Cover-title is "Fen and fell".   MPL

Verses from fen and fell. 2nd ed. Cambridge U.P. 1920.
xvi, 144p.
    Cover-title is "Fen and fell".   MPL

Whims and moods: [poems]. Cambridge U.P. 1930. xiii,
103p.   BM

THORNTON, Richard H.
War verses: August, 1914. Athenaeum P. 1914. [4]p.   IWM

THORNYHiLL, Winfrida see (29)

THORPE, Elphinstone
Nursery rhymes for fighting times. Everett. [1915]. 45p.
il. (by G.A. Stevens). BM

THRUSH, Arthur
The day of battle: an epic of war. Erskine Macdonald.
1915. 60p. (XXth century poetry series). BPL

THURMAN, John
Some products of an open mind from Sysonby Knoll: [poems].
Stockwell. [1934]. 184p. por. BM

THURSTON, Ernest Temple
Summer 1917, and other verses. Chapman & Hall. 1917.
69p. por. BPL

TICKLE, Barbara M.
The golden arrow: a quiver of poems. Stockwell. [1925].
112p. MPL

TIDMAN, Arthur, (Hart Dumartin, pseud.)
The new madonna, dedicated to the Singer of the Magnificat
and all true women the world over who hand-in-hand with men
strive for the uplifting of humanity; by Hart Dumartin. Torquay:
Author. 1919. [4]p.
  A limited ed. of 500 copies. BPL

Three war poems; by Hart Dumartin. Torquay: Author.
1918. [4]p. BPL

To the women of England: (an appeal); by Hart Dumartin.
Torquay: Iredale. 1916. 4p. BM

TILLIE, Violet see (64)

TILLYARD, Aelfrida
The garden and the fire: [poems]. Cambridge: Heffer.
1916. [viii], 78p.
  Author's profits to Serbian Relief Fund. BPL

Verses for Alethea. Cambridge: Heffer. 1920. 31p. BM

See also (28)

TIN OPENER, pseud. see **OPENER, T.I.N., pseud.**

TINDALL, Fedden
Dreams and ideals: sonnets. Bristol: Arrowsmith;
Simpkin, Marshall, Hamilton, Kent. [1919]. 40p.   BPL

TINDALL, M.C. see **GORDON, Hampden, & TINDALL,
M.C.**

TINKLER, Robert Nicolas
Honey-sight, and other poems. Erskine Macdonald. 1917.
46p. (Little books of Georgian verse).   BM

See also (52)

TIPUCA, pseud. see **WILSON, Theodore Percival Cameron,
(Tipuca, pseud.)**

TIPLADY, Thomas (Chaplain to the Forces. Served with the
London Territorials on the Western Front)

Beside the fire, and other poems. Epworth P. 1937. 72p.   BM

"In the trenches", and other poems. Hemel Hempstead:
Booker. 1916. 103p.   BM

Songs of pilgrimage: [poems]. Allenson. [1923]. 68p.
   Some written 'on the battle grounds of the Somme and
Arras' — preface.   BM

See also (2)

TITTERTON, William Richard
Drinking songs, and other songs: [poems]. With an intro.
by G.K. Chesterton. Cecil Palmer. 1928. xii, 64p.   BM

Guns and guitars: [poems]. Palmer & Hayward. 1918.
95p.   MPL

London pride, and poems for the forces, families
and friends. Douglas Organ. 1944. [ii], 58p.   BM

The madness of the arts, [and other poems]. Erskine
Macdonald. 1921. 48p.   MPL

Poems for the forces. Werner Laurie. 1943. [ii], 57p.   BM

See also (94)

TO fight the Kaiser. Blackpool: Laycock. [1914]. il.
   A postcard.   BM

TO hell with Yankee-Doodle. [1915].
  A postcard.   BM

TODD, Edith E. see (29)

TODD, Nicholas Herbert (Rifleman, Queen's Westminsters.
Killed in action in France, 7th October 1916)

Poems and plays. Sedbergh: Jackson. 1917. xiv,
122p. por.   MPL

TOLLEMACHE, Evelyn
The new crucifixion, and other poems. Stockwell. [1918].
40p.   BPL

TOLLEMACHE, Hon. Grace Emma
Don Quixote, and other sonnets. Ouseley. 1924. 96p.
por.   MPL

Lyrics and short poems. Elkin Mathews. 1914. x, 52p.   BPL

Poems and sonnets. Ouseley. 1916. 96p.   MPL

See also (19) (26)

TOLLY, Colin
Horizons at dawn and at dusk: poems. Hodder & Stoughton.
1918. x, 83p.   MPL

Knowledge and dream, and other poems. Hodder &
Stoughton. 1926. 64p.   BM

TOMBS, Joseph Simpkin McKenzie (Died of wounds, 11th
September 1915)

Critical moments: a collection of verse and prose.
Fisher Unwin. 1917. 150p. por.   MPL

TOMLINSON, Albert Ernest (Commissioned in Army)
Candour: first poems. Elkin Mathews. 1922. 96p. por.   BPL

TOMMY, pseud.
The alphabet of Mesopotamia: verses written by a "Tommy"
who has fought, suffered and triumphed in Mesopotamia, and
is still on active service there. [1917].
  A broadside.
  Reprinted from *The Syren and Shipping*.   IWM

If I goes west!: [poems]. Harrap. 1918. 47p.   BPL

TOMS, Alfred Augustus see (27)

TONOSO, pseud. see SMITH, Thomas Napoleon, (Tonoso, pseud.)

TORIEL, pseud?
A 1915 winter song. Printed Neath: Stacey. 1915. [4] p.   BM

TOUCHSTONE, pseud. see BURTON, Claude Edward Cole
Hamilton, (C.E.B.), (Touchstone, pseud.)

TOVEY, Duncan, (Glen-Worple, pseud.) (Sergeant, London
Scottish Regiment)

Grey kilts: a collection of war verses and other trifles
of the old territorial and volunteer days. *London Scottish
Regimental Gazette.* 1918. 94p. por.
     Some verses in Scots dialect.   BPL

See also (32)

TRACEY, C.B. see (20)

TRANTER, William (6th Battalion, Manchester Regiment)
Songs of the Sixth: [poems]. Alexandria : Whitehead,
Morris (Egypt). 1917. 15p.
     Dedicated to Lieutenant-Colonel C.R. Pilkington,
commanding 6th Battalion, Manchester Regiment.   MPL

TREDEGAR, Lord see MORGAN, Evan, Lord Tredegar

TREE, Iris
Poems. Bodley Head. 1920. 144p. il. (by Curtis Moffat),
por.   BM

See also (40) (41) (54) (61) (122) (123) (124)

TREMEARNE, A.R. see (27)

TRENCH, Herbert
Herbert Trench, poète anglais (1865-1923): notice sur
sa vie et ses oeuvres; [by] Abel Chevalley. Avec texte et
traduction de son poème "La Bataille de la Marne". Oxford
U.P. 1925. 55p.   BM

Ode from Italy in time of war: night on Mottarone.
Methuen. 1915. 18p.   MPL

Poems, with fables in prose. Constable. 1918. 2v.   MPL

Poems, with fables in prose. Cape. 1924. xvi, 204p.
por. (Collected works, v.1).   BPL

Poems, with fables in prose. Cape. 1924. viii, 212p.
(Collected works, v.2).
    3v. ed. of "Collected works". v.3 is a play "Napoleon".   BPL

Selected poems. Cape. 1924. xii, 158p.   MPL

See also (31) (32)(50) (104) (120)

TREND, William see (27)

TREVOR, George Herbert
Tributes in verse. Stockwell. [1926]. 112p.   BM

TRIPP, D. Howard (Lance-Corporal, London Irish Rifles)
see (19) (61)

TROTTER, Alys Fane
Houses and dreams: [poems]. Oxford: Blackwell.
[1924]. viii, 87p.   MPL

Nigel, and other verses. Burns & Oates. 1918. 48p.
por.   BPL

See also (87) (111) (112)

TROTTER, Bernard Freeman (b. Canada, but served as
2nd Lieutenant in 11th Leicesters. Killed in action in France,
7th May 1917)

A Canadian twilight, and other poems of war and of
peace. With an intro. by W.S.W. McLay. Toronto:
McClelland, Goodchild & Stewart. [1917]. 128p. por.   BM

See also (17) (18) (131)

TROUP, J.M. Rose- see **ROSE-TROUP, J.M.**

TRYFANWY, John Richard, pseud. see **WILLIAMS, John
Richard,** (John Richard Tryfanwy, pseud.) (3)

TUCKER, Alfred Nicholson
Dart, loveliest of rivers, and other Devon poems.
Ilfracombe: Stockwell. 1952. 80p. por.   BM

TUCKER, Mary see (29)

TUDOR-HART, Edith
Songs of the shadows, [and other poems]. Fowler Wright.
1927. 128p.   BM

TUNSTALL, Charles Onions
Some moods of a teacher in peace and war: a record of the
influence of the Great War on some common people in an
obscure corner: [poems]. Gloucester: Chance & Bland. 1919.
48p.   BPL

TURNER, A.T.
Farewell! and other poems. Drane. [1921]. 32p.   MPL

TURNER, Walter James (b. Australia. Came to London at
age of 17. Served as Lieutenant in Royal Garrison Artillery, anti-
aircraft section, 1916-18)

The dark fire: [poems]. Sidgwick & Jackson. 1918. 71p.   BPL

The hunter, and other poems. Sidgwick & Jackson. 1916.
77p.   BPL

[Selected poems]. Benn. [1926]. 32p. (Augustan books of
modern poetry).
   Bibliog. (author's works) 1p.   BM

Selected poems, 1916-1936. Oxford U.P. 1939. xiv, 212p.   MPL

See also (11) (22) (33) (35) (36) (50) (102) (112)

TURNLEY, Gertrude see (28)

TWEEDALE, Dorothy M.
Odds and ends: [poems]. Erskine Macdonald. 1915.
52p. (Little books of Georgian verse).
   'Dedicated to the memory of my kindest critic and
dearly-loved brother, Captain Maurice Tweedale, of the 7th
King's Liverpool Regiment, killed in action at Festubert, May
15th, 1915'.   BM

TWEEDSMUIR, Lord see **BUCHAN, John, Lord**
Tweedsmuir

TWELVE, I.Q., pseud.
Fifty years on: [poems]. Ilfracombe: Stockwell.
[1965]. 120p. il.   BM

TWOPENCE, pseud. see (110)

TYNAN, Katharine

Collected poems. Macmillan. 1930. xxiv, 381p.   MPL

Evensong: [poems]. Oxford: Blackwell. 1922. 60p.   BM

Flower of youth: poems in war time. Sidgwick &
Jackson. 1915. 80p.   BPL

Herb o'grace: poems in war-time. Sidgwick & Jackson.
1918. 120p.   BPL

The holy war: [poems]. Sidgwick & Jackson. 1916. 72p.   BPL

Late songs: [poems]. Sidgwick & Jackson. 1917. 96p.   MPL

Poems. Ed. with an intro. by Monk Gibbon. Dublin:
Figgis. 1963. [viii], 100p. (Chomhairle Ealaion series of
Irish authors, 6).   BM

[Selected poems]. Benn. [1931]. 32p. (Augustan books
of poetry).
    Bibliog. (author's works) 1p.   BM

Twilight songs: [poems]. Oxford: Blackwell. 1927. 63p.   BM

See also (12) (16) (17) (18) (19) (25) (26) (31) (32)
(51) (55) (63) (66) (95) (111) (112) (120) (121)

TYRRELL-GREEN, Margaret

More poems. Bristol: Arrowsmith. 1918. 83p.   BPL

Poems. Wells Gardner, Darton. [1917]. 52p.   BPL

See also (28)

UNDERDOWN, Emily

War songs, 1914: [poems]. Printed Riley. [1914]. 16p.   MPL

UNDERHILL, Evelyn

Theophanies: a book of verses. Dent. 1916. x, 118p.   MPL

See also (17) (18) (31) (32) (99) (100) (101) (111) (112)

UNDERWOOD, H.M.

Songs of the yonderland: [poems]. Printed Dulwich:
Greaves. [1918?]. 26p. il. (by Frideswith Huddart).   BPL

The **UNDISCOVERED** island, and other verses: in memoriam
J.T.T., born 22nd June, 1885, killed in command of his
submarine, 15th August, 1916. Printed Shield and Spring P.
[191-]. 12p.   EDR

UNEMPLOYED EX-SERVICEMAN, pseud.
Poem. Printed Victor Printing Co. [1919?]. [4] p.
   Title from cover.
   BM has several printings of this by Victor Printing Co.
with differing type and paper. Same poem as "Truthful poem"
by Unemployed Ex-Soldier, pseud.   BM

UNEMPLOYED EX-SOLDIER, pseud.
Truthful poem by an ex-serviceman. Printed Marlborough
Co. [191-]. [3] p.
   Title from cover.
   Same poem as previous entry by Unemployed Ex-Serviceman.   BM

UPCOTT, Emily see (90)

URWICK, Edward see (27)

V.A.D., pseud.
Colliton, and other verses; by a V.A.D. Bournemouth:
Cooper. 1924. 19p. il.   EDR

V., R. see (31) (32) (47) (48) (49) (63)

VACHELL, Horace Annesley see (30)

VAIZEY, Christine A.M.
"Homely bits" about the Great War: [poems]. Printed
Braintree: Joscelyne. 1918. 19p.   BPL

VAN BEEK, Theo (Lieutenant, Royal Field Artillery)
see (60)

VANSITTART, Robert Gilbert, Lord Vansittart
Collected poems. Lovat Dickson. 1934. xiv, 155p.   BPL

Green and grey: collected poems. Hutchinson. 1944.
216p.   MPL

[Selected poems]. Eyre & Spottiswoode. [1943]. 32p.
(Augustan poets).
   Bibliog. (author's works) 1p.   BM

VAUGHAN, Edith see (28) (29)

VAUGHAN, Gertrude E.M. see (31) (32)

VAUSE, Mrs. William
Britain's send off: recruiting lyric, with band accompaniment, composed and recited with great success by Mrs. Vause. Manchester: [Author?]. [1916?]. [4]p. por. — BM

VEASEY, Katharine see (29)

VERNE, Viviane
A casket of thoughts: poems. Simpkin, Marshall, Hamilton, Kent. 1916. 86p. — BPL

VERNEDE, Robert Ernest (Enlisted in 9th Royal Fusiliers, September 1914. Went to France as Lieutenant attached to 3rd Rifle Brigade. Killed in action leading an attack on Havrincourt Wood, 9th April 1917)

War poems, and other verses. With an introductory note by Edmund Gosse. Heinemann. 1917. 88p. por. — MPL

See also (4) (12) (16) (18) (33) (49) (50) (51) (59)(82) (83) (84) (99) (100) (101) (111) (112) (113) (119) (120) (121) (131)

VERNEY-CAVE, Alfred Thomas Townshend, Lord Braye
Lines in verse and fable. Longmans, Green. 1917. vi, 97p. — MPL

VICARS, Florence A. see (31) (32)

VICKRIDGE, Alberta (Voluntary Aid Detachment)
The sea gazer, [and other poems]. Erskine Macdonald. 1919. 58p. — BPL

See also (18) (19)

VINCENT, Charles
Coronel, and other war poems. Dent. 1917. vi, 93p. — BPL

VINES, Sherard
The kaleidoscope: poems for the people. Daniel. 1920. 47p. — BPL

The pyramid, [and other poems]. Cobden-Sanderson. 1926. xii, 61p. — MPL

The two worlds: [poems]. Oxford: Blackwell. 1916. 64p. ("Adventurers all" series, 6). — BPL

See also (96) (124) (125) (126)

VIR, pseud.
Murdering monsters. 1918. (Ruin'd rimes). ("Reflector"
series of lyrical post cards, 14).   BM

"Plutus imperator": or, the witches' den. [1918]. ("Reflector"
series of lyrical post cards, 3).   BM

**VISIAK, Edward Harold, pseud. see PHYSICK, Edward Harold,
(Edward Harold Visiak, pseud.)**

VOS, George Herklots
The Germans' place in the sun: a concise history in blank
verse of the Great European War that commenced in 1914, from
the declaration of war by England, 4th August, to the fall of
Antwerp, 9th October. Drane. [1914]. 48p.   BPL

VOSS, R. see (5)

W.A.C. see (110)

W., B.H. see (31) (32)

W.B.L., pseud. see **BRANTOM, William, (W.B.L., pseud.)**

W., C. see **WALSTON, Sir Charles, (C.W.)**

W., C.M.
Consolations: [poems]. McBride, Nast. 1915. [38]p. il.
   Only 1 page in 4 has printing.   BM

W.E.B. see **BERRIDGE, William Eric, (W.E.B.)**

W.E.K. see **K., W.E.**

W., E.S.S. see **WALLINGTON, Emma S.S., (E.S.S.W.)**

W.G.M.D. see **D., M.J. & D., W.G.M.**

W.G.S. see **SHAKESPEARE, William G., (W.G.S.)**

W., H.F. see (5)

W.H.O. see (31) (32)

W.H.P. see **P., W.H.**

W., H.W.B.
Union truce! Poole & Pemberton. [1917].
A broadside. BM

W., L. see **WHITMELL, Lucy, (L.W.)** (17) (18) (24) (31) (32)
(47) (48) (49) (51) (96) (111) (112) (119)

W.L. see (31) (32)

WADE-GERY, Henry Theodore
Terpsichore, and other poems. Waltham Saint Lawrence:
Golden Cockerel P. 1921. 69p.
A limited ed. of 350 copies. BPL

Terpsichore, and other poems. 2nd ed. Waltham Saint
Lawrence: Golden Cockerel P. 1922. 69p.
A limited ed. of 20 numbered copies on hand-made
paper and 350 other copies. MPL

WAITHMAN, Helen Maud see (64)

WALBANK, Sam see (29)

WALKER, Archibald Stodart- see **STODART-WALKER,
Archibald**

WALKER, Edith M.
Poems. Amersham: Morland. 1921. 36p. BM
See also (31) (32)

WALKER, John, (Rowland Thirlmere, pseud.)
Collected poems; by Rowland Thirlmere. Oxford:
Blackwell. 1934. xvi, 429p. por. MPL

Diogenes at Athens, and other poems; by Rowland
Thirlmere. Selwyn & Blount. [1918]. 128p. MPL

My dog Blanco, and other poems; by Rowland Thirlmere.
Erskine Macdonald. 1916. 60p. (XXth century poetry
series). MPL

New poems; by Rowland Thirlmere. Selwyn & Blount.
[1920]. viii, 102p. MPL

Polyclitus, and other poems; by Rowland Thirlmere.
Elkin Mathews. 1916. 76p. MPL

Tragedy: a few simple verses on a very serious subject;
by Rowland Thirlmere. Selwyn & Blount. [1918]. 12p.   BM

See also (16) (17) (18)

WALKER, Mary F.
1914. [1915].
  A broadside.   BM

WALKER, Thomas M.
Address to the nations (engaged in the European War).
[Govan]. 1915. 15p.   BM

Poems and songs. Printed [Govan]: [Cossar]. [1918].
40p. por.   BPL

Poems for the people. Printed Govan: Cossar. [1922].
[viii], 112p.   BM

Replies to pro-German American peacemonger [Edward
W. Evans], and other war poems and songs. Printed Glasgow:
Aird & Coghill. 1916. 45p.   BPL

To the immortal memory of our fallen heroes: [and],
Sonnet: The prayer of the angel of peace. Govan. [1919].
[4]p. il.   BM

WALKER, William Sylvester see (29)

WALKERDINE, Wilfred Ernest
Collected poems, 1900-1950. Newtown: Montgomeryshire
Printing Co. [1952]. xiv, 78p.   BM

Poems of the Great War. Simpkin, Marshall, Hamilton,
Kent. [1916]. 78p.   BPL

Selected poems. Favil P. 1935. 45p.   BM

WALL, Geoffrey (b. Liscard, Cheshire. Emigrated to
Australia. Returned to train as a Lieutenant in the Royal
Flying Corps at Oxford. Killed in aeroplane accident,
6th August 1917)

Letters of an airman. Melbourne: Australasian Authors'
Agency. [1918]. xvi, 248p. il., por.
  Includes verse and a prose fragment "The poetry of the war".   BM

Songs of an airman: [poems]. With a memoir by L.A.
Adamson. Melbourne: Australasian Authors' Agency. 1917.
[viii], 66p. por., facsim.   MPL

Songs of an airman: [poems]. With a memoir by L.A.
Adamson. 2nd ed. Melbourne: Australasian Authors'
Agency. 1917. [viii], 66p. por., facsim.   IWM

WALLACE, E.
The German song of hate against England; [by] Ernst
Lissauer; together with, The English reply;[by]
E. Wallace. [191-]. [4]p. il., por.   BM

WALLACE, Kathleen Montgomery
Lost city: verses. Cambridge: Heffer. 1918. 24p.   BPL

See also (20) (32)

WALLACE, P. see (115)

WALLINGTON, Emma S.S., (E.S.S.W.)
England's war song; by English born E.S.S.W. [Notting Hill]:
Author. [1914].
    A broadside.   BM

Our Queen. Notting Hill: Author. [191-].
    A broadside.
        Proceeds devoted to Queen Mary's Fund.   BM

WALSH, J. see **SAUNDERS, A., & WALSH, J.**

WALSH, Maud
The German pirate's end; and, Tommy's fag. Printed
Blackpool: King. [1916]. [4]p.   BM

WALSH, Michael
Brown earth and green: poems. Dublin: Talbot P.
1929. 32p.   MPL

The heart remembers morning: [poems]. Dublin: Talbot
P. [1931]. 43p.   BM

Walls in the grass, [and other poems]. Dublin: Talbot P.
[1943?]. 52p. il. (by Patrick J. Walsh), por.   BM

WALSH, William Sandford Pakenham- see **PAKENHAM-
WALSH, William Sandford**

WALSHAW, Mrs. R.J.
Cups of comfort: a little book of poems of consolation
for sufferers. Daniel. 1917. 56p.   BPL

For the lads: a war-time offering: [poems]. Stockwell.
[1918]. 37p.   BPL

WALSTON, Sir Charles, (C.W.)
1914; [by] C.W. Cambridge: Heffer. [1914]. [iv], 29p.   IWM

WARBURG, Joan Emma Violet (A schoolgirl in 1918)
Gossamer and honey: [poems]. Humphreys. 1918. viii,
51p.   BPL

WARD, Ethel M.
The weaver: a book of poems. Erskine Macdonald.
[1922]. 29p. il.   BPL

WARD, Frederick William Orde
The last crusade: patriotic poems. Kelly. [1917]. 40p.   BPL

Selected poems. Swarthmore P. 1924. 176p. por.   BM

Songs for sufferers (from a sick-room) : [poems].
Kelly. [1917]. 40p.   BPL

See also (27) (65)

WARD, John Sebastian Marlow
Poems of the Empire. Marlowe, Savage. [1924]. 60p. il.   BM

WARD, Leo (Worcestershire Regiment) see **STITT, Innes,
& WARD, Leo**

WARD, Lucy E. see (28) (29)

WARD, Will Warwick- see **WARWICK -WARD, Will**

WARD, William J.
Bosch: a collection of altogether Hun-necessary matter:
[poems]. Cardiff: Ward Maritime Publications. 1915. [7],
ix, 196p. por.   BPL

WARDEN, Roy C.
Songs of the Worcestershires, and other poems. Worcester:
Worcestershire Newspapers and General Printing Co. 1917.
26p.   BPL

WARDLE, Mark Kingsley (Captain, 1st Battalion, Leicestershire
Regiment) see **WARDLE, Mark Kingsley, & BUCHANAN-
DUNLOP, Archibald**

WARDLE, Mark Kingsley, & BUCHANAN-DUNLOP, Archibald
An alphabet from the trenches; by two infantry officers: rhymes. Hodder & Stoughton. [1916]. [59]p. il. (by A. Buchanan-Dunlop).
Printed on one side of leaf only.   BPL

WARING, John
The unknown warrior, [and other poems]. Stockwell. [1922]. 32p. por.   BPL

WARNER, Irene E. Toye see (28)

WARNER, Sylvia Townsend
The espalier: [poems]. Chatto & Windus. 1925. [viii], 103p.   MPL

WARREN, Clarence Henry (Private, Army Ordnance Corps)
Pipes of Pan: poems from Egypt. Erskine Macdonald. 1918. 30p.   MPL

The thorn tree: poems. Oxford: Dolphin Book Co. 1963. 49p.   BM

WARREN, Edith E. see (29)

WARREN, G.B.
For the sceptre of the sea: [poems]. Long. 1916. 62p.   BPL

WARREN, G.O.
The sword: poems. Oxford: Blackwell. 1919. [viii], 152p.   MPL

Trackless regions: poems. Oxford: Blackwell. 1916. [viii], 119p.   BPL

See also (17) (18)

WARREN, Gretchen
Humanity: twenty-six poems. Oxford: Blackwell. 1953. 40p.   BM

WARREN, Sir Herbert see WARREN, Sir Thomas Herbert
(19) (25) (55)

WARREN, Peter (2nd Lieutenant, Royal Flying Corps) see (32)

WARREN, Sir Thomas Herbert see (19) (25) (55)

WARRY, Isabel see (28) (29)

WARRY, William E.G.
Prayer for peace, August 4th, 1918; [and], Thanksgiving
for peace, July 19th, 1919. Printed Willis. [1919].
    A broadside.   BM

WARWICK-WARD, Will (Self-styled 'the English tailor-
poet of Hampstead')

Boycott Germany. Printed Finchley: Garden Workshop.
[1915].
    A broadside.
    Profits to the British Garment Makers' Guild.   BM

My soldier laddie. Printed Finchley: Garden Workshop.
[1915?].
    A broadside.   BM

WATERHOUSE, Gilbert (2nd Lieutenant, Essex Regiment.
Killed in action 1st July 1916)

Rail-head, and other poems. Erskine Macdonald.
1916. 62p.   MPL

See also (2) (16) (24) (56) (57) (96) (131)

WATERS, Bernard
Poems. Grant Richards. 1922. 46p.   BM

WATSON, Edward James
To our noble dead, [and other poems]. Bristol:
Arrowsmith. 1920. 47p. (Arrow booklets).   BPL

WATSON, Eleanor Whitmee
New patriotic poems; recited by Miss Mabel Suddaby at the
"Metropole", Hull, October 1st, 1914. Hull: Author. [1914].
[3]p.
    In aid of the Lord Mayor's War Fund and the Belgian
Relief Fund.   BM

WATSON, R.B. Marriott- see **MARRIOTT-WATSON, R.B.**

WATSON, Roger
Poems and prose. Cambridge: Heffer. 1915. [iv], 83p.   MPL

WATSON, T.
Barnardo's six hundred: verses. Dr. Barnado's Homes.
[191-].
  A broadside.
  'Canada is sending sixty thousand men fully equipped to
help the Motherland in the present crisis. Six hundred of these
are old Barnardo boys' — author's note.   BM

WATSON, Sir William (Given a knighthood in 1917 for his
propaganda poetry)

A hundred poems, selected from his various volumes.
Hodder & Stoughton. [1921]. x, 182p. por.   BM

The man who saw, and other poems arising out of the war.
Murray. 1917. 96p.   MPL

Poems, 1878-1935. Harrap. 1936. 302p. por.   MPL

Retrogression, and other poems. Bodley Head. 1917. 98p. MPL

Selected poems. Selected, with notes, by the author.
Thornton Butterworth. 1928. 336p. por.   MPL

The superhuman antagonists, and other poems. Hodder &
Stoughton. 1919. xii, 92p.   MPL

To the troubler of the world. *The Times.* 1914.
  A postcard.
  Reprinted from *The Times,* 6th August 1914.   IWM

See also (17) (18) (19) (23) (25) (26) (31) (32) (46)
(50) (51) (54) (55) (65) (82) (83) (84) (99) (100) (101)
(108) (109) (120)

WATT, Ernest
To Bertha, and other verses. Harrison. 1919. 120p.   BM

WATT, Lauchlan Maclean (Chaplain to the Forces)
Britannia's answer, and other war poems. Sampson,
Low, Marston. 1914. 64p.   BPL

The land of memory: [poems]. Hodder & Stoughton.
1919. [viii], 96p.   BPL

See also (12) (19) (107)

WATT, W.A.
Romar's journal: a souvenir of the Great War, 1914-1918:
[poems]. Privately printed. [1919]. [ii], 72p.   BPL

WATTS, Charlotte
Poems. Printed Wimbledon: Ellis. 1925. 99p.   EDR

WAUGH, Alec (Lieutenant, Dorset Regiment. Taken prisoner
of war in 1918)

Resentment: poems. Grant Richards. 1918. 62p.   MPL

See also (33) (60) (111) (112)

WAY-FARER, pseud.
Flash-lights: love lyrics. Stockwell. [1919]. 13p.   BM

WEATHERLY, Frederick Edward
Bravo Bristol! and other verses. Bristol: Arrowsmith.
1914. 40p.   BPL

[No copy of 2nd ed. traced].

Bravo Bristol! and other verses. 3rd ed. Bristol:
Arrowsmith. 1914. 38p.   BPL

Songs for remembrance: [poems]. With a foreword by Sir
Henry McCardie. Arrowsmith. 1930. 144p. por.   MPL

See also (51)

WEAVING, Willoughby (Lieutenant, Royal Irish Rifles.
Served on Western Front. Invalided home in 1915)

The bubble, and other poems. Oxford: Blackwell. 1917.
xii, 146p.   MPL

Heard melodies: [poems]. Oxford: Blackwell. 1918.
xii, 130p.   MPL

Purple testament: 'the purple testament of bleeding war':
[poems]. Oxford: Blackwell. 1941. 56p.   BM

The star fields, and other poems. With an intro. by Robert
Bridges. Oxford: Blackwell. 1916. xvi, 250p.   MPL

Toys of eternity: [poems]. Oxford: Blackwell. 1937.
viii, 110p.   BM

See also (33) (72)

WEBB, Frederick George
A little collection of "the stuff that rhymes" (the dunce's
definition of poetry). Printed Worcester: Herald Printers.
1921. [ii], 64p.

Printed for private circulation.   EDR

Sun and shadow: verses. Manchester: Heath. [1938].
128p.   BM

WEBB, Frederick John
Poems and verses. Edmonton: Author. [1954]. x, 35p.   BM

WEBB, Genevieve Gwendoline (A schoolgirl in the war)
Ten short poems. Printed [Birmingham] : [Whitty & Hooper].
1917. 7p.   BPL

WEBB, Mary
Fifty-one poems, hitherto unpublished in book form. Cape.
1946. 63p. il. (by Joan Hassall).   MPL

The spring of joy: poems, some prose pieces and the
unfinished novel 'Armour wherein he trusted'. Intros by
Walter de la Mare and Martin Armstrong. Cape. 1937.
383p. il. (by Norman Hepple), col. il.   MPL

See also (47) (48) (49)

WEBSTER, Frederick Annesley Michael (6th Battalion, South
Staffordshire Regiment)

For an ideal, and other poems. McBride, Nast. 1917. 32p.
   'Dedicated to that best of all comrades, A.E. Flaxman, 2nd
Lieut., 6th South Staffordshire Regt., wounded and
missing July 1st 1916'.   BPL

Songs apart: a collection of poems. McBride, Nast.
1917. 48p.   BPL

WEBSTER, Letitia Riddell- see **RIDDELL-WEBSTER, Letitia**
(28) (29)

WEDDELL, George
The battle of the world: verse. Elliot Stock. 1915. 50p.   BM

WEDGWOOD, M. Winifred (Devon 26 Voluntary Aid
Detachment)

Verses of a V.A.D. kitchen-maid. Torquay: Gregory &
Scott. 1917. 28p.   BPL

WEDMORE, Millicent
Collected poems. With intro. by Sir George Douglas.

Ingpen & Grant. 1930. 188p. por.   BPL

In many keys: [poems]. Elkin Mathews. 1921. 46p.   BM

WEIGHTMAN, -
Lord Kitchener is calling. [1914].
   A postcard.   BM

WELLESLEY, Dorothy, Duchess of Wellington
Poems; by Lady Gerald Wellesley. Murray. 1920. x, 65p.   IWM

WELLESLEY, Lady Gerald see **WELLESLEY, Dorothy,
Duchess of Wellington**

WELLOCK, Wilfred
The victory of peace: three poems on the times. Daniel.
1916. 15p.   BPL

WELLS, Frank Barber
A medley of verse. Collingridge. 1919. [vi], 105p. BPL

The roll of the drum, and other war verses. Harrap.
1916. vi, 88p.   BM

WEST, Arthur Graeme (Enlisted in the ranks. Served in
France, November 1915-March 1916. Commissioned
September 1916. Returned to France, and was killed by a
sniper's bullet in April 1917)

The diary of a dead officer: posthumous papers. Allen
& Unwin. [1918]. xiv, 98p.
   Includes "Poems".   MPL

See also (50) (80) (96) (105)

WEST, Henry
Britain's glorious army: God's day is marching on!: glory
song of the British Empire. Printed Patching. [1917].
[4]p.   IWM

"The children's hero": tragedy of the "Lusitania": a
dramatic patriotic poem. [1915]. [3]p.   IWM

Heroic King Peter of Serbia: a spirited loyal patriotic
poem. Printed Patching. [1915]. [4]p.   IWM

Nurse Edith Cavell, saint, martyr, and heroine, "the
victim of Germany's crowning infamy": a national

333

patriotic poem. Printed Patching. [191-]. [4]p. IWM

Victory as usual! Noble sons of the Empire!: a stirring
poem of triumph. Printed Wandsworth: Priestley. [1918].
A broadside. IWM

William the despot. 1914. [3]p. IWM

WEST, Zelda F.A. see (5)

WHEBLE, Arthur
Look forward for the best. [1916].
A broadside. BM

The terror of night. [1916].
A broadside.
Refers to Zeppelin raids. BM

WHEELER, Clifford
Fugitive poems, including elegies to Lord Randall Davidson,
Canon Mason, Dean Wace and Walter Cozens, Esq. Canterbury:
Author. 1931. 45p. por. BM

A metrical garland: twenty poems. Canterbury: Author. 1921.
27p. por.
Title from cover. BM

The solution of Armageddon. [191-].
A broadside. BM

WHEELER, Ethel Rolt see (64)

WHEELER, Leonard Richmond (Served with British West
Indies Regiment in the Sinai Desert)
Desert musings: verse. Stockwell. [1919]. 32p. BPL

WHEELER, Stanley Mortimer (Chaplain to the Forces)
Verses of peace and war. Sudbury: Marten. 1916. 25p. BPL

WHELAN, J.C.D. see (27) (29)

WHETHAM, Catherine Durning
An Exeter book of verse. Exeter: Eland. 1919. 39p. BM

Occasional verses in wartime. Cambridge: Bowes. 1918.
44p. MPL

Occasional verses in wartime. (Second series). Exeter:
Eland. 1919. 56p. MPL

Occasional verses in wartime. (Second series). 2nd ed.
Exeter: Eland. 1919. 56p.   WPL

WHITAKER, R.E.
Brands from the burning: [poems]. Westminster P. 1919.
40p.   BPL

WHITBY, C.H.
The light of life:a little book of religious verse.
Yeovil: Whitby. [1914]. 40p.   BPL

With myrrh and frankincense: an oblation in verse. Yeovil:
Whitby. [1916]. 64p.   BPL

WHITBY, Charles Joseph
The rising tide, and other poems. Elkin Mathews. 1920.
112p.   BPL

WHITCOMBE, E.L.
The queen's quest, and other verses. Bell. 1915. viii,
100p.   BPL

WHITE, Albert Clement
Love-letter lays, and some others. Heath, Cranton.
1916. 54p.   BM

Songs from the heart: verses in various moods. Forbes.
1915. 63p.   BM

WHITE, Bernard Charles de Boismaison (Lieutenant,
20th Northumberland Fusiliers. Killed in action 1st July
1916)

Remembrance, and other verses. Ed. with a memoir by
De V. Payen-Payne. Selwyn & Blount. 1917. 64p. il.,
por., facsim.   MPL

WHITE, Lucie Henley- see HENLEY-WHITE, Lucie

WHITE, Roma, pseud. see WINDER, Blanche, (Roma White,
pseud.) (72)

WHITEHEAD, T. see (27)

WHITEHOUSE, John Howard
Youth, and other poems. Oxford U.P. 1938. 28p.   BM

WHITEHOUSE, Peggy
Songs from the Sussex downs: [poems]. Erskine
Macdonald. 1915. 49p. (Little books of Georgian verse).   BM

WHITELEY, Alfred
Homely rhymes: local and otherwise. Printed Bradford:
Tetley. 1916. 80p.   EDR

WHITING, W.G.S.
"Cometh the song": [poems]. Erskine Macdonald. 1919.
54p.
    Written between January and May, 1918, when author
entered the Army.   BM

WHITING-BAKER, A.E. (2nd Lieutenant, 4th British
West Indies Regiment) see (2) (26) (110)

WHITMELL, Lucy, (L.W.) see (17) (18) (24) (31) (32)
(47) (48) (49) (51) (96) (111) (112) (119)

WHITNEY, T. see **CONSTABLE, M., & WHITNEY, T.**

WHITWORTH, Laura A. see (28)

WHYTE, Arthur J. see (55)

WIDEAWAKE, Captain, pseud.
Jovial jottings from the trenches. Harrap. 1915. [30]p. il.
    Cartoons with captions in rhyme.   BM

WIGRAM, Eirene see (64)

WILKES, H.E. see (87)

WILKINS, Helen F. see (28)

WILKINSON, Eric Fitzwater (M.C. Captain, Leeds Rifles,
West Yorkshire Regiment. Killed in the attack on
Passchendaele Ridge, 9th October 1917)

Sunrise dreams, and other poems. Erskine Macdonald.
1916. 48p.   MPL

Sunrise dreams, [and other poems]. [New ed.]. With an
intro. by Fitzwater Wray ("Kuklos"). Erskine Macdonald.
1918. 84p. por.   BPL

See also (2) (52) (56) (57) (58) (72) (131)

WILKINSON, Walter Lightowler (Lieutenant, 8th Argyll & Sutherland Highlanders. Killed in the attack on Vimy Ridge, 9th April 1917) see (18) (58) (96) (131)

WILL-O'-THE-WISP, pseud.
War! "To let". [1918].
  A postcard.   BM

WILLIAMS, Alfred
Selected poems. Erskine Macdonald. 1926. x, 180p.   MPL

War sonnets and songs. Erskine Macdonald. 1916. 86p.   BPL

WILLIAMS, Charles
Divorce, [and other poems]. Oxford U.P. 1920. 120p.   MPL

Poems of conformity. Oxford U.P. 1917. 128p.   BPL

WILLIAMS, Eliot Crawshay- see **CRAWSHAY-WILLIAMS, Eliot**

WILLIAMS, Huw Menai, (Huw Menai, pseud.)
Back in the return, and other poems; by Huw Menai.
Heinemann. 1933. xii, 177p.   BM

Through the upcast shaft: [poems]; by Huw Menai.
Hodder & Stoughton. [1918]. [vi], 95p.   BPL

[No copy of 2nd ed. traced].

Through the upcast shaft: [poems]. 3rd ed. Hodder & Stoughton. [1923]. 94p.   BM

WILLIAMS, Iolo Aneurin (Captain. Served in France and Flanders, 1914-1918)

New poems. Methuen. 1919. 44p.   BPL

Poems. Methuen. 1915. 48p.   BPL

See also (19) (33) (63) (85) (96) (102) (112)

WILLIAMS, John Richard, (John Richard Tryfanwy, pseud.)
see (3)

WILLIAMS, Llewellyn E. (Lieutenant, Royal Engineers)
Knights adventurers, [and other poems]. Simpkin,
Marshall, Hamilton, Kent. 1918. [viii], 40p.   BPL

WILLIAMS, Lucien see (27)

WILLIAMS, Morgan L.
On to Berlin!: to the Welsh army. Cardiff: Author.
[1914].
    A postcard.   BM

WILLIAMS, Richard Valentine, (Richard Rowley, pseud.)
City songs, and others: [poems] ; [by] Richard Rowley.
Dublin: Maunsel. 1918. [viii], 85p.   MPL

WILLIAMSON, David R.
Collected poems, 1928. Mitre P. 1928. 72p.   BM

See also (29)

WILLIAMSON, G.H. see (27)

WILLIAMSON, John Woolfenden
Helicon holidays: [poems]. Oxford: Shakespeare Head P.
1941. 80p.   BM

WILLIS, George
Any soldier to his son, [and other poems]. Allen & Unwin.
1919. 45p.   MPL

A ballad of four brothers, [and other poems]. Allen & Unwin.
1921. 43p.   BPL

WILLIS, J.A.
"Lest we forget": a poem intended to illustrate the signs
and events leading up to the Great War of 1914. [Bristol?].
[191-].
    A broadside.   BM

WILMOT, J.R.
Sunshine and shadow: random verses written on active
service. Amersham: Morland. 1919. [28]p.   BPL

WILSON, Bingley see (5)

WILSON, Charles
"Arouse! ye tyrants, bend your knee, don't do as devils
would decree". Willington: Author. [1915]. [3]p.
    Proceeds for Red Cross Fund.   BM

The battle of life. Printed Willington. 1914. [4]p.
    Proceeds to National Relief Fund.   BM

"Belgium's name let all proclaim", [and other poems].
Printed Willington. [1915]. [20]p.   BM

The bells of Rheims. Printed Willington: Coates. 1915.
[4]p.
    Proceeds in aid of widowed mother of Private Thomas W.
Dargue of Hurwick, who was killed at the Dardanelles, June
1915.   BM

"Billy's head has swelled and grown, it's too big for just
one crown". Printed Willington. [191-].
    A card.   BM

"Gone, but not forgotten". Printed Willington. [191-].
    A card.
    Refers to the Kaiser.   BM

"On sick leave, warriors three", and other poems. Printed
Willington: Coates. 1915. 24p. por.   BM

Poems by a pitman, Charlie Wilson. Willington: Author.
[1915]. [16]p.   BM

Poetical works. v.1. Stockwell. [1916]. 157p. por.
    No other v. publ. — BM.   BM

Time will tell. Printed Willington: Coates. 1916. 18p. por.
    'The whole of the profits will be given for the benefit of
Robert Foster, who has been totally incapacitated for several
months'.   BM

The unseen guest, and other poems. Printed Willington:
Coates. [1915]. 24p.   BM

"When duty calls", and other poems. Printed Willington:
Coates. 1915. 24p. por.   BM

When the lads come home again. Printed Willington:
Coates. [1916]. [4]p.   BM

Ye faithful Durhams, and other poems. Willington:
Author. 1915. [4]p.   BM

WILSON, Charlie see **WILSON, Charles**

WILSON, G.H.
War poems. Ossett: Cockburn. [1918?]. 23p.

Proceeds of sale to Soldiers' Comforts Fund at Dewsbury
Base Hospital. BPL

See also (27)

WILSON, Margaret Adelaide see (17) (18)

WILSON, Marjorie see (17) (18) (111) (112)

WILSON, Ronald W. (Served in Army Medical Corps. Died
of meningitis in France on day before 19th birthday)

On the threshold: a remembrance of R.W. Wilson, born
March 1st, 1896, died February 28th, 1915: [poems].
Printed Letchworth: Temple P. 1915. viii, 60p. il., por. EDR

WILSON, Susan
Xmas, 1918. Durham: [Author?]. [191-].
A broadside. BM

WILSON, Theodore Percival Cameron, (Tipuca, pseud.)
(Captain, Sherwood Foresters. Killed in action in the Somme
Valley, 23rd March 1918)

Magpies in Picardy, [and other poems]. Poetry Bookshop.
1919. 52p. MPL

See also (17) (18) (24) (31) (32) (33) (80) (96) (104)
(111) (112) (131)

WILSON, Thomas (Served with British Expeditionary Force
in France)

Hope of the dawn, and other poems. Stockwell. [1917]. 15p. MPL

WILSON, William V. (Private, 13th London Regiment. Severely
wounded by machine gun fire, 9th May 1915)

The lads of the Kensington Rifles (1/13 London Regiment):
verses; by one of them. [1916]. [4] p. BM

"Pals": verses. [1917]. [3] p. BM

WINCHESTER, Clarence Arthur Charles
Earthquake in Los Angeles, and other poems. Cassell.
1938. 46p. BM

Sonnets and some others. Taunton: Wessex P. 1928. 32p. BM

Poems of an air pilot. Wingwood Publ. Co. 1921. [19] p. BM

340

WINDER, Blanche, (Roma White, pseud.) see (72)

WINGATE, Walter
Poems. Gowans & Gray. 1919. xii, 92p.
  In Scots dialect.
    A limited ed. of 500 copies.   BM

Poems. 2nd ed. Gowans & Gray. 1919. xii, 92p. por.
  In Scots dialect.   BM

See also (91)

WINN, Leslie Hinchliff
Through two windows: poems. Palmer & Hayward.
1919. [vi], 57p.   BPL

See also (27)

WINNIFRITH, Alfred see (29)

WINSER, Ethel E.
Per ardua ad astra: war poems. Blackheath P. 1916.
[ii], 20p.   BPL

Thoughts in verse. Amersham: Morland. 1923. 39p.   BM

WINSER, Harold Albert
Life's autumn: a book of verse. Murby. 1927. x, 87p. por.   BPL

WINSTEN, Samuel (Conscientious objector. Went to prison)
Chains: poems. Daniel. 1920. 112p.
  Written in prison.   MPL

WINTERBOTHAM, Cyril William (Lieutenant, Gloucestershire
Regiment. Killed in action 27th August 1916)

[Poems]. Cheltenham: Banks. [1917?]. 32p. por.
  Printed for private circulation.   BPL

See also (72) (131)

WODEHOUSE, Ernest Armine (Lieutenant, Scots Guards)
Christmas Eve: a vision. Order of the Star in the East.
[1915]. 28p.   BM

On leave: poems and sonnets. With a foreword by Sir
Arthur Quiller-Couch. Elkin Mathews. 1917. 80p. (Vigo
cabinet series).   MPL

On leave: poems and sonnets. With a foreword by Sir
Arthur Quiller-Couch. 2nd ed. Elkin Mathews. 1917.
79p. (Vigo cabinet series, 43).   BPL

See also (2) (17) (18)

WOLFE, Humbert (An official in the Ministry of Munitions)
Early poems. Oxford: Blackwell. 1930. xvi, 126p.   MPL

The fourth of August. Eyre & Spottiswoode. 1935. [vi],
[33]p.
   Printed on one side of leaf only.
   A limited ed. of 725 numbered copies.   MPL

London sonnets. Oxford: Blackwell. 1920. 64p. ("Adventurers
all" series, XXVII).   BPL

Shylock reasons with Mr. Chesterton, and other poems.
Oxford: Blackwell. 1920. 64p.   BM

See also (112)

WOOD, Edward Harold Rhodes (Gunner, Royal Garrison
Artillery)

Splinters: [poems]. Erskine Macdonald. 1918. 62p.   MPL

WOOD, Frank Noble
Songs amid strife: a selection of poems written during
the Great War. 2nd ed. Hull: Johnston & Needham. 1917. [vi],
28p.   BPL

[No copy of 1st ed. traced].

**WOODBINE WILLIE see KENNEDY, Geoffrey Anketell
Studdert, (Woodbine Willie)**

WOODCOCK, Annie E.
Towards the light: [poems]. Bristol: Arrowsmith. 1923. 78p.   BM

WOODHOUSE, Reginald Illingworth
Confidence: patriotic and other poems. Erskine
Macdonald. 1918. 81p.   BPL

WOODLEY, Fabian Strachan (Served in the trenches in
France)

A crown of friendship, and other poems. Taunton:
Woodley, Williams & Dunsford. 1921. 62p.   BM

WOODS, James Chapman
A pageant of poets, and other poems. Elkin Mathews &
Marrot. 1931. x, 85p.   MPL

WOODS, M. Maud
The vision splendid: a poem. Printed Eastbourne:
Christian. [1929?]. 16p.
   'A tribute to our fallen heroes of the Great War, 1914-18,
and souvenir of the Kellogg Peace Pact, 1928'.   MPL

WOODS, Margaret Louise
The return, and other poems. Bodley Head. 1921. x, 131p.   MPL

See also (17) (18) (19) (25) (66)

WOODS, Mary
Reflections: [poems]. Elkin Mathews & Marrot. 1930.
xii, 65p.   BM

Sunshine and solitude, and other poems. Stockwell.
[1928]. 96p.   BM

WOODS, Mary A. see (28)

WORKMAN, A. Maud
The gate of life: [poems]. Epworth P. 1931. 47p.   BM

Poems. Stockwell. [1926]. 128p.   BM

See also (28) (29)

WOUNDED WARRIOR, pseud. see **LEVEY, Sivori,**
(Wounded Warrior, pseud).

WRENCH, Mollie Stanley- see **STANLEY-WRENCH, Mollie**
(64)

WRIGLEY, Maurice Jackson
A medley of songs: poems of yesterday. Liverpool:
Speirs & Gledsdale. 1927. 181p.   MPL

WYATT, Horace
Malice in Kulturland. *Car Illustrated.* 1915. [ii], 80p.
il. (by W. Tell).
   A parody of Lewis Carroll's "Alice's adventures in
Wonderland", in verse and prose.   MPL

Malice in Kulturland. 2nd ed. Richmond: Gillam. 1917.
[ii], 80p. il. (by W. Tell.)
    A parody of Lewis Carroll's "Alice's adventures in
Wonderland", in verse and prose.   BPL

See also (47) (48) (49)

WYATT, Samuel
The light of love: poems for life's pathway. Simpkin,
Marshall, Hamilton, Kent. 1917. 96p.   BPL

WYLIE, Georgina G. see (29)

WYN, Eifion, pseud. see **OWEN, David, (Eifion Wyn, pseud.)**
(3)

"X", pseud. see **CROSLAND, Thomas William Hodgson,**
("X", pseud.)

Y., J.L. see **YATES, John Lygo, (J.L.Y.)**

YATES, James Stanley (2nd Lieutenant, 3rd Battalion, Royal
West Kent Regiment)

War lyrics, and other poems. Oxford: Blackwell. 1919.
xii, 75p. por.   BPL

YATES, John Lygo, (J.L.Y.)
The Kaiser's plight and the allies' fight; by J.L.Y.
[Birmingham?]. 1914.
    A card.   BM

YEANDLE, Harold see (27)

YEATS, William Butler
Collected poems. Macmillan. 1933. xvi, 476p. por.   BM

Collected poems. [2nd ed.]. Macmillan. 1950. xviii,
565p. por.   BM

Later poems. Macmillan. 1922. xiv, 363p.   MPL

Michael Robartes and the dancer, [and other poems].
Dundrum: Cuala P. 1920. xii, 35p.
    A limited ed. of 400 copies.   BM

Poems. Variorum ed. Ed. by Peter Allt and Russell
K. Alspach. New York: Macmillan. 1957. xxxvi, 884p.

Bibliog. (author's works) 6p. MPL

Selected poems: lyrical and narrative. Macmillan 1929. x, 203p. por. MPL

Selected poems: lyrical and narrative. Macmillan. 1951. x, 203p. (Golden treasury series). MPL

Selected poetry. Ed. with an intro. and notes by A. Norman Jeffares. Macmillan. 1962. xxii, 232p. BM

The wild swans at Coole, other verses and a play in verse. Dundrum: Cuala P. 1917. xii, 48p.
    A limited ed. of 400 copies. BM

The wild swans at Coole, [and other poems]. Macmillan. 1919. x, 116p. MPL

The wild swans at Coole; Michael Robartes and the dancer; The tower; The winding stair, and other poems; From "A full moon in March"; Last poems. Definitive ed. Macmillan. 1949. xii, 308p. por. (Poems, v.2).
    v.1. does not contain war poetry. BM

See also (11) (33) (46) (53) (80) (105) (106) (112) (128)

YORKSHIRE GIRL, pseud. see (5)

YOUNG, Avery see (5)

YOUNG, C.E.
The day, and other poems. Heath, Cranton. [1920]. 32p. BM

YOUNG, Edward Hilton, Lord Kennet (D.S.O., D.S.C. Lieutenant-Commander, Royal Naval Volunteer Reserve. Served at Zeebrugge and Archangel. Wounded in 1918)

A muse at sea: verses. Sidgwick & Jackson. 1919. 36p. BPL

Verses: A muse at sea, and others. Sidgwick & Jackson. 1935. [viii], 44p. BM

See also (17) (18) (20) (33) (111) (112)

YOUNG, Francis Brett (Major, Royal Army Medical Corps. Served in the East African campaign. Eventually invalided home with fever and exhaustion)

Five degrees south, [and other poems]. Martin Secker. 1917. 47p. MPL

The island: [poems]. Heinemann. 1944. vi, 451p.   MPL

The island:[poems]. [New] ed. Heinemann. 1955.
xii, 451p.   MPL

Poems, 1916-1918. Collins. 1919. 88p.   MPL

See also (19) (33) (70) (96) (102) (104) (111) (112)
(120)

YOUNG, Geoffrey Winthrop (Served on the Italian Front
with the First British Ambulance Unit of the Red Cross)

Bolts from the blues: rhymes. Gorizia. 1917. 28p. il.
(by Sebastian B. Meyer).
     Title from cover.   BM

Collected poems. Methuen. 1936. viii, 246p.   MPL

Z., N.E. see (5)

ZANETTI, Celest
Through all the seasons: occasional verse. Selwyn &
Blount. 1922. 32p.
     Written while author was on active service.   BPL

ZANGWILL, Israel see (13) (14) (61) (66)

SECTION C: TITLE INDEX

Balkan fancies; by A.J. Mann

The ballad of Beaumont-Hamel; by N. Hill

The ballad of disdain; by H. Blaker

The ballad of Ensign Joy; by E.W. Hornung

A ballad of four brothers; by G. Willis

The ballad of Kaiser Wilhelm; by Anglo-American, pseud.

The ballad of St. Barbara; by G.K. Chesterton

Ballad of the bodkin and the musket; by E. Carpenter

A ballad of "The Gloster" and "The Goeben"; by M. Hewlett

The ballad of the iron cross; by A. Dodd

The ballad of the Royal Ann; by C. Garstin

A ballad of the war; by F. Coutts

Ballade of night — murder done!; by R.R. Hibbs

Ballades; by H.S. Mackintosh

Ballads and addresses; by J.E. Patterson

Ballads and carols; by R.L. Gales

The ballads of Ballytumulty; by S.S. McCurry

Ballads of battle; by J. Lee

Ballads of field and billet; by W.K. Holmes

Ballads of the Flying Corps; by G.R. Samways

Barbed wire; by Old Loot, pseud.

Barnardo's six hundred; by T. Watson

The barren tree; by L.W. Griffith

Base details; by S. Sassoon

La Bataille de la Marne; by H. Trench

Battle; by W.W. Gibson

Battle and beyond; by C.A. Renshaw

The battle fiends; by E.H. Physick

The battle of freedom; by H. Staunton

The Battle of Jutland; by W.C. Lovelace

The battle of life; by C. Wilson

The Battle of Mons; by S. Lewis

The battle of the world; by G. Weddell

Battle songs for the Irish Brigade; comp. by S. Gwynn & T.M. Kettle (43)

The Battles of Loos and Hill Seventy; by W.W. Russell

Bay; by D.H. Lawrence

"Be comforted"; by G.M. Bonus

Beasts royal; by D.M. Stuart

Beating shoes; by W.H. Coates

Beauty for ashes; by H. Roseveare

Before marching and after; by T. Hardy

The beginning and ending of the Great War; by T.L. James

Behind the eyes; by E. Rickword

Behind the firing line; by M. Herschel-Clarke

The Belgians' song of hope; by J.J. Lane

"Belgium's loss and Britain's gain"; by R. Temperley

"Belgium's name let all proclaim"; by C. Wilson

Belgium's refugees and Britain's open arms; by T.N. Smith

Bellicosities in prose and verse; by I. Firth

The bells of peace; by J. Galsworthy

The bells of Rheims; by C. Wilson

Berks 13, V.A.D. and the Great War; by C. Highet

Berries on a wayside hedge; by B.B. Baily

Bertha and Edith; by C.W. Scarr

Beside "Himself"; by E. Ottley

Beside the fire; by T. Tiplady

Between doubting and daring; by J. Barlow

Between sun and moon; by C. French

Beyond the dark; by F. Speaight

Beyond the sunset; by F.V. Luxmoore

Beyond the veil; by J.J. Lane

Beyond the war zone; by E. Coleman

"Billy's head has swelled and grown . . ."; by C. Wilson

The bird-catcher; by M. Armstrong

The birds; by J.C. Squire

Bits and pieces; by G. Gosselin

A black outlook; by J. Stone

The Black Watch bouquet; by Hackleplume, pseud.

The blind soldier; by A. Cooper

The blinded hero; by W.J. Rich

Blue sea ballads and chanties; by W.C. Reedy

Boabdil; by R. Gordon-Canning

The body's imperfection; by L.A.G. Strong

Bog-myrtle and peat reek; by P. Macgillivray

The Bolo book; by G.D.H. Cole & M.P. Cole

Bolts from the blues; by G.W. Young

The bomber gipsy; by A.P. Herbert

The bombing of Bruges; by P. Bewsher

A book of poems for the Blue Cross Fund (5)

A book of remembrance; by D. Barron

A book of twentieth-century Scots verse; comp. by W. Robb (91)

A book of verse of the Great War; ed. by W.R. Wheeler (121)

The book of William; anon.

Border songs; by M.J.D. & W.G.M.D.

Bosch; by W.J. Ward

The Bosch book; by R. Arkell

Bosh ballads; by J.H. Dumbrell

Bound in khaki; by L. Doyle

The boy hero; by G.M.L. Reade

Boycott Germany; by W. Warwick-Ward

Braggart of Braggadocia; by J. Gee

"Branches unto the sea"; by M.G. Collins

Brands from the burning; by R.E. Whitaker

Bravo, Bristol!; by F.E. Weatherly

The bridge of memory; by O.P. Downes

Brief words; by W. Soutar

Bright feather fading; by L.B. Lyon

Britain to America; by H. Burton

"Britain's debt to Belgium"; by H. Cole

Britain's defeat; by Bonavia, pseud.

"Britain's flag"; by J. Black

Britain's glorious army; by H. West

Britain's glory; by W. Frampton

Britain's might; by A. Adlington

Britain's send off; by Mrs. W. Vause

Britannia; by A. Muir

Britannia victrix; by R. Bridges

Britannia's answer; by L.M. Watt

British Boloism; by R.W. Rice

British boys; by W. Frampton

Britishers!; by S. Levey

A broadcast anthology of modern poetry; ed. by D. Wellesley (118)

Broken glory; by E. Gore-Booth
The broken melody; by H. Desmond
Broken music; by H. Key
The broken promise; by E.B. Terry
Broken shade; by J. Helston
Bronsil Castle; by T.E. Cole
Brookdown; by E.T. Sandford
Brother man; by E. Phillpotts
Brother o'mine; by A.J. Honer
Brothers; by I. Macdougall
Brought home!; by E.H. Rowe
Brown earth and green; by M. Walsh
"Brown studies"; by G. Seeby
The bubble; by W. Weaving
The bukshee ration; by W.C. Poulten
Bull; by D.S. MacColl
A bunch of Cotswold grasses; by E. Dobell
The burial in England; by J.E. Flecker
The buried city; by B.C. Hardy
The buried stream; by G. Faber
Burnley's war flame; by T.N. Smith
Burnley's winning Jennie; by T.N. Smith
But for the men; by F.W. Farrants
The buzzards; by M. Armstrong
"By Jaffa way"; by H.G. Mansfield
By Yser banks; by R. Fanshawe
Bydand; by J. Mitchell
Caesar remembers; by W.K. Seymour
"The call"; by T.E. Cole
The call; by G. Kendall
The call; by D. Macfadyen
A call from the trenches; by E.A. Fieldhouse
The call from the trenches; by G.M.L. Reade

Call not the laggard, but the brave; by T.E. Cole
The call of the miles; by L. Galletley
A call to arms; by L. Davis
A call to arms; by N. Richfield
The call to arms "Your king and country need you"; by H.C. Southam
A call to national service; by T. Hardy
A call to our men; by A. Campbell-Strickland
Call to the swan; by L.A.G. Strong
Cambridge poets, 1914-1920; comp. by E. Davison (20)
A Cameronian officer; by J.B. Lawson
A Canadian twilight; by B.F. Trotter
Candour; by A.E. Tomlinson
Captain Dimmer, V.C.; by T.B. Clark
The captive lion; by W.H. Davies
Cargo; by S.B. Gates
A casket of thoughts; by V. Verne
The castle; by C. Congreve
Casus belli; by C.R. Cammell
The cause; by L. Binyon
Cecil Spencer; by M. Baring
Cenotaph; comp. by T. Moult (66)
Chains; by S. Winsten
A challenge; by M. Hardyman
Chamberlain scheme; by R.W. Rice
Chambers's patriotic poems for the young; comp. by S.B. Tait (107)
Changing chimes; by E.H. Carlyon
A chant of affection; by T.W.H. Crosland

351

Chants in war; by W.S. Pakenham-Walsh

The chapman of rhymes; by J.B. Priestley

The charge at Loos of the 1/5 Lincoln Regt; by E.C. Plastow

The charge of the "London Scottish", Messines, October 31st, 1914; by M. Goodricke

The charge of the Ninth Lancers, August 24th, 1914; by M. Goodricke

Charing Cross; by C. Roberts

Charitas (a royal bull fight); by N. Davidson

Charles and Harry Bell; by A.H. Hadley

Charnwood poems; by A.F. Cross

Cheer up, brave hearts!; by E. Spaven

Children of circumstance; by A.J.E. Dawson

Children of fancy; by I.B.S. Holborn

Children of love; by H. Monro

The children's entente cordiale; by L.M. Oyler

"The children's hero"; by H. West

A children's painting book; by R. Arkell

Chimes for the times; by A. Bartholeyns

A choice of songs; by R. Kipling

Choice or chance; by E.C. Blunden

A Christmas card to the Kaiser; by J. Gilham

Christmas Eve; by E.A. Wodehouse

Xmas, 1918; by S. Wilson

Christmas 1914; by A.K. Sabin

Christmas roses; by F.W. Bourdillon

A Christmas story; by P. Pearce

Chronicles of man; by C.F. Coxwell

Chrysoprase; by E.C. Oliphant

The church militant; by H. Bloye

Cinquante Quatre (15)

The circling hours; by A.W. Smith

The city of fear; by G. Frankau

City songs; by A. St. J. Adcock

City songs; by R.V. Williams

Cleared for action; by H. Steele

Cloth o' gold for every-day wear; by E. Ling

Clouds and the sun; by E. Crawshay-Williams

"Clouds with silver linings"; by B.M. Stephens

The clown of paradise; by D.J. Baynes

Clowns' houses; by E. Sitwell

Clydeside melodies; by J. Millar

Coal and candlelight; by H.P. Eden

Coat of many colours; by T. Bouch

Cockney rhymes; by W.T. Millington

The cockpit of idols; by M. Stuart

Collected war poems; by E.H. Blakeney

Colliton; by V.A.D., pseud.

"Come now!" the appeal from the trenches in France; by H.R. Clyne

Come ye sons of Britain's glory; by A. Cooper

"Cometh the song"; by W.G.S. Whiting

Comfort the women; by D.S. Shorter

The coming doom of the Hohenzollerns; by G.M.L. Reade

Commentary on rations (with
some exaggeration); by T.B.
Clark
The common day; by S.
Southwold
Comrades; by P. Field
Comrades; by A. Robertson
Comrades! My comrades!; by
G.R. Harvey
Comrades of the Great War; by
R. McPherson
Confidence; by R.I. Woodhouse
Conflict and quest; by F.S.
Stevenson
The conflict of the nations; by
Britannia, pseud.
The conscientious objector; by
W. Frampton
Conscientious objectors of the
twentieth century; by G.M.L.
Reade
"Conscription"; by N. Davidson
Consider this!; by P. Field
Consolation; by A.S. Jupp
Consolations; by C.M.W.
Contemporary Devonshire and
Cornwall poetry; ed. by
S.F. Wright (129)
"The contest"; by N. Davidson
Copy of the Kaiser's will, issued
to the Allied Nations; anon.
Cordis flamma; by C. Gower
Corduroys or reefer jackets;
by W. Frampton
A Cornish chorus; by S.S. Hunt
A Cornish collection; by S.S.
Hunt
Cornish corners; by S.S. Hunt
A Cornish haul; by S.S. Hunt
Coronel; by C. Vincent
Cot 5; by E. Knoblock
Counter-attack; by S. Sassoon
The Country Life anthology of
verse; ed. by P.A. Graham (42)
The country of the young; by

M. Goldring
Country sentiment; by R. Graves
Country town; by W.J. Courthope
Coupon mad; by W. Frampton
"Courage!"; by J. Owley
Crimson skies; by N.R.E. Smith
Crimson stains; by A.N. Choyce
Critical moments; by J.S.M.
Tombs
The crooked world; by G.D.H.
Cole
A crown of amaranth; comp. by
E. Macdonald & S.G. Ford
(63)
A crown of friendship; by F.S.
Woodley
The Crown Prince's first lesson-
book; by G.H. Powell
The crowning purpose; by E.
Simms
Cry of the homeless; by T. Hardy
The crystal sea; by E. Emmons
The Cud; by L. de G. Sieveking
Cups of comfort; by Mrs. R.J.
Walshaw
Curtains; by C.H.B. Kitchin
Cypress and amaranth; by A.O.
Pughe
The dales of Arcady; by D.U.
Ratcliffe
Dangerous aliens; by R.W. Rice
Darien; by H.G. Dixey
The dark fire; by W.J. Turner
The darkened ways; by I.H.T.
Mackenzie
The darkest hour; by I.R.
McLeod
Dart, loveliest of rivers; by A.N.
Tucker
A Dartmoor village; by E.
Phillpotts
The dawn; by B. Green
Dawn; by E.G. Hoare
The dawn patrol; by P. Bewsher
The day; by H. Chapple

The day; by C.E. Young
Day dawn in rural England; by
    A. Morton
"The day is done"; by F.J. Lowe
The day of battle; by A. Thrush
"Day of honour"; by L. Lindgren
The day of national intercession;
    by H. Rollo, pseud.
The day of the dead; by R.
    Kipling
Daybreak; by A.M. Buckton
The day's delight; by G. Dearmer
Days of destiny; by R.G. Barnes
De bello; by W.N. Cobbold
The debt; by E.V. Lucas
'Delight'; by E. Phillpotts
Denunciation; by R.R. Hibbs
The Derbyshire Christian rhymes
    upon the present sinful times;
    by D. Bryan
The desert and the sown; by
    M.R. Adamson
Desert musings; by L.R. Wheeler
Desiderium, MCMXV-MCMXVII;
    by N. Davey
Desire of the moth; by W.H.
    Hamilton
Destroyers; by H. Head
Deveron days; by M. Symon
The devil and the Kaiser; by F.
    Sleep
The Devil's visit to the Kaiser;
    by S. Hall
Diabolus; by Junius Redivivus,
    pseud.
Diane; by H.E. Britton
The diary of a dead officer; by
    A.G. West
Died for his enemy; by J. Knight
Dies Dei; by M. Constable &
    T. Whitney
Dies heroica; by J.L.C. Brown
Diogenes at Athens; by J. Walker
The discharged soldier's appeal;
    by A.C. Hinton

Dislikes; by C.J.B. Masefield
Disunion spells disaster; by
    G.M.L. Reade
Ditchling Beacon; by A.B.
    Norman
Diverse verse; by R.F. Dalton
The divine drama; by L.A.
    Compton-Rickett
Divorce; by C. Williams
Don't; by A. Muir
Don't worry; by A. Muir
Does it matter?; by S. Sassoon
The dog; by V.W.W.S. Purcell
A dog hero; by J. Benjamin
Don Quixote; by G.E.
    Tollemache
Dooleysprudence; by J. Joyce
The dove; by V.W.W.S. Purcell
"The Dover Patrol"; by O.B.
The Dover Patrol; by F.C. Taylor
The dream; by J. Masefield
Dream-songs; by K.A.
    Braimbridge
The dreamer; by W.D. Cocker
The dreamer; by H. Stocker
Dreamers; by S. Sassoon
The dreaming antinous; by K.
    Everest
Dreams and ideals; by F. Tindall
Dreams and journeys; by F. Shove
The dried fount; by J.E.
    Matthews
Drinking songs; by W.R.
    Titterton
The drummer boy; by D.
    Millward
Drums of defeat; by T. Maynard
Duality; by V. de S. Pinto
Ducks; by F.W. Harvey
Dugout doggerels from
    Palestine; by J. More
Dunch; by U. Roberts
Dunstanburgh; by O.H. Ewing
Dusk of Avon; by L. Parish
Dust; by I. Hearn

354

Duty; by A. Ainger
Duty; by R.W. Rice
Duty and ease; by J. Miller
Duty or regret; by H. Stead
Duty's call; by L. Horswill
Duty's call; by R.W. Rice
Earth, dear earth; by J.A.
Mackereth
Earthquake in Los Angeles; by
C.A.C. Winchester
The East Devon route march; by
G.M.L. Reade
Easter at Ypres, 1915; by W.S.S.
Lyon
Easter lilies; by F.W. Bourdillon
The eaten heart; by R. Aldington
Echoes and evasions; by C.
Brooks
Echoes of the war; by C.A.
Salmond
"Economy"; by R.W. Rice
Ecrasez l'infâme!; by C.R.
Cammell
Edith Cavell; by D. Anderson
Edith Cavell in 1915 and 1919;
by R. Temple
Edith Cavell: inspiration words
before her doom; anon.
Edith Cavell, shot October 12,
1915; by E.S. Buchanan
Edith Cavell's last thought; by
H. Northcote & M.A. North-
cote
Eggs "eggs" traordinary; by
T.B. Clark
Eidola; by F. Manning
Eld; by H. Davison
An elegy; by E.C. Blunden
An elegy on the death of a mad
dog; by F. Norton
The elf; by W.R. Darling
The elfin artist; by A. Noyes
Empire; by P. Field
The Empire "one and all"; by
H.E.B. Sewell

The Empire our boys built; by
D. Brey
The Empire song book; by C.
Clark
The Empire's watchword not in
vain; by W. Frampton
Empty day; by T. Staveley
Emptyings of my ash-tray; by
G.H. Bushnell
An enchanted garden; by A.M.B.
Rosman
The enchanted wood; by F.
Newbolt
The end of a war; by H. Read
The end of the day; by S. Grant
England and her allies invincible;
by G.M.L. Reade
England, my England; comp. by
G. Goodchild (40) (41)
The England of my dream; by
S.G. Ford
England to Germany; by T.
Hardy
England's boys; by C.A. Renshaw
England's call, the Empire's
response; by G.M.L. Reade
England's greatest national debt;
by G.M.L. Reade
England's war song; by E.S.S.
Wallington
English poems; by E.C. Blunden
The English reply; by E. Wallace
"An Englishman's reply"; by
H. Cole
Epigrams; by H.W. Garrod
Erotia; by E. Hennesley
Escape; by R. Duffin & C.
Duffin
The espalier; by S.T. Warner
The eternal quest; by F. de C.
Hamilton & B.M. Stephens
Etincelles; by J. Millar
Eton faces, old and young; by
C.A. Alington
Eton lyrics; by C.A. Alington

The European War; by J.H.
Sayles
The European War 1914-1915;
by H.D. Rawnsley
"The evening hour"; by G.E.
Body
Evening on the Mawddach
Estuary; by L. Galletley
Evening reflections; by V.I.
Cuthbert & H.E.
Evensong; by K. Tynan
The exalted valley; by A.
O'Connor
An Exeter book of verse; by
C.D. Whetham
Exile; by R. Aldington
Exit homo; by A. St. J. Adcock
The exploit of the Clan
MacTavish; by J. Benjamin
Extremes; by Junius Redivivus,
pseud.
Fables and satires; by R. Ross
Facts and fancies; by N.
Richfield
Fairies and fusiliers; by R. Graves
Fairyland in 1918; by E.L.
Thomas
Fallen petals; by E. Petre
Falling leaves; by E.H. Blakeney
A famous war poem; by A.J.
Long
Fancies of a physician; by J.F.
Fergus
Farewell; by F.W. Harvey
Farewell; by A.T. Turner
Farewell my muse; by C. Bax
Farewell to Egypt; by R.
Coldicott
The farmer's bride; by C. Mew
Fate of the Lusitania; by J.W.
Cheetham
A father of women; by A.
Meynell
Fear not life's voyage; by J.E.
Smith

Fen and fell; by T. Thornely
Festubert; by W. Sewell
A few little verses about the war;
by G. Deverell
A few thoughts for our over-sea
cousins; by R.W. Rice
The fiddler's story; by T. Hardy
The fiery cross; comp. by M.C.
Edwards & M. Booth (25)
The fiery cross; by J. Oxenham
Fife and drum; by C.E.C.H.
Burton
15 patriotic songs; by A. Cooper
Fifty years on; by I.Q. Twelve,
pseud.
"A fight to a finish"; by S.G.
Ford
The fighters and workers; by
R.W.L.
Fighting lines and various rein-
forcements; by H. Begbie
Fighting men; by C.F. Smith
Fighting types; by H. Gordon
The final message; by
J. Benjamin
Finding; by H. Dircks
Finlay; by H. Jones
Firelight memories; by J. Preston
Fireside, countryside; by G.F.
Bradby
First and second love; by E.
Farjeon
First hymn to Lenin; by C.M.
Grieve
Five degrees south; by F.B.
Young
Five souls; by W.N. Ewer
"The flag of the free"; by J.
Black
The flagship; by T. Blakemore
Flak; by E. Crawshay-Williams
Flame-tears and heart-joy; by
J.S. Bailey
Flanders to Fowey; by S. Levey
Flash-lights; by Way-Farer, pseud.

356

God save the king; by J.E.
Flecker
God's bugle-call, Marne,
September, 1914; by M.
Goodricke
Gods of war; by G.W. Russell
Gold and ochre; by E. Morgan
The golden archer; by A.B.
The golden arrow; by B.M.
Tickle
Golden orchids; by H. Desmond
The golden rose; by H. Simpson
The golden thurible; by
W.R. Childe
The goldfinches; by S. Lynd
Goliath and David; by R. Graves
"Gone, but not forgotten";
by C. Wilson
Gone to the war; by B. Gilbert
Good Lord! what fools we be!;
by J. Baker
The good soldier; by F.M. Ford
Good will; by C.E. Sharpley
Goodwill; by E. Phillpotts
Gossamer and honey; by J.E.V.
Warburg
The grand reveille; by H.A.
George
The grand Stonewall Brigade;
by T.B. Clark
Grant us Thy peace; by D.B.
Payne & K.M.E. Lillingston
Grapes of thorns; by J.E. Stewart
Gratitude; by D. Hyman
The graves of France; by R.A.
Hayden
The great advance to ultimate
victory; by G.M.L. Reade
Great Britain and her allies
unconquerable; by G.M.L.
Reade
The great sacrifice; by A.L.
Holmes
The great sacrifice; by E. Sillito
The great sacrifice; by F.W. Smith

The Great War in verse and prose;
ed. by J.E. Wetherell (119)
The greater love; by E. Carter
The greater love; by R. Heywood
"Greater love hath no man than
this . . ."; by J.M.V. Hope
Greed and gain; by R.W. Rice
Green and grey; by R.G.
Vansittart
Green branches; by S.J. Looker
Green branches; by J. Stephens
The green copse; by G. Hadgraft
The green roads; by E. Thomas
Green ways; by D. Grenside
Greetings; by E.G. Sargent
The Gretna girls; by A. Burns
Grey kilts; by D. Tovey
The grumbling press; by G.M.L.
Reade
Guarding the line; by H. Gape
The Guards came through; by
A.C. Doyle
Guillaumism; by E.V. Lucas
The gunner's sacrifice; by J.
Benjamin
The guns; by G. Frankau
Guns and guitars; by W.R.
Titterton
The gutter and the stars; by
E. Crawshay-Williams
Gypsy love; by M. Mair
H.M.S.; by J.G. Bower
H.M.S. Mystery "Q"; by S. Lee
H.M.S. "Téméraire"; by P.
Thomas
H.M.S. "Vindictive" (the raid on
the Mole); by S. Levey
The hackle and the plume; by
Hackleplume, pseud.
Hail! Union of the brave; by
J.R. Penty
Half-hours at Helles; by A.P.
Herbert
Half-way; by H.S.V. Hodge
Halfway house; by E.C. Blunden

359

Hallow-e'en; by W.M. Letts
Hamewith; by C. Murray
The hand; by G.L. Barnett
Hands across the sea; by S.
Norton
"Hands off!"; by F.B. Dickinson
Hands up, obey!; by J.H. Partridge
The happy stillness; by A.
O'Connor
The happy tree; by G. Gould
The happy warrior; by A.H.
Cook
Hark! the trumpet; by G.M.L.
Reade
Harry, the hero of the Victoria
Cross; by Mrs. C.N. Jackson
Harvest; by T.W. Mercer
Harvest home; by A.
Lynnford-Smith
Harvest of youth; by E.L.
Davison
A harvester of dreams; by E. Orr
The harvesting; by W.F.
Robinson
Hasty verses of a "temporary";
by H.C. Lanyon
Hazards; by W.W. Gibson
Hazel leaves; by A.M. Colligan
He fought for me; by T.N.
Smith
Heard melodies; by W. Weaving
The heart of peace; by L.
Housman
The heart remembers morning;
by M. Walsh
Hearts courageous; by J.
Oxenham
The heart's journey; by S.
Sassoon
The heart's unreason; by E.L.
Davison
Heather ways; by H.C. Cole
The heavenly tavern; by H.
Hastings

Helicon holidays; by J.W.
Williamson
Hell let loose by the fiend of
Potsdam-nation; by S. Hall
Her last moments: tribute to the
memory of Nurse Edith Cavell;
by E.H. Rowe
Herb o' grace; by K. Tynan
Here comes she home; by G.F.
Fyson
A hero of Erin; by T.B. Clark
Heroes all; by J.S. Carroll &
K.M. Carroll
Heroes from the seething fight!;
by O. Hewett
Heroes in khaki; by T.B. Clark
Heroes of Neuve Chapelle; by
T.B. Clark
Heroic King Peter of Serbia;
by H. West
The heroic spirit; by A. Rees
A hero's son; by J. Benjamin
A highland regiment; by E.A.
Mackintosh
The highlander at the bridge; by
J. Silvester
The highway of Hades; by J.
Hogben
Hill and heather; by M.G. Cherry
The hills o' hame; by J. Donnan
The hills of home; by H.E.G.
Rope
Hilltops and song; by E.B.
Gilson
Hips and haws; by A.E. Coppard
His coming; by A.B.
His letter home; by F. Rigby
His soldier daddy; by J.
Benjamin
The history of England; by H.W.
Moggridge
Hits . . . and misses . . .; by
P.T. Kenway
Hits and misses; by J. Pope

An ideal England; by G.M.L.
Reade
Idle moments; by G. Israelstam
Idylls of life and love; by A.G.
Fraser
Idylls of the homeland; by G.
Savill
If I goes west!; by Tommy,
pseud.
If only!; by D. Hall
Ignatius; by A.C. Hay
Ils ne passerant pas!; by S. Levey
Images; by R. Aldington
Images; by A. Hay
Images and meditations; by
A.M.F. Duclaux
Images of desire; by R. Aldington
Images of war; by R. Aldington
The importance of art in war-
time; by O. Burdett
Impressions and depressions;
by W.K. Scudamore
In a cottage; by J.L.D. Howitt
In a rest-camp (near Ypres);
by A.C. Challoner
In Arcadia; by W.M. Dixon
In Britain's need; by R.S.S.
Ross-Lewin & R. O'D. Ross-
Lewin
In days of peace, in times of
war; by G.C. Guthrie
In divers moods; by J.C.
McCorquodale
In full flight; by E.V. Hall
In glorious memory of H.M.S.
"Vindictive"; by G.M.L.
Reade
In honour; by Father, pseud.
In lonely walks; by L. Bullock
In loving memory; by A.M.
Farrer
In loving memory of our fallen
heroes; by C.H. Clifford
In many keys; by M. Wedmore
In memoriam A.H.; by M. Baring

In memoriam Auberon Herbert,
Captain Lord Lucas; by M.
Baring
"In memoriam: E.M."; by W.
Bagshaw
In memoriam: Edith Cavell; by
W.S. Murphy
In memoriam: Kitchener of
Khartoum; by E.C. Plastow
In memoriam 'Lieut. Warneford,
V.C., R.N.'; by H. Cole
In memoriam: Miss Cavell,
murdered at Brussels, October
12, 1915; by J. Streaks
In memoriam Montague T.S.
Browning; by G.A. Browning
In memoriam of the "Empress of
Ireland"; by Mrs. Hayward
In memory; see EDITH Cavell:
inspiration words before her
doom; anon.
In memory of John Travers
Cornwell; by G.M.L. Reade
In memory of Kaiser Bill; by
C.H. Clifford
In memory of our beloved ones
embalmed by the seas; by
R.W. Russell
In memory of the late Lord
Kitchener; by R.W. Rice
In parenthesis; by D. Jones
In pastime wrought; by L.G.
Fison
In praise of life; by H.N. Spalding
In quest of the Holy Grail; by
C. Brumm
In shabby streets; by C.A.
Alington
In the camp fire smoke; by R.G.
Miller
In the day of battle; comp. by
C.E. Holman (47) (48) (49)
In the infirmary; by H. Davison
In the new world and the old;
by M.R.C.S.

362

In the open; by W.K. Holmes
In the town; by D. Goldring
"In the trenches"; by T. Tiplady
In the vale of years; by E.H.
  Blakeney
In the valley of vision; by G.
  Faber
In the wake of the sword; by
  P. Haselden
In time of "the breaking of
  nations"; by T. Hardy
In time of war; by E.H.W.
  Meyerstein
In time of war; by A. Romilly
In war and peace; by M.H.J.
  Henderson
In war time; by M.W. Cannan
In war-time; by M.E. Gladwell
Inasmuch; by P. Lawford
Increased cost of living; by
  R.W. Rice
"The indictment of 1914"; by
  G. Dibben
The Inn of Tranquility; by J.
  Galsworthy
Inspirations of Armageddon; by
  R. Berrill
Intercession; by A. Noyes
Interflow; by G. Faber
Interludes of an editor; by O.
  Seaman
Into battle; by J. Grenfell
The invisible sun; by V. de S.
  Pinto
Invocation; by R. Nichols
Invocation and peace celebration;
  by R. Nichols
Invocations to angels; by E.
  Rickword
The Irish Guards; by R. Kipling
Irish heroes in red war; by
  A.M.P. Cooke
The iron age; by F. Betts
The iron cross; by S. Hall
The island; by F.B. Young

Island lights; by G.F. Fyson
"It's a tough job to beat the
  allies"; by J.H. Sums
It is for man to choose; by G. de
  B. Bowen-Colthurst
"Jack" on the German Fleet;
  by A. Muir
A Japanese Don Juan; by F.T.A.
  A. Gwatkin
Jazzer's joy!; by S. Levey
Jean; by C. Ingledew
Jerusalem; by P. Field
Jesus of the Scars; by E.
  Shillito
A jingle on the times; by T.
  Hardy
"Jock"; by A. Muir
Jock McCraw; by J. Mitchell
"John Bull's Christmas party";
  by H. Cole
John Bull's game of cards; by
  H. Cole
John the Hermit; by S.S. McCurry
Join the R.F.C.'s; by W.
  Frampton
Jones's wedding; by A.H. Sidg-
  wick
Jovial jottings from the trenches;
  by C. Wideawake, pseud.
'The Judah 'ills'; by H.G.
  Mansfield
The judgement of Valhalla; by
  G. Frankau
"The judgment"; by N. Davidson
July XIX, 1919; by G.M.L.
  Reade
Justice; by R. Kipling
Jutland; by S. Leslie
"K.K." and the world-wide war;
  by T.N. Smith
The K.R.R.E.s; by T.B. Clark
"K.S.L.I."; by T.B. Clark
The Kaiser and the Bradda
  (Bradwell) lads; by I.M. Hall

363

The Kaiser and the Crown Prince; by G.M.L. Reade
"The Kaiser and the Emperor"; by G.M.L. Reade
Kaiser to Gott; by A. Muir
Der Kaiser von Potsdam; by H.B. Burton
The Kaiser's ambition; by M. Aston
The Kaiser's Christmas dinner; by J. Gilham
The Kaiser's doom; by S. Hall
The Kaiser's dream; anon.
The Kaiser's dream; by J.B.
"The Kaiser's dream"; by H. Cole
Der Kaiser's dream; by A. Muir
The Kaiser's dream; by J. Streaks
The Kaiser's dream of heaven; by H. Branson
Der Kaiser's end; anon.
The Kaiser's favourite song; by G.H.
The Kaiser's horoscope; anon.
The Kaiser's mistake!; anon.
The Kaiser's nightmare; anon.
The Kaiser's nightmare; by J.S. Norton
The Kaiser's ordeal; by N. Davidson
Kaiser's peace proposals; by G.M.L. Reade
The Kaiser's plight and the allies' fight; by J.L. Yates
The Kaiser's request, addressed to Old Nick; anon.
The Kaiser's sin; by A.H. Hadley
The Kaiser's soliloquy; by A. Morton
The Kaiser's telegram; anon.
The Kaiser's terms of friendship; by G.M.L. Reade
Kaiser's wish for peace; by G.M.L. Reade
The kaleidoscope; by S. Vines
Keep cool; by S. Levey

Keep smiling!; by E. Spaven
Kettle-songs; by H. Lulham
Khaki and blue; by T.E. Cole
Khaki characters and mufti monologues; by N. Easter
Khaki pal; by C. Long
Khaki soldiers; by M. Kenny
The Khud; by T.B. Clark
Killantringan; by A. Mackereth
Killed in action; by H. Burton
Killed in action; by W. Evans
"Killed in action"; by F.I. Harrison
Killed in action; by E. Sillito
Kilmore: the medicine man; by A.G. Dolden
A kind thought for the Army Service Corps; by R.W. Rice
"King Albert the brave"; by H. Cole
King Alfred; by S. Hancock
The king's "Contemptibles"; by Q. Cumber, pseud.
The king's high way; by J. Oxenham
The King's Royal Rifle Corps; by T.B. Clark
King's verse; by London University. King's College. Georgian Group (62)
Kitchener; by C.J. O'Shaughnessy
Kitchener calls you!; by E. Broxbourne
The Kitchener men; by E. Mills
Kitchener's army; by Colonial, pseud.
Kitchener's call to arms (answered); by S. Myers
Knights adventurers; by L.E. Williams
Knowledge and dream; by C. Tolly
Kultur and anarchy; by F.C. Owlett

Kultur and the German blunder
(buss); by H.R. Murray
Labour war chants; by A. Allen
The labyrinth; by J.W. Mills
The lads of the Kensington
Rifles; by W.V. Wilson
Lake and war; by A.S. Cripps
The lamp of freedom; by R.R.
Gibson
The "lamplighters"; by M.
Symington
Lamps in the valley; by E.
Newton
The Lancashire landing; by E.
Phillips
The land of memory; by L.M.
Watt
A lap full of seed; by M.
Plowman
The last chance; by A. Bennett
The last crusade; by F.W.O.
Ward
The last illusion; by C. Hurry
The last knight; by T. Maynard
The last line; by E.V. Hall
The last message; by A. Cooper
The last of four; by J.C.A.
Last post; by P.C.
Stacpoole-O'Longan
The last rebellion; by E. Haward
Last songs; by F. Ledwidge
The last will and testament of
H.I.M. the Kaiser . . .; anon.
The last will of the past Will,
to wit: — The Kaiser; anon.
Late lyrics and earlier; by T.
Hardy
Late songs; by K. Tynan
Later English poems, 1901-1922;
ed. by J.E. Wetherell (120)
Later songs from books; by
R. Kipling
The later Te Deums; by J.
Oxenham
Lauds and libels; by C.L. Graves

Lauds and loves; by H. Simpson
Laughing gas; by M. Few
Laughs and whifts of song; by
T. Maynard
Laurel and myrtle; by A. Barry
The laws of the Navy; by R.A.
Hopwood
Lays by the way; by R.B. Greaves
The lays of a labourer; by A.
Reeve
The lays of a limpet; by E.
McCurdy
Lays of stirring days; by D.M.
Nichols
The leaf; by R.D. Norton
The leaf burners; by E. Rhys
Leaves; by R. Cleworth
Leaves in the wind; by V.
Bartlett
The legend of Alompra; by
J. Macgregor
A legend of liberty; by F.C.
Palmer
"Lest we forget"; by G. De St.
Ouen
Lest we forget; ed. by H.B.
Elliott (26)
Lest we forget; by C.A. Renshaw
"Lest we forget"; by J.A. Willis
Lest we forget, U.B., 1914; by
J. Stone
Let's not forget them; by J.
McDonald
Letters of an airman; by G. Wall
Lieut. Guynemer, Viking of the
air; by W. Frampton
Lieutenant Tattoon, M.C.;
by E. Carpenter
The life I love; by W.K. Holmes
Life's autumn; by H.A. Winser
Lift high the flag; by R. Ashmore
The light of life; by C.H. Whitby
The light of love; by S. Wyatt
Lighten our darkness; by G.A.S.
Kennedy

"The likes of they"; by A.P. Herbert
Lilies of His love; by A. O'Connor
The lilt; by M.E. Angus
The lily of Malud; by J.C. Squire
Limehouse; by H. Mitcham
Lines in memory of my clansmen who fell in the Great War; by J. McDonald
Lines in verse and fable; by A.T.T. Verney-Cave
Lines of life; by H.W. Nevinson
Lines on the Fleet; by J.E. Hodgson
The lion; by C.A. Playford
A little book of quiet; by D.F. Gurney
A little book of verse; by J.P. Nott
The little brothers; by W.J. Ferrar
A little collection of "the stuff that rhymes"; by F.G. Webb
The little company; by A. O'Connor
The little peacemaker; by P. Wallace & others (115)
A little rhyme; by O.E. Lindsay
A little Te Deum of the commonplace; by J. Oxenham
A little . . . wooden cross; by E. Fielding
Livelihood; by W.W. Gibson
Lochaber's day; by M. Cameron
Lollingdon downs; by J. Masefield
London, one November; by H. Mackay
London pride; by W.R. Titterton
London songs; by M. Bell
London sonnets; by H. Wolfe
London stone; by R. Kipling
London town, (November 11, 1918-1923); by R. Kipling

The Londoner's chariot; by W. Thorley
The long retreat; by A.F. Graves
The long trail; ed. by J. Brophy & E. Partridge (6) (7)
Look forward for the best; by A. Wheble
"Look up!"; by F. Clifford
Look! We have come through!; by D.H. Lawrence
Looking on; by J. Howcroft
The loom of life; by M. St. John
Lord God of battles; comp. by A.E.M. Foster (30)
Lord Kitchener; by R. Bridges
Lord Kitchener; by G.M.L. Reade
Lord Kitchener and the British heroes of the Battle of Jutland; by G.M.L. Reade
Lord Kitchener is calling; by Weightman
The lord of misrule; by A. Noyes
Lord Rhonda, our new Food Controller; by R.W. Rice
Loss of the "Royal Edward" troopship; by J. Bradshaw
Loss of the S.S. "Lusitania"; by J. Bradshaw
Lost city; by K.M. Wallace
Lost or won; by C.M. Domleo
The Lothian land; by A. Dodds
Love and the stars; by W. Blathwayt
Love and war; by N. Malacrida
Love blossoms from my garden of dreams; by J. Fae
Love in a mist; by C.J. Arnell
Love in London; by W. Benington
Love-letter lays; by A.C. White
Love songs of a soldier; by E. Hennesley
Lovelit flames; anon.
A lover of the land; by F. Niven
Love's melodies; by M. Crosbie

Loyalties; by J. Drinkwater
The luck of the Navy; by O. Boulton
The "Lusitania"; anon.
Lusitania! Lo Satan near; by T.N. Smith
The lute of life; by W.H. Scott
The Lyceum book of war verse; ed. by A.E. Macklin (64)
Lyric earth; by J. Helston
Lyrical links; by L. Marcus
Lyrics and parables; by W. Davies
Lyrics and short poems; by G.E. Tollemache
Lyrics and unfinished poems; by L. Abercrombie
Lyrics for sport; by R.P. Keigwin
Lyrics from West Lothian; by I.W. Hutchison
Lyrics of life; by U. Bloom
Lyrics of life and thought; by E. Glazebrook
Lyrics of love; by N.R.E. Smith
Ma wee bit cot; anon.
Macedonian measures; by J.D. Macleod
Machines and men; by H. Stocker
The mad dog of Potsdam; by F. Norton
Mad moments; by E.T. Sandford
Made in England; by O. Seaman
Made in the pans; by A.W. Carmichael
Made in the trenches; ed. by F. Treves & G. Goodchild (110)
The madness of the arts; by W.R. Titterton
The Magians; by H.W. Moore
Magic; by E. Norton
Magpies in Picardy; by T.P.C. Wilson
Maid, mother — and widow; by J. Dareing, pseud.

The mailed fist; by H.J. Drane
The making; by G.R. Hamilton
The making of Micky McGhee; by R.W. Campbell
Malice in Kulturland; by H. Wyatt
The Malory verse book; comp. by E. Jenkinson (52)
A man; by H.F. Bristow
The man from Flanders; by E. Shanks
The man who saw; by W. Watson
Mandragora; by J.C. Powys
Many mansions; by R.G. Barnes
Many moods; by F.W. Howe
Many moods; by M. Philpot
Many voices; by E. Nesbit
Maple leaf men; by R.E. Sharland
Maple-leaf songs; by F. Niven
March evening; by L.A.G. Strong
The march of the Kaiser's men; by A. Muir
Margaret Atheling; by A.S. Lewis
Marlborough; by C.H. Sorley
Mars and Eros; by W. Boyd-Shannon
"The martyrs"; by N. Davidson
Mary in the wood; by D.K. Gardiner
Masks of time; by E.C. Blunden
Mater dolorosa; by A.E. Grantham
Matters in Macedonia; by T.B. Clark
Matters of love and death; by R. Gittings
Mattins; by G.H. Crump
Meditations of a country chiel; by J. Buchan
A medley of humours; by C. Granville
A medley of songs; by M.J. Wrigley

A medley of verse; by F.B. Wells

Memoir, 1887-1937; by G.R. Hamilton

Memories of childhood; by J. Freeman

Memories of 1915; by E. Lister

Memories of Peeko; by Don, pseud.

Memories of the Great War, 1914-1918; by E.F. Laxton

"Memories of the line"; by J. Baker

Memory; by A.N.Choyce

Men of my kin; by A. Ainger

Men who march away; ed. by I.M. Parsons (80)

The Menin road; by C. Oman

A merry new ballad of Dr. Woodrow Wilson; by D.S. MacColl

Mesopotamia; by J.G. Fairfax

Mesopotamia; by R. Kipling

Mesopotamian verses; by E.J. Thompson

A metrical garland; by C. Wheeler

Mice; by G. Bullett

Michael Robartes and the dancer; by W.B. Yeats

Mid-way tracks; by J. Horne

Midnight in Yarrow; by R. Quin

Midnight musings; by S.L. Lloyd

The mind of God with regard to the Great War; by D. Bryan

The minstrelsy of peace; comp. by J.B. Glasier (38) (39)

Mirrors and angles; by V.H. Friedlaender

A miscellany of poetry—1919; ed. by W.K. Seymour (94)

Miserere; by E.A. Mackintosh

Miserere Domine; by E.A. Mackintosh

"Mr. Private Khaki"; by P. Thomas

A modern Horatius; by J.M.Gibbs

A modern nursery tale; by C.W. Scarr

Modern poetry; ed. by G.N. Pocock (81)

Moments of vision; by T. Hardy

"The monsoon"; by A.M. Eteson

Moods; by J.D. Greenway

Moods and tenses; by H.L. Simpson

Moonset; by T. Blakemore

Moral tales in rhyme; by T. Sansome

More ballads of field and billet; by W.K. Holmes

More rough rhymes of a padre; by G.A.S. Kennedy

More songs from the moorland; by M.I.E. Dolphin

More songs of Angus; by V. Jacob

More Tommy's tunes; comp. by F.T. Nettleinghame (67)

More war poems; by J. Pope

Morn mist; by W. Lloyd

Morning-glory; by S. Sassoon

Morning mist; by J. Begbie

Moses; by I. Rosenberg

Mother Shipton's later prophecies; by F. Spafford

Mothers of England!; by J.E. Brame

Mothers of England! have ye mothered a man?; by J.E. Brame

Motley; by W. De La Mare

Mud and stars; ed. by D. York (130)

Mulvaney's gun; by M. Bent

The munition worker; by W. Frampton

Munitions; by Junius Redivivus, pseud.

The munitions brigade; by W. Frampton

Murdering monsters; by Vir, pseud.

A muse at sea; by E.H. Young
The muse in arms; ed. by E.B.
    Osborn (72)
The muse in blue; by J.S.
    Bailey
Musings and memories; by H.
    Nelson
Musings in verse; by T. Platts
Musings of a medico; by K.
    Rogers
My dog Blanco; by J. Walker
My dream, 1914; by D.
    Plimpton
My fifty versing years; by T.F.
    Royds
My lady's garden, planted and
    grown; by Hackleplume, pseud.
My quota; by J.E. Swallow
My soldier laddie; by W.
    Warwick-Ward
My window sill; by C. Carstairs
Myrrh; by H. Hastings
Mystica et lyrica; by C. Brereton
Naked warriors; by H. Read
Napoo!; by H. Hamilton
Narcotics; by C.A. Renshaw
The "national" post card; by
    L. Lindgren
National service; by G.M.L.
    Reade
The nation's duty; by R.W. Rice
Nations philosophy; by J.C.
    Richardson
The naval crown; by C.F. Smith
A naval motley; by N.M.F.
    Corbett
Near and far; by E.C. Blunden
Neighbours; by W.W. Gibson
Nennette and Rintintin (Paris,
    1918); by S. Levey
Neuve Chapelle; by H.A. Nesbitt
The new and delectable ballad of
    King Richard called Lionheart;
    by F. Betts

The new benedicite; by R.A.
    Kennedy
The new crucifixion; by E.
    Tollemache
The new madonna; by A.
    Tidman
The new morning; by A. Noyes
The new Navy; by R.A.
    Hopwood
New patriotic poems; by E.W.
    Watson
New times and old rhymes; by
    C.L. Graves
New voices; ed. by M.
    Wilkinson (127)
The new world; by L. Binyon
A New Year's eve in war time;
    by T. Hardy
Nigel; by A.F. Trotter
Nigella; by G.P. Dawnay
Night flight; by L. Taylor
The night guard; by H.L. North
The night sister; by C.T. Fox-
    croft
Night winds of Araby; by A.J.E.
    Dawson
Nil desperandum!; by J. Payne
The nincompoop, or slacker!;
    by G.M.L. Reade
1915; by W. Blair
A 1915 winter song; by Toriel,
    pseud.
1914; by R. Brooke
1914; by M.F. Walker
1914; by C. Walston
1914 and now; by D. Geddes
1914-18 in poetry; ed. by E.L.
    Black (4)
1914-1918: the darkness, the
    dawn and a vision; by Northern
    Celt, pseud.
1919; by N. Anglin
No more ghosts; by R. Graves
No one wants poetry; by E.
    Crawshay-Williams

No peace possible with
Hohenzollerns; by G.M.L.
Reade
No talk of peace till Prussian
militarism has been crushed;
by G.M.L. Reade
The noble slackers; by D.
Llewellyn
Nobody works in Britain (with
apologies to the Bolsheviks);
by F.J. Lowe
Noel; by G. Cannan
The nonsensical conjectors; by
E. Carpenter
The Norfolk recruit's farewell;
by C. Brereton
"The Norfolks"; by Grateful
Yorkshireman, pseud.
Norge; by C.E. Hammond &
C.R.A. Hammond
The North Sea; by H. de V.
Stacpoole
The north star; by L. Binyon
Northern numbers (71)
Nothing but eyes to weep with;
by R.D. Gibson
November; by H.B. Binns
November sunsets; by F.S.
Stevenson
Now and then; by I.S.M.
Hamilton
Now's the time; by S. Norton
Nursairy rimes; by D.C.M. Hume
Nurse Edith Cavell, saint, martyr,
and heroine . . .; by H. West
Nursery rhymes for fighting times;
by E. Thorpe
The nymph; by E.L. Gunston
Occasional poems; by H. Cust
Occasional poetic thoughts; by
A.C. Farrington
Occasional verse; by A.
Stodart-Walker
Occasional verses in wartime;
by C.D. Whetham

An octave of song, a rainbow of
hope; by M. Higgs
October; by R. Bridges
Odds and ends; by D.M.
Tweedale
Ode from Italy in time of war;
by H. Trench
Ode on the death of Lord
Kitchener of Khartoum; by
J.E. Swaine
An ode to Sergeant Samuel Meek;
by M. Dainow
Offered in aid of recruiting;
by A.L. Player
Oh! Glorious lads!; by H.W.
Southgate
Oh Lord, hear our cry; by E.H.
Mount
"Old England"; by R.W. Rice
The old home's calling me!; by
W. Frampton
The old huntsman; by S. Sassoon
An old proverb "It will all be
the same in a thousand years";
by D.S. Shorter
The old ships; by J.E. Flecker
The old way; by R.A. Hopwood
The old year and the new, 1916-
1917; by J.J. Lane
The Oldham flag song and
recitation; by J.W. Cheetham
Olton pools; by J. Drinkwater
The omega; by E. Shillito
On divers strings; by C.J. Arnell
On heaven; by F.M. Ford
On leave; by E.A. Wodehouse
On patrol; by J.G. Bower
On several occasions; by E.C.
Blunden
"On sick leave, warriors three";
by C. Wilson
On the coming of peace; by
C. Nicol
On the edge of the earth; by
E. Tee

370

On the Oxford circuit; by C. Darling

On the threshold; by R.W. Wilson

On to Berlin!; by M.L. Williams

On Vimy Ridge; by J.A. Ferguson

Once a hero; by A. Saunders & J. Walsh

Once through the alphabet; by T.B. Clark

One hour together; by E.G. Hoare

One hundred best poems on the war; ed. by C.F. Forshaw (27) (28)

One hundred of the best poems on the European War; ed. by C.F. Forshaw (27) (28)

One mother; by I.R. McLeod

One of them; by G. Frankau

The one voice; by J. Elyott

One-way street; by S.W. Powell

The only way; by G.M.L. Reade

Opals; by N.R. Edwards

Open eyes; by D. Grenside

"Or sing a sang at least"; by J.S. Carroll & K.M. Carroll

The orange and the green; anon.

The origin of war verses; by H.B. Chadwick

Orphans in Belgium; by A. Mee

The other side; by G. Frankau

The other side of silence; by H. Lulham

Otherworld; by F.S. Flint

Our air service in war; by R.W. Rice

Our air service value in war; by R.W. Rice

Our ally the war horse; by M.F. Larkin

Our bit; by A.C. Dacomb

'Our boys in brown and blue'; by H. Cole

Our brave boys; by W. Brantom

"Our dad"; by H. Branson

"Our economic boycott"; by R.W. Rice

"Our farm"; by W.J. Minter

Our girls in wartime; by H. Gordon

Our glorious dead; by G.M.L. Reade

Our heroes, (1914-1916); by A.E. Eagar

Our hopes and our aims; by A.L. Player

Our hospital ABC; by H. Gordon & M.C. Tindall

Our hospital Anzac, British, Canadian; by H. Gordon & M.C. Tindall

Our khaki boys; by A.N. Davies

Our mother land; by H. Oatway

Our own men; by F.M. Hay-Drummond

Our padre; by R.F. Eldridge

Our Queen; by E.S.S. Wallington

Our wounded; by M. Mail

Ourselves a dream; by H.G. Dixey

Out of the mists; by M.T. Parnell

The outcast; by C.L. Brodie

Outlaws; by N. Cunard

The outlaws; by R. Kipling

"Outpost"; by Defaulter, pseud.

Over the brazier; by R. Graves

Oxford and Flanders; by G. Alchin

The Oxford book of English verse; ed. by A. Quiller-Couch (88)

Oxford poetry (73) (74) (75) (76) (77) (78) (79)

Oxford, St. Bees and the front; by H.B.K. Allpass

A pagan shrine; by R. Gordon-Canning

A pageant of poets; by J.C. Woods

The pageant of war; by M. Sackville

372

Pilgrimage and battle; by E.A.
Stewart
A pilgrimage of the Empire; by
A. Crosfield
Pilgrim's joy; by A.S. Cripps
The pilgrims of the night; by
T.B. Clark
The pipe of peace; by A.M.P.
Cooke
Pipes of Pan; by C.H. Warren
The pity of it; by T. Hardy
Plain song; by N. Mardel
Plain song, 1914-1916; by
E. Phillpotts
Plain speaking; by Mrs. C.N.
Jackson
Play-hour lyrics; by A. Chambers
Play the game; by F. Bowman
Plea for continued unity; by
G.M.L. Reade
Plea for unity; by G.M.L. Reade
Plummets; by H. Allsopp
"Plutus imperator"; by Vir,
pseud.
A poem of the Great War; by
H.S. Hall
Poems and imaginings; by C.
Templer
Poems by a pitman; by C. Wilson
Poems for the forces; by W.R.
Titterton
Poems for the people; by T.M.
Walker
Poems from beyond; by R.
Mallett
Poems from history; by R.
Kipling
Poems from Punch, 1909-1920 (87)
Poems from the trenches; by
E.C. Melville
Poems, grave and gay; by A.R.P.
Poems in black and white; by
W.G. Raffé
Poems in captivity; by J. Still
Poems in Hampshire; by R.W.
Pressey

Poems in memory of the late
Field-Marshal Lord Kitchener,
K.G.; ed. by C.F. Forshaw (29)
Poems in peace and war; by
E.H. Blakeney
Poems in peace and war; by
L.D. Burke
Poems in wartime; by E.A.
Craven
Poems of a mother, 1914-1916;
by Mother, pseud.
Poems of a pantheist; by N.
Bomford
The poems of a patient; by
J.C. Amcotts
Poems of a private; by T.B.
Clark
Poems of an air pilot; by
C.A.C. Winchester
Poems of conformity; by C.
Williams
Poems of consolation; by J. Allan
Poems of dawn and the night;
by H. Mond
Poems of hope and vision; by
F. Mann
Poems of humanity; by N.R.E.
Smith
Poems of impudence; by E.G.V.
Knox
Poems of life; by T.H.
Collinson
Poems of London; by G. Skelton
Poems of love and loss; by D.
Stewart
Poems of love and war; by S.B.
Macleod
Poems of love and war; by A.
Reade
Poems of many years; by E.C.
Blunden
Poems of nature and war; by
C. Granville
Poems of 1915; by V. Gillespie
Poems of peace; by A. Beckett
Poems of peace; by R. Hill

Poems of peace and progress;
by J. Barlow
Poems of peace and war; by
F.B. Fenton
Poems of peace and war; by
I.B. Jenkins
Poems of peace and war; by
H. Ord
Poems of remembrance; by
T.B. Saunders
Poems of the Empire; by J.S.M.
Ward
Poems of the Great War (82)
(83) (84)
Poems of the Great War; comp.
by J.W. Cunliffe (19)
Poems of the Great War; by G.
Robertson-Glasgow
Poems of the Great War; by
W.E. Walkerdine
Poems of the love of England;
by W.H. Draper
Poems of the war and after;
by V.M. Brittain
Poems of the war and the peace;
ed. by S.A. Leonard (59)
Poems of two wars; by J.C.
Squire
Poems of Wales; by A.G.
Prys-Jones
Poems of war; by F.J. Doouss
Poems of war; by G.R. Newton
Poems of war and peace; by
S.G. Ford
Poems of war and peace; by
D. Macmillan
Poems on the war; by A.
Dobson
Poems on the war; by A.
Meynell
Poems on the war; by J.H.
Sayles
Poems, secular and sacred; by
J.S. Scotland

Poems, whisperings of love; by
J. Millar
Poems written at Ruhleben; by
T. Philip
Poems written during the Great
War, 1914-1918; ed. by B.
Lloyd (61)
The poet wanderer; by E. Gray
Poetic pilgrimage, 1929-1939;
by M.E. Layton
Poetical pictures of the Great
War; by H.T.M. Bell
Poetical tributes to the late Lord
Kitchener; ed. by C.F.
Forshaw (29)
Poetry in English, 1900-1930;
comp. by J.F. Sullivan (105)
Poetry of the First World War;
ed. by M. Hussey (50)
The poet's flower; by G. Kendall
The poets in camp; by E.W.
Hamilton
The poets in Picardy; by E. De
Stein
Polefield Hall Red Cross
Hospital, Prestwich, 1915; by
A. Peeler, pseud.
Policeman X, the man who did
not dare; by J. Oxenham
Policies in poem and parody;
by C.W. Hayward
The political outlook, past,
present and future; by A.
Morton
Polyclitus; by J. Walker
The ponderin's of Peter; by
F.S. Girdlestone
A poor man's riches; by C.
Dalmon
The poppied dream; by D.
Gurney
The poppies of Flanders; by
M. Thompson
Post-meridian; by W.E. Barnard

Rhythmic waves; by J.C.
Cohen
Richard Plantagenet; by D.
Davenport
The Rifle Brigade; by T.E.
Clark
Rifleman Mariner, V.C.; by
T.B. Clark
Right welcome, luckless
Belgians!; by O. Hewett
Rimes of the Diables Bleus; by
H. Baerlein
Ripples from the ranks of the
Q.M.A.A.C.; by I. Grindlay
The rising tide; by C.J. Whitby
The rivals, the swords and the
signs; by H.C. Corlette
The road of life; by I. Jerrold
The road to Calais; by A.B.
Scott
The road to ruin; by S. Sassoon
Roads and ditches; by J.
Peterson
The robin's-son; by F.H. French
The Roehampton reciter; by
S. Levey
Roehampton rhymes; by S.
Levey
The roll call; by S. Norton
Roll of honour; by M.
Aldington
The roll of honour; by K.
Mellersh
The roll of honour; by C.M.
Prevost
The roll of honour; by E.B.
Terry
The roll of the drum; by F.B.
Wells
Romance; by H.C. Mellor
Romar's journal; by W.A. Watt
Ronald W. Hoskier; by E.S.
Buchanan
Rosalys; by C.F. Kenyon

The rose of France (July 14th,
1918); by S. Levey
Rose Vaquette of La Boiselle;
by E. Knoblock
Roses, loaves, and old rhymes;
by A. Matheson
Roses, pearls and tears; by R.
Heywood
The Rosses; by J.S. Starkey
Rough rhymes of a padre; by
G.A.S. Kennedy
Roundels and rhymes; by A. Moor
The rubáiyát of a Maconochie
ration; by T.I.N. Opener,
pseud.
The rubáiyát of a ranker; by
Quiz, pseud.
The rubáiyát of Omarred
Wilhelm; by C. Fitzgerald
A rubáiyát of the trenches;
by De C.
The rubáiyát of William the war
lord; by St. J. Hamund
Ruhleben poems; by J. Balfour
Rumours of war; by J.M.
Staniforth
Rupert Brooke's grave; by C.E.
Byles
Russia re-born; by F.W.
Bourdillon
The sacrament; by J.A. Barry
The sacred way; by A.
Quiller-Couch
The sad years; by D.S. Shorter
Safety green; by H.B. Chadwick
Saga of the drifters, 1917; by
M. Kerr
The saga of the Seventh Division;
by H.E. Forbes
Sailors and mine-sweepers; by
R.W. Rice
St. George's Day; by H. Newbolt
St. James's Park; by F.O. Mann
St. Patrick; by E.K. Ellis

Some Sergeant-Major; by A.C.
Dacomb
Some thoughts in verse; by
Mrs. E. Harris
"Something"; by O.E. Lindsay
"Somewhere in France"; by
F. Ellis
"Son of mine"; by Mrs. C.O.
Dobell
Song in the whirlwind; by A.
Radford & E. Radford
A song of life in sonnets; by
H.C. Corlette
The song of the gay light cruisers;
by E.G.
A song of the guns; by G. Frankau
The song of the lathes; by R.
Kipling
The song of the Lewis gun; by
W.G. Thomas & A.S. Barnard
A song of the open road; by
L.J. McQuilland
The song of the plow; by
M. Hewlett
The song of the road; by M.
Sullivan
Song of the soldiers; by T. Hardy
Song of the unborn; by G.B.
Paget
Song of the young and old men;
by J.A. Mackereth
The song of Tiadatha; by O.
Rutter
A song of war; by Feathered
Heels, pseud.
Songs; by E. Shanks
Songs; by H.F. Taylor
Songs after sunset; by N. Cross
Songs amid strife; by F.N. Wood
Songs and chanties, 1914-1916; by
C.F. Smith
Songs and poems; by C. Clark
Songs and poems; by G.H.
Moore

Songs and shadows; by D.F.
Dalston
Songs and signs; by O. Davies
Songs and slang of the British
soldier; ed. by J. Brophy &
E. Partridge (8) (9) (10)
Songs and sonnets for England
in war time (99) (100) (101)
Songs apart; by F.A.M. Webster
Songs for remembrance; by F.E.
Weatherly
Songs for sufferers (from a sick-
room); by F.W.O. Ward
Songs for the times; by E.H.M.
Milligan
Songs for youth; by R. Kipling
Songs from a dale in war time;
by H.Allsopp
Songs from an Ulster valley;
by H.M. Pim
Songs from books; by R. Kipling
Songs from camp and college;
by A.A. Cock & J. Lodge
Songs from Dublin City; by I.
Adair
Songs from Tani's garden; by
M. Leigh
Songs from the heart; by A.C.
White
Songs from the moorland; by
M.I.E. Dolphin
Songs from the saddle; by
M.W.S. Bruce
Songs from the Somme; by
H. Rippon-Seymour
Songs from the Sussex downs;
by P. Whitehouse
Songs from the trenches; by
C.W. Blackall
Songs in captivity; by R.H.
Sauter
Songs in the darkness; by A.
Bennett
The songs of a broken airman;
by J. Howcroft

Songs of a chartered accountant;
by A. Bennett

Songs of a musician; by J. Millar

Songs of a new age; by A.T.
Story

Songs of a "Shiny" sergeant; by
E.C. Mudge

Songs of a subaltern; by D.O.
Lumley

The songs of a year; by W. Booth

Songs of all seasons; by T.
Hooley

Songs of an airman; by G. Wall

Songs of an islander; by D.
McDonald

Songs of defiance; by F. Ronald

Songs of deliverance; by A.
Dudley

Songs of exuberance; by O.
Burdett

Songs of faith and doubt; by
G.A.S. Kennedy

Songs of Glenshee; by D.E.A.
Ashmore

Songs of life and love; by E.
Leader

Songs of love and grief; by G.
Agnew

Songs of love and life; by D.
Sampson

Songs of peace; by F. Ledwidge

Songs of pilgrimage; by T.
Tiplady

Songs of protest; by F.L. Mitchell

Songs of seaside places; by
R. McDonnell

Songs of shadow-of-a-leaf; by
A. Noyes

Songs of the Ayrshire Regiment;
by W.F. Templeton

Songs of the Camerons; by
D.E.A. Ashmore

Songs of the cell; by H. Bottomley

Songs of the fields; by A. Dodds

Songs of the heather heights;
by W. Evans

Songs of the highlands and
islands; by H.G. Hill

Songs of the highway; by H.
Burton

Songs of the open; by T. Hooley

Songs of the red rose; by A.
Mackereth

Songs of the sailor men; by
W.M. James

Songs of the sea; by R. Kipling

Songs of the shadows; by E.
Tudor-Hart

Songs of the shrapnel shell; by
C.M. Horne

Songs of the Sixth; by W.
Tranter

Songs of the Specials; by E.W.
Fordham

Songs of the submarine; by
J.G. Bower

Songs of the trawlers; by
A. Noyes

Songs of the war and faith and
hope; by H.F. Byerley

Songs of the wayside; by S.J.
Looker

Songs of the winds and seas; by
V. Bartlett

Songs of the Worcestershires;
by R.C. Warden

Songs of the World-War; by A. St.
J. Adcock

Songs of the yonderland; by
H.M. Underwood

Songs of the younger-born; by
B.S. Bartlett

Songs of Ulster and Balliol;
by F.S. Boas

Songs of war and patriotism; by
K.K. Hallowes

Songs of wind and wave; by
A.L. Salmon

Songs of Yarrow; by G.W.T. McGown

Songs of youth and war; by P.H.B. Lyon

Songs on service; by E. Crawshay-Williams

Songs out of school; by H.H. Bashford

Sonnet on seeing on a newspaper bill . . . the words "Kitchener drowned"; by G.G. Napier

The sonnet song book; by C. Clark

Sonnet to the Kaiser; by J.J. Lane

Sonnets after loss; by D.L.I.

Sonnets and semblances; by H. Cloriston

Sonnets from a prison camp; by A.A. Bowman

Sonnets from Hafez; by E. Bridges

Sonnets in sand; by H.G. Dixey

Sonnets in war and peace; by H. Bagenal

Sonnets of many years; by J. Silvester

The sons of old Surrey; by A. Locke

Sons of the Empire; by J. Lyons

Sorrow of war; by L. Golding

The sorrow that whistled; by J.H. Stables

The sorrows of God; by G.A.S. Kennedy

A sough of war; by C. Murray

Soul of mine; by J.S. Bailey

Soul voices in the vigil; by H. Rollo, pseud.

Soul's belfry; by H.E.G. Rope

Sound, bugles, "all clear!"; by Mackenzie

Soundings; by H.G. Dixey

Sounds from another valley; by H.F. Sampson

South African harvest; by G.M. Miller

A souvenir of the war; by J.A. Gray

Souvenir: the 61st Division; by P. Field

The spacious times; by F. Coutts

"The sparrow hath found her an house"; by A. Elliot

Spindrift; by V. De S. Pinto

Spindrift and spunyarn; by W.C. Reedy

The spires of Oxford; by W.M. Letts

Spirits in bondage; by C.S. Lewis

The splendid days; by M.W. Cannan

Splinters; by E.H.R. Wood

The sponger of Strand.Alley; by W.C. Maxwell

The spot that wont rub out (real enamel); anon.

Sprigs of lavender from Algiers; by M.M. Curchod

The spring; by E.P. Cranmer

A spring harvest; by G.B. Smith

The spring of joy; by M. Webb

Spring songs among the flowers; by E. Emmons

Spring's highway; by C.J.R.

"Springtime of peace"; by R.W. Rice

Star-dust; by T. Blakemore

The star fields; by W. Weaving

Stars and fishes; by G.R. Hamilton

The station platform; by M. Mackenzie

Steel and flowers; by R.L. Carton

Still in my hand; by M. Smith

Stone trees; by J. Freeman

The Stonewall Brigade; by T.B. Clark

Stony limits; by C.M. Grieve

Storms in teacups; by T. Bouch

The story and glory of Ze[e]-
brugge; by M. England
The strafing section; by T.B.
Clark
Strange meetings; by H. Monro
The stranger; by B. McMaster
Stray shots from the
Dardanelles; by W.F. Rollo
Stray thoughts; by N. Hotblack
Strays; by D. Brey·
Strays in war-time and before
the war; by C.H. Grinling
Streets; by D. Goldring
Streets and starlight; by J.
Peterson
A study in starlight; by R.
McDonnell
Stuff— and nonsense; by I.Z.
Malcolm
A subaltern's musings; by A.J.
Mann
Such was my singing; by R.
Nichols
A summer day; by A. Thorne
Summer harvest; by J.
Drinkwater
Summer 1917; by E.T. Thurston
Summer songs among the birds;
by E. Emmons
A summer's fancy; by E.C.
Blunden
The summons; by G.M.L.
Reade
Sun and shadow; by F.G. Webb
Sun poems; by C.H. Pinnell
The sunken garden; by W. De La
Mare
Sunrise dreams; by E.F.
Wilkinson
Sunshine and shadow; by J.R.
Wilmot
Sunshine and shadows; by J.
Millar
Sunshine and solitude; by M.
Woods

The superhuman antagonists; by
W. Watson
Support coalition government;
by G.M.L. Reade
A suppressed poem; by S.
Sassoon
The supreme sacrifice; by J.S.
Arkwright
The supreme sacrifice; by J.J.
Lane
The supreme test; by R.W. Rice
Survival; by B. Purshouse
The survival of the fittest; by
J.C. Squire
The survivors; by G.F. Fyson
Sussex; by J. Harvey
Sussex at peace and war; by
W.E. Harker
Sussex at war; by A. Beckett
Sussex woods; by E. Parker
Swallows in storm and sunlight;
by R.H. Beckh
Swollen-headed William; by
E.V. Lucas
The sword; by G.O. Warren
A sword in the desert; by H.E.
Palmer
Swords and flutes; by W.K.
Seymour
Swords and ploughshares; by
M.I.E. Dolphin
Swords and ploughshares; by
J. Drinkwater
Swords for life; by I.R. MacLeod
Symphonie symbolique; by
E. John
Symphonies; by E.H.W. Meyer-
stein
The Taj Mahal; by Mrs. E. Harris
The taking of Bullecourt; by
D.C. Clarke
A talent of silver; by N. East
Tales of a "Tommy"; by T.B.
Clark
Tales of the sarai; by A.G. Shirreff

A talk with Kaiser Bill; by Briton, pseud.

The tapestry; by R. Bridges

Tapping the "War Lord's" claret; by W.H. Coates

The tavern of dreams; by C.H. Oldfield

The temple of Janus; by J.G. Fairfax

Terpsichore; by H.T. Wade-Gery

The terror of night; by A. Wheble

Thank you, from the wives, mothers and sweethearts of our Empire; by M.M. Leeson

Thanksgiving for peace, July 19th, 1919; by W.E.G. Warry

A thanksgiving hymn for peace; by J.R. Darbyshire

That boy o' mine; by A.E. Robinson

Their dead sons; by J.M. Hay

Their eyes off me; by T.N. Smith

Theophanies; by E. Underhill

There are no dead; by E. Coleman

There is a valley; by J.H.F. McEwen

There is no death; by R.M. Dennys

"There must be 'no next time' "; by G.M.L. Reade

These were the men; comp. by E.R. Jaquet (51)

They shall not pass!: by S. Levey

Things new and old; by V.T. Coats

Things new and old; by J.S. Phillimore

The things that count; by M. Crosbie

Think of mother; by A.J. Long

This for remembrance; by R.A. Hayden

This insubstantial pageant; by M. Gibbon

This is the hour; by A.G. Herbertson

This land I love; by R.B.Peck

Thistles and gorse; by F.J. Argyll-Dunn

Thomas Atkins, Esquire, writes home from the front; by W.N. Stedman

The thorn tree; by C.H. Warren

Thorns and sweet briar; by S.J. Looker

Thoroughfares; by W.W. Gibson

Thought blossoms; by A. Chambers

Thoughts; by C.M. Obbard

Thoughts and dreams; by E.F. Boulting

Thoughts in verse; by E.E. Winser

Thoughts in verse through many years; by A.E. McC.

Thoughts of a nature lover; by K. Rogers

Thoughts of home, written in the trenches; by G.W. Harley

Thoughts of mine; by M. Smalley

Thoughts on love; by C. Millar

A thousand strong; by J.C. Scott

The Thracian stranger; by E.J. Thompson

"Three crosses", Ypres, November, 1914; by M. Goodricke

Three days; by R. Macaulay

Three faces in a hood; by W.J. Ferrar

Three hills; by E. Owen

The three-rock road; by H.L. Doak

Three war songs; by P. Thomas

Three war poems; by A. Tidman

Through all the seasons; by C. Zanetti

Through cloud and sunshine; by W.S. Pakenham-Walsh

Through death to victory; by J.
   Macgregor
Through tears to triumph; by
   S. Grantham
Through the upcast shaft; by
   H.M. Williams
Through the window; by M.E.
   Connolly
Through two windows; by L.H.
   Winn
Tiadatha; by O. Rutter
The tidal town; by W. Benington
The tide at night; by E.Close
Tides; by J. Drinkwater
Time and place; by J.W. Hurrell
Time will tell; by C. Wilson
The tinker's road; by M. Angus
Tinkers twa in peace and war;
   by M.M. Dawson
' 'Tis simple mirth'; by W. Blair
Titans and gods; by F.V. Branford
To a fallen friend and poet; by
   G. Peel
To a nursing-sister; by E.
   Fuller-Maitland
To a soldier or sailor; by M.E.
   Bonus
To any dead officer (who left
   school for the Army in 1914);
   by S. Sassoon
To Belgium; by J.R. Marsh
To Bertha; by E. Watt
To Britain!; by G.M.L. Reade
"To der day!"; by H. Cole
To fight the Kaiser; anon.
To hell with Yankee-Doodle; anon.
To Ireland and the millions of
   true Irish patriots . . .; by
   G.M.L. Reade
To nature; by E.C. Blunden
To our brave soldiers now return-
   ing wounded from the great
   offensive in France; by
   G.M.L. Reade

To our noble dead; by E.J.
   Watson
To the day; by E.H. Blakeney
To the Duke of Portland, K.G.; by
   G.M.L. Reade
To the faint-hearted; by G.M.L.
   Reade
To the fallen; by R. Burnham
To the footballer at the front;
   by A. Muir
To the glorious memory of Gen.
   French's "contemptible little
   army"; by G.M.L. Reade
To the immortal memory of our
   fallen heroes; by T.M. Walker
To the level of the proud; by
   S. Milsom
To the living dead; by E.P.
   Cranmer
To the memory of Edward
   Thomas; by J. Guthrie
To the memory of Nurse Edith
   Cavell; by Mrs. T.T.
   Clatworthy
To the troubler of the world;
   by W. Watson
To the United States of America,
   the "Entente's" latest ally;
   by G.M.L. Reade
To the vanguard; by B. Brice-
   Miller
To the women of England; by
   A. Tidman
To V.C.'s and British soldiers
   and sailors all; by R.R. Hibbs
To Verhaeren; by W.K. Seymour
Toasts; by T.G.W. Henslow
Tod MacMammon sees his soul;
   by A. St. J. Adcock
To-day and yesterday; by V.
   Coats
Tommies of the line; by E.T.
   Cooper
Tommy Atkins, don't cher know;
   by E. Clifford

Tommy Atkins' requiem; by
    G.S. Maxwell
Tommy's ABC; by J.G.R. Harvey
Tommy's fag; by M. Walsh
Tommy's troubles; by T.B. Clark
Tommy's tunes; comp. by F.T.
    Nettleinghame (68) (69)
Tommy's vocabulary; by T.B.
    Clark
To-morrow; by I. Stitt & L. Ward
Topical Tommy's book o' the
    words; by J. Critten
Topical verses; by W. Murcott
Towards freedom; by W.R. Hall
Towards the dawn; by G. Thomas
Towards the light; by A.E.
    Woodcock
The tower; by H.A. Dalziel
The tower of harmony; by A.F.
    Cross
The town clock; by A.J. Long
The town on the hill; by R. Bain
Toys of eternity; by W. Weaving
Trackless regions; by G.O. Warren
The trackless way; by L. Taylor
Tragedy; by J. Walker
Tramp of eternity; by O. Baker
Trampled clay; by C. Mitchell
A treasury of war poetry; ed. by
    G.H. Clarke (16) (17) (18)
The trenches; by O. Burdett
Trenches: St. Eloi; by T.E.
    Hulme
Trentaremi; by J.R. Rodd
A tribute of love and
    gratitude . . .; by J. Mallett
Tribute to England; comp. by
    M. Gilkes (37)
A tribute to our brave British
    women; by G.M.L. Reade
Tribute to the memory of Lord
    Kitchener; by E.H. Rowe
Tributes in verse; by G.H. Trevor
The tricolour; by D.S. Shorter

Triolets from the trenches; by
    C.G.L. Du Cann
Triumph; by C. Chapin
The trumpet; by E. Thomas
Trust Lord Kitchener and the
    government; by G.M.L. Reade
Trust the Kaiser?!!!; by T.N.
    Smith
Truthful poem by an ex-
    serviceman; by Unemployed
    Ex-Soldier, pseud.
The tryst; by E.V. Rieu
The tulip tree; by R.J. Kerr
Turn fortune; by P.H.B. Lyon
The turn of the day; by M. Angus
The turn of the tide; by A.F.
    Graves
Twelve noon; by R. Church
Twelve poets (114)
Twelve war epitaphs; by J.M.
    Edmonds
Twentieth century harlequinade;
    by E. Sitwell & O. Sitwell
Twentieth-century psalter;
    by R. Church
Twenty; by S. Benson
Twenty-five trifles in verse; by
    J.B. Capper
The Twenty Seventh Division;
    by T.B. Clark
Twilight songs; by K. Tynan
Twittingpan; by E. Rickword
'Twixt dusk and dawn; by
    L. Henley-White
Two fishers; by H.E. Palmer
The two flags; by A. Lomax
Two foemen; by H.E. Palmer
Two friends; by P.E.T.F.
Two gardens; by J. Light
The two ideals; by G.M.L. Reade
Two Irish Fusiliers; by G.S.
    Holmes
Two kings; by P. Hookham
The two worlds; by S. Vines

U-boat warfare; by G.M.L.
  Reade
Ultimata; by D. Macmillan
Ultimate values, crudely expressed
  in verse; by H.E.E. Hayes
Uncivilized warfare; by W.H.P.
Uncle Sam's resolve; by R.W.
  Rice
"Under one flag"; by J. Black
Under the red lamp; by G.W.T.
  McGown
Undersongs; by W.C. Dunlop
The undiscovered island; anon.
The undying splendour; by J.W.
  Streets
Unheard melodies; by R.G. Barnes
Union is strength; by A.C.
  Dacomb
The union jack; by E.A. Carr
The union jack; by M.M. Curchod
The union jack; by F.J. Johnston-
  Smith
Union jack lyrics; by F.J.
  Johnston-Smith
Union true!; by H.W.B.W.
A united front; by G.M.L. Reade
Unity; by R.W. Rice
An unknown British soldier;
  by P. Field
The unknown God; by H. Meldrum
The unknown warrior; by W.H.
  Abbott
The unknown warrior; by E.C.
  Dee
The unknown warrior; by H.E.
  Palmer
The unknown warrior; by J.
  Waring
Unreturning; by K.M. Coates
The unseen guest; by C. Wilson
Unseen horizons; by F.A.H.
  Lambert
The unseen presence; by S.
  Grant

Until the dawn; by P.A.
  Robertson
Until then; by A.S. Jupp
The unutterable beauty; by
  G.A.S. Kennedy
Up the line to death; comp. by
  B. Gardner (33)
Up to the hills; by C.A. Renshaw
The upland field; by A.M. Allen
V.C. veteran to his son armed,
  1914-18 — 1949; by J.A.
  Mackereth
Vae victis; by E.J. Thompson
The vagabond; by R.C. Lehmann
Vagabond verses; by C. Garstin
Vain glory; ed. by G. Chapman
  (13) (14)
Vaincre ou mourir; by N.
  Davidson
Vale; by N. Orde-Powlett
Valediction; by A. Dudley
The valiant muse; ed. by F.W.
  Ziv (131)
The valley of dreams; by J. Mason
Valour and vision; ed. by J.T.
  Trotter (111) (112)
The vampire; by H.E. Palmer
Veil and vista; by E.M. Heath
Vengeance is mine; by E. Phillips
Verdun; by H.L. Doak
The verge of victory; by J.C.
  Frith
Verse and prose in peace and
  war; by W.N. Hodgson
Verse of valour; comp. by J.L.
  Hardie (46)
Verse or reverse?; by J. Campbell
Verses and ballads of north and
  south; by H.J. Boyd
Verses and versicles; by G.
  Radford
Verses appropriate to the war;
  by H.C. Foxcroft
Verses for Alethea; by A. Tillyard

387

388

War; by A.S. Jupp
War; by R. Le Gallienne
War; by R.C. Macfie
The war alphabet; by E.T.
"The war — and after"; by H.
  Branson
War and life; by W.J. Cameron
War and patriotic poems; by
  W.D. Birrell
War and peace; by A. Moss
War and victory; by E.P. Gill
War blasts; by J.B. Symons
War cartoon sonnets; by W.
  Dowsing
War daubs; by R.W. Kerr
War ditties; by W. Corah
War echoes; by R.W. French
War forced upon us; by J.F.
  Lambe
War harvest, 1914; by A.K. Sabin
The war in verse; by T.M.
  Babington
The war in verse and prose; ed. by
  W.D. Eaton (24)
The war loan; by A. Muir
War lyrics; by W. Kemble
War lyrics; by M. Roberts
War lyrics; by G. R. Samways
War lyrics; by J.S. Yates
The war men-agerie; by St. J.
  Hamund
War 1914; by L.N. Harrison
War no more; by W.Brantom
War Office rhymes; by E.R.
  Brown
War poems; by R. Bateman
War poems; by M. Betham-Edwards
War poems; by E.H. Blakeney
War poems; by R. Brooke
War poems; by A.W. Crampton
War poems; by T.W.H. Crosland
War poems; by G.V. Dodderidge
War poems; by J. Donnan
War poems; by T.G.W. Henslow
War poems; by M.L. Jacobs

War poems; by L. Marcus
War poems; by W. Phillips
War poems; by E.J.M.D. Plunkett
War poems; by J. Pope
War poems; by C. Powell
War poems; by C. Roberts
War poems; by S. Sassoon
War poems; by R.E. Vernède
War poems; by G.H. Wilson
War poems from The Times (108)
  (109)
War poems of a Northumbrian;
  by R.H. Forster
War poetry; ed. by D.L. Jones
  (53)
The war poets; ed. by O.
  Williams (128)
A war prayer; by A.S.E.D.
  Farrer
War-shrine fragments; by N.H.
  Romanes
War songs; by R.H. Banks
War songs; by A.G. Mitchell
War songs, 1914; by E. Underdown
War sonnets and songs; by A.
  Williams
War, the liberator; by E.A.
  Mackintosh
War thoughts for the Christian
  year; by C.E. Scott-Moncrieff
War-time; by O. Seaman
War time and patriotic selections
  for recitation and reading;
  comp. by C.B. Case (12)
War time and peace; by E. Lister
War-time ditties; by A.A. Grenville
War-time nursery rhymes; by
  N. Macdonald
War time poems; by J.H.
  Chadwick
War-time verses; by M. Du Deney
War-time verses; by R.L.O.
  & another
War! "To let"; by Will-o'-the-
  Wisp, pseud.

War verse; ed. by F. Foxcroft (31) (32)

War verse and more verse; by W. Holmes

War verses; by D. F. Fergusson

War verses; by I. Hammond

War verses; by R.H. Thornton

War verses and translations; by S.P. Rice

War! War! Bellona, the hell-sprite of war; by D. Dawson

War workers; by B. Gilbert

War writings; by R. Kipling

The warblings of a windy warrior; by R.L.B. Moore

"Ward 8"; by H. Davison

The warning bell; by J. Mitchell

War's echo; by R. Gurner

War's embers; by I. Gurney

War's surprises; by C.L. Graves

Wartime and patriotic selections for recitation and reading; comp. by C.B. Case (12)

The watch-tower; by H.W. Clark

The watchers on Gallipoli; by G.C. Duggan

Watching the war; by C.L. Maynard

Wavelets of the world-wide war; by T.N. Smith

The way of wonder; by M. Doney

Wayside treasure and poems, 1914-1918; by G. Ridgway

We fight or fall; by E. Drew

Wearing of the green; by L.P.C. Macquaid

The weaver; by E.M. Ward

Weeping-Cross; by A.H. Bullen

"Well done, Vindictive!"; by S. Lee

Welsh poems of the twentieth century in English verse; ed. by H.I. Bell & C.C. Bell (3)

Welsh poets; ed. by A.G. Prys-Jones (85)

West wind days; by M. O'Rourke

The western window; by E.G. Sargent

What can I do?; by G.M.L. Reade

What is life?; by A.H. Hadley

What the British Navy is doing; by E. Carter

What we are fighting for; by G.M.L. Reade

What will the harvest be; by G.H.

Wheels (122) (123) (124) (125) (126)

"When duty calls"; by C. Wilson

When England goes to war; by W. Macdonald

When good men meet as foe to foe; by M.E. Blood

When heaven was dark; by S.C. Hanning

When her soul awoke; by F.H. Hawthorn

When peace will come; by H.E.J.

When the Kaiser will invade England; by H. Jervis

When the lads come home again; by C. Wilson

When the robin sings; by R.H. Banks

When the Sammies marched through London (May 11th, 1918); by S. Levey

"When the trumpet is calling"; by C.L. Hancock

Whims and moods; by T. Thornely

Whin; by W.W. Gibson

White horses; by L.A.H. Shorter

The white ribbon of honour; by W. Frampton

The white roads; by R.B. Ince

Whither goest?; by E. Richardson

"Who won the war, and why!!";
by J. Morris
Why is the red blood flowing?;
by H. Bottomley
Why war?; by M. Friedlander
Wide horizons; by J. Oxenham
Wild roses; by J.E. Matthews
The wild swans at Coole;
by W.B. Yeats
Wilhelm and his God; by W.
Hudson
Will they never come?; by S.
Smirk
Will you forget?; by C.J. Brown
William in the looking glass; by
H. Butt
William, Kaiser, by the grace of
the—; by A. Horspool
William the despot; by H. West
Willie dear; by A. Muir
The wind in the temple; by E.
John
The wind on the downs; by M.
Allen
Windmill Hill; by A.W. Nightin-
gale
Windrush and evenlode; by H.
Baerlein
The wine drop; by W.M. Marsden
Winged chariots; by A. Agius
Winged victory; by C.H.B.
Kitchin
Wings; ed. by H.G. Bryden (11)
Wings of the morning; by R.G.
Barnes
Wings of youth; by L. Taylor
The winners; by L. Housman
The winnowing-fan; by L. Binyon
The Winstonburg line; by O.
Sitwell
A winter fragment; by W.G.
Shakespeare
Winter songs among the snows;
by E. Emmons
Winter sunshine; by A. Fry

Winter words, in various moods
and metres; by T. Hardy
Wishes from home, for Tommy
and Jack; by A. Ainger
With courage; by H.J. Bulkeley
With double tongue; by S.A.
Robertson
With myrrh and frankincense;
by C.H. Whitby
With the eagles; by W.N.
Stedman
With the organ to the trenches;
by T.N. Smith
With the season's greetings; by
E.A. Carr
With the years; by C. French
The wizard's loom; by B.
Malaher
Wolf's-bane; by J.C. Powys
"Woman, clever woman"; by
A. Hillcoat
The women's message; by M.
Peterson
Wooden crosses; by T.E. Cole
Wooden crosses; by E.W.
Hornung
Wooden crosses; by L.B.
Solomon
The Worcesters at Gheluvelt;
by T.E. Cole
The Worcestershire Hussars; by
W. Corah
Word pictures of war; by W.F.
de B. Maclaren
Words by the wayside; by J.
Rhoades
Work-a-day warriors; by J. Lee
The world in travail; by A.H.
Owen
The World War; by J. Oswald
The world's greatest war; by
S.G. Field
The world's new birth; by A.
Cooper
The world's war; by W. Long

391

Worms and epitaphs; by H.W.
Garrod
Worple flit; by E.W. Tennant
"Worthy of his name"; by A.H.
Hadley
Woven arras; by E. Spurway
Wraith and wrack; by D.J.
Robertson
A wreath of immortelles; by
I. Colvin
The writing on the wall; by
J. Mallett
The written lie; by E. Feasey
Wycollar Dene; by P.J. Nuttall
Wylins fae my wallet; by G.
Abel
Yankee boys; by W. Frampton
Ye faithful Durhams; by C.
Wilson
A year and a half of war; by
A. Morton
A year of war; by M.R. Adamson
The years between; by R. Kipling
Years following after; by J.
Leftwich
Years of peace; by G. Elton
"Yepres"; by J. Mitchell

Yorkshire lyrics; by D.U.
Ratcliffe
"You mothers of England!";
by I.B. Heathcote
The young captain; by M.I.
Bedford
The young guard; by E.W.
Hornung
A young soldier's "De profundis";
by H.H.V. Cross
Younger poets of to-day; comp.
by J.C. Squire (103)
Youth; by L.P. Jones
Youth; by I. Rosenberg
Youth; by J.H. Whitehouse
Youth and age; by C.C. Abbott
Youth at arms; by L. Barnes
Youth in the skies; by H.
Asquith
Youth's heritage; by B. Hill
Ypres; by W.G. Shakespeare
"Ze[e]brugge", April 23rd,
1918; by Mr. Holthusen
The Zeebrugge Mole exploit;
by A. Morton
Zoar; by H. Bosanquet & B.
Bosanquet

SUPPLEMENT

WAR POETS OF OTHER
ENGLISH SPEAKING NATIONS

Key: AU   Australian
CA   Canadian
NZ   New Zealand
SA   South African
US   American

AU A., A.N.O., pseud.,
    (i.e. Allan Douglas)
AU A.N.O.A., pseud., (i.e.
    Allan Douglas)
AU? ABBOTT, J.M.H.
NZ ADAMS, Arthur Henry
US ADAMS, Katharine
NZ ADAMSON, Bartlett
SA ADAMSON, Sir John
    Ernest
US AIKEN, Conrad
CA AL PAT, pseud., (i.e.
    Alexander Callow
    Joseph)
US ALEXANDER, Julius
    Myron
US ALLABEN, Frank
US ALLEN, Hervey
AU ALLEN, Leslie Holds-
    worth
US ALLING, Kenneth Slade
US ALLINSON, Brent Dow
US? ALSOP, Charles F.
US ANDERSON, Melville B.
AU ANDREWS, James
US ANDREWS, Mary R.S.

US APPLETON, Everard Jack
AU ARCHER, Bernard Joseph
US? ARCHER, E. Margaret
    Du P.
US ARMSTRONG, Hamilton
    Fish
CA ATHERTON, John Joseph
CA ATKINSON, Elmina
AU AUSTEN, Peter
CA BAILLIE, Oliver E.
US BAKER, Karle Wilson
CA BANNELL, Charles
    Samuel
US BARBER, Emma Cowan
CA BARKER, John Richard
US BARNEY, Danford
US BATES, Brainard Leroy
US BATES, Katharine Lee
CA BELCHER, Alexander
    Emerson
NZ BELL, Henry James
US BELLINGER, Alfred
    Raymond
US BENET, William Rose
US BENNETT, Henry
    Holcomb

AU BERESFORD, Claude
    Richard de la Poer,
    (Seebee, pseud.)
AU BETTS, Margery Ruth
AU BEVAN, William Austin
CA BIDWELL, Edward J.
US BISHOP, John Peale
AU BLACK, George
AU BLUEGUM, Trooper,
    pseud., (i.e. Oliver
    Hogue)
US BODENHEIM, Maxwell
CA BOURINOT, Arthur S.
AU BOYD, Martin
AU BOYES, W. Watson,
    (Oyster, pseud.)
US BRADFORD, Charles Hall
US BRADFORD, Gamaliel
US BRALEY, Berton
AU BRENNAN, Christopher
    John
AU BRERETON, John Le
    Gay
AU BRIDGE, Horace
US BRIDGMAN, Amy
    Sherman
US BRODY, Alter
US BROOKS, Ames
US BROOKS, Fred Emerson
CA BROWN, Frank S.
CA BROWNE, Thaddeus A.
US BUCK, Howard
AU BULL, John James
CA BUNBURY, Charles John
US BUNKER, John
AU BURDEN, E.
US BURNET, Dana
AU BURNS, James Drummond
US BURR, Amelia Josephine
US BURROWS, E.
US BURT, J.B.
US BURT, Maxwell
    Struthers
CA BUSCHLEN, John Preston
US BUSH, David V.

US BUTLER, F.E.
US BUTLER, John
US BYNNER, Witter
AU? C.J.N.
CA CALL, Frank Oliver
SA CAMPBELL, Ethel
AU CAMPBELL, Norman
CA CAMPBELL, Wilfred
US CARBAUGH, Frank
CA CARMAN, Bliss
US CARPENTER, Rhys
US CARRINGTON, Mary
    Coles
US CHALONER, John
    Armstrong
US CHAMBERLIN, Henry
    Harmon
AU CHANDLER, Alfred
US CHANNING, Grace
    Ellery
US CHAPMAN, John Jay
CA CHILD, Philip
US? CHILD, Oscar C.A.
CA? CHRISTIE, Robert A.
NZ CLARK, Alfred
SA CLARK, John,
    (Poscimur, pseud.)
US CLARK, William F.
CA CLARKE, George
    Herbert
US CLEVELAND, Reginald
    McIntosh
US COATES, Florence Earle
US COLCORD, Lincoln
AU COLE, Muriel Beverley
CA COLEMAN, Helena
CA COLLINS, Alice Helen
SA COLVIN, Ian
US CONE, Helen Gray
US CONKLING, Grace
    Hazard
US CONVERSE, Florence
US COOPER, John Crossan
US CORBIN, Alice
AU CORNEY, Henry Bickerstaff

CA	COSENS, Abner, (Wayfarer, pseud.)
US	COWAN, Ella F.
AU	COWLISHAW, Miss, (Pro Patria, pseud.)
AU	COXHEAD, Mrs. G.R.
AU	CRAMER, Violet B.
US	CRANDALL, Charles Henry
US	CRAWFORD, Charlotte Holmes
US	CREW, Helen Coale
US	CROMWELL, Albert
US	CROMWELL, Gladys
AU	CROSS, Alan
AU	CROSS, Zora
CA?	CROW, Currie
US	CUMMINGS, E.E.
US	CURRIE, George Graham
CA	DALTON, Annie Charlotte
AU	D'ARCY-IRVINE, Gerard Addington
US	DARGAN, Olive Tilford
US	DAVIES, Ernest E.
US	DAVIES, Mary Carolyn
AU	DAVIS, A.C.
US	DAWSON, Emma Frances
AU	DAYBREAK, pseud., (i.e. Clement Gray)
AU	DELAHUNTY, J.P.
US	DELL, Floyd
AU	DENNIS, Clarence James
SA	DE WAAL, Daphne
US	DILLENBACH, Lucia
AU	DILLON, D.
US	DIVINE, Charles
US	DODD, Lee Wilson
CA	DODWELL, Claude
CA	DOLLARD, James B.
US	DONALDSON, Robert A.
AU	DOUGLAS, Allan, (A.N.O.A., pseud.)

AU	DOWNES, Marion
US	DRISCOLL, Louise
US	DUFFIELD, Kenneth Graham
CA	DURKIN, Douglas Leader
US	DYKE, Henry Van
US	DYKE, Tertius Van
AU	DYSON, Edward George
US	EARLS, Michael
CA	EASSIE, R.M.
US	EATON, Walter Prichard
CA	EDELSTEIN, Hyman
AU	EDMONDS, Harry Moreton Southey
AU	EDWARDS, H.E.
US	ELLIOT, Gabrielle
NZ	ELLIOT, Wilhelmina Sherriff
US	ERSKINE, John
US	EUWER, Anthony Henderson
SA	FALLAW, Lance
US	FARRINGTON, Harry Webb
AU	FERGUSON, Ernest Adie
CA	FIELD, George Blackstone
US	FINCH, Lucine
US	FINLEY, John
US	FIRKINS, Oscar W.
AU	FISHER, Lala
US	FISKE, Isabelle Howe
SA	FLEMING, Leonard
AU	FLEMING, William Montgomerie
US	FLETCHER, John Gould
US	FLORINE, Margaret Helen
AU	FORREST, M.
US	FOSTER, Jeanne Robert
US	FOULKE, William Dudley
US	FRANK, Florence Kiper

US FRANK, Henry
US FROST, Robert
AU FULTON, J.B.
US FURMAN, Alfred
    Antoine
NZ G., J.
US GARESCHE, Edward
    Francis
AU GARLAND, Hugh Gordon
US GARRETT, Erwin
    Clarkson
US GARRISON, Theodosia
CA GARVIN, Amelia Beers,
    (Katherine Hale,
    pseud.)
AU GELLERT, Leon
AU GERARD, Edwin,
    (Trooper Gerardy,
    pseud.)
AU GERARDY, Trooper,
    pseud., (i.e. Edwin
    Gerard)
US GIBBS, Jessie W.
US GIDDINGS, Franklin H.
AU GILES, Joanna E.
CA GIRLING, T.A.
AU GLADSTONE, James
    Jerome
US GLAENZER, Richard
    Butler
AU? GODFREY, R.J.
US GOETHALS, Gus L.
US GOETZ, Philip Becker
US GOING, Charles Buxton
CA GORDON, Alfred
AU GORE-JONES, Alice
    Muriel
SA GOULDSBURY, Cullen
US GRANT, Robert
CA GRAVES, Joseph
    Waddington
US GRAVESTEIN, Kate
    Evans
US GRAY, Agnes Kendrick

AU GRAY, Clement,
    (Daybreak, pseud.)
US GREGORY, Leo
US GRIFFES, James
    Hartness, (Luke North,
    pseud.)
US GRIFFIN, Bartholomew
    F.
US GRIFFIN, Gerald E.
US GRIFFITH, William
AU GROSS, Alan
US GUEST, Edgar Albert
US GUINEY, Louise
    Imogen
AU GUMSUCKER, pseud.,
    (i.e. M.J. Keogh)
AU GUNNER 379, pseud.,
    (i.e. Henry Weston
    Pryce)
US GUNSAULUS, Frank W.
AU? H.R.
US HAGEDORN, Hermann
CA HALE, Katherine,
    pseud., (i.e. Amelia
    Beers Garvin)
US HALL, Angelo
SA HALL, Arthur Vine
US HALL, James Norman
AU HAMBIDGE, George R.
AU HARKINS, J.M.
CA HARPER, T.M.
AU HARRINGTON, Edward
US HARRISON, A.R.
CA HARRISON, Stanley
CA HARRISON, Susie
    Frances, (Seranus,
    pseud.)
US HARVEY, James
    Clarence
US HAVILAND, C. Augustus
AU HENERIE, J.E.S.
US HENSON, Nellie Parker
US HEROD, William Pirtle
US HERSCHELL, William

SA LEFEBVRE, Denys
US LEONARD, William Ellery
US LEVERIDGE, Lilian
US LEVIS, William Bittle
US? LILLARD, R.W.
US LINDSAY, Vachel
US LINEBARGER, Paul Myron Wentworth, (Paul Myron, pseud.)
US LIPPMANN, Leonard Blackledge
AU LISTON, Maud Renner
AU LITTLEJOHN, Agnes
CA LIVESAY, Florence Randal
CA LOGAN, John Daniel
US LOWELL, Amy
AU LYALL, James Robert, (Patroclus, pseud.)
AU ? M.R.
AU MACARTNEY, Frederick Thomas
US McCARTNEY, Richard Hayes
CA MACCONNELL, H.B.
AU McCRAE, Dorothy Frances
AU McCRAE, George Gordon
CA McCRAE, John
US MACDONALD, Francis Charles
AU McDONALD, J.A.
AU MACDONALD, William John
AU McDONALD, William Michael
CA MACDONALD, Wilson
AU McDOUGALL, Catherine
CA McEVOY, Bernard
AU McFADYEN, Ella
US McGROARTY, John Steven

CA MACINNES, Thomas Robert Edward
CA MACINNIS, Edgar Wardwell
AU McJANNETT, Robert
CA MACKAY, Angus
CA MACKAY, Isabel Ecclestone
US MACKAYE, Percy
AU MACKINNON, Eleanor
US MACLEISH, Archibald
SA MAGRAW, John Edward
US MARBURG, Theodore
US MASON, Harrison D.
US MASSON, Thomas L.
US MASTERS, Edgar Lee
US MASTIN, Florence Ripley
AU MATTHEWS, Harley
CA MAURICE, Furnley, pseud., (i.e. Frank Leslie Thomas Wilmot)
AU MEYNELL, Florence Elizabeth
AU MIDDLETON, Arnold Safroni-
CA MIDDLETON, J. Edgar
US MILLER, J. Carson
US MILLS, William Hathorn
US MITCHELL, Frank A.
US MITCHELL, Ruth Comfort
CA MOFFATT, Warneford
SA MOME, pseud., (i.e. G. Murray Johnstone)
US MONROE, Harriet
US MORGAN, Angela
US MORISON, Mrs. John Archibald
US MORLEY, Christopher
AU MORRIS, Frederick Pitman
AU MORRIS, H.W.
US MOWRER, Paul Scott

AU MOYNIHAN, Cornelius
NZ MULGAN, Alan Edward
US MYRON, Paul, pseud.,
  (i.e. Paul Myron
  Wentworth Line-
  barger)
AU? N., C.J.
US NOPPEN, Leonard Van
US NORTH, Luke, pseud.,
  (i.e. James Hartness
  Griffes)
US NORTON, Grace Fallow
US O'BRIEN, Edward J.
US ODELL, Minna, (Minna
  Irving, pseud.)
AU O'DONNELL, J.P.
CA O'HAGAN, Thomas
AU OLIVER, R. Mill
AU O'NEILL, C.T.
US OPPENHEIM, James
AU ORIEL, pseud., (i.e.
  John Sandes)
US OWENS, Vilda Sauvage
AU OYSTER, pseud., (i.e.
  W. Watson Boyes)
US PALMER, Fanny Purdy
AU PALMER, Vance
AU PATRIUS, pseud.
AU PATROCLUS, pseud., (i.e.
  James Robert Lyall)
AU PATTERSON, Henry
US PAULL, Charles
US? PEABODIE, W.G.
US PEABODY, Josephine
  Preston
CA PEACOCK, Harold
US PEELE, R.E.
US PERCY, William
  Alexander
AU PERRY, Dorothy Frances
AU PETERSEN, Christian
  Olaf
CA PHILLIPPS-WOLLEY,
  Sir Clive

AU PHILLIPS, Frederick
  Wynne
US PICKENBACH, Harry
  Edward
CA PICKTHALL, Marjorie
  L.C.
AU PINN, Mrs. E. Power-
SA POSCIMUR, pseud.,
  (i.e. John Clark)
US POUND, Ezra
AU POWER-PINN, Mrs. E.
CA PRATT, Edwin John
AU PRETTY, V.
AU PRIMROSE, Maud V.
AU PRO PATRIA, pseud.,
  (i.e. Miss Cowlishaw)
AU PRYCE, Henry Weston,
  (Gunner 379, pseud.)
US PULSIFER, Harold
  Trowbridge
NZ PURNELL, Charles
  William
AU QUIN, F.W.
AU? R., H.
AU? R., M.
US RAVENEL, Beatrice
  Witte
CA REDPATH, Beatrice
AU RENTOUL, J. Laurence
AU RETURNED SOLDIERS,
  pseud., (i.e. C. Ryan
  & J. Ryan)
US RICHMOND, Charles
  Alexander
NZ RIFLEMAN'S MOTHER,
  pseud.
US RINEHART, George
  Franklin
CA? RIPPON, Albert
CA ROBERTS, Sir Charles
  George Douglas
US ROBERTSON, Donald G.
AU ROBERTSON, Mary Ann
AU ROBERTSON,
  Philadelphia N.

US ROBINSON, Edgar L.
US ROBINSON, Edwin Arlington
US ROCHE, John Pierre
US ROCHESTER, Edith Grensted
CA RODDICK, Amy Redpath
US RODMAN, Selden
AU ROSE DE BOHEME, pseud., (i.e. Agnes Rose Soley)
AU ROWSELL, Dorothy C.
AU RYAN, C., & RYAN, J., (Returned Soldiers, pseud.)
AU SAFRONI-MIDDLETON, Arnold
US SANDBURG, Carl
AU SANDES, John, (Oriel, pseud.)
US SANGER, William Cary
CA SARSON, H. Smalley
AU SCANLON, H.
US SCHAUFFLER, Robert Haven
US SCOLLARD, Clinton
CA SCOTT, Duncan Campbell
CA SCOTT, Frederick George
AU SCOTT, Kenneth
AU SEAGER, Mrs. A.
AU SEEBEE, pseud., (i.e. Claude Richard de la Poer Beresford)
US SEEGER, Alan
US SEITZ, Don Carlos
US SEIVER, Elizabeth R.
CA SERANUS, pseud. (i.e. Susie Frances Harrison)
CA SERVICE, Robert William
CA SHEARD, Virna
US SHEPARD, Odell
US SHERMAN, Stuart Pratt

AU SHORT, Lionel G.
AU SIEBENHAAR, William
CA SILCOX, Claris Edwin
AU SIMPSON, Helen de Guerry
AU SKEYHILL, Tom
SA SLATER, Francis Carey
AU SMITH, Elizabeth A.
US SMITH, Gertrude
US SMITH, Lewis Worthington
NZ SMITH, Lucy Evelyn
US SMITH, Marion Couthouy
AU SMITH, Quintin H.R.
CA SMITH, W.R.
CA SMYTHE, Alfred
US SNOW, Wilbert
AU SOLEY, Agnes Rose, (Rose de Boheme, pseud.)
US SPICER, Anne Higginson
US SPIERS, Kaufmann Charles
US SPINGARN, Joel Elias
CA SPRECKLEY, R.O.
AU? SPRENT, James
CA STEAD, Robert James Campbell
AU STEPHENS, W.H.
US STERLING, George
AU STEVEN, Alexander Gordon
US STEVENS, Thomas Wood
CA STEWART, A.C.
AU STEWART, H.W.
US STIMSON, Saxe Churchill
US STONE, J.O.I.C.
AU STRONG, Archibald T.
CA STUART, Mabel L.
CA SULLIVAN, Alan
US SUTTON, Edward Forrester
SA SWEMMER, Benjamin Northling

US SWIFT, Elizabeth Townsend
CA TAIT, Robert Holland
US TAYLOR, Belle Gray
US TAYLOR, Edward Robeson
US TEASDALE, Sara
AU TERRILL, S.
US THAYER, Sigourney
US THOMAS, Edith Mathilda
CA THOMAS, Hartley Munro
SA THOMPSON, Owen Richmond
AU THOMSON, Boyd Cunningham Campbell
US TORRENCE, Ridgely
US TOWNE, Charles Hanson
AU TROOPER BLUEGUM, pseud., (i.e. Oliver Hogue)
AU TROOPER GERARDY, pseud., (i.e. Edwin Gerard)
US TUCKER, Allen
US TUCKER, Louis
US TUCKERMAN, Fleming
CA TURNER, Jack
US TYRRELL, Ada
US UNDERWOOD, John Curtis
US UNTERMEYER, Jean Starr
US UNTERMEYER, Louis
US VAN DYKE, Henry
US VAN DYKE, Tertius
US VAN NOPPEN, Leonard
US VAN VORST, Marie
SA VEE, Roger
US VIERECK, George Sylvester
US VIETT, George Frederic
US VORST, Marie Van

SA WAAL, Daphne De
NZ WALL, Arnold
US WALLIS, J.H.
CA WARDEN, Horace W.
US WARREN, Lansing
CA WATSON, Albert Durrant
CA WATSON, Isabella B.
NZ WATT, W.M.W.
US WATTS, Harvey M.
SA WAY, William Archer
CA WAYFARER, pseud., (i.e. Abner Cosens)
US WEEKS, Raymond
CA WEIR, Robert Stanley
US WEITBREC, Blanche
AU WELSH, Alexander Carl
AU WESTBROOK, Frank E.
CA WETHERALD, Ethelwyn
US WHARTON, Edith
AU WHITE, Gilbert
AU WHITE, Godfrey W.
CA WHITE, Isaac S.
US WHITE, Wilton E.
US WICKERSHAM, J.H.
US WIDDEMER, Margaret
US WILCOX, Ella Wheeler
US WILDER, Amos Niven
US? WILDER, John Nichols
US WILLIAMS, Oscar
US WILLIAMSON, Paul
CA WILMOT, Frank Leslie Thomas, (Furnley Maurice, pseud.)
NZ WILSON, Anne Glenny, Lady
US WILSON, Eugene E.
US WILSON, McLandburgh
CA WINLOW, Alice Maud Dudley
US WITHINGTON, Robert
CA WOLLEY, Sir Clive Phillipps-
AU WOOD, John James O'Hara

401

US WOODBERRY, George Edward

US WOODWORTH, George W.

AU WYATT, Mary L.

US YBARRA, Thomas Russell

AU ZEKLE, pseud.

AU ZEPHYR, pseud.